THE
MAN
WHO
CARRIED
CASH

JULIE CHADWICK

THE
MAN
WHO
CARRIED
CASH

Saul Holiff, Johnny Cash, and
the Making of an American Icon

DUNDURN
TORONTO

Cover image: Courtesy of Jonathan Holiff. Photograph by Jorgan Halling/Saul Holiff Collection.
Printer: Webcom

Library and Archives Canada Cataloguing in Publication

Chadwick, Julie, author
        The man who carried Cash : Saul Holiff, Johnny Cash, and the making of an American icon /
Julie Chadwick.

Includes bibliographical references.
Issued in print and electronic formats.
ISBN 978-1-4597-3723-5 (softcover).--ISBN 978-1-4597-3724-2 (PDF).--
ISBN 978-1-4597-3725-9 (EPUB)

        1. Holiff, Saul, 1925-2005. 2. Cash, Johnny. 3. Concert agents--United States--Biography.
4. Concert agents--Canada--Biography. 5. Country musicians--United States--Biography. I. Title.

ML429.H732C43 2017   782.421642092   C2017-900762-9
                                                    C2017-900763-7

1   2   3   4   5   21   20   19   18   17

 Conseil des Arts   Canada Council    ONTARIO ARTS COUNCIL
du Canada   for the Arts   CONSEIL DES ARTS DE L'ONTARIO
                                                      an Ontario government agency
                                                      un organisme du gouvernement de l'Ontario

We acknowledge the support of the **Canada Council for the Arts** and the Ontario Arts Council for our publishing program. We also acknowledge the financial support of the **Government of Ontario**, through the **Ontario Book Publishing Tax Credit** and the **Ontario Media Development Corporation**, and the **Government of Canada.**

Care has been taken to trace the ownership of copyright material used in this book. The author and the publisher welcome any information enabling them to rectify any references or credits in subsequent editions.

— *J. Kirk Howard, President*

The publisher is not responsible for websites or their content unless they are owned by the publisher.

Printed and bound in Canada.

VISIT US AT

dundurn.com | @dundurnpress | dundurnpress | dundurnpress

Dundurn
3 Church Street, Suite 500
Toronto, Ontario, Canada
M5E 1M2

FOR RUBY AND ROWAN

CONTENTS

INTRODUCTION

The story of Saul Holiff and Johnny Cash first arrived in my inbox as an email with a subject line marked "CONFIDENTIAL." I was a cub reporter at my hometown paper in Nanaimo, British Columbia, and had also recently been promoted to editor of our weekly entertainment section, The Hub. In journalism many a tall tale comes across one's desk, and part of the birth story of any piece begins with separating the wheat from the chaff. But unlikely as it seemed, this story was immediately compelling.

The man writing to me was Jonathan Holiff, whose father, Saul Holiff, had officially worked as Johnny Cash's manager for thirteen years. Before his death in 2005, "at a time of his own choosing," as the subsequent obituary in the *Globe and Mail* had so eloquently put it, he had lived out his last years in Nanaimo.

Since then, Jonathan had written, produced, and directed a documentary film about his father's life and relationship with both him and Johnny Cash, and was writing to me regarding the gala opening of the film that was about to take place in Nanaimo on his father's home turf.

It was a story that held immediate intrigue, and in the years since, its grip on my imagination has only intensified.

Following his father's death, Jonathan returned to Nanaimo from his home in Hollywood, where he worked in the world of celebrity endorsements as managing director of the Hollywood-Madison Group.

Overcome with conflicted emotions around his father's death, these feelings were soon exacerbated by the incessant calls of journalists who were curious about his father, as renewed interest in Cash swirled around the imminent release of the Joaquin Phoenix and Reese Witherspoon film *Walk the Line*. It seemed he couldn't escape the spectre of his father. In the midst of this chaos, Jonathan's mother, Barbara, offered her son the key to his father's storage locker in the hope that, by going through his belongings, it would give him some form of closure.

What it marked was the beginning of a multi-year journey of discovery for Jonathan, who, in his own words, was "searching for his father in the shadow of a legend." What he found in the storage locker was a vast archive of materials his father had saved during his time as Johnny Cash's manager. As he waded through the archive, a picture began to emerge of a person he never knew — who was not only his father but also Saul Holiff, a man personally possessed of a rich and troubled internal life, but who outwardly was a major figure in the history of Canadian and American music.

The result was *My Father and the Man in Black*, a highly personal documentary that was as much about managers and superstars as it was about fathers and sons. When the film had its hometown opening, I was assigned to write the cover feature story on it. Over time, Jonathan and I began to discuss the possibility of a book that delved even deeper into the mystery of Saul Holiff, the man, and his career as manager of one of the legendary bad boys of American music.

From the beginning, I could see that the material that Jonathan and the Holiff family had granted me access to was impressive. Saul was meticulous, a list-maker, highly organized and fastidious both in appearance and in personal habits. This was reflected in the vast quantity and quality of the records he kept. Of particular significance was a large scrapbook of the type that was built to hold newspaper broadsheets, on the front of which were a series of gold letters: *L-I-F-F*, as though once intended to spell out Saul's last name. Perhaps the other letters had fallen off. However, on closer inspection it could be seen that the final letter had been amended with a pen to become an *E*, so instead the letters read *LIFE*.

Herein was Saul's own collection of newspaper cuttings, letters, and photos he found personally significant, and it provided a sort of key to the other materials within the archive. There were detailed financial records, contracts, audiotaped phone calls with Cash, audio and written diaries, letters, posters, and hundreds of photos both candid and professional. Many of the recordings and diary entries were recorded within hours, weeks, or months of events, which in turn served to inform the book on an as-it-happened level.

Though fascinating and historically significant, it is also worth noting that Saul Holiff never intended for this archive to become public. In fact, up until his death he was busy with liquidating much of it; most of the gold records he had earned previously as Cash's manager had been sold or auctioned off to charity, and each year he would go down into the storage locker with a garbage bag to weed out items into the trash, with a promise to his wife that he would soon whittle it down to almost nothing. It is not known how much was lost in this process, but what survived is still considerable.

Through the years, into his retirement, Saul toyed with the idea of writing a book about the entertainment industry and the quirky personalities within it, but a tell-all memoir about his famous clients like Johnny Cash was never his intention. He wanted to write something that would have served as a sociological study from an insider's point of view. Not only was it not his style to do a tell-all, but also, as a highly private individual like many men of his generation, Saul rarely, if ever, revealed the turmoil, pain, and insecurities that lay behind his facade of refined success — even to those closest to him. As such, I feel it is important to view his diaries and letters with a sense of reverence in that, though they paint a fascinating and complex portrait of a man and his tumultuous relationship with one of the most iconic figures in American music, they are also the very personal musings of a man who did not imagine that one day these thoughts would become public.

Here, it might be worth making a note on style: Much, if not all, of Saul's thoughts that I have included are written in italics, and come from Saul's own diaries or were stated in interviews. Though these are not in quotes, I attempt to stay as close to his own exact wording as possible. The scenes in the book are described as closely as possible to what factually transpired, with some minor allowances for creativity, and are based on newspaper clippings, quotes, diary entries, letters, and information from other books, but as with any scenarios based on memories, they often involve differing accounts. In some of these cases I defer to Saul's perspective and descriptions, as until this point, his story has largely gone untold.

It is also important to note that this book is not intended to be a definitive biography of Saul Holiff, or of Johnny Cash, for that matter. There are far more qualified and intrepid writers who have shouldered the task of crafting Cash biographies with skill and nuance, and will continue to carry that story far into the future. This is, rather, the tale of a relationship between two men, in friendship and in conflict, and is as much a look into the world of music during the era of the 1950s, 1960s, and 1970s — on both a personal and professional level — as it is a meditation on modern masculinity. Perhaps it is even a cautionary tale of sorts. What stood out for me as I researched these two men's entangled lives was that though they eventually achieved the outward success and triumph they so fervently sought, it did little to heal their internal strife. Therein lies a tragedy, but also, perhaps, a warning.

I hope you enjoy the story of Saul Holiff and Johnny Cash.

PROLOGUE

The sun was setting as Saul Holiff crossed the living-room floor, his shadow falling on the neatly packed bookshelves as he rounded the corner and entered his study. He looked trim in his tailored black slacks and cashmere sweater; his stride was smooth and purposeful. Despite his seventy-nine years, he was in fairly good health, aside from a heart condition that was controlled with medication. Pulling a set of keys from his pocket, he unlocked the top drawer and pulled it open. He removed the kit from a small black leather bag and placed it on top of the desk. Methodically, he began to remove his jewellery and place it in the drawer.

First he slipped off the slim Piaget watch from his left wrist, then the thin gold wristband from his right. He struggled to loosen the wedding band that had been a fixture on his hand for forty years. The wallet was last.

He reached for the keys, just as he had done in every practice run. But something had changed. He studied the keys in the palm of his hand. Locking the drawer was pointless. He dropped them into the drawer and closed it.

The curtain of dusk began to fall. As he returned to the living room, he flicked on a single lamp, which threw off just enough light to see. The leather sofa squeaked slightly as he sat. The kit, he placed in the centre of the glass coffee table in front of him.

He went over his checklist:

Sit in an upright position (*check*).

Eat a little food to prevent vomiting (*check*).

Drink a small amount of alcohol to augment the action of the drug (*check*).

He unzipped the kit and parted it against the surface of the table. A television flickered in the corner but was silent. The bottle of pills clicked as he placed it on the table. He removed a black garbage bag and a large elastic band.

He separated a number of gelatin capsules and lightly tapped their contents into a crystal glass, forming a mound of fine reddish powder. Using a long spoon, his actions measured, he mixed in a liberal amount of Stolichnaya, his favourite vodka, and topped it off with a splash of orange juice. Then he lifted the glass to his lips and drank its contents without stopping.

The garbage bag lay beside him, edges rolled up carefully over the elastic band. This part, he had practised a number of times, unrolling and re-rolling the bag until it could be brought down over his face in one smooth action. His wife, Barbara, was on the couch next to him. He turned to meet her eyes and spoke his last words: "Remember what we agreed. You stay in the bedroom and don't come out, no matter what, until this thing is over."

He pulled the bag over his head and filled it with air, before quickly placing the large elastic band around his throat to create a seal.

Barbara was in the bedroom when she heard the noise. Perched on the edge of her mattress, plucking at a stray thread on the bedspread, she raised her head at the sound, hoping she had just imagined it. Straining to listen over the pounding of her heart, it came again, a muffled shout. The third cry brought her to her feet, and instinct forced her out the door and into the living room, toward the sofa. *Do not leave the bedroom, no matter what.* His last words echoed in her mind. She froze.

The Seconal, a fast-acting sedative used to calm patients before surgery, was beginning to hit his bloodstream in a vodka-enhanced flood. Barbara watched in horror as Saul's arms rose and lagged in the air. She wanted nothing more than to tear that wretched thing off his

14

head, if only to stop the sound he was making, a sound that was now etched into her mind.

She stood rooted to the carpet for a moment, her hands trembling, then turned mechanically and walked back into the bedroom. The lamp on her bedside table remained dark. She turned her wedding band around and around on her finger. *I promised I wouldn't interfere. If I revive him and he ends up a vegetable, or maimed in some way — no, it is impossible, he would never forgive me.* As night fell, the patches of silence in the living room expanded until their edges bled together seamlessly. It was over.

It was March 17, 2005.

After what seemed like hours, Barbara emerged from the room. The slumped figure on the couch did not stir. She knew everything had to be left exactly as it was, so she touched nothing except to gently hold her husband's hand, already cooling to the touch. She remained there for a moment, feeling the tears on her cheeks. Then, she slowly rose and called the police.[1]

1

THE WHITE COAT

Two girls huddle in a modest wood-framed house in the village of Dmytrivka, not far from Ukraine's capital city of Kiev. The shouts of men on horseback grow louder, and soon they hear the sound of hooves in the mud outside. Then the screams, as the house next door erupts in flames.[1] "It's time to run," their mother says in Yiddish, and throws each of them a coat — one white, one brown.

The screen door claps shut behind them, and they tear off toward the cornfields that lie flat and green on the horizon. The youngest, Ann, sees the men on horseback out of the corner of her eye as she runs. There are seven or eight of them. The sound of a gunshot cracks through the air. Her sister falls. Ann keeps running.

For four days Ann hides amongst the cornstalks with the other children, drinking cow's milk from a makeshift cup and subsisting on what grain and scraps are around until she can return home. Schuncha, her older sister, survives, but not for long; the bullet wound in her stomach becomes infected. About a month after she was shot, she dies.

"It could have been me," Ann said later. It was the coats; they were accidentally switched. "I got the brown one; she got the white one. There was only a year and a half difference between us, so either one would have fit. And that's when she was shot, because the white coat stood out." It was a sentiment also echoed by her aunt, who murmured, "Isn't it too bad that the beautiful child had to be taken?" when she thought Ann was out of earshot.[2]

Ann's father was an intellectual, she was told. He worked as an *advocaat*, something like a lawyer. This made her proud. When the shadow of the First World War loomed, her father, Joel Holiff, was one of a flood of villagers who abandoned their dwindling *shtetl* to avoid being conscripted into the army. He left his homeland and travelled across the ocean to build a new life for his family in Canada, and his attempt to find work there was executed with single-minded determination. Not long after his departure, Jews in the Ukraine were pummelled by large-scale anti-Semitic pogroms and brutal raids that ground on in the lead-up to the Russian Revolution of 1917 and continued for years after. Tens of thousands of Jews were murdered by Bolshevik armies and Ukrainian nationalists.[3]

It would be almost eight years before Joel's wife, Esther, and daughter Ann were permitted to join him in Canada. During that time, life for Ann and her mother was simply a matter of survival, as the sound of horses drove them, breathless, into hiding among the dusty feed bags. The fear of discovery hung dark over their days like the sacking over the broken windows. The men would ride into the village and take over, stay a day or two, get drunk, rape and terrify the villagers, and then move on. Ann watched silently one afternoon as a man went into her house carrying a scythe and entered the bedroom where her grandmother lay dying. In a senseless act of cruelty, the man swept the weapon across the old woman's nightstand and sent all of her medicine bottles shattering to the floor. It was incomprehensible to Ann, who replayed the scene in her mind for years after. *My grandmother didn't do any harm to him,* she thought. *She didn't even open her mouth.*

The underground shelters weren't much better. At first they would make their escape carrying a few household items, uncertain how many days they would be gone or what would remain when they returned. However, their valuables were eventually all pillaged. The winters were so harsh, the cold gnawed into Ann's toes and made her bones ache. Ann's mother strained to quiet the noise of the little ones. She feared for herself also, as the attractive lines of her face and her long hair meant she was a target for the marauding men. Fear hung in the air, high and sharp, mingled with sweat and mouldering damp. During one pogrom, more than two hundred people crammed into the shelter. When one of the infants began to squall, Ann watched as a man took a pillow and wordlessly suffocated the baby so it wouldn't give them away.

Ann helped out when she could, and stood guard at the cellar door to watch for military police while her mother made bootleg liquor in the basement and then hid it in the wall to later sell to the *goyim*. This, along with some sewing work, allowed Esther to provide for the children and her bedridden mother, as all the money Joel sent home from Ontario was confiscated by the Russian authorities.

At least three times their escape plan seemed set, their passage guaranteed, only to have it unravel at the last minute when the Russians refused to let them leave. Finally, in 1921, with exit visas in hand, Ann and Esther boarded a train in Kiev destined for Hamburg. Thin and sickly, Ann tried to keep her strength up so she could pass the immigration examinations. At one station stop, Esther got off the train and went to find a pharmacy to get her daughter some medicine. On her way back along the platform, the train started to move. Ann, watching from the small train window, began to scream as she saw her mother break into a run. As she tried desperately to catch up to the train, her mother's long hair, held up with bone hairpins, started to fall. Just then, two men reached out and pulled her onto the train. Ann was in tears. She had nearly gone to Hamburg without her mother.

While switching trains in Germany, an elegant woman approached Ann and Esther on the platform. "You have too much luggage to carry by yourself. Let me help you," she said with a smile. A moment later they turned back to find she had disappeared, along with the two small bags containing all of Esther's valuables, purchased or bartered for through years of sewing and bootlegging. All that was left was their large wicker travelling trunk.

"My mother sat down and cried her heart out," Ann later remembered. "She wanted to show her husband she wasn't exactly a pauper, that she earned monies herself."

At Hamburg, they boarded the ship that would take them to Montreal. Three weeks of travel across the roiling Atlantic Ocean followed, as the pair was packed in steerage with hundreds of retching passengers and nothing to eat but herring, sour cream, and onions. The entire boat was crawling with lice, and upon their arrival in Montreal the immigration officials doused them in kerosene and roughly sheared their hair.

Then came the medical examinations.

"I remember vividly about a dozen people were put on the small boat to go back to the big ship and be taken back to Europe, because they had different diseases. We were fortunate. They let us through," said Ann.

Free to leave, they were swallowed up in the push of bodies leaving the immigration hut; struggling with their wicker luggage, they merged into the river of other passengers streaming onto the train station platform.

A man, eyes searching behind circular-framed glasses, stood tall and immutable amidst the jumble of bodies, derby hat clutched in his hand. "This is your father," Esther said to Ann in Yiddish as they approached him.

Husband and daughter stood staring at each other. Joel wore a double-breasted topcoat, all buttons, and underneath, a vest and high-necked shirt. A tie was just visible, held down with a tiny sparkling pin. His face was smooth and inscrutable, though this moment marked the culmination of days that had run into weeks and months and years. Time had blended together in an endless ream of rolled-up rugs and sacks of dried goods hefted door to door. It was nights measured by the clink of his fork as he ended the day at Wong's Garden, the old Chinese restaurant on Richmond Street. It was the creak of springs as he fell into bed at the boarding house where, he would later confess to his son Saul in a rare moment of intimacy, the woman who ran it once tried to lure him into a "compromising situation." And here, now, on the train station platform was his child — a virtual stranger.

Joel's arrival in London, Ontario, in 1913 had been swiftly followed by news of the war, which clouded out all else except the grinding years of waiting and working. Cent by cent the original fifty-dollar loan he had taken out was repaid, and dollar by dollar he trudged unwaveringly toward the goal of freeing his family. At first, he peddled goods on a bicycle; then, he moved to a horse and buggy until he scraped together enough money to purchase a panel truck.

By the time he led his wife and remaining child out of the train station, it was to the open door of a convertible Essex automobile, in which they drove to a trim little house on Rectory Street, which was furnished and complete with a wiggling bulldog puppy for Ann. Her old doll, fashioned from a linen kitchen towel, was replaced that day with a new one.

Ann remained an only child for two years until her brother Morris was born in 1923. Two years after that, her mother came home from the Salvation Army hospital across the street with a new baby they called Israel — and who later went by his middle name, Saul. The family soon moved from Rectory Street into a large apartment above the ladies' ready-to-wear shop they owned, where both parents toiled for thirteen hours a day. Ann was left to raise the boys, who were both still in diapers. Serving as nursemaid and housekeeper, cooking, making formula from scratch, and washing diapers, thirteen-year-old Ann often resented the lack of choice in her position as second mother. She juggled this role alongside the adjustment to life in a new country, where her family members were dismissed as "greenhorns," and in which she was so ashamed of her inability to speak English that she often didn't speak at all.

Saul was a boisterous six-year-old when his sister, Ann, was first courted by Sam Paikin, a man from Hamilton who would later become her husband. Adored and admired in equal measure, Sam captivated Saul. When Sam came to visit, it was the high point of Saul's day, and the two soon developed a game in which Saul wheedled nickels and dimes from him. It always took a different form, but when Sam arrived, Saul would race out to meet him as he emerged from his car.

"Look, Sam! I found a billfold, and there was a nickel in it," Saul would call to him.

"Only a nickel, Saul? What'll that buy you?"

The way the game unfolded, Saul would typically end up triumphantly clutching two quarters. Throughout his life he viewed Sam as a mentor, though Saul struggled with insecurities that were exacerbated both by his father's constant belittling and Sam's impatience and criticism. Even when pushed away, Saul continued to watch Sam from the corners, taking note of his style and flair, his dominant personality and ability to turn a room to his favour with magic tricks and jokes. The way Sam jostled and traded barbs with his own siblings was curious to Saul. It stood in stark contrast to the pressurized, reserved atmosphere in his own home. Proper inhibition was the tenor of their household, and physical affection was in short supply. At times, Saul would become tongue-tied around his brother-in-law — Sam would tell a joke, and Saul wouldn't get the point. If Saul tried to be a smartass, Sam could cut him up and down with just a few words. Like a shamed dog, Saul would put his tail between his legs and run off. Over time, though, Saul went from feeling intimidated by Sam to wanting to emulate him.

By the beginning of the 1930s, Saul's parents were struggling to make ends meet at the dress shop. It was as though Joel and Esther were sliding into a pit, and no matter how hard they squirmed to get out, it only seemed to make them sink faster.[4]

Aware of this, six-year-old Saul conspired with his brother Morris, and the two boys took to the streets. They slipped into the backyard of one of the nearby houses, raided their pear tree, and then went out and sold the fruit along Dundas Street. One of their customers turned out to be the very owner of the pear tree whence they had obtained their wares, a man who had a ladies' wear store nearby.

The two boys became adept at shoplifting from the variety store and the Loblaws supermarket down the road from their house, and would regulary load up their windbreakers with jelly beans and licorice and chocolate maple buds. This continued until Morris brazenly bounced a huge beach ball away from the front of the store and was caught.

The boys also got newspaper routes, and Saul took pride in his notoriety as the youngest carrier in London. They did what they had to do, Saul later recalled with a sense of pride. More or less, the two boys were growing up on their own; but as self-sufficient as they were, times were going to get even tougher. By May of 1933, the bottom had dropped out of the business and the family faced bankruptcy. After much agonizing, Joel shut down the clothing store, and with Sam's help moved the family into a home at 315 Wharncliffe Road North, which they rented for $33 a month. Though small, their new home still allowed each of the kids to have their own bedroom. They also had a nanny — though she was faced with her own financial problems and would drink Saul's daily milk allowance until he came down with a case of rickets.

In addition to the strain of the family's finances, there was also a discernible atmosphere of anti-Semitism that was pervasive in the city at that time. The schoolyard bullies the boys had to push past every morning on their way to Lorne Avenue School were incessant in their torment. Particularly brutal were the Wiley family boys, the biggest being Tor Wiley, who took great delight in burying Saul in the schoolyard sandbox. The Holiff boys would spend the last two periods frozen by fear of what inventive taunts might lie in wait for them once the bell rang. The Italians had recently invaded Ethiopia, so some taunts involved strange slogans that associated Jews with Ethiopians somehow — a twist that was so bizarre Saul thought it verged on poetic. One Halloween, Esther went to answer the door and had a bag of flour thrown in her face. Before it slammed shut, Saul heard a voice call out, "Dirty Jew!"

As the boys waded through the challenges of the Great Depression, there was little time for distractions or hobbies, though they would often play street hockey until midnight, or strap on roller skates and head down Dundas Street to Queen's Park to watch buskers entertain the jockeys as they trained their racehorses.[5]

Saul's father also found time for his own small pleasures. Well-read and highly skilled at chess, Joel continually lobbied the local paper to devote more of their coverage to the game via letters to the editor and articles. "It is better than Latin for teaching young minds to think," Joel once told a reporter, "and it will keep young men and women off the streets at night." As president of the London chess club and one of the top players in the district, Joel played both locally and internationally, by correspondence. Forms with chess moves would come in the mail from far-off places like Belgium, and Saul would watch his father as he set up the board and logged his own moves on the sheet. When Saul was eleven, Joel invited twelve-year-old chess prodigy Daniel "Abe" Yanofsky to stay at their home, and young Saul was awestruck by the boy's abilities. Yanofsky not only simultaneously played thirty games of chess, including one against Joel at the London Public Library, but he also demonstrated to Saul how he could read a page of the Bible and remember it word for word, a feat he explained by saying his head worked like a recording machine.

By this point, Saul and Morris had taken up serious gambling of their own with a dreidel, and were engaging in every other kind of competition they could think of: gin rummy, poker, and matchstick races in the gutter runoff down the streets. The instincts were to kill, to win, to exploit, and Morris always prevailed and pressed Saul to play just one more game — and typically came out the winner.[6]

Dark, awkward, and uncertain of his place in the world, Saul was regularly subject to comparisons with tall, fair, and affable Morris, which didn't help their sense of rivalry as they entered their teens. Saul often had the impression his mother favoured him, though his father was toughest on him by far. This tendency of Joel's was most evident in the aftermath of conflicts that inevitably arose as a result of the boys' regular competitions. One time, while on a trip to a family member's farm outside London, Saul tricked Morris into a barn on the property and then locked him inside. When Joel found out he beat Saul so severely he was hospitalized. Another afternoon when a fight erupted between the brothers in their bedroom, Saul suffered two broken front teeth. The punishment meted out by Joel was so severe that Saul rarely talked about it afterward; it was another of his father's episodes that he later preferred to keep hidden. That incident was the beginning of decades of dental work and a lifelong self-consciousness that rendered Saul almost incapable of smiling. "Which seems to suit my personality anyway," Saul later liked to joke.[7]

Though she moved to Sam's hometown of Hamilton once they were married, Saul's sister Ann continued to be a firm and loving force in his life, and provided guidance that his parents were simply too busy to offer. As Saul stumbled from childhood into adolescence, he became aware that he was not terribly happy, one reason being the realization that he was woefully unprepared to become an adult. Ann had to take him aside on more than one occasion to inform him he should be wearing underarm deodorant, and if not, he should be showering more frequently. "Clean up your act," she advised him, and then proceeded to outline the basics he so desperately needed. It took years for Saul to understand how to operate in the world of adults, and Ann couldn't bear to watch him flounder.

Although Saul was aware that he once had another older sister, he was never told the full circumstances of her fate, nor that of his grandmother, and as an adult he confessed in his diary that he thought they had died of diphtheria. Ann never talked about the sister they had lost, but did her best to be all things to everyone, and continued to be close to her younger brothers as they grew older.

At fourteen, Saul's life was small, as were his joys. Hockey on the radio. Glazed honey-dipped donuts and fresh coffee for fifteen cents at the White Spot on Richmond Street, next to the shoeshine parlour. Aside from Sam Paikin, his hero was Gerry Siegel of the Siegel Fruit Company. It was a small life, but it wasn't always simple.

As they did when they were children, Saul and Morris sensed once again that their help was needed at home. This time they planned to drop out of high school to sell fruits and vegetables door to door, but on a more professional basis like the other vendors in London. It was a difficult scenario; Saul already knew he wanted to finish school and continue on to university. On hot summer days he sat on the veranda at the Wharncliffe Road house and watched with jealousy as the long procession of expensive cars driven by well-groomed locals and out-of-towners made their way to Western University, dreaming of the day he would be a student there. It represented everything he desired in life.

Something else entered Saul's life at this time that offered him his first glimpse of a larger world. Ann would often say their house was "so quiet you could hear a mouse," but by the time he was thirteen, Saul had developed a keen interest in music — specifically jazz, classical, and the big band swing music that expanded in popularity just as he was emerging from boyhood. Not unlike his fascination with Sam's family, the contrast it offered to his own life bordered on magical. Through his teenage years he ventured out to see big band leaders like Glenn Miller, Duke Ellington, and his all-time favourite, Artie Shaw, who had just been dubbed "the new King of Swing."

After the shows, Saul liked to wander the silent streets home to Wharncliffe Road and reflect on what he'd seen. One clear evening in

1939, it was well after midnight when Saul emerged from an Artie Shaw performance at the London Arena and proceeded to walk up Dundas Street. The roads were empty. On the left he passed the looming facade of Joe McManus's Hotel London. And as he passed Muirhead's Restaurant, Saul happened to glance in the window. He did a double take. On a stool, alone at the soda bar, sat Artie Shaw, looking completely dejected. It was unbelievable. Saul stood and studied the slumped figure for a moment.

Temperamental, brilliant, and a perfectionist, the clarinetist was often immersed in turmoil about his work and how commerce was occupying an increasingly dominant space in the world of music. Recently, he had dismissed his jitterbug-dancing fans as "morons," though he later clarified he found it hard to understand "why kids paid for a ticket to hear the band, and then stood in front of it and yelled at the top of their voices for the whole night." Saul, who attended shows alone, was not one of those fans. Every move Shaw made onstage or in life, Saul followed — especially how he pulled together innovative bands that combined stars like Billie Holiday and Buddy Rich, only to swiftly dissolve them again to form something new.

Saul's ears felt warm as he pulled open the door. The bell faintly jingled. With typical chutzpah, Saul slid onto the stool next to Shaw, uninvited. The two began to chat. Born Arthur Jacob Arshawsky, Artie Shaw was a twenty-nine-year-old Jewish boy from New York — short-tempered, imperial, and sophisticated. He would soon marry actress Lana Turner. By contrast, Saul was a gauche and inept teenager; by his own estimation, "strictly small potatoes." The two immediately hit it off.[8]

Not yet sixteen, and therefore too young to get a driver's licence, every morning at 5:30 a.m. Saul would slide into the passenger seat of the Holiff Brothers delivery van beside Morris to hit the market. Their father, by some miraculous means, had been able to continue putting money into two policies he'd taken out when they were born, and when both policies had a mature value of about a thousand dollars, he agreed to turn that money over to purchase Louis Averbach's fruit and vegetable business. Hauling cases and bags of produce, the brothers delivered to boarding houses and grocery stores until late in the evening. "Invariably, we would wind up with things like raspberries or strawberries or other fruit that could not be kept overnight. We did not have refrigeration. So no matter how hard we worked, the leftovers usually wiped out our profit and the day was just for nothing," Saul later recalled.

When Morris joined the air force in 1942, Joel took over his sons' business and continued to sell fruits and vegetables while Saul drifted through a variety of unappealing jobs. While toiling more than fifty hours a week in a menswear store near the old Palace Theatre in London, he discovered he had a knack for selling, but little else. He stayed in boarding houses and eventually wound up living in his sister's attic, where Ann continued to look out for him, securing him a variety of jobs through Sam (whom Saul still considered his mentor) at the Paikin Brothers steel businesses in Hamilton. Although it was hard labour at the scrapyard — working the scales, clearing stoppages on the conveyor belt, and loading dump trucks with scrap glass for transport to Dominion Glass — the job allowed him to observe the Paikin family and their dynamics at an even closer vantage point, and he never tired of their rancorous and passionate interactions. It was unlike anything he had ever experienced in his own family, and he was drawn to it. One time Saul was recruited to chauffeur Sam's father, Ora, on a buying trip to the scrapyards around Kitchener and Waterloo. As he drove, Saul realized he was being judged by the older man about his lack of knowledge of the Jewish religion. By the time he managed to cluelessly order bacon from a roadside diner in Hamilton, Ora had given up, and for the remainder of the journey his communication dwindled down to little more than withering looks aimed at his driving companion.

Directionless, Saul decided to follow in Morris's footsteps and enlist with the Royal Canadian Air Force, where Morris was working his way up to becoming a general. The next few months were tough, as he waited to be called up. In the meantime, a job was secured at Silverstein's, where he was paid a pittance to haul halibut out of freezer cars, with part of his paycheque going toward the purchase of his own cotton gloves, which wore out at the rate of about two or three pairs a week. It was frigid, miserable work. Finally, word from the air force came, and he travelled to New Brunswick, arriving on May 7, 1943, after a train ride in which he lost all his savings — several hundred dollars — shooting craps with people he later realized were professional con men.

Soon after he arrived on the East Coast, he started a diary. Paper was in short supply at that time, so he wrote on the backs of envelopes that had held letters from home. Many of the entries focused on working out his insecurities and his perceived lack of inclusion among the other RCAF members.[9]

"I shall never make a success if I always incite the anger of my fellow airmen. It seems no matter what I do, I either lose the friends I make, or make enemies of mere acquaintances. Why, I don't know, but as my sister once told me, 'Fifty thousand people can't be wrong, I guess.' I better start taking inventory. The conclusion is: talking too much, showing off, and inferiority complex," he wrote. "Pete gave me a going-over. Told me I talk too much, ignorant, push myself, bad manners, possessive, use words I don't know and always try to grab the limelight."[10]

But Saul soon discovered a way in which the air force, where he was now a tail gunner on the Lancaster bombers, could supply the means for him to pursue his musical education. His brother had explained how, whenever he got a pass, he would finagle it to travel from New Brunswick to New York or Chicago for free. "All I did was to get 'Permission to visit U.S.A.' typed on my pass and get on the train to New York," advised Morris. As a result, Saul saw more first-class music and theatre than some people observe in a lifetime. Harbouring a clandestine habit, an interest that could feed and enrich his life, lessened the sting of loneliness. These adventures were then relayed to Morris, who by this point felt obligated to offer his little brother some more advice about how to better work his passes and handle himself in the Big Apple.

"If they ask you how much money you've got, you say about four dollars in Canadian money. You show them your pass and say that you're going to visit your uncle. They know that you're full of shit anyways, so they don't say anything," Morris wrote. "If you haven't already gone to New York, by all means see Hazel Scott at the Café Society Uptown. But stand at the bar — don't sit at a table or it will cost you an extra $3. Also, go to 52nd Street where all the nightclubs are next door to each other.

But watch out for these smart looking dames who will approach you. They're nothing but pros and will take you for every cent you've got."[11]

The travel also fostered an intoxication with America itself. "In New York City on Easter Sunday," Saul wrote in his diary on April 9, 1944, "trotting down 5th Avenue with eyes wide open. American people are for me. They're spending, earning and enjoying life. Saw Ted Lewis at the Versailles Club, Billie Holiday at the Onyx. Saw Phil Spitalny broadcast, etc., etc. Everything I'm seeing for the first time."

By the time Saul received an honorable discharge from the air force in 1945 (despite having gone AWOL the previous month to catch a Bob Hope show), he was hungry for more showbiz. Expected to return to London, he lied to the discharging officer and said his parents had moved to Vancouver so that they would send him to British Columbia. Now armed with a flight sergeant's rank, which gave him some perks on the train, he took a lower berth for free and headed out west. Tucked in his pocket was a book of stamped passes given to him by Morris, who had risen to the position of navigation bombardier instructor, which came with the authority to issue passes.

After a short stop in Banff, where he chased a girl for a bit, Saul ended up in Vancouver, and wandered into a jewellery store. There was nothing to lure him there beyond the name of *London Jewelers*, which seemed serendipitous given his point of origin, but it was a start. Before long, he struck up a friendship with the woman who ran the store and confessed an intention to hitchhike to Hollywood. "Wouldn't you just know it? I have a connection in Hollywood," she told him with a grin. "A Jewish jeweller, he belongs to a famous club there called the Masters Club, made up of Irish character actors who are famous, recognizable — not necessarily mega-stars, but you get the idea." For the adventurous twenty-one-year-old Saul Holiff, that was all the connection he needed.

It was pouring rain as Saul stood on the edge of the highway out of Vancouver in a blue battledress jacket adorned with his air gunner's badge. It hung wet above a pair of beige pants, from which he attached a long keychain to hang down in a way he thought was fashionable. In his pocket was thirty-eight dollars. As he shifted from one foot to the next in his air-force-issue shoes, with one thumb out, the other hand pushed rain from his eyes. *Here I am heading off for California with no money, no brains, no destination ... but I have a key thing, I have a Hollywood connection,* thought Saul.

It turned out to be one of the most exciting connections in his entire life.

2

"SHOWBIZ HAD TO BE MY LIFE"

After an overnight ride in a truck, Saul emerged from the downpour of Vancouver into the record-breaking heat of a clear Hollywood morning. White houses rose up from the sidewalk, peculiarly massive and palm-fronted. Passersby confronted him with their friendliness and exuberant clothing in a manner that both rattled and dazzled him, and USO service members of all shapes and colours roamed the streets. By noon he had tracked down the Masters Club on Sycamore Street and was mixed into a crowd that was about 90 percent *goyim* and 10 percent Jews. Seated next to him were seasoned Hollywood actors like Jimmy Gleason — whose last role had been a small part alongside Cary Grant in *Arsenic and Old Lace* — Guy Kibbee, Pat O'Brien, and Eddy Arnold. It was surreal. Just days before, Saul had watched Arnold play blind detective Duncan Maclain in *The Hidden Eye*. As he ate lunch, Saul kept glancing at Arnold and wondering where his guide dog was, before he sheepishly remembered that he was not actually blind.[1]

During the lunch, Saul asked around about work and secured the phone number of a man named Max Factor, who ran a cosmetics business over on Highland Avenue. Originally named Frank, he was the son of the original Max Factor, a Polish-Jewish wigmaker and former cosmetician to the imperial family of Russia, who escaped to America in 1904. Carried aloft by the burgeoning Hollywood film industry, Factor's specialty was the creation of innovative products for film that were lighter and far more subtle than the heavy greasepaint that was a staple of the stage.

Trained in the business alongside his siblings, all employed at various levels of the company, Max Jr. apprenticed alongside his father in the laboratory. By the time he was poised to take over the cosmetics empire, they had together developed the original formula for Pan-Cake makeup — one of the company's crowning achievements. Many film stars were reluctant to depart from black-and-white film and appear in the new Technicolor movies because the existing facial cosmetics were so unflattering and greasy. Spurred on by Factor's innovations in makeup (a term he coined), Pan-Cake became the industry standard and looked so good, even off-camera, that starlets often pocketed it at the end of shooting. Once it hit drugstore shelves, public demand soared. With the subsequent release and wild success of Max Factor Jr.'s new Tru-Color indelible lipstick, by 1945 the company's fortunes were such that it employed hundreds of workers. It was into this mix that a young Saul Holiff strode, and was hired to work in the factory as a "puddler." Not unlike those employed in steel mills, his job was to ensure makeup ingredients were properly funnelled down a trough so that the mixing machine didn't back up.[2]

Saul soon insinuated himself into the Factor family to the point that they invited him to celebrate Rosh Hashanah at the Bouchard Boulevard Temple with them. As Rabbi Edgar Magnum conducted the ceremony, Saul squirmed. Raised as an atheist, there had been no ceremony to mark his bar mitzvah, and he certainly didn't feel as though he belonged in any *schul*. "I was an imposter, but as long as I kept my mouth shut I was Jewish and nobody recognized me for an imposter, so no one threw me out," he recalled. This connection with the Factor family only further widened a door that had begun to reveal a glittering landscape of opportunity. Hollywood was leagues away from London, Ontario. In addition to Max Factor, Saul was awestruck by the examples around him of powerful Jewish entrepreneurs, directors, distributors, writers, actors — risk-takers, visionaries — real-life moguls who weren't ashamed of who they were or where they came from. And they often came from poverty, like him. There were legendary names like Marcus Loew, who founded Metro-Goldwyn-Mayer, and Paramount Pictures founder Adolph Zukor, who emigrated from Hungary to the United States in 1889. Or the Warner family, Jews who fled Poland in the late 1800s and went on to establish Warner Bros. Studios. Moreover, even though he was uncertain and naive and unworldly, he felt included. They were kind and welcoming, offered him access into their world, and it was nothing short of intoxicating. Further passage into this milieu was next secured via the book of passes Morris had issued him.

"Each pass was a book of one hundred or something or other forty-eight-hour passes, and they went on for like eight months and he stamped each one of them legally, so as each date expired I'd tear it out. If any MP or American equivalent, police officer came up to me, in this ridiculous uniform, they weren't quite sure what the hell it was, they didn't know if I was a circus performer or a parachute jumper. But in any event it all looked very fancy with my air gunner badge and my key chain and this crazy hat at a strange angle," Saul said. "But as long as I had a valid pass no one would bug me, and so for months every time I was queried, out came my passbook, valid pass. That valid pass gave me free food at the Hollywood Canteen, free street car or bus rides, free tickets to plays, dinner."

Co-founded by Bette Davis and John Garfield, the Hollywood Canteen was an ambitious home front nightclub that provided free food, entertainment, and socializing to service members from both the United States and overseas. The club was housed in a converted barn and staffed primarily by volunteers from the motion picture and show business community, so it wasn't unusual on any given night to find Rita Hayworth in the kitchen serving sandwiches, Hedy Lamarr and Betty Grable on the dance floor with soldiers, and Marlene Dietrich or Bob Hope entertaining onstage. The Canteen also had a blackboard where messages would be posted, and this led to all kinds of interesting developments for Saul.[3]

One of them was a girl by the name of Molly Polland, the personal secretary to iconic American film director Cecil B. DeMille. This connection gave Saul access to Paramount Studio and eventually an introduction to DeMille himself.

"It meant going to the commissary and watching people who I'd heard of all my life just casually goofing around having lunch. It led to watching endless movies in the process of being made. One of them was *Monsieur Beaucaire* with Joan Caulfield and Bob Hope and Bing Crosby," he said. "Watching countless different situations as they developed, I would return to the studio. I remember Bob Hope playing a part of the barber and he decides to act silly and he takes the puff, that was used to dust all over in eighteenth, seventeenth century France, and he decides to put it all over Crosby's face. Which broke everybody up but of course brought the scene to an end." When it was a wrap, Saul managed to go off with Hope for a Coke and stood with him for a photo.[4]

Saul Holiff and Bob Hope at Paramount Pictures, Hollywood, 1945.

At nightfall, if there wasn't much happening in the Canteen, Saul would return to his bug-infested dormitory behind Jimmy Gleason's house on Cahuenga Boulevard and crawl into bed, his head spinning. It felt lonely and strange. He stared at the ceiling. This was like nothing he had ever encountered. *I have to stay*, he thought, *but where is my place in all this?* It was tough, and competitive. *Maybe I can be an actor myself, or a radio disc jockey.* He rolled over and scratched. Perhaps he could go home and prepare to return again, when he was ready to stay for good. One thing was certain: he had to focus on making connections here and ensure they were solid.[5]

Though Saul was thoroughly taken with the tinsel of Hollywood, there was trouble brewing under its facade. In the spring of 1945, tensions within the labour movement built to a head and more than ten thousand unionized studio workers walked off their jobs. Sparked by union infighting among set directors, the action hit many of Hollywood's major studios and theatres. Led by former boxer and studio painter Herb Sorrell of the Conference of Studio Unions, battles were pitched against the rival International Alliance of Theatrical Stage Employees union.

As spring turned to summer the struggle escalated, and by fall the picketers were still out in force. Clashes escalated between the unions, and the leadership of the Screen Actors Guild, which included Ronald Reagan, voted to cross the picket lines. Some actors, such as Humphrey Bogart, then did so. But many others, like Bette Davis, did not. The conflict got so heated at one point that, fearing reprisals, Reagan would lie awake at night in bed with his gun, ear cocked for noises outside. By October, days of unrest and mass picketing outside the Warner Bros. studio erupted into a full-scale riot when more than three hundred strikers attempted to block the main gate. Several cars that tried to pass the picket line were turned over by picketers and tear gas bombs unleashed by Warner's armed security guards. Conflict erupted among the firefighters, who were asked to turn their hoses on the strikers, and the crowd swelled to thousands. Police, security, picketers from other unions, and non-union scabs all descended into a brawl of fist fighting with chains, lead pipes, and monkey wrenches.[6]

It was at this time that Saul decided to visit the Warner Bros. studios armed with the rather naive idea that he would try to work his way into a face-to-face meeting with founder Jack Warner. He surveyed the striking throng, an obstacle he hadn't anticipated. Tenacious as ever, he negotiated through the angry crowd as they as they moved in and out of the front gate and called for strikers to spike the gas tanks of vehicles with sugar. With no regular way to get into the studios, as they were closed up tight, Saul somehow wormed his way through to the office door. Glancing over his shoulder, grateful to be away from the noise, he approached the front desk.

Somewhere, he thought he had heard company president Jack Warner was born in London, Ontario. *That makes us practically brothers,* Saul thought with a smile. It was a stretch, but it might work as an "in" to get through the fortress gates. The secretary looked at him expectantly as he approached. "Ah, this is very difficult to explain, but my name is Holiff and I'm from London, Ontario, and Mr. Warner is from London, Ontario, and … I thought he might like to see me," Saul blurted out.[7]

The woman blinked and then began to laugh. When she recovered, a buzzer was pressed and Saul was told that a person would be right out to attend to his request. The man who soon emerged introduced himself as Milton Sperling, son-in-law of Warner Bros. founder Harry Warner. After some chuckling at Saul's explanation, he confirmed that a meeting with Jack wasn't going to happen. But he could offer him a chance to check out the premises. "I never met Jack or Harry Warner; I never got into the inner sanctum at all. But I was invited in to wander around, any time I wanted, in the studio lot. Those connections in that studio were actually very valuable to me. While wandering in there, I came across and chatted with Cary Grant as he drove his Cord convertible beige car," said Saul. It was a marvelous time, and that made it for him. *Show business, one way or another, come hell or high water — it has to be my life,* he thought feverishly.[8]

Unfortunately, life had other plans for Saul Holiff, and he soon fell ill with a severely infected wisdom tooth. In unbearable pain, he weighed his options. To get treatment would blow his cover — he was permitted to wear a uniform for only thirty days following his discharge, and it was already weeks past that point. He was in the United States illegally, wearing his uniform illegally, perusing the Canteen illegally, with a pocketful of illegal passes. No, he was certain that if he attempted to go to a veteran's hospital under the guise of warranting treatment in the States, he would be discovered.

With a heavy heart he decided to return to Canada, consoling himself with the thought that he could surely find his way back to California when he felt up to it. In the meantime, he decided to follow through on his aspiration to become a radio disc jockey, and secured an audition with London's CFPL Radio. By the time he arrived back home and went for treatment at Westminster Hospital, it turned out that not just one but all of his wisdom teeth were infected. During the subsequent painful extraction, the dentist — a tiny man with bifocal glasses who operated on clients while standing atop a little cart — cut down into his jawbone and muscle. Forty-eight hours later, Saul could barely open his mouth. "I was so unsure of myself, so certain that if I postponed the audition that I would screw it up and that would be the end of it, that I went and had the audition and I spoke, virtually strangling on every word," remembered Saul. "I didn't get the job. They waited until I was finished before they threw me out, mind you."[9]

The failed audition marked the death of that particular dream, but not the end of his Hollywood ambitions. It was impossible to forget the way those weeks in California had illuminated his imagination. Though terribly insecure, Saul possessed a unique ability to bluff, to project an outward show of confidence, and the risks involved in travelling alone had only further developed this trait. Upon his return to London, he began to hone another skill that would take him even further: the art of self-promotion. Taking a page from his father's book in how he had pursued chess coverage in the media, Saul contacted the local newspaper and it subsequently ran a piece on him and his adventures, titled "Blue Uniform Key to Hollywood Visit." "Those people out there are the most willing and most generous hosts one could hope for or imagine," he told the reporter.[10]

In the ensuing years, Saul drifted through a variety of jobs with moderate success, but none held deep appeal. In 1947, he completed a year-long accounting course and worked briefly as a bookkeeper for a plumbing and appliances company before securing a position as a waiter at the Windsor Hotel in Hamilton, the first restaurant-bar in Ontario to legally reintroduce liquor following the prohibition. Though he didn't receive any training, he managed to save a thousand dollars within a year. "It was a disaster, but I made a lot of money," Saul recalled. Despite the cash, Saul was not particularly service-oriented, so he answered a help-wanted ad posted by a shoe salesman and became his driver, hitting stores all over Ontario and Quebec. It somehow felt natural to be on the road; the endless driving suited his directionless mindset, and connections flourished with a variety of business owners throughout the province. But if he needed security or safety, there was none to be found at home. For whatever reason, his father made it clear he was not welcome to return.

"Not only myself, but mother also is fully convinced that if you ever decide to come and stay home, your life will be so miserable that you will be glad to leave as fast as you came," Joel wrote to Saul in May of 1947. "I am not referring to weekends. You can come home any weekend you wish, but as for staying here permanently, I warn you accordingly, and I mean it. Now it's up to you to act accordingly."

London was clearly not an option, so using the contacts made through the driving job, within two years Saul went into business for himself. He bought his first car, a brand new 1949 Chevrolet Coach, and sold ladies' dresses wholesale throughout northern Ontario. But he soon received another letter from his parents, and this one requested that he come home immediately.[11]

"It finally happened — my father had a heart attack after almost forty years of excellent health. They want me to go home and take over. It makes me think of a few years ago when he told me not to come home from Hamilton. Then, I needed moral support and strength more than anything," Saul wrote in his diary. It sent him into a deep reflection about the nature of home, family, and the strained relationship with his father.

"I never heard the word [love] when I was growing up. It made me feel acutely uncomfortable when I did," he later mused. "We never saw a display of affection, never experienced hugs and all that stuff. It just wasn't part of our family scene. Being properly inhibited was. I always thought people using the word love were exhibitionists, or phony, or both. Something Holden Caulfield here. But if I thought about it at all, and if anybody ever said that they loved me, the statement was always suspect in my mind."

Despite mixed feelings, he did return, and shouldered the small clothing business his father had nursed along since 1933. Saul renamed it Store at Your Door and rented a showroom and some facilities.[12]

The business did well, and Saul both made a living for himself and supported his parents at the same time. But it was both a blessing and a curse. For the next five years, Store at Your Door was just that — Saul would conduct business at customers' homes, and he hated it. In 1956, having saved enough money, Saul renamed the business Saul Holiff Kustom Klothes and opened a showroom above a furrier downtown on King Street. With an innovative flourish, he christened the front part of the loft The Swatch Bar, and fashioned an area where customers could relax while perusing books of fabric samples. In the back, he carved out

Saul Holiff greeting patrons at his Swatch Bar (London, Ontario, 1957).

a tiny bachelor pad to cut down on costs. Weekly newspaper ads carried a variety of the catchy slogans and phrases he coined, such as: "If Your Clothes Aren't Becoming to You, You Should Be Coming to Us."

Inexplicably, it was at this point that Saul fell into a deep depression. The store was up and running, but he had gone into debt to open it, borrowing money from his brother-in-law Sam, among others. The anxiety around this was crippling, and his tranquilizers weren't cutting through it. Consumed by darkness, he wrote out a Last Will and Testament by hand on his Holiff's custom stationery and then penned a suicide note. "Please go up the back stairs. You shall find my door open, and inside, my body. Please be kind enough to inform my brother, so that he in turn might inform my parents," he wrote. On a separate sheet, he drafted a note to his family.

June 13, 1956

To my family —
Please forgive me!!!
    I guess I'm a misfit or just a plain fool. Whether I am, life seems to have become too involved for me. I've caused you enough pain and upset. If anything or anybody is to blame for my situation, I suppose the fault is with myself.
    Have courage to face this last source of unhappiness that I shall inflict upon you.

All my love,
Saul.[13]

Something changed his mind, however. Perhaps the note itself provided some catharsis, but after putting his thoughts to paper, Saul voluntarily sought out the assistance of a psychiatrist at London's Victoria Hospital and was admitted to the psychiatric floor that evening. Over the next few months he was subjected to electroshock therapy; with help from the psychiatrist and his friends, Saul slowly surfaced from his self-imposed seclusion at the hospital and felt he could return to his life. "I emerged from a very serious blue funk, came to realize that I had unrealistically magnified my problems totally out of proportion and had completely distorted my financial situation in my own mind," Saul later wrote. "I also came to the realization during that period, that my vanity (always a big factor), an oversized ego, and of course my biggest nemesis, self-deception, had led to and was responsible for most of my problems."[14]

Back in the game, as the last vestiges of his youthful awkwardness faded away, Saul became attuned to the nuances of fine clothing and dressed in the latest fashions from New York. The outside world responded in kind. Respected by other men, he also began to receive attention from women who recognized him from the swarthy headshot splashed across most of his newspaper ads. Saul had always fared well with the opposite sex — while still in the family home on Wharncliffe Road, he somehow convinced his mother to allow his Dutch girlfriend to live in his room with him, despite her frustration at continually finding lipstick smeared all over his pillowcases. But now it seemed that every other week he had a different girl on his arm. Never one to retain what he learned only for himself, Saul then sought to pass on his knowledge of women to his nephew Larry Paikin, Sam and Ann's son.

"If you want, I'll take you out and get you laid," Saul told Larry, who at nineteen years old was still a virgin and lived in a university frat house with about ten other guys, all of whom were big on talk and short on experience. Larry readily agreed, and, along with two friends, travelled with Saul to the nearby tobacco farming town of Tillsonburg, where there were a number of brothels.

"He took us to this farm house that had no electricity, they had kerosene lamps, and we walked in and sat down. I remember it was five dollars a shot. I went in and came out about ten minutes later with a big smile on my face and the second guy went in and came out, and the third guy went in and came out and the second guy went in again," said Larry.

While all this was going on, Saul, ever the entrepreneur — and whose trunk was full of women's clothes — seized the opportunity to offer some of his wares to the waiting prostitutes. "He sold all his samples to the girls while we were screwing our heads off," remembered Larry with a laugh.

As Saul was growing up, his family had the rare distinction of being the only Jewish household in an all-gentile neighbourhood of wealthier and educated families, and as a result, Saul had long harboured a sense of inferiority that he channelled into a dedication to self-improvement and self-education. Deep into philosophers like Friedrich Nietzsche and Arthur Schopenhauer since he was a teen, he consistently pushed himself ever further in his reading habits, and began to visit estate sales to add to the significant collection of books that was becoming his personal library. A subscription to *Reader's Digest* offered him a monthly quota of new words that he regularly devoured and then worked to incorporate into his lexicon. Well-versed in a variety of topics, Saul soon developed into an adept conversationalist, which further broadened his affiliations. However, there were some circles that would always be closed to him, no matter how successful or charismatic he became.[15]

One day Saul decided to apply for a membership at the local YMCA, where he was active in a variety of capacities, such as their Speakeasy Club, Co-ed Club, and Fitness Club. On occasion he also modelled for a women's organization. At his request, he was curtly informed there were "no openings." Suspicious, he invented a different name and identity as an executive with General Motors Diesel, which had just set up shop in London, and phoned another department. Immediately the voice on the other end replied, "Come on in. Delighted to have you." Armed with this evidence of discrimination, Saul took it to the board of the YMCA and, in the ensuing scandal, became their first Jewish member. But the exclusion stung, and it wasn't the only example.

By then his clothing store had taken off, and Saul was a strong and regular customer at the Bank of Montreal. Naturally, he thought nothing of it when an invitation was extended for a special dinner at the long-standing London Club across the street from the bank. However, the hospitality would not last. "Some clerk had made an egregious error, and when they realized they had invited one of their clients that was

Jewish, all hell broke loose as to how they could diplomatically un-invite me, so as to not cause some Colonel Weldon to have an upset stomach," Saul later said in his diary.[16]

Amidst a sense he would never quite fit in no matter what level of success he achieved, the allure of Hollywood lingered. But what would his place be within that world? Saul decided to test his abilities onstage, and joined the London Little Theatre, where he performed in several plays, including *Teahouse of the August Moon* in 1957. "Saul Holiff, essentially a good actor and possessed of an easy stage presence, fell victim to a fault I have commented on earlier. This play was satire," the *London Free Press* theatre critic said in his review of Little London Theatre's production of *The Torch-Bearers*. "Mr. Holiff's approach to the role was far too heavy. I wish he would smile now and then to let us know that he, too, is being made fun of by the playwright." Of course, the reviewer couldn't have known how his broken teeth made smiling an unpleasant endeavour.[17]

It felt as though the world was a finely tuned machine and Saul was the mechanic, with the success of his store and his venture into acting, which allowed him to finally enjoy the sensation of being liked — if not by all the reviewers, then at least by his fellow actors. But he soon began to wonder if the position he was destined to inhabit wasn't on the stage, but behind it.

With that in mind, he turned to the emergence of a new music scene in Canada: rock 'n' roll.

Teenagers in Canada were first introduced to rock 'n' roll music via the radio, and there was no one more integral to this awakening of their senses than radio disc jockey Red Robinson. Based in Vancouver, Robert Gordon Robinson landed his first radio show at the age of seventeen, after he prank called CJOR's afternoon teen show to deliver a spot-on impersonation of actor Jimmy Stewart. When the *Vancouver Sun* picked up the story as real, Robinson called again, in character as Peter Lorre, and host Al "Pappy" Jordan figured out the ruse. Invited on as a recurring guest, Robinson was then offered the show when Jordan left in 1954.

Immediately, Robinson began turning his audience on to doo-wop and rock 'n' roll, and was one of the first white DJs in the country to play music by African American artists. "It was all black music, and this is where I faced a whole bunch of bullets — not real bullets, but verbal bullets. 'How can you play all that nigger music?' That's what they said to me. And I said, 'Because I happen to like it.' And the kids at school liked it, I mean, that's where I got the inspiration to play rock 'n' roll, was the kids at school," recalled Robinson, who wielded enormous power with his show and commanded an unprecedented 50 percent of the local audience.

The first-ever rock 'n' roll concert on the West Coast took place in June of 1956 and featured Bill Haley & His Comets at the Kerrisdale Arena in Vancouver, emceed by none other than Robinson. "It was a rock 'em, sock 'em, knocked-out bunch of kids going crazy. It was nuts," he said.

Out east, Saul thought he'd try his hand at promotion — and Bill Haley, whose smash 1955 hit "Rock Around the Clock" garnered him wide credit as the father of rock 'n' roll, was high on his list. But first, he convinced two Hamilton-based businessmen to each invest $1,500 to bring jazz trumpeter Louis Armstrong to Buffalo, New York, for a one-night engagement. Once the venue was secured, Saul felt he had a surefire winner on his hands. Armstrong was huge, and Saul was a fan himself. Then disaster struck. Elvis Presley was booked to play Buffalo on the same night, at the Memorial Auditorium. If there was a star bigger than Armstrong, or pretty much anyone in the biz at that time, it was Presley. It was a loss for all the promoters, and a personal embarrassment for Saul, as he had invited his brother Morris and his wife Joyce to attend the show. Ever the gambler — he was currently deep into penny stocks on the Toronto Stock Exchange — he shrugged off the losses and steeled his determination.

The next month, he scored the show with Bill Haley & His Comets and brought them to the London Arena for the first time. "In Britain they waited for hours to see the Bill Haley rock 'n' roll show. He got the biggest welcome Britain's ever given to a show personality.... And now he's coming to London Arena," crowed the radio spot Saul purchased on CFPL to advertise the show. "Join the crowd, see rock 'n' roll at its best with the King of Rock, Bill Haley, when he appears in London with his Comets May 24."

Saul Holiff stands with early rock 'n' roll pioneer Bill Haley, whom he promoted extensively in the late 1950s. London, Ontario, 1957.

The crowd was near capacity, but after the cost of promotion, posters, and rent of the arena, Saul made a grand total of $54. Undaunted, he pressed on, and by early August he hosted a dance marathon at the Lucan Arena with the Everly Brothers — who were currently enjoying the success of their song "Bye Bye Love." The first marathon in the district for thirty-five years, the catch was that this one would feature four bands that played only rock 'n' roll music, Saul told columnist Dick Newman. Judged by a panel, first prize was a new hi-fi recording set, and the venue featured a glass-enclosed mezzanine floor and modern air-cooling system that consisted of huge blocks of ice set in front of blower fans.[18]

Later that month Saul went on to promote a double bill with pop singer Jimmie Rodgers and a sixteen-year-old Canadian teen idol named Paul Anka. The son of an Ottawa restaurant owner, Anka was riding the wave of his monster hit "Diana," penned when his friend Diane Ayoub asked him to write a song about her while they were at a high school party in Toronto. Saul felt certain about this show, and about Anka himself, who in his mind was destined to be another George Jessel.

Billed as a "rock 'n' roll costume ball," the show's advance ticket sales included a draw for one lucky girl to have dinner with Anka and then dance with him at the arena. Despite the robust advertisements and Anka's popularity, the show flopped. Clearly learning on the job, Saul continued to lose money on his promotions most of the time, and if he made anything at all, it was usually less than a hundred dollars.[19]

Despite this he remained convinced there was money to be made; he just needed to figure out how. And though he was personally more partial to the horns and strings of jazz and classical music, the challenge of promotion itself appealed to him more than selling clothing. He would soon learn that there were also other nuances, aside from the finances, such as the finicky and unpredictable nature of artists.

Edgy and zany, musician Little Richard caught Saul's attention with a string of hits he released through the 1950s, like "Tutti Frutti" and "Long Tall Sally," so he phoned his manager and booked him for two dates in December. Two months before the shows, Little Richard's management in New York phoned back to inform Saul that though the contract had been signed, these dates — and all others he had scheduled on his tour — were cancelled. While on a record-breaking tour in Australia, Little Richard had experienced an epiphany after a ball of fire soared overhead as he played at a stadium in Sydney. It was the launch of the Russians' *Sputnik 1*, but already exasperated with the pressures of touring and the need for spiritual regeneration, Richard took it as a sign. Abruptly, he decided to leave his rock 'n' roll lifestyle, change his ways, and become a preacher.[20]

"I have a great favour to ask. This afternoon, Gale Agencies in New York phoned to tell me that two dates that were signed and sealed for Little Richard and his orchestra in London and Kitchener on December 20th and 21st, plus all of his other bookings, have been cancelled. It appears that besides needing psychiatric treatment, Little Richard has become a monk," Saul wrote to Everly Brothers manager Wesley H. Rose. "I had made extensive arrangements for these dates, such as the securing of highly desirable auditoriums in both Kitchener and London and have now been left holding the bag. I know that Don and Phil are not booked for these dates and would appreciate having them appear for me at that time."[21]

The Brothers were unable to fill the shows, as they wanted to be home for Christmas, but despite these setbacks, Saul persisted. The following year, he expanded to nearby cities and bought three dates for Alan Freed's ABC-TV summer series *The Big Beat*, a show featuring Buddy Holly, Chuck Berry, and Jerry Lee Lewis. It was a smash, and the venue was packed to the rafters with more than four thousand wild, sweaty teenagers. By the summer of 1958, Saul promoted his first tour with the Everly Brothers and booked them for eight dates across Ontario and Quebec. Saul drove the boys to each city himself, during which he caught a glimpse of their notoriously acrimonious relationship and watched in the rear-view mirror as they fought bitterly "like cats and dogs" in the back seat the entire time.[22]

More dates followed with some of the most prominent names in rock: the Ink Spots, Sam Cooke, Frankie Avalon, Duane Eddy, Bobby Helms, Kitty Wells, Brenda Lee, Marty Robbins, Buck Owens, Hank Snow, Jim Reeves, Ferlin Husky, Faron Young, and Carl Perkins of "Blue Suede Shoes" fame. When rock 'n' roll acts first began their crossover into

Saul often postered his car to advertise the shows he was promoting. In the background is the theatre that advertised a contest to win a trip to Mexico, which Barbara Holiff won. Ontario, 1961.

Canada, they frequently travelled as package shows, primarily because many of them had only a few songs in their entire repertoire. As such, it wasn't unheard of to have up to fifteen performers in a two-hour show.

In the early days, Carl Perkins performed in a country trio with his brothers Jay and Clayton, often touring with drummer W.S. "Fluke" Holland and the Isley Brothers, who were soul gospel singers. The first time they played in Canada they drove up in a brand new 1956 Fleetwood Cadillac for a date in the old mining town of Trail, nestled in southern British Columbia.[23] "It was dirt roads, and not because it was muddy or anything, but because there were deep ruts in the road where people had been driving through and we all had to climb out of the Cadillac because it kept bottoming out. In some places we had to push that car," remembered Fluke.

Saul soon booked them for a show in Ontario and got a first-hand initiation into the dynamics of wild rock 'n' roll personalities. "Clayton Perkins, he's Carl's younger brother — craziest dude I ever heard of or met since then. We showed up, and Saul was standin' out in front of the hotel, waitin' on us, and we all said, 'There's Saul Holiff.' And Clayton got out of the car and he ran up to Saul and jumped into his arms and bit him on his ear. The funny thing about that is, somebody like Saul — sophisticated, alligator shoes and all this kind of stuff, and someone we were all lookin' up to — and this crazy boy gets out of the car, and Saul never forgot it. Every time I saw him after that, I'd always say, 'Hey, Saul, how's that ear of yours?'"[24]

With contacts firmly established with many big-name musical acts, Saul then turned to the business of making money. There had to be a way to utilize their star power in a way that was more lucrative for him than typical promotional work.

By the spring of 1959, Saul had expanded his other entrepreneurial endeavours and opened Sol's Square Boy, a drive-in restaurant and the first in Ontario to offer push-button voice ordering from the comfort of your car. As a gimmick, everything in the restaurant was square — "including the owner," Saul liked to joke — from the cube-shaped signage to the ice cream scoops and even the hamburgers. Square patties were advertised with the clever slogan that it was "four extra bites for your money." A partnership project several years in the making, promotion for the restaurant was kicked into high gear and at times edged into the ridiculous. The grand opening of Sol's Square Boy featured a full-page fake news story about a pair of gorillas that had escaped from the set of a jungle movie and were "cavorting" in the restaurant. It included a photo of Saul restraining men in gorilla suits, who were going after a couple of horrified "square girls" — employees at the restaurant. "You may not have to be a member of the ape family … but you'll have a lot of fun monkeying around at the official opening of Sol's Square Boy Drive-In," ran the caption underneath.[25]

The grand opening day itself featured men dressed in gorilla costumes bouncing on trampolines outside the restaurant to illustrate the "crazy prices," and a woman staged so that she appeared to be frozen in a giant block of ice to promote their ice cream floats and milkshakes.

Aside from posing yet another challenge and source of revenue, the restaurant also provided Saul with the perfect venue for cross-promotional ventures. It seemed a no-brainer to make the burger joint work together with the rock shows to draw in the lucrative teen demographic. A proviso was quickly embedded into the performers' contracts that required they visit Sol's Square Boy afterward to sign autographs; an event that would in turn be advertised on the radio. As London was a rather obscure Canadian city to the big acts from the States, to combine rock 'n' roll music with hamburgers would not only allow the artists to forge closer ties with the very people who would buy their records but also increase the business at Saul's restaurant as teens flocked there en masse after a show.

It was around this time that another American musician came on Saul's radar. While negotiating further dates around an upcoming Carl Perkins show in London, manager Bob Neal brought up another possible client — a rising star named Johnny Cash. The charismatic young country singer had joined the Sun Records lineup in 1955 and was enjoying some popularity with his hit song "I Walk the Line," written as an ode to his wife, Vivian Cash, to assuage her concerns about dalliances with other women on the road. This wasn't the first time Saul had heard of Cash, who was on a whirlwind fifteen-day tour of Canada to promote his latest single, the rather saccharine "Ballad of a Teenage Queen." Just a month prior, he had received complimentary tickets to Cash's show at the Palace Pier in Toronto with an offer that, as a rising figure in the world of promotions, Saul would have a ringside table and be introduced to the crowd by the emcee from the stage.

There was no mistaking that Cash was swiftly becoming a hot act in Canada. Given the volatile nature of promotions — so much so that he eventually named his business Volatile Attractions, though that was more of a reference to the stock market — Saul needed a musician who was a sure thing. Maybe this Cash guy would fit the bill.[26]

3

WHEN SAUL MET JOHNNY

As with so many things in his life, Saul's ascent in the world of music promotion was built on a foundation of research. In this case it meant regular trips to Heintzmann's, the record store on Dundas Street, where he would walk his fingers through records for hours. It was a musical hub for not only London but also all the surrounding districts. At the epicentre of its teenage section stood Dave Roberts, a sixteen-year-old music aficionado with a deft ear cocked toward what was up-and-coming, who reigned over Heintzmann's back counter and listening booths, where teens flocked to check out the latest records.

Initially a customer, Roberts made incessant musical requests that eventually landed him a job at the store after the employees realized he knew more about what the kids were listening to than they did. He was a smart kid, and had a deft handle on what was hip. From there he grew to become a source for radio DJs and promoters on which records were moving fast and who was going to be the next big thing. Clever enough to know what he didn't know, it wasn't long before Saul realized Roberts had what he needed.

"I knew a lot about what could make a hit and what didn't, so I did get called on," said Roberts. "Saul used me as a sounding board to say, 'What's cooking? What should we be doing?'"

Saul wanted to know about Johnny Cash, who first caught his ear when he heard "Five Feet High and Rising," his ode to a childhood flood, on a jukebox a couple of years earlier. Bob Neal had set down a solid offer for an August 16 date for Cash, at the cost of $1,250, and he needed to know more. Primarily in charge of overseeing the pop section, Dave was the first to notice when hits like Cash's "Walk the Line" began to make their crossover from country. The trend was clear, and it was Dave who first insisted that, as an avid listener of a variety of stations, like WSM out of Nashville, it was imperative that Saul look into expanding his promotions to include country musicians. The names of country stars like Merle Haggard, Johnny Horton, and Eddy Arnold were still unfamiliar to Saul, but that was about to change. In return for Dave's help, Saul would often take the teenager out to shows with him in style, picking him up at his modest home in west London in a white fin-tailed Cadillac Eldorado. The image of Saul's elegant car coasting to a stop outside Dave's house was a sight the young man never forgot.

One night after Saul promoted a package show in Kitchener that featured Duane Eddy and the Rebels and Buddy Holly and the Crickets, Dave and Saul headed back to London and decided to stop to get something to eat. "We pulled into a restaurant along the highway. As we settled into a booth we looked across the restaurant and saw Buddy Holly and his band at another table. We then joined them for an after-show burger," said Roberts. Shy and nervous, Buddy answered all those who directed questions at him with "Sir," and it soon struck fifteen-year-old Dave that the singer did not seem to have any idea just how big a star he was.[1]

By 1958 Johnny Cash had officially joined Columbia Records, for whom he had been recording new songs all summer. Saul watched as the artist took the stage for a show in London. As an onstage presence, Johnny's enigmatic electricity was unmistakable, and to see him was an experience that far surpassed his recorded material. Though still uncertain of himself, he commanded the stage in a manner that made it hard to look away. Not quite as pretty as Elvis, his dark hair and tall, lithe frame draped in white satin nonetheless cut a striking figure. Possessed of a charismatic darkness, it granted him a depth unlike other artists of his genre. Together with bassist Marshall Grant, with a face as happy and open as a Christmas ham, and guitarist Luther Perkins, eyes askance like a dog that had just eaten his master's dinner, they painted quite a picture onstage. Though the

Johnny Cash, backstage in London, Ontario, 1958.

music wasn't as nuanced and technically complex as the music Saul typically favoured — the Tennessee Two's musical abilities were rudimentary, and their stage presence stiff — that signature boom-chicka-boom sound, mixed with Johnny's rich, unusual baritone, provided a certain warmth he could appreciate. *It's like the Bible*, he thought. *It does something for some people, and that's fine.* Most important, it was what the kids liked, and they were the ones who would follow Johnny like he was the Pied Piper into Saul's restaurant.

Saul recognized potential when he saw it, and Cash had it in spades.

After the performance, Cash — in a large cowboy hat — kept to himself and glowered the entire time. When introduced to Saul backstage after the show, he "perfunctorily" dismissed him, Saul later recalled. It was a rejection Saul remembered as painful, as he didn't usually seek out people and had made a special effort for Cash. Apparently the darkness Saul had sensed in the performer wasn't just an act, and the two "did not hit it off at all."[2]

The following year, Saul booked Johnny for a show at the Lucan Memorial Arena. After three twenty-five-minute sets, Johnny prepared to depart to Saul's restaurant as agreed in the contract, though in this instance Johnny stipulated that his presence not be advertised in advance. Everything proceeded as planned, but before he and Marshall departed for the restaurant, they wanted to discuss finances with Saul, so the three men pushed into the arena's cramped box office.[3]

Though it concerned only a trifling amount of cash, a difference in the range of forty dollars, the animosity that had merely simmered during Saul and Johnny's first encounter erupted into an argument. The two haggled over interpretations regarding Johnny's contract and whether advertising expenses were to be taken off the top prior to the performer's cut being calculated (they were). The disagreement irked Saul, who considered himself a principled man who rarely made mistakes when it came to specifics. He was also hard-nosed, and wasn't about to be pushed around by some young country singer, rising star or not.

Saul fiddled with a cufflink and stared at the men while he collected himself. He couldn't help but reflect on all the piddling negotiations he had been required to hash out over recent years. The previous summer he had hosted Jerry Lee Lewis at a net loss in London, and two weeks earlier he had promoted hard-drinking honky-tonk singer Faron Young. Laid up for weeks afterward with hepatitis, Saul had been required to phone Young from his hospital bed to explain why the 15 percent non-residence tax for performers — which Young was refusing to pay — was, in fact, a requirement. It had been a dreadful experience; to top it off, Young was both egotistical and "one of the worst shit disturbers" Saul had ever seen in his life.[4]

Many artists simply had no idea how much sweat went into guaranteeing promotion that went off without a hitch. And that was exactly Saul's specialty: a smooth, seamless experience that appeared effortless. Despite his better judgment, the complaints and hairsplitting felt like ingratitude.

"You're just like the rest of them," he snapped at Johnny, regarding him with something approaching disdain. The comment gave Johnny pause. He prided himself on his distinction from other performers, many of whom he, too, felt were shallow and had a lackadaisical attitude toward music and performing. He didn't like to think of himself as being like anyone else. Just the week prior, he had announced his departure from the Grand Ole Opry and moved his family across the country to California, in part to pursue a career on the screen, but also to distinguish himself from the rabble in Nashville. He was his own man. The two men regarded each other silently in the stuffy room. Johnny slowly nodded, and then cracked a half-smile. *This is a man who stands up for what he believes*, Cash mused. Saul felt something shift. Johnny suddenly recognized him as a man in his own right, and an outspoken one at that — a distinct entity rather than just "some passing face in the night." The two men shook hands.[5]

"Come as you are & eat in your car," proclaimed the cube-shaped neon sign as "Old Gray," Cash's Cadillac sedan, joined the other Cadillacs and VW Beetles lined up in the drive-in parking lot. After making an appearance, Cash asked if there was somewhere else to eat, so Saul drove him to a nearby steak house, wisely concealing any insult he may have felt.

Finances on the Cash shows had worked well, so Saul negotiated a mid-November tour with Johnny's new manager, Stew Carnall, for a couple of dates in Kitchener and Peterborough. After the final show in Peterborough, band members Marshall Grant and Luther Perkins were eating at a restaurant with cowboy singer Johnny Western and fiddler Gordon Terry when they noticed a man outside in the bitter cold, pacing beside his Cadillac convertible. Looking exasperated as he approached the restaurant, they realized it was Saul. The door jingled faintly as he came in. After he called a tow truck, Saul approached the table and chatted with the men, who were surprised and pleased at how friendly the promoter's demeanour was. They began to warm to this city slicker. Stung by their previous encounter and the haggles over finances, Saul had been reluctant to engage with Cash and refused to speak to him for the entire two and a half days, taking care to avoid his dressing room. However, outside of business negotiations, Saul now seemed friendly to the men, even funny. And the shows had been a success, of that there was little doubt — Saul was back in the black, but only barely.[6]

Once the car was functional again, Saul picked up a friend, real estate magnate Keith Samitt, and the two hit the new 401 expressway to Montreal. As the highway unrolled in the headlights, his mind pored over his finances. The proceeds from the latest shows were a relief; the previous month he had promoted Marty Robbins in a disastrous tour that had sunk him, with more than two thousand dollars in lost revenue. Robbins had, of course, been gracious about the whole affair, and even gone so far as to attempt to adjust the contract so that Saul wouldn't be out of pocket.

"That Marty Robbins tour didn't go over so well," Saul said to Keith, thinking out loud.

"Yeah? But he's got that big song out, don't he?"

"'El Paso.' I know, I thought it was a safe bet. He's a good guy, Marty. Luckily, I don't owe anything, but boy, I lost every liquid nickel on that tour," said Saul, clenching his jaw and glancing at the speedometer. They were doing at least eighty miles an hour, but the highway was empty. He was broke. He had to think of something. "Marty said he'd arrange something so I could make a few bucks on the next tour. Maybe I oughta take him up on that now."

He glanced at the car phone, a gadget he adored and used at every available opportunity. It made him feel a bit like Lyndon B. Johnson, who he heard also had a wet bar in his car.

"Hey, Saul. You said these shows you just did went over well. Why don't you just get some more dates for Johnny instead?" said Keith.

Saul glanced at him, and then back at the road. Of course. He lifted the phone. "Get me Stew Carnall," he said, and pressed his foot on the gas.[7]

Carnall had previously managed Johnny in a partnership with Bob Neal, but had bought him out in the beginning of 1960 and had since taken over full managerial duties. A start-up promoter from southern California, he was a prep-school boy who came from money, drove a brand-new Cadillac convertible, and kept himself busy booking small country packages. Four years earlier, he had come across Johnny's music while swilling a beer and thumbing through songs on a jukebox and was immediately hooked. Initially, the seeming sophistication of tall, blond Carnall in his fancy shirtsleeves and vest put Johnny and his bandmates on edge; they were accustomed to eating at greasy spoons and setting off firecrackers in hotel rooms. However, after a few tours Carnall gave in and became as wild as they were.[8]

Carnall's burgeoning friendship with Cash rose just as Neal's relationship had begun to cool, and he became more of a central figure, but often in the role of friend and party companion. They had experienced their share of outrageous ideas that were often successful, like the time he booked Cash for New Year's Eve shows in three different California-based cities — and then chartered a plane to pull it off — but Johnny was also in desperate need of someone reliable. By this point he was non-stop touring, performing almost three hundred shows a year to audiences of thousands. A racetrack junkie, Carnall had convinced Johnny to invest in a racehorse with him they named "Walk the Line," and though he never managed to place better than third, it seemed that Stew had been spending more time hitting the tracks than he had managing Johnny.[9]

Saul took note of the slack left behind by Carnall and began to keep tabs on all aspects of Cash's career and what his management entailed. After he called Stew from his car, both men agreed to work as partners on an eleven-show tour of Ontario in May, the largest Saul had yet organized

Johnny Cash, at home in California, circa 1960.

for Johnny. Everything had to be in place. Though Stew came from money and could cut as impressive a figure as Saul did, he was so accustomed to their haphazard ways — carrying wads of cash in paper bags, showing up for flights only ten minutes before they left, and regularly trashing hotel rooms with paint, axes, and handmade explosives — that the litany of details Saul regaled him with during their negotiations must have both dazzled and irritated him. It may have also made him wonder if his days were numbered.

"Please forgive my long-windedness, but I feel that, to avoid any misunderstanding, I should be quite thorough concerning our arrangements," Saul wrote in a four-page letter to Carnall regarding every nuance of the upcoming tour, from the receptivity of audiences in different areas of the country to the cost, availability, and suitability of venues — factoring in seating capacity and whether multiple shows were required to serve demand — and the price of local radio advertising in various cities, calculated down to the cost per second. In some cases, he averaged out the audience Johnny had drawn the last time he had played in a venue, even if it was years prior, and accounted for that also. "If you will examine the foregoing information you will find that it varies only slightly from your proposition, and that certainly it would make me feel like rolling up my sleeves and making this one helluva promotion," Saul concluded.[10]

JOHNNY CASH

Johnny Cash. This publicity photo, circa 1958, reads, "Saul Holiff, 'World's Greatest Promoter' Your Friend, Johnny Cash."

Johnny put a dime in the hockey arena pay phone again and stabbed in the numbers. They were at a date in North Bay, Ontario, and near the end of the tour Saul had organized with Stew. It was May 18, 1961, and a business venture had arisen that couldn't wait. Once again, Stew was nowhere to be found. Finally, he picked up.

"I've been trying to get a hold of you," said Johnny, shifting his weight from one long leg to the other, uncertain of how to begin. "And I know where you've been, you've been at the track." There was a pause. "Now, I know, but we blew off this deal, and it was very important to me," answered Johnny. He took a breath. "Stew, it's over."

In tears, Stew desperately tried to sway him, and handed the phone to his wife, Lorrie Collins, who was eight months pregnant with their first child. It was a cheap move. For years, Johnny had been besotted with Collins, a rock and roll singer with whom he had toured in his early years and performed, along with her brother Larry, on the Los Angeles television show *Town Hall Party*. Though he was still married to Vivian, Johnny's infatuation with the teenage Collins had become so intense that, consumed with guilt, he confessed his feelings to fellow musician and long-time touring companion Johnny Western while the two were on a drive in the Mojave Desert. Alarmed, Western implored Cash to consider all that he stood to lose: a burgeoning music career that had just taken flight, and his wife and growing family.

"For God's sake, Johnny. I know you like Western movies. Well, just like in the Western movies, you gotta ride out into the sunset by yourself on this one," said Western. "It'll end your career and your family at the same time, and you'll be finished."[11]

Stew Carnall began to chase Collins himself, and by the time she was seventeen, she had impulsively eloped with thirty-five-year-old Carnall — a scandal they narrowly avoided by adding a couple of years onto her age in media reports and subtracting several from his. Rumours circulated that she had married Carnall to avoid torching Cash's career, but nonetheless, disaster was averted. This time, however, even Lorrie Collins wasn't about to sway Cash.

"Get off the damn phone, Lorrie. Stew's fired, and he's going to stay fired, and there's nothing you can do to save his job. It's over," Johnny said, and hung up the phone.[12]

Western, who stood beside Cash as the whole scene unfolded, was secretly pleased. A long-time performer with the king of the cowboys, all-American singer and movie star Gene Autry, Western was most famous for "The Battle of Paladin," a theme song for the popular television series *Have Gun — Will Travel*. Fair-haired, husky, and gorgeous, he was also a real-deal cowboy — a guitar-playing, sharpshooting, Old West aficionado who was possessed of a near-photographic ability to recall events. One of his earliest memories was of sitting on an uncle's horse at eighteen months of age, a feat that flabbergasted his mother when he told her. Unable to drink due to an allergy, Western was often one of the sharpest and most sober-minded of the group, and had kept a keen eye on Saul's meticulous professionalism for months. At that point Saul was merely handling Cash's bookings, though his attention to detail was a skill Cash sorely needed.

The extended tour had allowed Saul time to speak more deeply with Johnny about his career and where he felt it was headed. Saul tried to impress on Cash that he truly thought a man of his presence and talent was destined for much larger venues, and his label should be throwing more effort into promoting him as a pop act, not just as a country star. It was a niche category, he said, and country hits were often noticed only when they crossed over into the pop charts. With Cash-composed songs racking up millions in sales in his first four years, and more than a million with "Walk the Line" alone, Cash was destined for bigger things. In Saul's eyes, that was more than enough reason to start pressuring Columbia Records to deliver.[13]

It was food for thought. Until that point Johnny had felt pretty happy with his lot, blessed even. Who else had this kind of opportunity — to do what they loved to do and get paid for it? But Saul Holiff's ideas pushed things to a whole new level. "Think about it, John. Instead of just ballrooms and dance halls around the United States and Canada, you could be aiming at Europe, the Orient," Saul told him. "And big venues in the U.S. like Carnegie Hall or the Hollywood Bowl. Why not? And that could be just the beginning."[14]

The Canadian tour also permitted them time to hit it off on a personal level, as Saul saw it. At one point while the two men talked at length in his car, Cash confessed he was worried about Vivian, who was pregnant with their fourth child. When Saul produced his car phone so that Johnny might call home and ease his mind, the generosity and luxury of it impressed him to no end. This seemed to be a man who made things happen.[15]

The men may as well have been from different ends of the earth, but the two found they had striking similarities, too. Left desperate by the ravages of the Depression, Johnny's family had relocated to Dyess, Arkansas, when he was three years old to farm cotton as part of Franklin Roosevelt's New Deal program. Beyond the childhood poverty that gave them both a determined edge, both men also grew up in families that had suffered the early and violent loss of a child — Cash's older brother Jack had died at the age of fourteen when a table saw slashed through his abdomen, a defining incident that haunted Johnny for the rest of his life. Both men had also struggled with overbearing fathers who had belittled and singled them out for harsh reprisals, and to whom they always felt they were a disappointment. A stint in the military shaped both men's youth, and each had sold goods door-to-door and found early solace and escape in the arts.

Their differences were remarkable, too, and once the tour finished the two continued to correspond regularly via telegrams and letters throughout the summer of 1961, displaying an increasing affection and amusement regarding these contrasts. They began to collaborate on plans for the future, much of which centred around an extensive upcoming tour of eastern Canada, including a sponsored hunting and fishing trip in Newfoundland, and even talked over the particulars of financing Saul to travel to the Far East on a reconnaissance mission so that they might plan a tour — a particularly ambitious prospect Saul had dreamed up. In early June, he jotted off a telegram about his progress on both projects.

> STILL HOPEFULLY AWAITING YOUR CALL. IN
> MEANTIME I CONTACTED HARMON AIR FORCE
> BASE IN NEWFOUNDLAND TO INVESTIGATE
> A CUSHIONED GUARANTEE TO HANG OTHER
> DATES AROUND. [...] AWAITING YOUR FURTHER

INSTRUCTIONS AS TO APPROXIMATE EAST COAST DATES AND NEWFIE PROPOSAL. HAVE ACCUMU-LATED MUCH INFORMATION ALREADY ON THE FEASIBILITY OF YOUR FAR EAST APPEARANCES. WHATEVER HAPPENS, I REGARD YOU AS ONE OF THE NICEST PEOPLE I KNOW. SAUL HOLIFF.[16]

As he composed another longer and more detailed letter, which was sent around the same time, Saul took time to express his gratitude for the opportunity Cash had given him; privately, he felt insecure about his capabilities. This was all new territory to him, and he felt a deep-seated need to impress Johnny. "Rest assured that I will put every effort and energy at my disposal into making this tour [of eastern Canada] a success. I feel the arrangements are fair, and I consider it a privilege to work on behalf of you, and appreciate the confidence you have shown in me. You can be sure that whatever the nature of the deals made in each city, they will be made with your best interests in mind," Saul wrote on July 4. Enclosed within the letter was a bundle of photos of Johnny, that had been snapped at a recent concert in Guelph, and a long list of cities for the eastern tour, complete with the population of each location and when Johnny last played them, if ever. Near the end of his letter, Saul paused. There was something else that had come up that he wanted to address — the mens' behaviour on the Ontario tour, during which Cash and Gordon Terry, an Alabama fiddler and frequent supporting act, had made prank phone calls.

The way it worked was that the boys would gather around in the hotel room after their show, go through the phone book, and call a random number, no matter what time of the night it was. Disguising his voice, Gordon Terry would then pretend to be a delivery service driver.

"We got a truckload of baby chicks from Bandera, Texas, here," Gordon would say.

"It's the middle of the night; I'm not comin' down there for no baby chicks!" the person on the other end would shout back.

"You'd better come down here, or we're gonna put these chicks in a taxi cab and send them to your house," Gordon would reply, at which point the entire room would fall about laughing.

Recalling these events, Saul added a postscript to the letter: "I haven't yet fully recovered from Gordon Terry's Negro imitations with the special sound effects courtesy of Johnny Cash, and I don't think the people who received those calls will ever recover." His distaste didn't extend much further than an addendum, but the event may have reminded Saul of his own struggles with anti-Semitism.[17]

Though he chose to address the issue in a lighthearted manner, Saul privately thought the behaviour of the men while on the road was alarming and distasteful. Hotel-trashing bad boys before it became rock-star fashionable, their tours were notoriously rowdy. Bassist Marshall Grant regularly carried a circular saw with him for shortening the legs of hotel room tables and chairs, and all the men sported holsters and Colt .45s, which they would load with blanks and then use to stage gunfights down the hotel hallways.[18]

Their pranks ran the gamut from dropping water balloons, eggs, and furniture from hotel balconies to more complex antics, like tying all the doors on a hotel floor together with rope, or painting the doors (or sometimes an entire hotel room) a different colour. On two separate occasions they axed down the wall between their rooms and flushed a cherry bomb down the plumbing — which took out an entire wall of toilets below.

A long-running joke of Marshall Grant's was to sit at a long diner counter, order a big piece of pie with a mountain of meringue, dig in his fork, and then slam it with his hand to splatter the person next to him. On one early tour, the person next to him happened to be Saul, who was mortified. As they left the diner and returned to the road in two cars, Johnny asked Saul to speed up next to Marshall's vehicle so that he could lob pies at him. In retaliation, Marshall handed the wheel to another driver and sped past, blasting Saul with a cap-and-ball pistol that he had loaded with baloney. Thoroughly rattled, Saul pulled the car over to the shoulder of the road and asked one of the other passengers to drive. It was like nothing he had ever encountered. If he thought the Paikin family was charmingly unbridled, these men were like wild animals.

"Saul was completely mortified by the deal because that was his territory where we worked those shows: Peterborough, Kitchener, Sudbury. He was so straitlaced, he couldn't imagine anyone doing that,"

Saul Holiff, Luther Perkins, Gordon Terry, and Johnny Cash on tour in 1962, having a bite to eat at a roadside diner in San Antonio, Texas.

remembered Johnny Western. "He'd never seen anything like that. He was used to ladies and gentlemen, and there weren't any on that tour."

As he grew closer to Cash, Saul also learned to keep his distance; he began to book himself in at separate hotels and avoided the mayhem backstage by hovering about the box office, where he could keep a keen eye on audience numbers and the night's takings. The all-cash world of promotions in those days was notorious for rip-offs, an aspect of the business he loathed. In his mind, business dealings were to be undertaken in good faith, and he adhered to a sense of honesty in such negotiations with a near-spiritual reverence. It was the grease that kept the entire machine running.

Two days later, Johnny replied to Saul's message on letterhead that read, "A Few Very Rural, Badly Phrased But Well Meant Words From Johnny Cash." Typed across the bottom of each page were the words

Singer — Song Writer — Guitar Picker — Cotton Picker. He began by addressing Saul as "Mr. Volatile," and thanking him for the photos he had included. At that time, Cash's publicist was a man named Howard Brandy, so he noted that if Saul needed anything in the promotional department, Howard was his man. The points Saul had raised regarding the proposed tour of eastern Canada and Newfoundland were agreeable, continued Cash, and a trip to the Far East to check out the possibility of a tour was also something he was willing to pay for.

In personal news, Johnny wrote that he had just laid the foundation for his new home in the hills near Ojai in California, where he would live with Vivian, still pregnant, and their three little girls. In total, the property was fifteen acres, situated on the lower slopes of a mountain that overlooked a beautiful valley, with room for stables to house bulls for hamburger in the winter, Cash wrote. In a postscript he added, "Gordon went to Las Vegas over the weekend, won $1,000 playing dice. I went to the mountains with a friend and my 30.06 Winchester. We dry-gulched two deer. Had venison all week."[19]

Saul swiftly composed a letter in return.

June 12, 1961

Dear Mr. Singer, Song-Writer, Guitar Picker and
Cotton Picker …

You've got more titles than an Arabian Sultan, but I think your stationery is terrific! In any event, here are a few very suburban, horribly phrased but terribly confused words from Mr. Volatile.

I appreciate your prompt and thorough answer to my letter of June 4th. I'm glad you liked some of the pictures, and will order the ones you requested, immediately. I'm also very happy to hear that Howard Brandy is doing a good job and have made a note of his address for any contributions to his publicity file. I assume that you are aware of the story in *Billboard*, on Page 6 of the

June 5th issue, concerning your acquiring rights to *The Jimmie Rodgers Story*. I do hope you will go on to produce it, and if there's a part for a dissipated, constipated, overweight, over-wrought, oversexed, and overbearing promoter, I'd like to read for it. [...]

Sorry to hear you are suffering from laryngitis; I wonder if the venison had anything to do with it. I do hope your illness is short-lived and that it doesn't force you to cancel your Texas date.

The description of your new home sounds like a Paradise and the fulfillment of a dream. It's exactly what I would like, only I'm still dreaming.

It's great to hear of Gordon's win in Las Vegas. I wonder if he tells you about his losses.... Incidentally, what does "dry-gulched" mean?

Recently when I spoke to you, you mentioned that you were going to Colorado with your father and Merle Travis, and, to quote you, you were "aimin' to breathe air that ain't never been breathed before." I was so intrigued by the thought behind that statement that, while in Toronto, I called the Entertainment Editor of the *Toronto Star* and he felt as I did, and quoted your remarks in the paper. If you knew what the air is like most of the time in Toronto, you would realize what impact your statement had on those who read it.

Very happy to have received your O.K., plan on meeting Columbia officials in New York next week, and hope to leave for Tokyo around the 5th of July.

Keep well, and good hunting! Your Chicken Pickin' Friend, Saul Holiff.

P.S. Have you ever played England, and if not, would you be interested?[20]

With Carnall out of the picture, Saul had seized the initiative and arranged a flight to New York to meet with Columbia executives in mid-June on Johnny's behalf. What he and Dave Roberts had discussed was true: country stars had a draw, and at least as comparable an appeal as rock 'n' roll acts. With Johnny's charisma and star power, Saul was convinced he needed to be treated as much more of a top-level act. Imploring Cash to also think of himself as a bigger star, he now needed to persuade him that Saul Holiff was the man to take him there. And one way that was going to happen was to build his international presence. Part of the trip to meet with the Columbia executives would be to pressure them to support his idea for a tour for Johnny in Japan. Hell, maybe he could get Elvis to go along, too. Before he left, Saul jotted off a quick telegram.

MEETING COLUMBIA OFFICIALS IN NEW YORK CITY NEXT WEDNESDAY. THEY APPEAR ENTHU-SIASTIC AND COOPERATIVE ABOUT ORIENT PROSPECTS BUT HAVE DONE LITTLE TO PLUG YOUR RECORDS THERE IN THE PAST. JOHNNY HORTON "ALASKA" NUMBER SIX IN TOKYO THIS WEEK. IF I HAVE MY WAY YOU TOO WILL BE IN TOP TEN BY THE TIME I'M FINISHED THERE. PLAN TO LEAVE APPROXIMATELY JULY 4 AS VISAS ARE NOW OKAY. MAY I BE OF ANY SER-VICE TO YOU WHILE IN NEW YORK? HOPE YOU FEEL BETTER. REGARDS, SAUL.[21]

The mere mention of Horton in the telegram — he had been one of Johnny's closest friends — likely stung. Johnny was still reeling from Horton's fiery death in a car accident just seven months earlier, after a drunk driver plowed into his car. It was Cash who had gone to retrieve his body in Texas, arranged the funeral, and then assisted his grieving wife, Billie Jean Horton, and her three children. Dark-haired, devastatingly beautiful, and a renowned singer in her own right, Billie Jean was now a widow twice over, having previously been married to country legend Hank Williams.

Even worse, Cash was also mired in his own secret revelation that he was in love with Billie Jean, and had been so for months. The three were the best of friends and had often gone fishing and hunting together, and Cash considered Johnny Horton's character to be of the highest integrity. Billy Jean was not only lovely to look at, but as a veteran of the country music scene, she was also filled with her own convictions, ideas, and humour, and wasn't afraid to speak up to add them into the conversation. Consumed with grief, the two had grown even closer in the wake of the funeral, where Cash had delivered the eulogy. For months afterward he doted on the devastated Billie Jean, and took her on a three-week shopping excursion to New York, where he had wined and dined her in fine restaurants to lift her appetite and spirits. She soon became like a second wife to Cash, who divided his time between her home in Shreveport and his in Casitas Springs. The affair even went so far that he asked Billie Jean to marry him, though his spiralling dependence on pep pills and his marriage to Vivian finally gave her pause.[22]

First introduced to him by Gordon Terry in 1957, the pills — amphetamines with the trade names of Dexamyl, Benzedrine, and Dexedrine — were often used on tour to help musicians endure the endless hours of driving through the night to get from show to show. "You know, I think some of these promoters would get a map of North America and just throw darts, and wherever the dart hits, that's where you're gonna go next. With a thousand miles between concerts," Cash once mused.[23]

Even Johnny Western, who largely abstained from drugs and alcohol, had to admit that the use of amphetamines had likely saved their lives more than once by preventing drivers from falling asleep at the wheel. Johnny discovered they had another use — they electrified his performances and eliminated his shyness onstage. However, the drying affects of amphetamines could also wreak havoc on his voice. And as much as they pumped him up, they began to twist his personality. As he began to consume more, he would be awake all night, pacing and nervous or brooding and moody. He would have deep, insightful conversations in which he was very much lucid and present, but would then forget them the following day. At times it was like there were two people inhabiting his body.[24]

To cope with the stress of Horton's death, Cash had begun to turn more and more to pep pills, though the truth was that it was these pills that caused him to act strangely about Horton's death, not the other way around. Whatever the case, the drugs were more than likely the culprit that had caused Johnny's laryngitis, rather than the venison Saul had joked about.

If Saul was aware of the pills at this point, it wasn't a primary concern. For now, foremost in his strategy was the need to convince the officials at Columbia that Johnny was worth further investment. Just prior to Saul's departure, Cash jotted off a letter to advise him about who to look out for — namely, people who had been kind to him: Debbie Ishlon, head of public relations, Dave Kapralik, Peter Freund, Bill Gallagher, and Columbia president Goddard Lieberson, whom Cash referred to as "The Great White Father." If there were any problems, Cash added, he could be contacted on the road care of "the leading motel" in Eureka, California. With that out of the way, Cash added that though he was feeling a lot better, the smog in Encino was burning all of their eyes out. "Can't wait to get into the new place, and out of it," Cash signed off.[25]

It was a short trip to the Columbia offices, and upon his return Saul excitedly filled Cash in on what had transpired. "Just returned from New York last night; met Gallagher, Kapralik and many others. They erroneously thought I was your manager, and although I emphasized that I'm not, they all appeared to be happy about the recent change and felt that I might be an influence for the good. I only hope that they are right," Saul wrote on June 23. "Bill Gallagher tells me that you wrote a song especially for him, and he was as pleased as punch about it. Kapralik is now the main cog under Lieberson."

He had pressed the men on the importance of solid promotional materials to back up some of Cash's upcoming U.S. performances and then engaged them in a discussion about various details of publicity, including a plan to increase the frequency with which his singles were played in jukeboxes. This in particular was significant, as Saul's own first exposure to Cash had come via jukebox.

"They all think you're great, and send their best regards," Saul concluded. "I can't get over how prompt you are in replying, and the fact that you are pounding out letters left and right. I mentioned this in New York and they think you have been reborn. All kidding aside, I do appreciate the business-like way you've attended to my requests. Keep up the good work; it's bound to be worthwhile."

He thought for a moment, and then included a postscript: "Still don't know what the hell 'dry-gulched' means!"

Things had gone even better than expected at Columbia, and though Saul's inexperience had made him nervous, the brass there had treated him with respect, even going so far as to express how pleased they were that Cash appeared to be in solid hands.

Following Carnall's departure, however, Cash's management situation had in fact gone from bad to worse. Though Carnall was still booking some dates, in the absence of his other duties, Cash had decided to manage himself. Upon their return home from Canada in the spring, Johnny Western had walked to Cash's Los Angeles office to find him answering the phone and booking his own shows. Knowing Cash was never much of a businessman, even at the best of times, Western decided it had gone far enough. In the months leading up to Stew's firing, Western had been gunning for Johnny to go with Saul, and told Johnny the promoter had already offered him more management on the road than he was paying Stew Carnall or Bob Neal to do.

"I'm seeing stuff — the *t*'s are crossed, the *i*'s are dotted, all the ducks are in a row," Western said. "And he's just booking your shows — he's not managing you and he's not picking up 15 or 20 percent. This is incredible. You need to either get Saul or get someone exactly like him."

However, Cash had ignored Western's advice and was now facing disaster. Even Carnall had been better than no manager at all. If Cash wouldn't approach Saul, perhaps Saul would step in of his own accord. Desperate, Western sat down and composed a letter.[26]

July 1, 1961

Dear Saul,
Many thanks for your nice letter of June 16.
I have meant to bundle up some things and send them on to you for some weeks now and have either

been busy or have done the typically American thing and "put it off until tomorrow." The package of records enclosed are releases of mine that I wanted you to have for your personal record collection. I'll have another for you before you return from the Orient as my new record of "Paladin" will he released very shortly.

Enclosed also are the photos and bios for the next tour. I'm really looking forward to working with you again, Saul. I hope on this next trip that you can reach some sort of management thing with Johnny as he is wandering in a fog, so to speak, now.

He is trying to keep his business affairs together and is also booking himself, neither of which is even a little bit successful. He is not a good businessman nor can he, or should he, be on the phone when the bookers call for a Cash show. He is in serious need of expert advice on what to record and what to release, Saul, and if ever there was a big star on the brink of disaster, it's Johnny right now unless he has some qualified help immediately. He has a new publicity outfit that is doing great things for him and doesn't have so much as a liaison man between himself and this office. I personally feel, Saul, that when you return from this trip that you should lay your cards on the table with John and at least offer a management deal as whether he takes it or not, he needs you.

I may have stepped out of line where Johnny is concerned in the above paragraph, however I feel that it is in his very best interest that I made mention of this need. You'll have to take it from there.

Till I see you again then, I remain
Gratefully, your friend,
Johnny Western.[27]

It was just the catalyst Saul needed, and only confirmed the impression that he was on the right track. The same day, Cash responded to an idea Saul had passed by him. Always mulling over what new directions he could take Cash, Saul had a vision of broadening the show in a more established sense. Cash often travelled with Johnny Western and Gordon Terry, and had shared the bill with other star performers like Merle Travis, but Saul wanted something bigger — a sort of travelling country extravaganza. Most important, he wanted a woman up front with Johnny to add chemistry. The perfect time to launch this would be on their eastern Canada tour, and the most likely candidates were Bob Luman, a country singer-songwriter from Texas, and Rose Maddox, a powerful vocalist who started out performing with her brothers and had successfully moved on to a solo career. She had toured with Cash on shows before and was a solid performer who gave it her all onstage, with glittering costumes made by a bona fide rodeo tailor and finished off with white rhinestone cowboy boots.[28]

After completing a mid-June tour in Lubbock, San Antonio, and El Paso, Johnny settled into his bed late one night and scrawled out a handwritten response to Saul's letter about his trip to New York. "Glad the 'wheels' at Columbia were kind. Don't repeat it, but I'll be damned if I remember writing a song for Bill Gallagher," he wrote by way of introduction, and then addressed the issue of Bob Luman and Rose Maddox, which revealed where his true allegiance now lay — and it was not with Stew Carnall. Prefacing his words by saying they were "STRICTLY CONFIDENTIAL," Cash said he had asked Carnall how he might get in touch with Bob and Rose for booking purposes, to which Carnall responded, "Why not let me sell them to Holiff so I can make a commission?" Cash agreed. This was where his warning came in.

"HINT #1: (TOP SECRET)," Cash wrote to Saul. "I never paid Rose Maddox more than $150 per day, and usually $125 per day and she was constantly available. HINT #2: (TOP SECRET) Bob Luman has never worked a tour with anyone but me, and we paid him $150 to $200 per day."

Most important, Cash added, was that "Stew will try to 'snow' you."

As he nodded off, Cash wrote that he would be travelling to Anchorage, Alaska, on July 6 and then be off bear hunting, before telling

Saul that to "dry-gulch" meant to sneak into the mountains and kill deer, out of season.[29]

Though not yet officially Johnny's manager, the letter's advisory illustrated a clear and crucial shift in Johnny's loyalties, and Saul didn't miss a beat.

"Appreciate your 'top secret' and confidential hints regarding Luman and Maddox, which will remain confidential as you requested," Saul responded on July 2. "I won't do anything definite about extra talent until I've investigated and made sure that they would be the right people and would prove helpful. It may be that Rose Maddox or someone along the same lines would prove sufficient to give the show more depth and avoid too much in the way of extra cost."[30]

On July 11, Saul departed for Japan and managed to secure some connections for what he envisioned as a series of one-nighters in the Philippines, Singapore, and Japan, which he hoped could be scheduled for that November. As he kept the Far East pan warm in the fire, he struggled to finalize the last dates for the tour of eastern Canada and Newfoundland (which was in the midst of a wildfire outbreak that had raged for weeks). Saul was frustrated by the lack of progress. As the heat of summer bore down, both men then also became entangled in intense life circumstances that grappled for their attention.

In mid-August, Saul received news that his father had died, just months after the family had been rocked by the sudden death of Sam Paikin. Only fifty-one, Sam had suffered a heart attack while playing golf at the Beverly Golf and Country Club in Hamilton. Two days later, as the family was forced to carry on with the first birthday party for Sam's grandson, Steve, Saul's sister Ann was in a daze. Within a month, she sold their house and moved into an apartment. The blow to her identity as "Mrs. Paikin" was severe. Saul said very little to anyone about either death, simply writing to Johnny that his father had passed away and "as you can well appreciate, it has somewhat upset my working tempo," though the loss of both his father and mentor must have cut him deeply.

Saul also inquired after Johnny's wife, Vivian, who had given birth to their fourth child, Tara, on August 24. Johnny saw the new baby only briefly before he hit the road to play a weekend show at the Indiana

State Fair in Indianapolis. The tension among the needs of his expanding family, his passion for other women, like Billie Jean Horton, and his burgeoning career was beginning to overwhelm him. "Hi Saul, am rushing, getting junk taken care of so I can leave for Indianapolis," Johnny scribbled a week after the birth, and reassured him that both Vivian and baby Tara were fine. Though earlier Johnny had expressed to Saul that he couldn't wait to get away from the smog and into his sprawling new home in Casitas Springs, in reality the family had scarcely moved their belongings into their opulent new house before Johnny had disappeared again on tour.[31]

Sensing the strain Johnny was now under with four young children at home, Saul continued to write to ask about Vivian and his domestic life, mailing trinkets for the older siblings and a silver dollar memento to commemorate Tara's birth. "I re-read your autobiography last night," Saul wrote to Johnny on September 4, after he had confirmed that all the dates for the Newfoundland tour were finally set. "It is much more revealing than I first realized, and certainly provides a clear insight of the many stages that you have passed through up 'til now. I believe that any time you get dejected or despondent you should re-read it yourself."[32]

The twenty-one-day tour of eastern Canada and Newfoundland was sponsored by *Field & Stream* magazine and included a multi-day moose hunting trip, during which photographer Richard Fiske snapped *au naturel* photos of Johnny in prime hunting territory, engaged in one of his favourite pastimes. In advance of the tour, Saul and Johnny stopped over in New York on October 3, where they met with Columbia executives to renegotiate Johnny's contract. Just prior to their departure, Saul organized a quick show at Massey Hall that met with middling reviews. The show was sold out three days in advance and more than a thousand people were turned away at the door, but the next day's newspaper declared the show to be a "Big Letdown." The incessant upselling of merchandise, constant assurances that they were going to have "a good show" by emcee Johnny Western, and syrupy praise of Canada throughout the performance was frankly insulting, said *Toronto Daily Star* reviewer Wendy Michener.[33]

"Mr. Cash himself did not appear until the end of the evening's program of popularized folk and western music, and then for only half an hour," she wrote. "A cold, or throat trouble of some sort took the resonance out of his low-pitched voice, and the zip out of his performance. Those rhymed stories of his, so reminiscent of Robert Service, were falling apart at the seams despite good support from his trio." The greatest portion of her praise was reserved for the Tennessee Three, Gordon Terry — "spectacularly dressed in white with rhinestones" — and Rose Maddox, who, Michener felt, delivered the "meatiest" performance with "lots of real singing and little chin-wagging."[34]

There was that throat trouble again. It was becoming a problem, but Saul didn't have time to consider the implications, and if he did, it still seemed like Cash had a handle on it. No, he had to focus. The return trip to Columbia Records was to be a trial by fire of sorts, his chance to show not only the executives there — but also Johnny — that he truly meant business.

I'm like a mystery guest. I'm a completely unknown entity, Saul thought, as they entered Columbia president Goddard Lieberson's office. Everything seemed to slow down, as though he could observe the proceedings from outside himself. An aristocrat and consummate classical music fan, Lieberson not only cut an elegant figure himself but also was married to a stunning Norwegian ballerina dancer of considerable fame. It was intimidating, but Saul had at least one card he could play, and it was that he knew Lieberson either possessed or pretended to have great personal interest in Johnny. Arguably one of the most influential and powerful men in the recording industry, it was British-born Lieberson's visionary nature that led the label to sign Johnny in 1958. Under his leadership, the company had doubled their sales. But he was much more than just a suit. An accomplished composer, he had written more than a hundred pieces of music, and was also a pianist, producer, and novelist. *To Goddard Lieberson, I must be the equivalent of an irritating mosquito,* Saul mused.[35]

It was there, feeling completely out of place in Lieberson's spacious office, his heart racing, that Saul had a moment of realization: it was then, right then, that he needed to assert himself. *It's now or never,* he thought. He made his move.

"You're just going through the motions," he declared. "Actions speak louder than words, and so far it's all words. You don't appreciate your talent. You're not doing what can be done for him."

At that, Lieberson stood up, stormed out of the room, and didn't return.

At that moment, Saul felt his relationship to Johnny become an actual reality. "I think he realized that I was either one of the world's best actors from a small town that ever existed, or else I rose to the occasion. I never dreamed I could, but I made my point. I got him sufficiently upset. The renegotiation took place," he later told author Michael Streissguth.[36]

This renegotiation included a push from Saul for a new arrangement in which Cash's records would no longer be selected in Nashville, but in New York by Mitch Miller, Columbia's influential head of Artists and Repertoire in their pop division. How a musician was categorized was critical, and if Johnny remained pigeonholed in the Nashville country genre he would never get the radio play he needed and therefore never become as big a star as Saul envisioned. The move to New York would mean that his songs would then be largely chosen for their pop appeal.

On Thursday morning, Saul and Johnny left New York to fly into Halifax for the tour in eastern Canada, a trip that though neither of them yet knew it, would prove crucial to both of their careers.[37]

It was Johnny's first time in Newfoundland, and he brought Johnny Western, Merle Travis, and Rose Maddox, among others, along for the trip. Both Johnny and Saul had grown fond of Maddox, who had travelled with them both in their plane to New York and on to Newfoundland. Convincing Maddox to come on the trip had taken some work — on September 29, en route to meet Cash for a show in Boston, the landing gear on Maddox's plane had failed and sent the aircraft into Boston Harbor. She had escaped unhurt, but the accident had rattled her, and she became terrified to fly afterward, though the rest of the troupe had pitched in to comfort her. Cash took her shopping to replace her stage clothes, and she went to sleep each night in Cash's pajama bottoms and Johnny Western's pajama top.

There was another issue, however, which was that she thought Saul might have an amorous interest in her. Cash had only recently left his last manager, and if this was true she didn't want to cause any trouble in his venture with a new promoter. Feeling protective, Cash had coaxed her into facing her fears and all but pushed her onto the plane, where she reluctantly agreed to travel with the two men. This concern displayed by Cash seemed to offset any attraction Saul had toward her, she later said, though it's not clear whether it was real or imagined.[38]

Upon their arrival, the group settled into a cabin in Gander, and played all the venues they could in the province, from fishing villages to the Harmon Air Force Base in Stephenville. It was well after midnight when the latter show wrapped up and the troupe emerged from the base, jazzed from the show and not the least bit tired. The boys piled into their car outside the venue and turned on the radio. Jimmy Dean's new single "Big Bad John" came on, and they all looked at each other. It was the first time any of them had heard it. "That's going to be a smash hit," mused Johnny Western. "It's going to be a monster."[39]

When not playing shows, much of their time was spent holed up in the cabin, sharing stories, drinking, and taking drugs. Merle Travis favoured barbiturates, and downed so many pills it could have "knock[ed] an elephant to its knees," remembered Western. "He was barely able to perform, but he was still up there."

Saul did his best to hang out with the other guys, though trampling through the bushes with high-powered rifles was not something he was accustomed to, nor had much interest in. He had never fired any kind of gun in his life outside of the military, and when his turn came, the rifle's recoil bashed him in the forehead with such force it left a scar. The effort eventually paid off for Cash, who bagged a moose and then excitedly communicated the news to Merle Travis through the walkie-talkies that were a sponsored feature of the trip. The show dates were not always ideal in crowd turnouts, but they were ticking along nicely when their first setback of the tour occurred.[40]

Vivian, home alone in the mountains with her new baby and three young girls, called Johnny in a panic.

"He owned the whole side of a mountain and his friend Curly Lewis had built this beautiful home up there, but it backed up to this hillside and there were rattlesnakes all over the place up there," said Western. "These rattlesnakes were coming down into the yard, and of course with the four little girls there everybody was petrified. Vivian was just scared to death of snakes and so were the kids, and they were real live rattle-snakes, in the backyard. She just said, 'I can't be with this.'"

Johnny, who had a phobia of snakes, immediately boarded a flight from Corner Brook, Newfoundland, to Los Angeles and tossed a promise to Saul over his shoulder that he would return for the second half of the tour, no matter what. Four days later, true to his word, he did return, and he made an overture that formalized an idea that had been on both men's minds since their meeting at Columbia.[41]

Not long after he disembarked from the plane, Johnny called Saul over and told him he had something he wanted to discuss. In his hand was a pad of coffee-stained, yellow, legal-sized stationery. Scribbled out on the paper was the outline of a management deal. Johnny then asked Saul to be his manager, and Saul agreed. They negotiated that Saul was to receive 15 percent commission on all income that Johnny earned, from one-night shows to record royalties, and that all of Saul's road expenses would be taken care of. Then they shook hands.[42]

It was a significant move that — though executed casually — would come to characterize and define the men's relationship and lives for the next decade to come.

4

THE SINGIN' STORYTELLER

As Johnny and Saul boarded the plane at Los Angeles International Airport, the manager couldn't help but feel relieved at the clear-headed and articulate manners of his travelling companion. En route to a series of dates at The Cave Supper Club on Hornby Street in Vancouver, Saul had been troubled by Johnny's erratic behaviour of late. Just over a month after Saul was named as Cash's manager on an official basis, Cash was out on the town in Nashville with songwriter Glenn Douglas Tubb and got arrested for public drunkenness.

Though not entirely scandalous — the two were picked up at 3:30 a.m. near Printer's Alley on November 15 and released on bond after a four-hour incarceration — Saul nevertheless felt compelled to extract a guarantee from Tennessee ex-governor Frank G. Clement that the charge would be dropped and the incident kept out of the papers. Despite this, a minor story appeared in the *Nashville Banner* after Tubb and Cash forfeited their bonds. It bothered Saul, and he wanted a retraction.

"The unfortunate publicity that resulted from this incident was directly contrary to the assurance that Johnny received from ex-governor Clement that this would not occur. I would appreciate a note from you as to what our position would be not only demanding a retraction from the newspapers involved, but also what action could be instigated against both the Police Department and said newspapers," Saul wrote to Bill Morgan of the Nashville-based Morgan-Shelley Music Company. "Since the charge against Johnny was not only not proven, but apparently erroneous in nature, your comments would be very much appreciated."

It's unclear why he thought Morgan would be of use, but he seemed to have possessed enough connections to assist with the night in question: Saul went on to thank Morgan for his kindness during the "unfortunate episode," and added that "I, too, as Johnny's manager, appreciate your thoughtfulness and graciousness to Johnny. As long as there are people like you left in this business, things couldn't be too bad."[1]

In any case, that issue thankfully seemed to have died out. Saul looked sidelong at Johnny in his airline seat, engrossed in an issue of *Time* magazine, which he soon tossed on the empty seat next to him. *He must have read it cover to cover in just about three minutes,* he mused. *I suppose he doesn't waste time on the articles that one shouldn't waste time over.* Saul voraciously consumed magazines and newspapers himself, often ripping out articles and stuffing them into his briefcase for later perusal. He glanced at Johnny again. Maybe there was no need for concern, after all. Perhaps these worrying incidents, though unfortunate, were simply anomalies.

For his own part, Cash had his own concerns to think about. Not particularly fond of nightclub shows, he was not looking forward to his performances at The Cave. He happened to know that Billie Jean Horton would be in town at the same time, as part of a showcase at the Queen Elizabeth Theatre. Furthermore, she would also be staying at the Hotel Georgia. He didn't quite know what to think. She had been distant recently, put off by his pill-popping, and he hadn't seen her in some time. She loved him, he knew that, but Johnny Horton had shunned drugs and alcohol, and Cash's substance use alarmed Billie Jean. She had been through the wringer with Hank Williams, and either she didn't know how to handle it or didn't want to; but whatever the reason, she had begun to withdraw from Cash.

Still married to Vivian, a situation that was becoming more untenable all the time, and with his marriage proposal to Billie Jean rebuffed, Johnny had grown bitter and penned "Sing It Pretty, Sue." It was a song many suspected was about Billie Jean, who aspired to a music career of her own, because it references a woman who cares more about her career than love.[2]

Known for its spectacular jazz and elaborate striptease performances, The Cave was an upscale supper club venue with high-end, quirky decor that featured velvet curtains, fool's gold sparkling in dark corners, and stalactites hanging from the ceiling. Tuxedoed ushers greeted patrons at the door to escort them to their tables. With a capacity of about eight hundred, it was typically packed, especially on nights with big-name stars like Lena Horne.

Upon their arrival at the hotel, Johnny immediately went for his pills. Swiftly the calm, rational man that Saul had made note of on the airplane disappeared and was replaced by what Saul observed to be an entirely different person. By the time he stumbled backstage, Johnny was bouncing drinking glasses off the dressing room walls, leaving a wake of broken glass.

In between shows, Johnny went into Red Robinson's Vancouver studio for an interview, though it was short-lived. "All of a sudden, I look over — I asked him a question, no answer — he's fallen asleep at my desk because he's gassed," said Robinson.[3]

On the evening that Billie Jean was in town, Cash returned to the hotel and stormed down the hallways in search of her room. Pounding on the door, he threatened to break it down. The two argued, and she pushed him from her doorway and locked it. Enraged, Cash turned and ran the length of the hallway, shattering all the antique chandeliers hanging in his path.[4]

"True enough, they should have been smashed because they had to redo the whole hotel anyway. Certainly after he left, they had to redo it," Saul recalled. To his credit, Johnny paid for the damages before their entire entourage was then thrown out of the hotel. By the next day, just as dramatically, Johnny settled back into his role as a pleasant travelling companion. The two men flew to Los Angeles and rented a car, and as they drove from LAX to Johnny's mansion in Casitas Springs, they calmly discussed future career moves and Johnny's possible purchase of a new car. Saul studied his client's profile as they drove. It was curious. Once again, everything had changed. It seemed as though there was never any certainty about just who, exactly, you were speaking to at any given moment.[5]

At this juncture Saul had his work cut out for him. Not only did he already feel drawn to become Johnny's protector and defender in a capacity that extended far beyond typical management duties, but Cash's career was also lagging. Though he and the Tennessee Three had enjoyed regular performances on a wide variety of music shows like *American Bandstand*, and were more recently featured on *Five Star Jubilee* and *Here's Hollywood*, attempts to branch out into television and film as a bona fide actor had fallen flat. A lead role in the ultra-low-budget crime drama *Five Minutes to Live*, in which he invested twenty thousand dollars of his own money, had floundered, and the reviews were scathing.

Musically, he was also adrift, and the dismissive *Toronto Daily Star* review wasn't a one-off. The amphetamine-induced weakness in his typically rich baritone got so bad that criticism was trickling in from radio DJs, who until this point had been Cash's greatest fans. "Tell Cash that if he ever makes another record as bad as 'Locomotive Man,' don't even send it, because I'm not ever going to play it on the radio," prominent Des Moines–based promoter and DJ Smokey Smith told Johnny Western. The pills also interfered with Cash's motivation and ability to record. It had been two years since he had released a hit album, and in the spring of 1961, Cash wasn't on any charts, country or otherwise. Earlier that year, in May he relented to Columbia's request that he take a 50 percent cut to his royalties on the sales of his next two records.[6]

Despite this, ex-manager Bob Neal wrote to Cash on October 24, pleading with him to revive their partnership. Neal had fallen on hard times. Previously a DJ on Memphis station WMPS, he had managed Elvis until Colonel Tom Parker elbowed him out of the picture. He struck gold again with Cash in his early days at Sun Records, but was soon edged out in much the same manner by Stew Carnall. In 1958 he decided to buy radio station KCIJ in Shreveport, Louisiana, but three years later he ran into trouble. Desperate, he reached out to Cash.

"I waited all day the other day for your call," Neal began the letter. After some preliminaries of asking how Cash's tour of eastern Canada went, he then explained that he wasn't doing so well himself. In fact, he was in way over his head at the station; "hanging on by his teeth" after losing everything he had in the venture. The possibility that he would have to turn the station back to its previous owner looked imminent. With this established, he made a plea to Cash: "Have you thought about the possibility of putting together our old Winning Team again? You know, with your talent and ability and my knowledge of the business, we had it going mighty good for a while," he wrote. "I don't know yet why we fell apart, but I do know that everything I built and was building for you was based on good solid realities."[7]

Johnny replied almost immediately on stationery that indicated the address of the new office he had just opened on Main Street in Ventura, California. The tour had turned out well, he wrote back, despite the sheer lack of people in Newfoundland. He had a new promoter working for him, a Mr. Saul Holiff, who had already done a great deal on his behalf. Not only had Saul recently travelled to the Far East to look into a tour, Cash wrote, but he had also practically set a date for him at Carnegie Hall. "Also, he went with me to New York about three weeks ago and raised a lot of hell on my behalf, resulting in a relationship with Columbia Records that is and has been needed for a long time. I honestly think things are really going to swing now. Columbia is getting behind the Carnegie Hall deal as well as all the other things we laid out."

That was about as far as Cash went in directly answering Neal's request for a reconciliation, but his position was clear: For now, Saul was his right-hand man. Throwing Neal a bone, Cash added that he had some upcoming dates in Iowa and Wisconsin and had suggested to Saul, who would join him in Ventura in about two weeks, that they could perhaps arrange for Neal to promote those shows.[8]

Despite Johnny's lukewarm status, Saul was still determined he would be a superstar far outside the conventional confines of country music, and, as Cash mentioned in his letter, Carnegie Hall was the next stop on the road map to getting him there. During the Columbia meeting Saul made sure to mention it as a signal of his intentions, and he had to make good on his promises, not least because of the burning sense of insecurity that fuelled much of them.

"I guess I felt that I never should be his manager," Saul later confessed to a reporter. "This is as close to the truth as you're ever going to get from me. I couldn't find any way to justify why I was doing what I was doing, so I thought I had to keep performing. As a non-performer, I still thought I had to perform. And the only way that I thought I could perform was to come up with something that hadn't been done before that would excite him, and that I was part of the reason he got excited."[9]

Within weeks of the official managerial announcement, Saul moved to California and continued to mull over just how to package Johnny in a way that shifted him outside the confines of country music. He wasn't anxious to play up the "country" label, because labelling was serious — if an artist became lumped into a certain category, it meant restricted airplay.[10]

He rolled the issue over and over in his mind. There was something that had hooked him when he had first heard Johnny's music, as country wasn't his taste. *What was that unique quality that I heard, the thing that elevates him to a place where people relate to him?* he wondered, rewinding back to the first Cash song he had heard on the jukebox in 1957. He pored over what his own feelings had been. And just as quickly, he knew. *He's a storyteller.* That's the way he approached putting a song together, like "Five Feet High and Rising," and the reason he chose to sing songs about subjects like farming and poverty in the rural south. That's what his people lived. And that's how he should be portrayed — "America's Singing Storyteller." It was perfect, and just nebulous enough. Beginning with a bold red, white, and black palette, he swiftly envisioned a press kit package built around this idea.[11]

Modelled on an Old West poster, it featured an intense close-up of Johnny's face — primarily his dark eyes — overlaid with a shot from the waist up, playing the guitar. Above, it read "Wanted" in Old West–style font, and underneath, "Johnny Cash: Americana's Most Wanted Singin' Storyteller." In case there was any doubt, smaller text below that assured Cash was a "Song Singin', Gun Slingin', Cash Register Ringin', Entertainer.... Here is a man who packs 'em in every time he calls a meetin' … a man whose face and voice are known the length and breadth of the land … a man whose arrival in any city, town, or village starts people to talkin', whistlin', and toe tappin', in anticipation of seeing and hearing him."

The moniker of "Singin' Storyteller" stuck, and it took on different incarnations over the years as others picked up the catchy phrase and ran with it. But it was innovative and did the job.[12]

The Carnegie Hall show was the next piece of the puzzle Saul needed to lock down. As a venue, it was the perfect backdrop to crystallize what had become his grand vision of a travelling country music extravaganza. Who else could he imagine on that stage? There was no question that women filled out the show and offered both a balance and an edge to the performance. This presented a dilemma, however. On the Newfoundland tour there had been another significant setback, and this one involved Rose Maddox. Halfway through the tour she had received news from her husband, Jimmy, that their son had signed up for the U.S. Marine Corps. Devastated and concerned for his safety, she told Cash she had to leave immediately and dropped everything to fly home to Oceanside, California, in an attempt to stop him. She never returned, and it was the last tour she ever worked with the troupe as their featured female singer.[13]

There had been other issues, too; though she was unaware of Cash's growing drug problem, Maddox was beginning to tire of his unreliability and the rescheduling of show dates it entailed. When he flew off to placate Vivian during their Newfoundland tour, it had simply driven a point home — that his domestic conflicts were not improving. There was also a sexual tension between Maddox and Cash that had gone unrealized, until one night in a hotel room after a show in Calgary. Lying beside her in a bed, Cash tossed and turned and finally left, saying, "I'm goin' back down to my room. I can't stand bein' this close to you."

Surprised by his interest, Maddox later confronted Cash, who tried to convince her to be with him. "I want you completely or not at all," he said.

Maddox curtly informed him she had no intention of cheating on her husband, but he continued to pursue her, which only added to her discomfort and eventual decision to leave.[14]

Fond of Maddox and appreciative of her reliability and talent, if nothing more, Saul was at a loss. Aside from the designs he had on Carnegie Hall, they had a number of upcoming performances peppered with notable venues like the Dallas Sportatorium, which was to host the *Big D Jamboree* in Dallas in early December, and the KRNT Theatre in Des Moines, Iowa. He needed someone reliable, and a crowd-pleaser. Patsy Cline was a possible replacement. "One of the boys," as Johnny Western liked to say. She was a hard-drinking, dirty-joking road veteran with a wide smile and raucous laugh, and had toured with Cash previously. Renowned for her emotional delivery, her popularity was swiftly rising. "I Fall to Pieces" had hit number one on the charts earlier in the year, and she was the first female performer in that era to both demand and receive equal billing with her male counterparts.

The year 1961 had been a whirlwind for the singer, from the birth of her second child to her growing star power, which was highlighted when she joined the Grand Ole Opry and then took the stage with more than a dozen Opry performers at Carnegie Hall in November of that year. A near-fatal head-on collision in June had sent Cline to the hospital for a month and left her with a severely scarred forehead, after which she soon hit the road again — on crutches — and made it back into the studio by mid-August to record "Crazy," penned by little-known singer-songwriter Willie Nelson. She first heard the song when her husband and manager Charlie Dick drove Nelson out to their house at 1:00 a.m. and pulled Cline out of bed to listen to it.[15]

Likely Saul's first choice for the upcoming *Big D* show on December 9, Cline probably turned down the invitation due to exhaustion: by mid-December the singer had been diagnosed with "a nervous breakdown" and was prescribed two weeks of bed rest. Besides, once the knockout success "Crazy" — a pop hit as well as a country one — climbed the charts, she began to command top dollar, which made her a little pricier than Maddox. However, Saul kept her in mind as an asset for the bigger shows like the Country Music Extravaganza he was planning for the Hollywood Bowl. In the meantime, they needed someone quick for the Dallas performance on the *Big D Jamboree* in Dallas on December 9; someone who was affordable, charming, and possessed of an enigmatic stage presence.[16]

"We need a girl singer on the show," Saul said to Johnny when they next spoke. "They want more than just you and your band."

"Well, get one," said Johnny.

Saul thought for a moment. "What do you think about June Carter?"

Clever and confident, June had been a veteran stage performer since the age of ten and hailed from the legendary Carters, considered one of the founding families of country music, though their reach and influence had waned in recent years. Johnny had grown up hearing June's voice on XERA radio, a border station with a strong signal out of Del Rio, Texas, and the first time he had ever seen June onstage at the Grand Ole Opry he'd been just a teenager. On a field trip with his classmates from Dyess High School, he watched enraptured as she sang and played guitar and five-string banjo, and performed a sort of comedy routine alongside the Texas Troubadour, singer Ernest Tubb. It seemed funny now in hindsight, because the songwriter with whom Johnny had recently been carousing in Nashville was Glenn, Ernest Tubb's nephew.

Johnny grinned at the memory of June's onstage antics. "I've always been a fan of hers. Get her if you can," he told Saul.[17]

In the days leading up to his performance on the *Big D* radio show, Johnny may have reflected on another meeting he'd had with June Carter, which later became one of his favourite stories. On July 7, 1956, he visited the Opry again, but this time as a performer. After an introduction from June's husband, country singer Carl Smith, Johnny launched into a performance of "So Doggone Lonesome" in a sombre black suit and ruffled white shirt, a contrast to the sea of cowboy hats and checkered flannel. It was the first number of a three-song set, but it was backstage that was most memorable for him. That was where he ran into June, who recalled that while they talked his "black eyes shone like agates."[18]

Already familiar with Johnny Cash, June had heard his music while touring with Elvis as part of the Carter Family, Elvis's opening act. While on the road, Elvis would incessantly pump nickels into jukeboxes and listen to Cash's songs whenever they stopped to eat at diners. Elvis also tuned his guitar by singing the opening line to one of Cash's songs.[19]

Like June, Cash was also married, and his "I Walk the Line" ode to Vivian was then climbing the charts. The way Cash told the story of that first meeting is that he walked right up to June and told her he was going to marry her someday. "Well, good," she said with a laugh. "I can't wait."[20]

It would be five years until the pair met again on the *Big D* show, and Johnny was late.

Aired from a large multi-purpose arena called the Sportatorium, the *Big D Jamboree* was a barn dance and radio program fashioned in the manner of the Grand Ole Opry and Louisiana Hayride. The barn-like venue featured an octagonal seating arrangement that could hold more than 6,300 spectators, though it was primarily used to host wrestling matches. Aside from seating the audience, the arena offered performers an opportunity for exposure through its radio show on KRLD, which had such a wide range it reached listeners in forty states. By the early 1960s, competition with television had begun to affect audience turnouts and interest in country music variety shows had begun a slow decline. Despite this, Saul felt it remained an important tool for exposure.[21]

Busy with the band's two sets, Johnny didn't even see June until after the show. Bound for a show in Oklahoma City later that night, Cash, Johnny Western, Gordon Terry, and Marshall Grant prepared to bundle up into one car. As she was also booked for the same show, between sets June had asked Marshall Grant — whom she had just met — if she could tag along for the ride. When he hesitated, thinking of how crowded the car would be, she assured him she would be happy to just sit on someone's lap. By the time the gig was finished and Johnny realized what was going on, he quickly volunteered to share his seat. The group piled into the car, and June sat on Johnny's lap. En route, snowflakes began to descend slowly outside the windows, eventually becoming a swirling snowstorm. By the time the car chugged to a stop outside their venue in Oklahoma, the performance had been cancelled due to the weather. Their show may have been over, but June's long-term association with the Johnny Cash Show had just begun. And perhaps more importantly, a seed of attraction between her and Johnny had been planted.[22]

By mid-December of 1961, Johnny had given Saul power of attorney over his affairs. As Christmas approached, Saul decided to formally invite June to become a permanent part of their show; in fact, he would eventually request that she bring on the whole Carter family of musicians. It was a nod to bona fide country royalty, which both he and Johnny liked, but for now at the very least he needed June. She was a dynamo onstage, and damn funny. She was also professional and reliable, an increasingly

Saul Holiff and June Carter in the back of a limousine after a show, circa 1962.

valuable commodity as the complexity and calibre of their shows was incrementally raised.[23]

The next performance was at the KRNT Theatre in Des Moines, and it would be an even larger and more extravagant affair than the *Big D*. Saul needed to be certain of June's presence. Even more important was the Carnegie Hall show, for which he had now confirmed a date in early May. Cash had no arguments with Saul's plans with June, and had so thoroughly enjoyed the car ride to Oklahoma that he made certain to tell the other guys in no uncertain terms that when it came to her, it was "hands off."

"Don't mess around with June Carter," Johnny told them. "I'm watching over her like a big old rooster." Though it sounded funny, he wasn't laughing.[24]

With no objections from Cash, Saul went ahead with pulling June in on a more permanent basis and picked up the phone. To his delight, she was open to the idea. Carnegie Hall was likely a go for her as well, she said, if he'd type out the request and terms of agreement and send it to her in a letter. This would make two female singers for Des Moines, as

Saul had just heard back from Patsy Cline, and she was also on the roster. It was all proceeding swimmingly. As Christmas Day dawned clear and bright, Saul sat down and composed a letter.

December 25, 1961

Dear June:

It was very nice talking with you the other night, even though I did make like a remonstrative paternal father.

This letter will confirm your appearance at the KRNT Theatre in Des Moines on January 28th. As we discussed by phone, your return transportation is to be paid by JOHNNY CASH, and if we draw as well as the previous engagement there, an additional $100. [...] This time, as you know, we have George Jones, Carl Perkins, Patsy Cline, and, of course, June ("The Heel") Carter. (Smokey Smith already is pushing "The Heel" like crazy; he has got his "heel" and "sole" in it.)

I would also like to confirm the appearance of you and all your assorted relatives at Carnegie Hall, Thursday, May 10th, with the fee to be $500 for you and your family, plus cost of transportation by car from Nashville to New York and return, and I might even buy you a steak as an additional bonus.

It is understood that you will arrive in New York on May 7th in order to have ample opportunity to assist in the last-minute exploitation of the May 10th appearance.

I will endeavor to fill any additional dates if at all possible, and will advise you subsequently.

I will also try to arrange an appearance in New York at the Village Gate so that an extra source of revenue, plus exposure, may be secured for you and your family.

The very best to you and your family for the new year, and I do look forward to seeing you once again in Des Moines.

Yours for Bigger and Better Heels
JOHNNY CASH INC.

Saul Holiff
Personal Manager[25]

Within days he would hit the road for a short trip to Las Vegas, but before he departed there were some issues to discuss with Johnny.

With much effort, they were finally getting his jumbled affairs into some semblance of order at the office in Ventura, as various wrinkles left over from Stew Carnall were ironed out. The office itself was a modest affair on 433 East Main Street, which Saul had furnished with a few minimal items: a lamp, a teak desk, and a wooden swivel chair. Behind the desk he mounted a huge map of the United States that took up much of the wall, which not only gave the space the feeling of a war room but also allowed them to map out upcoming tours.

Tasked with the process of streamlining operations was their new office assistant Betty Siegfried, whom he instructed to implement a new filing system for cheques, finances, records, and publicity materials. Cash's finances were in an incredible state of disarray, and the previous accountant had essentially "filed" items by tossing them into cardboard cartons. There had been no attempt to put them in order, or submit any tax returns for at least three years. *I have inherited a massive headache and an extraordinary mess,* Saul thought when he first surveyed the wreckage. It would take some untangling to make it functional, but with Betty's help he felt up to the task.

The move to Los Angeles had been personally stressful. Upon Saul's midnight arrival at LAX, Cash was nowhere to be found, so he had hailed a cab to travel the almost one hundred miles to Casitas Springs. As they pulled up to the driveway, he rummaged around in his pockets and realized with a sinking feeling that he hadn't brought any American money with him. The cab driver simply shook his head when he offered Canadian bills. So, although it was about 3:00 a.m., he had to bang on the door and wake up Vivian.

It was a rocky start to a life that Saul feared he might be ill-equipped to handle. Now dividing his time between London and Los Angeles,

Johnny Cash and Saul Holiff at the Johnny Cash Incorporated office in Ventura, in the fall of 1961.

living in a motel, without a car, and with net assets at about four thousand dollars, it was a struggle to keep his insecurity at bay. And in the midst of it was the sickening realization that he had entered a bit of a madhouse. Johnny's marriage was obviously troubled, and he appeared to have some kind of manic-depressive issues due to (or exacerbated by) his pep pill addiction. In addition to the protective inclinations

Saul felt — as Johnny was lucid and eminently likeable when he was sober — he could see that this job would require him to be a counsellor, accountant, adviser, agent, and psychiatrist, among other things. Was he ready? He didn't know.[26]

Johnny's Christmas in Casitas Springs was celebrated with typical extravagance. Decorations were trailed all the way up the hillside outside their home to the mountain peak, where he installed a ten-foot light-up aluminum cross. Oblivious to how much their family already stood out as a beacon of wealth, perched above the modest, tiny community in a five-thousand-square-foot mansion, he had proceeded to blare Christmas music from an amplifier on his roof every year until the neighbours complained. At one point, sheriff's deputies were dispatched to deal with the noise.

"I didn't think there was a Scrooge left," Cash muttered in response, and yanked the plug out halfway through "Joy to the World."[27]

At their office in the city, Saul waited for June's reply and feverishly looked for ways to occupy himself as the holidays slowed the flow of work to a muddy pace.

He lit a cigarette and began to dictate a letter to Johnny, as Betty scrolled paper into the typewriter. "Dear Small, Sad Sam," Saul began. He exhaled. "Enclosed are a few things I thought might interest you." They were listed off in order: First, a poem that his girlfriend Barbara Robinson had composed about him that had fluffed his ego. "Thought you might enjoy it," he noted nonchalantly. Also included were some articles on Goddard Lieberson that he had sent for and had finally arrived, and a clipping that included a description of a fabulous new tranquilizer he had on order for delivery. Now for the items of business.

First up were issues with Columbia executive Dave Kapralik, Lieberson's second-in-command, which had gotten under his skin. Pressure had been maintained on the Columbia executives regarding when and how Cash's albums were to be released for maximum exposure, and Kapralik was now throwing roadblocks up in front of the plan. They had clashed in particular over "The Big Battle," a Civil War–era song Johnny had recorded in March, which covered the topic of war in a way he felt passionate about.

"Summarized below are some ruminative thoughts, plus some new developments," Saul said as Betty typed. He began to pace. "One. Kapralik — he told me in Nashville, and then again in New York, that he would check with Law regarding 'The Battle' after Don was discharged from hospital. Now he tells me that only Don Law is responsible for your releases and that, as far as he knows, no artist has final say as to when a release should be made or, for that matter, what release will be made. Apparently it is a mutual situation."

He paused, recalling Kapralik's tone.

"He rather snottily advised that it takes at least sixteen weeks from the time material is complete to get an album on the market. He spoke in a spooky fashion," he said, waving his hands around, trailing smoke. "*Condescendingly* — and got me mad. I'm afraid I expressed my anger. Suggested you could and would write a sequel to 'Ride This Train' for Carnegie Hall if Columbia would record at the Hall. Told him this was my idea and wasn't a prerequisite to your doing the sequel. However, it might give you the impetus nevertheless to do so. He replied by saying that you shouldn't need any encouragement to come up with additional material. I got madder. So much for Kapralik."

Saul stubbed out the cigarette in his desk ashtray and ran a hand across his dark, wavy hair, which he had recently cut quite short. Dressed in his trademark black, he had taken to wearing short sleeves to better deal with the heat in California. It was nothing like the chilly, snowy winters he was used to in London.

I'll call Don Law in Johnny's presence, thought Saul, divining how he might approach the issue differently. Johnny's producer at Columbia and head of their country music division, Law seemed to be providing little direction for his client, preferring to let Johnny do just as he pleased, rather than take the reins and offer guidance. Saul lit another cigarette as Betty blinked, fingers hovering above the typewriter keys. *He will have to go,* he thought, making a mental note. Next on the agenda: Carnegie Hall.

"Two. Will write Lieberson about plans for Carnegie, plus giant Johnny Cash 'thank you' Caribou Cocktail Party in New York. Plans for this party have jelled in my mind, and I am sure it will set the industry on its musical ear. I'll fill you in next week and see if you concur," said Saul. It put him in a better mood to think about plans for the pre-Carnegie party, the aftermath of which he felt certain would reverberate in their circles for some time. Finished with business, he decided to remind Johnny of some personal issues they had discussed during their many long car rides between LAX airport and Casitas Springs. Though he was clearheaded at the time, Johnny often had a hard time recalling these conversations.

"I'm so pleased with your new attitude toward our future plans, but after doing some extensive reading on other artists I have come to the overpowering conclusion that an artist, to properly flourish and prosper, absolutely must be concerned with self-discipline, and even more concerned with the need to grow and mature with the passage of time." Saul scratched his jaw, thinking. He began to tread the carpet again. "This, in my opinion, calls for an honest appraisal of what the artist really wants. If he is truly ambitious and admits it, then it means work, concentration and a level head. I sincerely believe that you are capable of great things — far in excess of what you have accomplished up to date — providing you keep a level head and an even perspective. Forgive me for lecturing and preaching, but this is how I feel."

"See you soon. Happy New Year," said Saul. He nodded at Betty, and a smile hovered at the corner of his mouth. "Sign it, 'Preacher Holiff.'"[28]

This reflective tone continued upon his return to Los Angeles after the Vegas trip, where he spent New Year's Eve alone in his motel room ruminating on all that had come to pass in the last few months, and all that would shortly come to pass. He often missed his girlfriend, the kind, insightful secretary Barbara Robinson. She was beautiful, too — refined, with a wide smile, a long, slim neck, and tidy chestnut hair. The poem she had written about him, which he had forwarded to Johnny, was titled "Mister 17," and was inspired by his obsession with the number seventeen. Though he knew better than to engage in such superstitions, the number seemed to recur as a prominent "thing" in his life. "You're a practical sort of fellow / Who believes in Logic only / While astrology and tea-cup reading's / Balm for the lonely," she had written. "But isn't it peculiar / That you never fail to notice / Any time the number 17 / Might come within your focus?"[29]

The intimacy of her overture had touched him, and it was clever. He liked that. As his management of Cash expanded, he sought Barbara's assistance and opinions in many areas of the business, and she was already becoming near-indispensable to him in that capacity.

It was back in November of 1957 that Barbara had traded her hometown of Winnipeg for London, Ontario, and worked her way into a job at the *London Free Press*. It was the city's daily paper, and she served as the personal secretary to their dynamic advertising director, Charles Fenn. For years, Saul had visited the newspaper's offices to purchase ads — first for his clothing store and then later to promote Sol's Square Boy and his rock 'n' roll shows. Not long after Barbara's arrival, Saul immediately noticed her, though he wasn't certain she had noticed him back. In fact, he had first seen her outside of the newspaper office, in a booth at the nearby Greek restaurant where the newspaper staff took their coffee breaks. As she laughed with the other secretaries, Saul sidled up to owner Victor Mahas to ask if he knew who "that woman" was. Feeling protective, Mahas looked Saul up and down and shook his head no, though she was in fact a friend. As Saul departed, he hoped he would get another chance.

A short while later, Barbara was in her office — a windowless cube on the upper floor near the copy services section — immersed in the discussion of an advertising contract with one of the newspaper's part-time temps. A shadow crossed the page they were focused on. She glanced up just in time to see a man pass by the open door of her office.

"Who was that?" Barbara asked her co-worker.

"I can't remember his name. I think he's a tailor?" She shrugged.

Hours later, Barbara was bent over her desk at work when she heard a voice behind her.

"So, what kind of music do you like?"

Startled, she looked around. She hadn't heard anyone come in. It was the man, the one who had passed by earlier. She thought for a moment. *No "hello"? No introduction? And that's a funny question for a tailor to ask.*

"Well, I like pretty well anything, except country music and rock and roll," she said with a smile. At this, he laughed.

"Don't you know who I am?" he said. A smile lingered around the edges of his mouth.

"No, I haven't seen you until today." The question made her nervous. Executives' secretaries were supposed to know everything and everybody.

"My name's Saul Holiff. I promote concerts in the area," he said, hands in his pockets. "They're usually country music or rock 'n' roll."

"I guess that's why I've never met you before," she said, and then allowed herself to laugh.

Just before the end of the day, the phone rang. It was Saul, calling to ask if she would like to come over to his apartment and listen to the new hi-fi equipment he had just got installed. A music lover herself, she had heard about the advances in sound that this new technology had promised. Curious, she accepted.

Little did she know that this was not the first time she had encountered Saul, either. As they began to date she realized why he looked familiar — years earlier when she had first moved to the city, Barbara had been in the audience when Saul performed with the Little London Theatre's production of *The Teahouse of the August Moon*. The acting wasn't the best she'd ever seen, but he had a brooding quality that was so charismatic she couldn't take her eyes off him.

By the next year, the two had grown close — Saul now regularly consulted her advertising expertise on everything from Johnny's press kit, which she designed with her colleague Jerry Davies, to his new stationery that featured flashy gold embossing and a JRC logo in the shape of a crown — but at times she had doubts about her dynamic, intoxicating new boyfriend. Though he respected her intelligence enough to take her advice, he was also pushy and impossible to disagree with. Unyielding, even. It seemed at times that if she said black, he'd say white — just for the sake of it. And no amount of arguing would convince him otherwise. When she needed to leave at the end of a date, he'd always convince her to stay. *Just one more show; just ten more minutes.* Sometimes it seemed attentive, but at other times it felt oppressive. And then there was that trip to Mexico.

At the end of October she had won a trip to Mexico through a promotion with a local theatre company. Saul immediately assumed his inclusion on the journey as her plus-one, but it then provided a unique dilemma for Barbara. Only newly dating, she was reluctant to involve herself in a scandal by travelling alone with a man who was not yet her husband. It just wasn't done. Saul suggested a variety of excuses, people she could say she was going with, including his mother or a girlfriend, but the possibility of lying made Barbara even more uncomfortable. The prize included a double hotel room, so eventually she caved, and with the explanation that they were soon to be married, managed to clear it with the hotel and at least arrange separate rooms. Incensed, Saul then refused to pay for his own room, which she found ridiculous.

The obnoxious behaviour continued once they arrived. Saul soon made his acquaintance with the local pool boy, and over the next few days he delighted in challenging him to a round of competitive poolside push-ups. Exasperated, Barbara filled her days with walks on the beach, often to escape his company (though she was loath to admit it) and clear her head. Typically, the two spent their evenings dining together at the local restaurant, after which they would arrange to borrow a jeep from the head server.

One evening, after the two had gone on a tour of the local area together, they returned to find Barbara had received a letter from the head server, proposing marriage. Flattered but confused, she demurred with the explanation that Saul was her fiancé and they would soon be married. "Married? I thought you were his secretary," the head server wrote back.

Barbara was floored. Had he told everyone she was his secretary? And neglected to inform her? There was no risk of scandal at this point. Was he embarrassed to be with her? She felt as though she were under water. It was clear she was already in over her head with this man, whose powerful personality easily overwhelmed Barbara's sensitive, empathic nature. Naturally a giving person, she had begun to notice a predatory quality in the way Saul operated, and it made her uneasy. Though she already knew she was on unequal footing with him, there was one person who seemed, strangely, a match for Saul Holiff. A man who also saturated the air of a room when he entered it — and that was his new client, Johnny Cash.

When Saul had first told her of his agreement to become Cash's manager, Barbara was concerned. The scandal of Jerry Lee Lewis's marriage to his thirteen-year-old cousin was all over the news. *What kind of people are these, exactly?* she had wondered, with a sense of both curiosity and caution.

She would find out soon enough.[30]

Johnny Cash and fans, backstage in London, Ontario, 1962.

Though Saul had taken up residence in Hollywood to keep a close eye on the comings and goings at their Ventura-based office, he retained a small bachelor apartment on King Street in London to serve as his Canadian base. It was here that Barbara first encountered Johnny at the end of a ten-day tour through Ontario, earlier that year. After their final show in Sault Ste. Marie, Saul had asked Barbara to be on hand at his flat that evening to help serve drinks and snacks to the entourage while he showed off his new hi-fi stereo system.

The apartment was so tiny that his primary sink was the one in the bathroom, so Barbara had decided she would wash the limited dish supply in there as she went along. Excusing herself, she had just about finished a sinkful when, from the corner of her eye, she saw Johnny enter the bathroom. For a moment she had figured he'd mistakenly barged in, and kept washing. The door was slowly pushed behind him until it clicked. She stared at the dish in her hands and kept the cloth moving across its surface. *What do I do?* She glanced at him.

"Hi," she offered, hands still immersed in the water.

She began to re-rinse the dishes. Johnny had remained in front of the door, an awkward expression on his face, and began to chatter. Something about his gun collection. Barbara had stared past her reflection at him and tried to focus on his words, but there were few topics less interesting to her than guns. *Is he trying to test me? See if I'll throw herself at him like all the other girls?* She pulled out the plug. *Maybe he wants to create the impression that he'd had another conquest. And with Saul's girlfriend, no less. Nice try.*

She held her breath and willed him to stay where he was. Years earlier, it had seemed his track "Don't Take Your Guns to Town" always came on the radio right when she arrived to work. It was uncanny. At the time she had found the song strangely compelling, not least because of the sheer originality of his voice and style. It was unlike anything she had ever heard before. However, by this point Cash was little more than a name, another client upon whom she and her colleague Gerry Davis expended a fair amount of creative energy to design press kits and fancy letterhead. And now that the body had been linked to the name, she needed it to move out of the way.

Gathering up the dishes, she had turned with the stack in her hands. To her relief, the knob turned behind him and he released the door.[31]

5

CARNEGIE HALL AND JUNE CARTER

Saul was in a great mood. Determined that 1962 would be their big year to build on the momentum set in motion during the preceding months, he felt it was off to a fine start, indeed. In less than six weeks he had three significant performances lined up that were all crucial to his broader career plans for Johnny. June had promptly responded to his letter, and revealed that under the airy, affectionate Southern persona she was in fact a tough negotiator.

"I have signed the letter and am returning it. As we discussed on the phone, this is our tour price, and it was planning on as many as four days. At this rate, we can come out on this — otherwise we will just about make expenses. You know what the rooms are in New York etc. Let's hope that the other dates come through," she wrote on January 3, in looping cursive on card paper that featured a cartoon Siamese cat over a pink backdrop.

"I am anxious to do this New York date, even if just for the one day. Let's pray for a wonderful show. I am still holding the Feb. dates and waiting to hear from you. When I see you, we will discuss the management deal. Regards to John — Fluke, Marshall and Luther as I love all of you — June."[1]

All the names after "John," written hastily underneath as the card ran out of room, seemed like an afterthought. Saul smiled. Under any other circumstance the haggling over costs might have been irritating, but with her agreement to the immediate tours and a potential managerial contract with her underway, Saul couldn't help but feel impressed by June's business acumen. She would be a welcome addition to the tour.

There was much to attend to immediately; most pressing was a January 28 show at the KRNT Theatre in Des Moines, Iowa. Not only was June on board, but Saul also felt a sense of anticipation about acquiring Patsy Cline for the show. Cline was off her bed rest and on a two-week tour through a variety of cities, including Kansas City, Omaha, Joplin, and Wichita, before she'd meet them in Des Moines. It was already clear that her record *She's Got You*, released January 10, would deliver her third hit song in a row. Both sides were popular, and the song "Strange" was getting heavy play. Also along for the tour with Cash, Patsy, and June were all the usual suspects: George Jones, Carl Perkins, Gordon Terry, and Johnny Western. But this time, there would be an unusual added attraction.

"Got a 12-year-old girl who plays steel guitar out of this world. My ole ears have never heard anything like it," Patsy wrote to her friend Louise Seger days before the KRNT show. "She also plays a sax and sings. Looks like a blonde doll. And boy, what a show-woman. She's great. Her name is Barbara Mandrell. Wish you could hear her." Aside from the concerns of more level-headed members regarding the chaotic party atmosphere that little Barbara would be thrust into, there were legalities that needed to be sorted out. Both Saul and Johnny had seen Mandrell cut her teeth as a performer a couple years back on *Town Hall Party*, though this was her first time ever on tour.[2]

Underage by a long shot, Mandrell had just turned thirteen on Christmas Day and was not legally allowed to tour on her own. As a result, Saul came up with the solution that he could become her legal guardian. The necessary paperwork, completed by January 16 and signed by her father Irby and a notary public for the State of California, declared that Barbara was authorized to go with the Johnny Cash Show under the personal direction of Mr. Saul Holiff. Little Barbara was thrilled, and if she noticed any strange behaviour from her travelling companions, she likely didn't understand the implications.[3]

During their flight — her very first time in an airplane — she crawled up into the seat next to Cash, who could barely keep his eyes open, and leaned over him to look out the window.

"Oh, Mr. Cash, they look like ants down there!" said Barbara, her eyes dancing. "Oh, look! Are we going to fly over that mountain?"

Cash willed his lids to stay open and studied the small figure.

"You know, they'll give you all the Coca-Cola and peanuts you want?" she continued, with a grin.

"Yak, yak, yak, yak, Mr. Cash. Yak, yak, yak, Mr. Cash," he said with a smile, and yawned.

She laughed. Barbara adored him, not just because of his talent and stature, but for how gentle he was with her. "No drinking, no cussing, no wild talk, as long as I was in sight. That was his code," she later wrote in her memoir. And boy, did he encourage her as a performer. To be included on this tour, as a "nobody," was almost beyond what she could comprehend. She watched as he drifted off to sleep. It was nice. A lot of the time he was so fidgety. It was like he couldn't keep his hands or his eyes in one place. At one of the truck stop diners they had visited on the road, she noticed he couldn't stop picking at the torn Naugahyde upholstery on the booth seat. By the time they'd finished eating he'd ripped the whole thing apart. When he went to pay for the meal, she saw he had confessed and paid for the damage he'd done — he always paid for the damage — but it was a bit spooky, she thought.[4]

Patsy sought to shelter Barbara from the more raucous antics of the boys. George Jones was a heavy drinker, and volatile when drunk. Riding high on the success of his monster hit "She Thinks I Still Care," he would host all-night parties in his camper. One night when the party invitation was extended to Barbara, Patsy was incensed. It was unacceptable. In all likelihood it was an innocent overture, but one she did not take to kindly, possibly due to her own history of childhood sexual abuse. From that moment on she insisted on being Barbara's chaperone and that they were to share a room. The two grew close, initially sharing a bed like sisters, until Barbara's sprawling sleep patterns drove Patsy crazy and they got twin beds. One day, they went on a shopping spree and got their hair done, but by the time they got back to the hotel "Miss Patsy," as Barbara called her, felt unhappy with the way her hair had turned out, so Barbara — skilled at hairstyling from a young age — offered to brush it out and redo it. This ritual soon became routine, and little Barbara became Patsy's unofficial hairdresser on the road.[5]

Reluctant to travel in Cash's car with "the world's worst driver," as Johnny Western called him, Patsy made the decision early on to ride almost exclusively with Gordon Terry and Western. "I love him dearly, but I'm not riding with him if there's any chance that he's driving," said Patsy, who punctuated the comment with a loud laugh as she squeezed into the back seat of Terry's white Cadillac sedan to drive to their next stop in Iowa. This suited Terry and Western just fine, as her brassy, take-no-nonsense attitude (she often referred to herself as "The Cline") and off-colour jokes made her just about the best road buddy they ever had. She was also no princess, travelling with a face bare of makeup, in a basic one-piece flight suit. When the boys tried to assist with her luggage and wig boxes, she would just laugh and wave them off.[6]

On this tour in particular, Patsy made certain that Barbara also rode in the car with them. Accustomed to singing only during rehearsals and performances, the young musician was captivated by the impromptu way Patsy sang her heart out while they drove. When little Barbara fell asleep in the back seat, Patsy and Johnny Western used the long hours on the road to engage in conversations about their rocky marriages.

"Patsy and I became closer than Saturday was to Sunday. I became Patsy's confidante. She was having a lot of trouble with her marriage, and so was I," said Western. "She was still married to Charlie Dick ... and she was telling me what a rotten SOB he was and the crappy things he had done to her. He beat her up. She was telling me, 'One of these days, I'm gonna divorce him.'"[7]

By the time the crew arrived in Des Moines, they had bonded in a variety of ways. Virtually everyone was either secretly or openly thinking of June Carter, who was set to join them at this stop. To Barbara, she was nothing less than a country legend who hailed from the great Carter family of southwest Virginia. For Patsy, who still felt vulnerable in the wake of her recent accident, June was a comforting presence, a confidante who knew many of her darkest fears and secrets. It was June she often turned to and called in the middle of the night for advice. They had first met on a plane from New York to Nashville, and had performed live together many times since. It was often just the two of them onstage, as well as on television and radio, and each did their thing — June on the autoharp and banjo, and Patsy with her inimitable voice, and then they'd finish up with a duet of old Carter songs, or a few numbers that Patsy liked.

"We don't step on each other's toes," Patsy once said to June about the complementary nature of their performances. Both women understood the tribulations of navigating the "man's world" of country music, and each found a sort of solace in the other. They also found comfort in their shared personal experiences; both women endured divorces in an era when it was still frowned upon, and knew the heartache of leaving young children at home so that they could perform on the road.[8]

Upon their arrival in Des Moines, Patsy regarded the frozen cement outside the car with terror. Though now off crutches, the car accident had left her with hip injuries, and as they exited the car she asked Barbara to hold her arm. As they traversed the icy sidewalk toward the theatre, Barbara was deeply touched that Patsy would reach out to her for support. *Miss Patsy's looking out for me on this trip, but in a way, she needs me to look after her, too,* she thought.

They had arrived late, so there wasn't any time to get ready at the hotel; most of the performers had to be content with dressing and preparing for the show backstage. The two were soon enveloped by June, who set upon Patsy's dress with a travel iron, while Barbara unpinned her hair and gently combed it. Patsy was self-conscious about the extensive scarring on her forehead, so June used her expertise with powder and makeup to help her disguise the marks.[9]

Both women spotted Johnny as he bustled by in a rumpled lavender shirt. They exchanged a look.

"Johnny," June called after him. "Hand me that shirt."

"What shirt?" he said, turning. His heart raced a little faster at the sight of June.

"That one you got on," she said, hands on her hips. "You're not goin' onstage with your shirt all wrinkled up like that."

Within minutes, Gordon Terry returned with Johnny's shirt and trousers, which June pressed, making a neat crease down the front. June's trajectory into being the boys' road mama — among other roles — had begun.[10]

With the crew finally in order and ironed out by June, the show opened to a roaring, sold-out crowd that filled the 4,100-seat theatre to capacity. It was the first of three performances that KRNT radio jockey Smokey Smith had scheduled for the day, and typically opened with Johnny Western's Old West material, which included his classic "The Ballad of Paladin." Moving into the role of emcee, he then introduced June, who sashayed out and got the crowd laughing with her novelty songs and stories, followed by Carl Perkins (of "Blue Suede Shoes" fame), and then Barbara performing with her steel guitar and saxophone. Next up was George Jones. Though a rising star in his own right, if he felt insulted about being billed under a child performer, he didn't show it. In fact, when they were backstage after the first stop of the tour he called Barbara over to ask her if she would perform with him, as most of the singers didn't travel with bands and were simply backed by the Tennessee Three.

"Would it be all right, when you come off, they'll introduce me and I'll do one song and then I'll call you back out and ask you to play steel for me?" asked Jones. "Most of my records have steel guitar on them."

Barbara regarded the iconic singer, letting the weight of his words sink in. "Yes, sir, I'd be glad to," she said finally. "Just give me a list of the songs and what key they're in."[11]

With near-equal billing to Johnny, Patsy usually opened the second act as their feature performer. Introduced by Johnny Western as simply "the one and only Patsy Cline," she took centre stage in a long evening gown, with glittering earrings and red lips, lit by a single spotlight. As she sang she slowly spread out her fingers and pushed them down her hips, as though smoothing out her dress. She was breathtaking. Every time "She's Got You" began, Johnny Western would find himself inexorably drawn to the stage from wherever he was, and he would watch, transfixed, for the remainder of the song. After the lights came up the audience would often remain rooted in their seats, spellbound and dabbing their eyes with handkerchiefs.[12]

Saul surveyed the crowd from the back of the theatre. It was a routine he had become comfortable with: the silent observer. His skill at reading a crowd had become so nuanced he could conjure up an accurate head count within minutes just by scanning. It was crucial to getting an honest payout from the promoter at the end of the night, and combined with his observations from the box office, it typically gave him ample ammunition to forcefully negotiate a good return.

Though Patsy and June complemented each other — June made the audience roar with laughter, while Patsy's ballads brought them to tears — he worried Patsy might be almost *too* good.[13] With her rising status and star power, she already headlined her own shows; at this rate he wouldn't hang on to her for long at six hundred dollars a day. And that was good money, the best they could offer. Perhaps it was wise to focus his energy on June. A natural fit with the other members of the troupe, June had a palpable chemistry with Cash, and along with George Jones, expressed serious interest in a management deal with Saul. It was no small thing that she could bring a talented, venerated family into the mix — Mother Maybelle and sisters Anita and Helen. No matter what chaos ensued with Cash, she was professional and flexible enough to work around it. She already had a demonstrated gift for riffing and extending her set with improvisations. This was especially crucial given Johnny's increasingly unstable behaviour; another level-headed person was an asset. Hopefully she'd look out for Cash like bassist Marshall Grant often did.

The amphetamines, as intended, allowed Johnny a confident persona onstage, but their drying effect on his vocal chords meant his voice simply couldn't keep up. Saul continually trimmed his performance time as the tour went on, from an hour down to about forty minutes, in the hope he could finish before it gave out completely. As emcee, Johnny Western kept up playful references in his introductions, and prepared the crowd at KRNT with an insinuation that Cash was simply too ill to be there. "He should really be in a hospital," he began, but was bravely determined to make the show go on. Excuses aside, from then on throughout the show, Western billed him as nothing less than "The Fabulous Johnny Cash."

Overall, if the performance at KRNT was something of a dress rehearsal for Carnegie Hall, by all indications they were on good footing.

The three performances pulled in more than eleven thousand patrons, which broke all existing attendance records for the venue. The shows also met with "unanimous acclaim," which "exemplifies the esteem and respect that Johnny Cash, a superb showman, commands throughout the country," said theatre manager, Gerald E. Bloomquist.[14]

Something about the way the acts fell together felt right. It represented everything Cash loved about country music, which was that it was a brotherhood, a sisterhood. "We share the music, and we share the songs and we share the feelings and emotions," Johnny said. "We do it — we cry on each other's face if we want to."[15]

The close-knit nature of the troupe bled into their performances, and by all accounts they were hitting it out of the park. Another successful group show was completed on February 24 at the *Louisiana Hayride*, a live radio show broadcast by KWKH out of the Municipal Auditorium in Shreveport, Louisiana.

"There is no need for me to tell you what a whopping success our first show of the season was. My only regret is that we couldn't seat those 2,000 or more people who couldn't get into the Municipal Auditorium. Paid attendance showed 4,000 people and the auditorium seats only 3,582, so you can see we did some stretching," *Louisiana Hayride* producer Frank Page wrote to Saul after the show. "There wasn't a bobble from your end, which is some kind of a record considering it was your first show here, and our first show of the Spring season. I am looking forward to working with you on succeeding shows with the same profitable results."[16]

When they were apart between shows, Johnny felt as though he couldn't wait to see June again. *Here is this vivacious, exuberant girl — as talented and spirited and strong-willed as they come*, he mused. *She brings out the best in me, and it feels wonderful. She's like a tonic for the whole crew.* For the first time since his infatuation with Billie Jean, he felt there was a woman who understood the music industry like he did — who knew life on the road and all its attendant joys and irritations, and he wasn't going to let her go.[17]

Days later, Saul was officially named the manager of both June Carter and George Jones, and was given a limited power of attorney over Jones's affairs. However, any illusions he may have harboured that Jones could add to a sense of reliability within the troupe were soon shattered. At least as much of a handful as Johnny, Jones swigged Texas-sized bottles of liquor, had also played prisons and roadhouses, and was equally fond of pranks — a favourite involved emerging from a coffin, carried in as part of the performance. He also tore up hotel rooms, fired guns, and shattered instruments. Liquor regularly made him aggressive and hostile, even toward friends, which led to frequent fist fights and brawls on the road or even backstage before shows. When Johnny and George ended up on tour together, the combination was downright explosive.[18]

One spring night in Gary, Indiana, George retired to the Holiday Inn after the show with Cash and Merle Kilgore. A recording artist and songwriter, Merle's song "Wolverton Mountain," which he co-wrote with singer Claude King, had just launched Claude's career and was a huge hit. The song stuck in his head, George sang it incessantly throughout the night, to the point that Cash and Kilgore got so irritated they ditched him and hid in their room.[19]

Stumbling around until he found them, George began to discuss the logistics of the tour with Johnny, whose manager he now shared. It needled a potentially sore point between both of them. Though Johnny had reassured Saul he had no objection to his managing Jones, there was often a palpable strangeness around it that Saul couldn't quite pinpoint. If he didn't know better, he'd say it felt akin to jealousy. Though Johnny never came straight out and said it, he made comments that insinuated he perceived Saul's attentions were now divided. Without a definitive complaint, however, Saul simply had to chalk it up to the mercurial nature of his client, which in Cash's case he felt was quite significant.[20]

During the conversation, Jones became increasingly incensed over an aspect of the Johnny Cash Show he disliked — the focus on Johnny as the show's central figure. In his autobiography, Jones later described how as his fury mounted, a fight erupted, in the midst of which a lamp was accidentally knocked over. Stalking across the room, Jones picked it up and threw it on the carpet again.

"One broken lamp," Cash said. "That will be forty-five dollars."

The tension broke as Kilgore, Jones, and Cash all burst out laughing. Jones drunkenly seized the other lamp and slammed it on the floor.

"Two lamps," said Johnny with a sigh. "Ninety dollars."

Kilgore looked on, unable to predict what was coming next. Johnny had obviously seen this all before, but trashing hotel rooms was something entirely new to Merle. Down came the curtains, which Johnny pegged at three hundred dollars.

Furious at what he perceived to be an exorbitant amount to pay for curtains, George lurched into the bathroom and pulled the porcelain lid off the back of the toilet. He hurled it into the bathtub, where it shattered.

"One commode top, one hundred seventy-five dollars," Johnny said, from where he lay on the bed. George continued to trash the room.

At the end of the tour, the men lined up in Saul's hotel room as he counted out their take on the bed and dispensed the cash.

"Now, George," said Saul, "before I pay you, I want you to know there's a few deductions here."

In his typical style, every broken item was itemized and precisely accounted for, down to the last dollar. But what amazed George was that almost all of Johnny's estimations had been exactly correct. The only error was the lamps, which were listed as forty-five dollars for both.

"Those lamps were beautiful," said George sheepishly, as he accepted his significantly diminished payout. "That's a real good buy."[21]

Carnegie Hall was a fitting venue for Johnny Cash's launch into the annals of country music history, but not only because he would be the first country music star to ever headline his own show there. Built in 1891 by Andrew Carnegie, who was then one of the richest men in the world — if not *the* richest — the venue's construction was part of a wider philanthropic push by the wealthy industrialist to endow his fortune to a variety of institutions focused on "the improvement of mankind." As a boy he was deeply inspired by the generosity of Colonel James Anderson of Pittsburgh, who encouraged Carnegie and other working boys in his area to freely access his four-hundred-book library. This act formed part of Carnegie's later "gospel of wealth" philosophy — which held as its central tenet that "the man who dies rich dies disgraced." It also inspired him to fund the construction of thousands of "free libraries" around the world, so that "other poor boys might receive opportunities similar to those for which we were indebted to that noble man."

Carnegie's rise to wealth was a tale as quintessentially American as that of Cash himself. Born into a family of handloom weavers in Dunfermline, Scotland, Carnegie relocated to the United States with his family when the introduction of steam-powered looms drove his father out of work. It was there that his new career trajectory began — from his start as a bobbin boy in a cotton factory to his pinnacle as the magnate of Carnegie Steel, an empire so vast it eventually produced more metal than all of Great Britain. In this sense, Carnegie's humble beginnings and near-vertical ascent to prominence were not so different from Johnny's own journey from humble Arkansas farm boy to refrigerator salesman in Memphis on up into chart-topping American country artist.[22]

Following its construction, Carnegie Hall was swiftly crowned as one of the most prestigious concert halls in the world — by virtue of its appearance, which featured Italianate neo-Renaissance construction, and its venerated performers, who ranged from opening night performer Pyotr Ilyich Tchaikovsky to Duke Ellington. By 1962 the quality of the Hall's acoustics — which the *New York Herald*'s opening night review pronounced as "perfect" — were well established, as was the Hall's reputation for positioning the musicians who played there as among the world's very best.

The Main Hall seated 2,804 people — not the largest venue they had ever played, but certainly the most significant — and Saul was anxious to ensure the seats would be packed with the right people. The plan for this was executed with precision and his usual flair for detail, though the social and professional circles within New York City were not the most accessible to navigate, even for a consummate professional. And for a former burger joint magnate from London, Ontario, at times it felt next to impossible.

"To be trying to set up a show as an unknown from nowhere in Carnegie Hall is not easy. I mean, just getting there and booking the hotel and talking to the right people, that wasn't easy," Saul recalled. Tying up the logistics took months, and was sandwiched between other tasks and projects that demanded his attention. Immersed in the plotting out of other shows, his own ongoing visa application with the U.S. Consulate, a lawsuit filed against Johnny by former manager Stew Carnall over back royalties, the construction of a new "house on the hill" for Barbara and himself on Jarvis Street in London, and the finalizing of the rental details of a new apartment for himself in the Hollywood Hills, he was overwhelmed.[23]

"I am absolutely snowballed at the moment, so this letter will sound like a drunken James Joyce. A sore throat and bad cold plus fatigue and what seems to be a mountain of work combine to create a feeling of utter panic at the moment, and I'm not joking," Saul wrote to Barbara on April 13, after a trip to New York to fine-tune some details of the show. "New York was furious, hectic, bewildering, amazing, confusing, disturbing, frightening, exhilarating, stimulating, nauseating — but I got quite a bit done."[24]

Following his move to the States, Saul had grown close with performer and emcee Johnny Western, and they often mapped out plans together for upcoming tours as they worked in the L.A. office or in the evenings over dinner. Consumed by incessant work and hotel living, Saul was lonely at times, and grateful for Western's low-key company and keen observations. Saul had taken to relying on Western to fill in the gaps when Johnny arrived at a venue high and the show began to unravel. At this point most performances were plotted months in advance, with extensive publicity efforts spread out over radio, newspapers, handbills, posters, and even aerial banners. But Cash was always the unknown factor.

Over the last few months their discussion zeroed in on the Carnegie Hall preparations in May, and then the Hollywood Bowl in June. Cash had already begun his crossover into a mainstream audience, Saul told Western, and this show would serve to fix him in that position.[25]

"We'll present that in the most prestigious place in America, we'll take this completely out of the realm of 'country boy,' and take it to a brand-new level," Saul said. "We're going to do something that'll knock the socks off of the ordinary country music show."

"'Johnny Cash at Carnegie Hall' — that separates the men from the boys right there," Western agreed.

Though members of the Grand Ole Opry had performed in a group show at the venue, Western was well aware that at this point no country music performer had yet pulled off their own show there as a headliner. Until Cash came along, none had yet been popular enough. Western thought that Saul's persuasiveness in driving this point home to anyone who would listen — that Cash was ready — was admirable. Specifically, Saul was adamant that Columbia must record the night's performance as a special live album, in the same vein as Harry Belafonte's live double album *Belafonte at Carnegie Hall*, which had been nominated for a Grammy the previous year. On this point he was unrelenting, and leveraged all the clout he had in the pursuit of it. The executives finally agreed, and producer Don Law was given the green light to record.[26]

Souvenir programs were drawn up with a simple black cover and a single image of Johnny front and centre. Underneath, Saul continued his deliberate and careful marketing of Johnny with the phrase "America's Foremost Singing Story Teller."

Two nights before the show, Saul asked Johnny Western if he would like to go with him to see a Broadway show. On a visit to the William Morris Agency he had secured some free tickets to *I Can Get It for You Wholesale*, starring Elliott Gould, which marked the Broadway debut of a nineteen-year-old singing sensation named Barbra Streisand. Western readily agreed, as it would be the first time he had seen anything on Broadway.

As the two watched Streisand finish her knockout solo performance of "Miss Marmelstein," one of the few songs she had in her minor role, Saul leaned over to Western. "Within a year's time she's going to be the biggest thing in the world," he whispered. Western looked at what he thought was the somewhat homely girl onstage and laughed. He glanced at Saul, but he wasn't laughing.

"Saul, it's not going to happen," he said, chuckling.

After the show, the two went for dinner at Lindy's restaurant. Saul was edgy and agitated. A waiter in tuxedo and tails approached their table. Saul turned to him. "Tell you what," he said.

"Yes, sir?"

Saul leaned back, pulled out a wad of cash, and peeled off a twenty-dollar bill. Carefully, he tore the bill in half and handed one half to the startled waiter. "You can't cash that one half, but if we get good service at this table tonight I'll give you the other half for your tip," he said.

The waiter, who had likely never seen a tip that big before, swallowed hard and nodded. Johnny Western watched as he slunk away.

"That's the way you've got to treat these guys," Saul said when he saw Western's face. He lifted his drink. "I'm telling you. Otherwise, they'll eat you alive. They'll treat you like dirt."

It must simply be an example of "the New York attitude," Western surmised, and true enough, from that moment forward the waiter bowed and scraped and waited on them hand and foot.

Saul got to the matter at hand. If Carnegie marked the emergence of "a new Johnny Cash," it didn't appear that his client had received the memo. It was only days before the performance and he was haggard and his voice was weak. The stress of this only made him lean on the pep pills more, which in turn made everything worse.

"Johnny's voice is just awful. Unless there's a miracle recovery, I don't see it getting any better by Thursday night," Saul told Western. His jaw clenched. "Listen. You're emceeing this thing. Let's just make sure the best of everything happens before the finale of the show, because the finale is not going to happen."

Western rubbed his forehead. By now he knew that when Johnny's voice went, it sometimes took a week to get anywhere near back to normal. He looked up at Saul and nodded.

The final piece of Saul's plan involved a high-profile cocktail party thrown the night before the concert, so that Johnny could rub elbows with all the major players and industry insiders in the New York music business. At Saul's insistence, Columbia secured the top floor of the Time & Life Building, where he had heard publisher and chairman Henry Luce held his board meetings. Saul had recently heard of an attempt in Wyoming to popularize buffalo meat in small steaks, so he orchestrated an elaborate menu of hors d'oeuvres that included fillets of buffalo, buffalo salami, and elk summer sausage flown in from the Rocky Mountain Packing Company. Columbia was then asked to utilize their buses to round up the VIPs they had invited and drive them to the party.[27]

Located on Sixth Avenue in Manhattan's Rockefeller Center, the seventy-eight-million-dollar Time & Life Building had been completed just two years prior and boasted a spectacular modernist lobby adorned in the abstract works of Fritz Glarner and Josef Albers. Heels clicking across the terrazzo-style floor tiles, which fanned out in undulating waves of grey and white, Saul and Johnny Western strode toward the bank of elevators, which were sheathed in a checkerboard of alternating stainless steel panels designed to complement the floor.

As the two men were whisked up to the forty-eighth floor, Western fiddled with the collar of the sport coat Saul had advised him to wear. With his initials emblazoned on the pocket, it was a departure from the jackets Western usually wore, which he had custom-made from Aztec blankets. Eyes fixed on the floor numbers as they rose, he hoped he had dressed the part. They emerged on the forty-eighth floor, home of the Hemisphere Club and Tower Suite, the highest restaurant in the city, with accompanying spectacular views of the New York skyline.[28]

After they entered the suite, Saul went to find Cash while Western picked at hors d'oeuvres. A young golden-haired representative from Columbia Records approached him. The label had picked May 10, 1962 — the day of the concert — to release Western's album *Have Gun, Will Travel*, for which Cash had written the liner notes, and on which Western was backed by the group Sons of the Pioneers.

"I've really wanted to meet you because I've been working on some of your records," the man said, by way of introduction. A smile emerged from under his handlebar moustache. "I had to take one verse out of your song called 'Cowpoke.' I hope you don't mind, but they were insisting that we get that song down around three minutes for radio play."

"You guys are the bosses. Whatever," Western shrugged.

"My name's Terry Melcher," the man said, and offered Western his hand.

"Hell, you're Doris Day's son," said Western with a grin, pumping his arm. Only twenty years old, Melcher had just joined Columbia as one of their A&R producers. Within the next few years he would rise to prominence as one of their wonder boys, considered an A-list talent for his work with the Byrds and, later, the Beach Boys. Of course, neither man knew then that before the decade was out, Melcher's work with Columbia would also lead him to an aspiring rock singer named Charles Manson and into one of the country's most notorious murder cases.[29]

The event at Time & Life was virtually seamless; a Saul Holiff production from top to bottom, with nothing left to chance. Both Johnnys, Western and Cash, addressed and thanked the music luminaries warmly and expressed their excitement both about their inclusion on the Columbia label and the attendance of their executives at the upcoming performance. Hosted early in the evening, the party wound to a close at a respectable hour, and Western watched Saul whisk Cash away, presumably to bed so he might get a good rest for the following night.

However, no amount of rest — were it even possible with the amount of amphetamines Johnny was consuming — would have prevented the impending disaster. "It was one of the worst nights of my life," Western later recalled, with a sigh.

After the Columbia Records party, he had gone out to perform at an open mic of sorts at the Bitter End nightclub in Greenwich Village. Along for the ride with Western was Tompall Glaser of Tompall & the Glaser Brothers, a band on the following night's bill at Carnegie Hall, who were known for their unique sound that blended folk and rock 'n' roll. Western had never performed at the Bitter End, but he was acutely aware of how significant it was to the American music scene, which was becoming the centre not only of a powerful folk music revival but also, peripherally, of a burgeoning civil rights movement.

"All the folkies were there, the Joan Baezes and Peter, Paul and Mary, all the people who got popular later on when the folk music thing really hit big, they all appeared at The Bitter End," said Western. Owned by Fred Weintraub, the club's emcee that night was Ed McCurdy, a hard-drinking and critically acclaimed folksinger who was big on the New York circuit. Despite the enticing scenario, Western managed to make it back to the room at the Barbizon Plaza in ample time to sleep well and get ready for the show.

Weeks earlier, Saul had asked Western to emcee as usual, but to ditch his regular cowboy clothes. "I need you to be neutral, and not 'Johnny Western,'" Saul had said. "What have you got in the way of civilian clothes?"

Recently back from a seventeen-week tour to entertain the troops in Vietnam, Western had had a three-day stopover in Hong Kong during which he had commissioned a custom-fit pinstriped Italian suit in black from the city's finest tailor, complete with silver buttons.

Cash would play with a range of performers on the bill, from George Jones and the Carters to Mac Wiseman, the Glaser Brothers, Gordon Terry, and the last-minute surprise of Merle Kilgore, and Saul wanted the night's emcee to project a classy image that could provide a cohesive thread through the entire performance. The Italian suit would be perfect, Saul had told him.

Though the minor details were settling into place, by the next day it was clear that, as anticipated, their star attraction was in trouble. "All afternoon for rehearsal — we didn't have a dress rehearsal, we just had a run-through so we could do a sound check and all that — he wasn't talking. He was writing notes to his secretary, hoping he could save his voice, but of course it was unsaveable at that time," said Western. The other performers simply looked on in horror.

"This is never going to happen. He can't even talk, much less sing. He's just rasping," fiddler Gordon Terry murmured to Western as Johnny frantically scribbled notes to secretary Betty Siegfried, who had travelled in from Los Angeles to assist with the show.

"It sounds like he's gargled with household cleanser," Western heard another member of their entourage say.

Perhaps feeling the inspiration of the venue's prestigious aura, Cash had decided to use the performance to serve as a tribute to one of his heroes, Jimmie Rodgers. A founding father of country music, Rodgers was a former railroad brakeman who sang movingly of the American countryside, the rail lines that stitched its surface, and the culture that welled up around them. Though he enjoyed only a short career and died young, he left a lasting legacy of music that inspired Cash and many others who followed.

"I'd thought up something special. Mrs. Rodgers, before she died, had given me some of Jimmie's things," wrote Cash in his second autobiography. This included an old railroad hat, jacket, and lantern that Rodgers had worn previously for performances.

In addition to popping amphetamines "like popcorn," in advance of the show, Cash had also consumed quantities of diet pills in the weeks leading up to the performance. "He had starved himself down to 158 pounds so he could put on that outfit, and Jimmy Rodgers was tubercular so he probably weighed 130 pounds, and Johnny starved himself down so he could get into that 1930s railroad outfit and come out on stage like that wearing these clothes," said Western. "That had only added to how bad his voice was."

On the day of the performance, Saul was well aware that his star performer was in rough shape, but said little about it. "I think Saul tried his best to try and tell him," said Western. "[But] at the time, you couldn't talk to Johnny about it. He had his mind set on doing these things, and it was like, 'My way or the highway.'"

Once again, Saul turned to Western for backup.

"I'm the one who had to go out on the stage and say, 'Folks, he really belongs in a hospital.' Which he really did. I mean, he was just a scarecrow," said Western. No one had seen or heard from Cash since that afternoon's rehearsal. With only minutes to go, he finally showed up backstage, noticeably dirty and unkempt.[30]

For Cash, the evening unfolded like a bad dream. The main hall went black as the lights were dimmed. As Johnny emerged into the darkness with only a lamp, few in the audience made the visual connection to Jimmie Rodgers. His emaciated frame, ill-fitting, worn-out clothes and deeply lined face made him look bizarre. As he made his way to the microphone, voices in the crowd called out for his song "Folsom Prison Blues."

Quickly Cash handed the lantern off, deciding to turf the Rodgers routine and start off with his regular number. But when he opened his mouth to sing, nothing came out. At first the audience laughed, but as the chuckles died out, the realization that it was not a joke slowly rippled through the crowd. The drugs had taken their effect. No matter how many glasses of water Cash downed, his voice was gone.

"I have laryngitis tonight," he whispered. "I have no voice. I don't know if I can sing anything."[31]

"He sat on a stool with just his guitar and whispered 'I Walk the Line,' and you could hear a pin drop," said Tompall Glaser. "It still chokes me up." Horrified, Don Law from Columbia quickly instructed the recording crew not to bother turning on the machines.[32]

The elation from that evening's knockout performances, that had preceded Cash's, deflated as Western watched from backstage in his fitted Italian suit. Merle Kilgore had shown up that afternoon, to their delight, and was snuck onto the show at the last minute by Cash, who wanted him to perform "Johnny Reb," a song Merle had written and Johnny Horton had recorded. "So Cash sent him down to a costume shop in New York, and he got a rebel uniform from the civil war," Johnny Western said. On the spot, Western ad libbed Kilgore's introduction and dubbed him a "surprise guest." Unexpected performers and veteran staples of the stage included, it had all gone off without a hiccup.

As Cash desperately mouthed along through "Give My Love to Rose," Western's heart felt heavy. He had seen Cash at his very best, when he stalked the stage like a panther and sang for two hours without so much as clearing his throat. *Now he looks like the wraith of God*, he thought, cringing.

When it was over, Johnny retreated to his dressing room and snapped at anyone who tried to comfort him, including June Carter. She had appeared onstage as a vision in white, Cash later remembered in his autobiography, with a heart sewn into her robe. The only one who could reach him was singer Ed McCurdy, who had attended the show and knew all too well that the cause of Cash's public humiliation was amphetamines, likely Dexedrine. He recognized it immediately. After the show he snuck backstage and managed to engage Cash in conversation about it, drawing him in with both his folk credentials, which Cash was aware of, and his own experience with drugs.

"You know, man, you can learn to sing around laryngitis a little bit. I'm a writer and a singer, I've been in this business all my life, and I've learned some stuff like that," McCurdy said. "If we spent a little time together, maybe I could show you how to take care of yourself a little better." Cash took him up on the offer, and the two took off.[33]

By noon the next day, Western heard a knock on the door of the hotel room he shared with Gordon Terry. He opened it to find Cash standing there with a sheepish expression on his face. "I'm sorry it turned out like that," he said, looking at his shoes. "I took it out on everyone but myself. This was my own fault. I should have done this last night right after the show, and apologized, but I just couldn't."

Western had never seen Cash so contrite. Typically he avoided them if he screwed up, and rarely admitted responsibility. But there was no doubt his apology was sincere.

As they continued the tour, Cash's voice began to clear, but buried in the wake of pain and disappointment was the sober realization for many within their travelling troupe that Cash was now truly in deep trouble with the pills.[34]

"When I took my first ones, I said, 'This is what God meant for me to have in this world. This was invented for me,' you know? I honestly thought it was a blessing — a gift from God, these pills were," Cash later told Larry King. "Then I finally found out I was deceiving myself. That this was one of those things that have a false face — that it's the devil in disguise that has come to me."[35]

6

"MY CAREER IS ZOOMING"

Saul stood on the balcony of his apartment, nestled in a lush Japanese-style complex perched on Sycamore Street, and surveyed the "electric orchard" of Hollywood that unrolled below him in glittering strands. The apartment was perched above a pool, formerly a lake that had once housed rare black Australian swans back when Yamashiro, which means "mountain palace" in Japanese, was a private hilltop mansion. A few years ago, before Saul moved in, they had used it as a set for the 1957 Marlon Brando film *Sayonara*.

It was the early morning of June 28, 1962, and it was already warm, though the evenings in Hollywood were remarkably tolerable, at times even cool. And there weren't any insects, which he found delightful. *It seems the only bugs in Hollywood are the people*, he mused, though he knew that was somewhat unfair. Generally speaking, the majority of the people he had met thus far were pleasant and the atmosphere unhurried, with a slight touch of sophistication, an air of well-being, and a basic friendliness.[1]

It was a rare moment of calm. The touring and one-nighters since Carnegie had been near-incessant, with scarcely time to breathe between shows. The Carnegie performance, of course, had been devastating, and decades later Saul would characterize the incident by simply stating that it gave him "horrible memories." *Part of the joy of being a manager and a promoter*, he would offer flippantly. But it was a blow. And like a coach who experienced a loss, there was little choice but to shake it off and move forward.[2]

Fortunately, music critic Robert Shelton from the *New York Times* held back somewhat in his assessment the following day. Cash's performance was difficult to judge, he wrote, as he was suffering from a throat ailment, and added that "the hoarseness of his voice and the incohesiveness of his performance suggest that another hearing is needed." All considered, he said Cash still "came highly endorsed by reputation and a series of successful recordings" and was known as a singer-songwriter "in the vein of some of the country's greats, such as the late Jimmie Rodgers and the late Hank Williams," a comment which no doubt pleased Cash.[3]

Thankfully, there hadn't been much time to brood too heavily on the failure. On June 15, scarcely a month later, the Hollywood Bowl had been booked for a show Saul produced and presented in partnership with the KFOX radio station. Dubbed "The First Annual Giant-Folk-Western Bluegrass Musical Spectacular," it had gone decidedly better. Essentially the West Coast equivalent of Carnegie Hall, the Hollywood Bowl was not a typical country venue by any means, and once again Saul steered clear of the "country" labelling and went with a classic aesthetic, drawing up posters and flyers in red, white, and blue. The lineup was one of their most impressive yet: Patsy Cline, Marty Robbins — always a pleasure to work with — bluegrass stars Flatt & Scruggs, George Jones, pop-country singer Leroy Van Dyke of "Walk on By" fame, the Carter Family (with June, of course), novelty singer Sheb Wooley, bluegrass tenor Mac Wiseman, Gordon Terry, Tompall & the Glaser Brothers, and an opening act with Gene Davis and the Hollywood Square Dancers.

This time there was a team of emcees. Johnny Western was retained as both performer and announcer, though his organizational skills were also utilized as the show's stage director and coordinator. Earlier that year, Saul and Cash dreamed up a scheme to distribute "Johnny Cash Awards of Merit" to various industry luminaries, with the rather exhaustive description that it was intended for those who had "done the most to intelligently and honestly present country and western talent in a manner calculated to upgrade such presentations." Their first recipient was Cracker Jim Brooker, a DJ with WMIE radio out of Miami. At the

Bowl, three more awards would be presented to special guest stars Lorne Greene from *Bonanza*, Stuart Hamblen, for his contributions to the field of gospel singing and writing, and Gene Autry, for his considerable additions to the field of western music.[4]

With so much going on, a strict schedule was written up prior to the show and issued to all the artists, with the explicit instruction that they were to follow the time allotted to the minute, or face penalties. "Note to talent: Out of respect for those in the latter part of the show, it is imperative that artists adhere to time allotted to them. Otherwise, talent performing later in the evening will be faced with a restless and inattentive audience," Saul noted at the bottom of the schedule. "Bowl penalty for overtime is a severe 2 1/2 % of gross for every 15 minutes of overtime. Please understand the necessity of limiting your time on stage." On average, artists were each given eight to ten minutes. Gaunt and hoarse, Cash was still in rough shape, and it was difficult to engage him in conversation for more than three minutes in the days leading up to the show. Anticipating the worst, Saul kept him on a tight half-hour leash, slotting him onstage at 10:40 p.m., before the all-artist finale at 11:10 p.m.[5]

Sweating profusely, Johnny Western had raced around backstage to ensure all the musicians were on and off the stage with only minutes to spare. Then Faron Young showed up for his set. Though he was not even billed as a performer in the show's promotions, Saul shoehorned him in at the last minute for a strict seven-minute set — three songs and then out.

"Faron always had this idea that he was kind of a pop singer and stuff, and here he was, in front of a huge crowd in Hollywood, California, not Nashville, Tennessee, and he got out there and did seventeen minutes. I couldn't get him off the damn stage," said Western. "He really screwed the pooch. He was my main problem with that show."

After peacocking about and crooning to the crowd, "like he thought he was Dean Martin or somebody," Faron finally ended his set, said Western.

"You son of a bitch," Western said, standing in his path as he had exited the stage. "You wrecked the rest of the show."

"I don't give a damn. I'm never coming back here, anyway," leered Young, stepping around him with a grin. In a mad dash, Western sought out the bigger artists like George Jones and Leroy Van Dyke to ask them if they'd cut a song from their sets, an obligation he found mortifying.[6]

By the time Cash took the stage for his set they had managed to get back on schedule, and he eked out an acceptable performance that at least did not further diminish his reputation. But it was an incident after the show that later gave Saul cause for concern, this time for different reasons. Secrets were difficult to hide in their close-knit group, and the growing affection between Johnny and June was apparent to most within their vicinity since she had joined them on the road. After Carnegie Hall, they had travelled to the Mint Casino in Las Vegas for an eight-day stint, and June had joined them for the final five days. It soon became clear to everyone that their flirtation had become a full-blown affair.[7]

"Like anyone at the top in country music or any other field, he set out to conquer whatever he could conquer. If he had the chances, he took them," Saul later explained to writer Steve Turner. "I don't know of very many people either in country or any other field of music who remained chaste."[8]

Though a certain amount of fooling around was par for the course, Saul wholly disapproved of where this business with June was headed. When he finally advised Johnny to end the affair, his worst fears were confirmed.

"You shouldn't be with June anymore," Saul had counselled. "You're going to go through a living hell."

"I know, but I'm not gonna live without June," Cash said.

This was obviously not a simple road fling, and its implications concerned Saul. Though not particularly close with Vivian, Saul was fond of her and was often the one on the other end of the phone who heard her anguish when Johnny hadn't returned home. He knew her husband's absences were tearing her apart.[9]

Johnny's statement, and the trouble it entailed, had swiftly come into focus after the Hollywood Bowl show. Vivian, who hadn't seen Johnny in months, had attended the concert and waited for him in the performers' parking lot after the show with the girls and his parents, Ray and Carrie Cash. By this time she was apprehensive; she had never liked June, and whenever the two were on tour together it made her uneasy. Their marriage seemed to have changed drastically in the last six months, and she simply wanted to see her husband before he left for the tour's remaining dates in Arizona. When Johnny finally emerged, he slid past Vivian and his children with a cursory greeting before he jumped into the back seat of a Cadillac. Next came June Carter, who breezed past and got into the back seat next to him. She waved to Vivian and the girls as they raced off, leaving Johnny's wife standing in the parking lot, humiliated.

"She didn't say anything. She just had this look of total devastation on her face, like, 'My God, I'm his wife and he's not coming home. He's going to Tucson with June Carter,'" said Johnny Western, who watched the whole scene unfold from behind the wheel of Mother Maybelle's Cadillac. In the back seat were June's sisters, Anita and Helen. Though he was horrified by what had just taken place, they had planned to travel as a convoy to Arizona, so there was little that Western could say to Vivian except to bid her goodbye. "I couldn't believe it," he said.[10]

Now that the show was finished, and he could relax and reflect in the silence of his apartment, Saul felt in fairly good spirits and health — though the desire to quit smoking was nagging at him. Just six days earlier, on June 22, he had celebrated his thirty-seventh birthday. With the dilemma of Johnny, June, and Vivian weighing on his mind, he realized it had been some time since he had written to Barbara. After attending to paperwork at the office, he decided to jot down a letter before he headed off for a business trip to San Francisco.

June 28, 1962

Dear Barb,

I know I don't exactly take first prize for letter writing but I think you'll agree with me that the one-nighters we've been on recently consume quite a bit of time. I certainly enjoyed getting your letters, however, and hope you forgive the prolonged silences on my part.

The Hollywood Bowl show was a success in spite of the worst weather that Hollywood has had for years. It rained early in the day and then went on to be the coldest evening in the last 25 years. At 9 PM the temperature had dropped to 61 degrees. I like air-conditioning, but what the hell. In spite of the Western Fair October feeling — in spite of the fact that some women had turned slightly blue — the general opinion is that the show was a huge success. It looked well, the sound was great, and the timing left nothing to be desired. The party that Columbia threw two days prior to the 15th was a success beyond my wildest imagination. It was held at the main building (inside and out) where I live — the Hollywood Hills Apartment Hotel. The food, the view, coupled together with some fine singing by Johnny and others melded and synthesized into what some people considered the cocktail party of the year. Incidentally, I ended up emceeing a healthy portion of the program and it seems that I did pretty good.

Once again I'm under pressure out of necessity to make this letter as short as possible since I just have a few hours before leaving for San Francisco, then off to Daytona, and then home. It means I'll be absent from the office for many days. The work-load that has accumulated here is almost frightening and I simply must get on to it. I'll ramble on with observations and comments and dashes, and hope that you can make sense of it.

Glad you enjoyed your trip to Michigan with my mother — you shouldn't thank me because a thousand of these trips couldn't repay you for the help, consideration and understanding you have shown me. [...] Thank you for your suggestions concerning Johnny. You seem to be in good spirits — I read "The Carpetbaggers" — it's probably the most vivid, the most sensual book that I read in years — Suggest you read an absolutely charming and delightful book called "To Kill a Mockingbird." [...]

Give my love to my mother — My birthday was celebrated on top of a trailer in Salt Lake City with ice cream and cake behind a ballroom — Marshall hit the ice cream with the flat of his hand — everybody had ice cream. Thank you for you kind sentiments and cards — never did get the wires — Keep well — See you soon.

Love, Saul.[11]

Later that summer, Cash released a rather lacklustre album, *The Sound of Johnny Cash*, recorded earlier in the year. It contained a variety of cover songs in a somewhat incoherent mix — "In the Jailhouse Now," by Jimmie Rodgers, which peaked at number eight on the *Billboard* Country Singles, "Mr. Lonesome," by Tompall Glaser, and "Cotton Fields," by Huddie "Leadbelly" Ledbetter. Perhaps the most interesting feature of the album is the photo of Cash on the cover. Taken in April of 1962 by photographer Leigh Wiener at his studio, it is a clear and striking image of the singer, with a neatly greased pompadour and guitar held upright against the floor as he gazes intensely into the camera. The image is enhanced by head-to-toe black clothing against a black backdrop.

Nowhere is the myth and the reality of Johnny Cash more muddled than in the history of his legendary image as the "Man in Black," and the cover of this album serves as one of the definitive moments where the musician began to establish this trademark look. Earlier in his career, Johnny was known to wear a variety of colours, including white suits sewn for him by Vivian, which she had trimmed in hand-stitched silver down the lapels, sleeves, and pants. The Tennessee Two often used a variety of tailors for their clothes, one of the most popular being rodeo tailor Nudie Cohn, the original rhinestone cowboy out of North Hollywood.[12]

In the early days, when the band were earning about ten dollars a day, Marshall, Luther, and Johnny would buy their shirts down on Beale Street in Memphis, where shirts and trousers of fair quality were cheap. Black was often a natural clothing choice, as it didn't show dirt, required less cleaning, and looked good onstage. Cash also frequented a store called the Clothes Horse in Portland, Oregon, but according to Johnny

Western, he rarely chose clothes in black back then. By the 1960s, it made sense that Saul had some input into the way the band looked, given the energy he put into his own appearance and his background in clothing, which included his own "Holiff's" label. Though he'd begun to move out of the clothing business by 1962, he still had a hand in ordering custom-made clothes for artists like Marty Robbins.[13]

"He designed all of our band costumes," said W.S. "Fluke" Holland. "He had a clothing store back then, and he made the outfits we wore in the early days." Saul made up matching suits for the band and different suits for Johnny, he added. Tommy Cash, Johnny's brother, recalled that Saul once offered to take him to his store to get a fine custom suit. "He picked out a very expensive brown and black striped suit, and he didn't charge me full price for it; it was like half price. I never forgot that. I thought that was really cool," said Tommy.[14]

If there was one person in particular who contributed to Johnny's iconic look besides Nudie Cohn, it was the designer Manuel. One day Saul escorted the band to his storefront in North Hollywood, to get suits made. The way Saul remembers it, when Johnny was measured for his suits, Manuel told him that he had a surplus of black fabric on hand, so Johnny replied, "Just make all mine in black, then." Though Manuel doesn't recall when exactly he began making black clothes for Johnny — maybe 1959 — it did involve a sale on black fabric.

"He called me and he said, 'You know, Manuel, I need more clothes, this business is really picking up,'" said Manuel, who then took an order from him for nine suits. "I made them and then mailed them on the road to him, and he got on the phone and said, 'I received the clothes. I like them fine, but how come they're all in black?' and I said, 'Well, we had a sale on black fabric, so I went for it and made you those suits.… I think black is appropriate for you.'"[15]

Things puttered along throughout the summer of 1962, and the mountain of office and administrative work Saul often faced on his return from touring seemed to have subsided, though perhaps he was also more relaxed because Johnny's performances had improved remarkably over the summer. With an almost fatherly affection, Saul saw fit to encourage and affirm this turning over of a new leaf for the musician.

"I was proud of you in Daytona. No temperament — hard, sincere efforts on stage regardless of the size of the crowd," he wrote to Johnny on July 13, referring to a recent show. "This has been in evidence on practically all the dates we've played recently, and differs drastically from last year. A lot of newly won composure and maturity — much easier to be with — evident efforts to settle down and re-establish yourself at the top … where you belong."

He signed off, "Your obedient Director of Planning."[16]

The feeling that things were ticking along well was apparently mutual, as around this time Johnny felt compelled to pen his own handwritten thank-you letter to Barbara, in which he raved about Saul's performance and the "million-dollar" letterhead she and Jerry Davies had designed, which he felt gave the impression of top billing.

"I feel that my association with Saul over the past few months is the foundation for the new lease on life I have found," Cash wrote. "As a

Johnny Cash and Saul Holiff in Saul's Hollywood apartment, 1962. Pictured is *The Sound of Johnny Cash* album.

matter of fact, I know it…. Not only have I begun to enjoy life but I am happy and excited about the way I think my career is zooming."[17]

Despite the seeming cohesion on the surface, that summer the two men had their first serious argument. On August 10, Saul received a letter from Cash that he interpreted as an accusation of sloppy bookkeeping. Worse, it alluded to extravagance on his behalf — even dishonesty — in his handling of finances.

Listed in numerical order — a style Saul favoured in his own business dealings — were a variety of complaints and new directives from Cash. These ranged from the cancellation of their order of special gold-embossed stationery (which he now seemed to be having second thoughts about) and shock over its cost, which he found "sickening and ridiculous," to confusion over the hotel bill at the Barbizon Plaza Hotel and the price of the Carnegie Hall and Hollywood Bowl programs, which he thought had already been deducted from his funds long ago, to the payment of a nine-hundred-dollar *Billboard* magazine ad. Included with the letter was a package of invoices, bills, and statements that seemed to belong to Saul but that Cash viewed as confusing because he did not have access to all the records.

Simmering below the specifics, the George Jones issue surfaced again.

"This office is not a talent agency. Betty was hired by myself to take care of my business and my fan club. George Jones' business, as well as all his bills, should be handled by someone else. You're welcome to handle their business through my office in your name but you'll have to arrange another girl to take care of it. George Jones is not a Johnny Cash Enterprise," Cash wrote. With the letter, he enclosed a receipt from June Carter for $1,440 that Saul seemed to have forgotten to get from her, with the instruction that from then on any talent costs should be paid for by cheque. In addition, Cash wanted all contracts for his personal appearances to specify that payment was to be issued to "Johnny Cash," not "Johnny Cash Enterprises" or "Johnny Cash, Inc." as there was, in his words, "no such organization."[18]

Insulted beyond measure, Saul took a moment to compose himself before writing back to Johnny, care of his brother Roy in Tennessee. Evidently, his occasional visits home to Vivian were becoming even more sporadic.

Dear Johnny:

After reading your letter, my only conclusion is that in my absence I've been TRIED, JUDGED and FOUND GUILTY, WITHOUT a HEARING. You have many good and bad characteristics. I always believed one of the good ones was fairness.

Your letter unmistakably challenges and attacks my integrity, character and honesty. Worse than that, it appears now that any confidence and faith you had in me is now at an all-time low. PLEASE ALLOW ME THE COURTESY OF READING THIS LETTER THOR-OUGHLY AND IN A PLACE OF PRIVACY SUITED TO DIGESTION OF ITS CONTENTS WITHOUT INTERRUPTION.

If what you say in your letter of August 10th is cor-rect; particularly in reference to the New York hotel bill and the souvenir program books, then that makes me guilty of a clear-cut case of misappropriation. This is a criminal offence, and if the positions were reversed, I would be sorely tempted to prosecute such a person; moreso if that person had been the recipient of many wonderful opportunities and generous actions as in the case of your treatment of me.

Saul then issued Johnny a challenge: if, after reading the letter and giving a thorough assessment of all the pertinent records, by an accoun-tant of his choice — there was even a "shred" or "particle" of truth in his accusations, Saul would forfeit all the record, BMI, and music publishing royalties due him for the first six months of 1962, which amounted to several thousand dollars.

"Judging from your letter, it would appear that it was my intention to literally and figuratively steal money via the New York hotel bills and the souvenir programs," he continued. "If this is proved the case, I should be dismissed. Briefly summarized below is my rebuttal, point by point, to your letter. These points all will be substantiated down to the smallest detail and to the last copper when the records are examined."

Each accusation in Johnny's letter was then examined in excruciating detail, down to the expense of the gold-embossed stationery — which was, in fact, a five-year supply of paper, and which had elicited such a fantastic response that recipients of letters from their office were stapling them to their walls. This was the one area in which he may be guilty of extravagance, Saul admitted, but it was his firm belief that the materials served to enhance and broaden Johnny's image in both the business world and with his fans.

"The news release stationery has resulted, by its use and my efforts, in continuous monthly articles on your activities in all trade papers over the last ten months," wrote Saul, who added that it was in fact at *his* recommendation that Cash dispense with his publicist Howard Brandy (whose work Saul then largely took on himself), a move that easily saved him four thousand dollars in wages — which in turn more than sufficiently covered the cost of the printed materials that Cash was upset about.

"Incidentally, of all the various office equipment purchased, only two items involve my personal use — an office chair and a desk lamp. The reception room couch serves other purposes in addition to the fact that I paid 50% of its cost," Saul wrote. The advertising bill with *Billboard*, he continued, was paid only after every other avenue to get Columbia to pay for it had been exhausted.

His exasperation began to subside somewhat.

"As a so-called business manager, and in consideration of the fact that you have frequently indicated that you preferred to leave these matters up to me, I felt that I was not being out of line in authorizing the payment of this account. Apparently I had an erroneous conception of my position, and therefore I apologize for not consulting you," Saul wrote, and began to painstakingly describe the new filing system he had established at their office; the way it functioned, why monies were withdrawn at various times, and what they were used to pay for.

There was that issue with George Jones again, buried in all these trifling details, thought Saul. Yes, he had directed Betty Siegfried to oversee a variety of tasks associated with Jones, but that had all been cleared with

Johnny six months earlier. They had discussed it over a meal at a restaurant on Vine Street, next to Music City — he recalled it clearly. Later, Saul had been careful to itemize any expenses George incurred, and made sure to pay for a portion of the rent, Betty's extra time, and any long-distance calls involving George out of his own pocket. Suddenly, it seemed clear that perhaps the nebulous jealousy he had perceived earlier was the real issue. Maybe it had shaken Johnny's trust in him. He thought for a moment.

"Everything I have mentioned in this letter can be supported beyond a reasonable shadow of a doubt and withstand the most intensive investigation. I have had, and still do have, the highest regard for your talent and for you personally," Saul wrote. The next part, he underlined: "I have said it before, and I repeat again, that, no matter where I am, and no matter what I am doing, my first loyalty has been, and will continue to be, to you. Please bear in mind that I function as follows: When I have a lot to do, I can do a lot. I thrive on pressure, and it wouldn't matter if I had ten artists; none of your affairs would ever be neglected in the slightest way. Yours truly, Saul."[19]

The reassurances apparently worked ... to a degree. However, Johnny moved ahead with plans to shift both Betty and the operations now housed in their Ventura office to Nashville, where he would share the space with his brother Tommy. This potential move mystified Saul, and he wrote home to Barbara about it. "It means of course that the office routine re: cheques, records, etc. which was so painfully built into a workable system will be screwed up immediately," he told her. Moreover, Johnny had also instructed Saul to book him for dates only up until January 1964, pending further discussion. This detail also made him uneasy.[20]

As the troupe prepared to depart in late October for their USO tour of Japan and Korea, Saul couldn't help but feel frustrated that his plans to include Elvis Presley on the tour hadn't come to fruition. It didn't entirely make sense. On a trip to Las Vegas in the days before New Year's Eve, he mentioned the idea to Elvis himself, who had responded with enthusiasm. In a subsequent letter on January 17 to Colonel Tom Parker, Elvis's

manager, Saul then laid out the case in persuasive terms that were difficult to refuse.

"After several days in Tokyo and much discussion with various Japanese
agents, one thing became overwhelmingly clear — Elvis Presley would
break any existing show business records anywhere by an appearance in
Japan," Saul wrote, and then listed all the reasons it was a good idea, while
simultaneously addressing any problems or excuses Parker could conjure
up. There was even a chance to stop over in Manila, where Elvis could play
to several thousand Filipino fans if he so desired, Saul added.[21]

A couple of weeks later, Parker's assistant Tom Diskin issued a terse
refusal, advising that "for some five years now we have several standing offers for personal appearances there, and in fact have not taken any
requests for additional appearances for the past two years due to the
great backlog now on file."[22]

Everyone in the business knew that Parker was a hustler to the *n*th
degree. This was not an anomaly in the promotions business by any
stretch, but negotiations for Elvis were typically judged first and foremost by their dollar value. And Japan was a no-lose venture — Saul
clearly offered to take on all the sticky particulars of accommodations,
travel (he detailed exact routes in the letter, and their time commitment
— down to the half-hour), possible venues (and their capacities), and all
publicity and promotion. There was little else for Parker to do but come
along to collect the paycheque. Moreover, the market for Elvis was likely
even larger than Saul had estimated. By 1957 Elvis was already the biggest star not only in Japan but in Germany also, according to journalist
Alanna Nash.

What Saul also didn't know, however, was that Elvis *couldn't* leave the
country — because Parker didn't want him to.

In *The Colonel*, Nash's biography of Parker, she details how despite
being offered millions to take Elvis abroad on European tours, his manager always staunchly refused. Born Andreas van Kuijk in Holland,
Parker had first entered the United States illegally in 1929 and lived in
fear of the discovery that he lacked the necessary paperwork to re-enter
and would be deported. Though he had served in the U.S. army, by 1932
he went AWOL. After serving months in military prison for desertion,

he was diagnosed as a psychopath and discharged. But his illegality was a strange dilemma. By the time he helped nurture Elvis to superstar status, the Colonel's extensive power and connections within the U.S. government meant the process of naturalization shouldn't have been too arduous; he counted Lyndon Johnson among his personal friends. However, in her book Nash speculates wildly that Parker may have in fact fled Holland to escape arrest for the bludgeoning death of a greengrocer's wife in his hometown, which would explain the intense effort to cover up his past.[23]

Whatever the case, Parker would not leave the United States, which meant Elvis didn't either. And other than a few Canadian shows in 1957 that the Colonel did not attend, Elvis would never tour outside the States for the remainder of his career.[24]

It was October 24, 1962, when Saul, Cash, June Carter, Johnny Western, Gordon Terry, Marshall Grant, Luther Perkins, and W.S. Holland boarded their Japanese Airlines plane from Los Angeles for a fifteen-hour flight to Tokyo. After some negotiation, the USO had agreed to fly June

Marshall Grant, W.S. "Fluke" Holland, Saul Holiff, Johnny Cash, and June Carter in a plane over Korea en route to their first Far East tour. Note Saul in the back, hard at work. 1962.

and "the babies," as she affectionately called the Tennessee Three, out to their point of embarkation so that they could all depart together, which only added to the festive atmosphere.[25]

Encouraged by his successful work at the Hollywood Bowl, Saul's role during the trip was not only to oversee the entire affair as manager but also to serve as an emcee. With thirty shows scheduled during the two-week tour, it was a gruelling run, with many of the gigs tacked on after the interest Saul had gauged as "frantic" prior to their departure was upgraded to downright explosive upon their arrival. Though it was the first time any of them had toured in Asia, it was also the first time country and western musicians had performed in front of a non-English-speaking audience in this area.[26]

In a remarkable move that was also a first, Saul went to great efforts to involve the State Department, the USO, and AT&T in his arrangement of a two-way-call direct broadcast from Japan during the Country Music Festival in Nashville, so that Cash and the ambassador in Tokyo might greet Tennessee's governor Frank Clement from where he was stationed with the Grand Ole Opry.[27]

Whether motivated by patriotism or not, overseas trips such as these offered an opportunity for Cash and Presley to "single-handedly do more to improve [the] relationship between our countries than all the efforts combined up to date," Saul had written in his initial proposal to Parker, and he wasn't far off the mark. A consummate jazz fan, Saul was acutely aware of the existing efforts of the State Department to do just that, with their Jazz Ambassadors program. Initiated in 1956, the program utilized musicians like Dizzy Gillespie, Dave Brubeck, Louis Armstrong, Duke Ellington, and Thelonious Monk, among others, as representatives sent abroad to countries in the Middle East, Africa, and eastern Europe to promote some of the finest culture the States had to offer.

There was no reason why these efforts couldn't be extended to include country music, and other countries, Holiff thought. Why not Russia, for example? Country artists were already beginning to branch out into countries overseas with great success. The previous summer, musicians Chet Atkins, Jim Reeves, and Floyd Cramer had played a string of successful shows in South Africa.

"Many kinds of American musical art have been represented in the cultural exchange program with the Soviet Union over the course of quite a few years," Holiff told *Billboard* magazine, as the tour wound to a close. "But never has country music had its chance. I will personally do all that I can to see this come about and I'd love to get other interests in the field active in the project too."[28]

A show at the Korakuen Auditorium in Tokyo brought out a crowd of more than three thousand Japanese fans and was televised to millions via NTV, Japan's leading television network. "On stage he's a jangling, floor scuffing contradiction, ranging from boyish, caught-in-the-cookie-jar shyness to sweat-drenched virility that fairly leaps across the footlights," gushed writer Al Ricketts in his On the Town column from Tokyo. At the Tachikawa air force base, the troupe was accompanied by four Japanese country bands. An air force plane then flew them all to Korea on November 2, where they entertained twenty-six thousand GIs over seven days and played twenty-six shows instead of the original twelve they had scheduled.[29]

The tour was the first on which June played the banjo, which the troops loved, according to Cash. In South Korea, they played at the Camp Howard military base in the mountains above Seoul.

"So many of the boys hadn't been home in so long and hadn't seen an American girl in I don't know when," June later told Pete Seeger in an interview. "I had this cute little trick where I would take the microphone and sing this little song, and throw the mic into the footlights, and yank it back real quick. Well, it always came back. And that day it really came back. It hit me right in the mouth and knocked teeth everywhere." Unsure of what to do next, June felt she couldn't disappoint the men, who had lined up for miles to watch the show. Ever the road trooper, she said she just grabbed her banjo, propped her foot up on a chair, and finished the show with a toothless grin.[30]

"Japan and Korea were unqualified successes. Johnny behaved and performed beautifully at all times, in spite of frequent exhaustion and other handicaps. The TV show was videotaped in front of a live audience consisting of close to 100 percent Japanese people. Their response was fantastic. I might proudly add that because of the language barrier, I literally and figuratively produced and directed the show," Saul wrote to Barbara on November 23, upon their return. Staying at the Cashes' house, he had just enjoyed a large meal and was recuperating from a cold.[31]

As far as personal enjoyment went, as much of the tour's details were executed months beforehand, the trip afforded Saul some time to sample Japan's wares, from the decorated geishas and attractive hostesses to private Turkish baths and Kobe beef — the flavour and allure of which so impressed him that for some time afterward he entertained the idea of opening a Kobe steak house in Los Angeles.

As the holiday season bore down upon them, Saul gave himself some credit for what he had told Johnny would be a "year of renewal." It had, in fact, been a remarkable first year on the job, and Saul had successfully transitioned from a small-town clothing salesman and part-time promoter to major up-and-coming player in the music business.[32]

The gruelling pace of the Far East tour took its toll on Johnny, however. Upon his return he contracted acute laryngitis and was hospitalized, after which his voice disappeared for weeks. Though he had held up admirably on the tour, it had only served to distract him from the pressing reality of home life in Casitas Springs, which had come ever more unglued since the scene at the Hollywood Bowl. Increasing time spent in Nashville with June, and at his brother's place in Memphis, didn't help.[33]

Though only seven years older than Johnny, Saul couldn't help but adopt a paternal role at times. By example and through specific recommendations, Saul helped Johnny develop good reading habits, to which Cash credited "a lot of growth mentally and spiritually." Fond of utilizing the most verbose words to describe things, Saul's use of adjectives could be exhausting, but he also took time to explain or define what he meant. In a letter sent in the new year, after a long list of upcoming shows and performers, Saul paused to define the word *eunuch* for Johnny, as according to the *Concise Oxford Dictionary*.

His paternality was rarely condescending, and besides, it was simply good business. As Johnny's manager, he needed a fully functioning performer for all the upcoming tours and dates he had planned; television was also still a possibility Saul wanted to explore further, with a certainty that it was the key to launching Johnny into superstar status. Without a number one hit for some time now, he was anxious to keep his client on top, and rumours of instability and suspicious bouts of laryngitis were not helpful toward that goal. At times his efforts to fight these innuendos or counter them with positivity were somewhat odd, such as the news release he sent to the trade papers that detailed how Marshall Grant "has never consumed an alcoholic beverage in his life, is a non-smoker and rarely has he tasted the aromatic flavours of coffee." Or that Luther Perkins "may consume two drinks a year, if that many," and that in addition to being "a lifelong abstainer" of all these things, W.S. "Fluke" Holland was "the antithesis" of the public's concept of drummers — whatever that meant. Needless to say, an editor receiving the release likely thought the manager doth protest too much.[34]

As both men confronted the spectre of 1963, Saul suggested Johnny join him in writing down their personal goals for the year, with the idea they could work to help each other keep their resolutions.

Personal Goals:

1. To completely, absolutely, positively give up smoking.
2. To reduce to a healthful, suitable, comfortable weight.
3. To eliminate candy in any form.
4. To eliminate coffee.
5. 50 pushups by January 1964.
6. To arise every A.M. by 7 and get mobile immediately with hot water, orange juice, push-ups, and a walk.

In the year to come, Saul would see to it that he stuck to the resolutions they had laid out. Johnny, on the other hand, would not.

7

THE FLAMES WENT HIGHER

Around suppertime on March 5, a single-engine Piper Comanche plane got caught in strong winds and went down in the woods five miles west of the Tennessee River, about twenty yards from a fire tower station. Patsy Cline was on board. Also in the plane were Grand Ole Opry stars Hawkshaw Hawkins and Cowboy Copas, as well as Patsy's manager, Randy Hughes, who was serving as pilot. There were no survivors. As details on the tragedy began to emerge, a wave of devastation spread from their musical community in Nashville out to California, where Saul and Johnny Western both got the call.

"I cried like a baby," remembered Western.

It didn't seem possible she could be gone. Just two months earlier they'd met up on set for the filming of a TV show for KCOP on Channel 13. The two had stood together and watched as Patsy's husband, Charlie Dick, elbowed his way onto the set in his sport coat and ascot and proceeded to order the lighting and sound crew around.

"Lookit there, 'Mr. Cline.' What an asshole. These Hollywood people do this for a living every day of their lives, and this clown comes in and is trying to tell these people where to set the microphones and how to set the lights," she had said to Western with a sigh. "I really am going to divorce him one of these days."

And now she was dead. Strangely, she had often predicted her demise to close friends, stating with a calm certainty that she would never live past thirty. After Patsy and Johnny Western wrapped the taping of the television show, Patsy had hit the road to tour with June Carter. On the drive out of Oxnard, California, one night, she had turned to June and asked her to remember what she was about to say. Certain that she would "go out soon" in a tragic manner, Patsy then detailed who she wanted to take care of her children after her death, and that she wanted her body to come home. It wasn't the first time Patsy had talked to her this way, but this time it seemed different. Chilled by her serious tone, June had rummaged around in the dim light for a pen. Though she couldn't understand how Patsy seemed so certain about her fate, she had done as she was asked and had written everything down.

Tension had recently surfaced between the two during a plane trip with Cash and Johnny Western. En route to Shreveport, Louisiana, to meet with a Columbia executive, June had been absorbed in her Bible when she'd looked up from her reading to catch Patsy's eye. It seemed as fine a time as any to lecture Patsy on her various road romances.

"You know, Patsy, you've got to stop your runnin', jumpin', and playin'," sighed June. "It's gonna hurt your career up and down the line. One of these things is going to catch up with you and it's going to be in the papers."

"I'll just have to take that chance, I guess," Patsy had said with a sigh, and looked out the window. June's Bible-thumping was tiresome at times. When it later became clear to the whole entourage that June and Johnny were an item, Patsy nudged Johnny Western. "Remember June chastising me? Well that's just like the pot calling the kettle black, isn't it?" she had said to him with a laugh. It didn't help June's guilt that her first marriage, to Carl Smith, had ended after he had had an affair with singer Goldie Hill, whom he subsequently married.[1]

Of course that was behind them, and all that remained now was the great hole Patsy Cline's death created. During the funeral, June stayed behind at Patsy's house and watched her children. Her mind churned. She knew Patsy was right, her love for Johnny was hypocritical, and wrong, and against everything the Bible taught her. It seemed like nothing would save her from its all-consuming intensity, no matter how often she wore out her knees praying. The torment was epic, poetic even, and for months she had turned to writing to process her feelings. During some of the tours,

June took time out with Merle Kilgore, who encouraged her writing, to collaborate on songs. In the later months of 1962 he came around to her house in Madison to pen some more music. They sat at her kitchen table trading ideas, and it led to the swift completion of a song that seemed to just about perfectly capture the way she felt: "Love's Ring of Fire."

"June had found a letter or something from an old friend who was going through a divorce, and it said, 'Love is like a burning ring of fire, I'll never get married again,'" said Merle Kilgore in the documentary *Half a Mile a Day*. Long before the Kilgore session, June had driven through the streets of Nashville at night in a haze of angst over what to do about her affair with Cash, when the idea crystallized. The letter merely put words to what was already taking shape in her mind.[2]

Initially, June offered the song to her sister Anita, who was seeking one last track to finish her debut album for Mercury Records. Released in January of 1963 and sung in a lilting folk style, Anita's version of the song didn't chart at all, though it was selected as a "country and western spotlight" pick by *Billboard* magazine in their January 12 issue. Desperate for a hit, Cash immediately noticed the song and told Anita that he would give her "five or six months," and if it didn't burn up the charts, he wanted to record it his own way.

With his contract set to expire at the end of 1963, Cash couldn't afford to waste any time, and scheduled a recording session in the first week of March regardless. Columbia was starting to lose interest in Cash, who hadn't recorded anything new in months or had a hit record since 1959. Hedging his bets, Saul had even begun to research other labels in case Columbia dropped Cash, who was summoned to New York and sternly advised that he needed to get his act together. Cash was no longer the golden boy he once was when they had signed him, but producer Don Law begged the executives for one last chance, and they gave the okay for a one-day recording session.

Set for the first week of March, the session was delayed in the wake of Patsy's death and put off until March 25, which only heightened the tension and gave it more weight. Shaken by the death of his friend, Cash was also anxious because he wanted —*needed* — the session to go well, and was uncertain whether Don Law was the man to take him there.[3]

"Cowboy" Jack Clement had just eased himself into the bath at his home in Beaumont, Texas, when the phone rang. One of the star producers and engineers at Sun Records, Clement was responsible for many of the company's high points in the late 1950s. This included the discovery of Jerry Lee Lewis, which came about when the receptionist at Sun came back to Clement's office and told him there was a man at the front desk "who says he plays piano like Chet Atkins."

A songwriter of significant skill, Clement played guitar, dobro, ukulele, and bass, and had penned some of Cash's most successful songs with the label, including "Ballad of a Teenage Queen" and "Guess Things Happen That Way." After a fight with Sam Phillips in which he was fired for "insubordination," Clement had a brief stint in Nashville as a producer and then moved south to set up his own operation: the Gulf Coast Recording Studio and Hall-Clement music publishing company.[4]

Heaving himself from the bath, he padded to the phone. To his surprise, Johnny Cash was on the other end of the receiver. They hadn't worked together in a professional capacity since Johnny's Sun days.

"June and Merle Kilgore have written a song called 'Ring of Fire,'" Johnny told him. "I had a dream about hearing these mariachi horns in it, and I want you to come to Nashville to help me produce it."

The request put Clement in an awkward position. Johnny needed him to take the reins on this one, and truth be told, if Johnny asked him to do something, he did it. It was clear to Clement why Johnny came to him for help — Don Law was a nice old gentleman, but he didn't really know what was going on. He wasn't hip. But all the same, if he participated, he'd have to walk a fine line with his involvement to ensure Law wouldn't feel alienated.

Upon his arrival in Nashville, Clement went to the studio where Johnny and the session musicians had gathered. He immediately changed the microphones on the drums and then regarded horn players Bill McElhiney and Karl Garvin, standing awkwardly in front of music stands that held blank sheets of paper. Clement thought for a moment and then hummed what would become the iconic opening horn lines to the song. He told them to write it down. Then he walked over to the stool and picked up the guitar. The way Clement tells it, it was simple: they then recorded "Ring of Fire." But the results were explosive.[5]

Fuelled by those strange Mexican trumpets and Cash's tweaked lyrics, the song took a dark, intense turn — which was Cash's particular forte. Columbia rushed it out for April 19, and by early summer it had soared to number one on the country charts and number seventeen on the pop charts.

"'Ring of Fire' is a hit, and an unqualified one," Saul wrote to Barbara on June 6, hardly able to contain his excitement. "Sales are outstanding and the song is high on the pop charts in every trade paper. Reports received today indicate that the record has broken wide open in Canada, especially Winnipeg and Toronto. An album also called *Ring of Fire* will be released immediately to capitalize on the strength of this single."

In the midst of all this action, Saul couldn't have been more pleased. Not only was it their first bona fide hit as a team, though he had had little direct involvement, but it also vaulted Cash ever closer to the

Saul Holiff hard at work in his Hollywood apartment, 1963.

goal of mainstream pop success. What was more, it came at a moment when Saul finally felt a sense of confidence and finesse as a manager that until now had eluded him. The hit was well-timed and offered further ammunition with which he could renegotiate Cash's contract with Columbia.

It was all going more or less according to plan, which made it all the more shocking when, the following month, Johnny decided to fire Saul.

July 11, 1963

Dear Barb, .

What I've always considered was inevitable happens to have finally happened. Johnny has suddenly and rather abruptly advised me that he would like to discontinue our present arrangement. However, he has indicated that he would like me to go on booking him.

The suddenness of his decision has of course upset me considerably, especially since it comes at a time when everything is shaping up so well. Even though I may sound immodest, I feel that the June tour was handled professionally and thoroughly, which is a direct result of the trial and error and experience resulting from the last many months.

Recently I negotiated a new music publishing contract which was very favourable to Johnny and managed to squeeze out an extra concession that should bring in between $6,000 and $8,000 extra a year, plus a 50% increase in the fan club, a thoroughly organized business office; not to mention constant useful news releases and a continuous stream of letters apologizing for or attempting to rectify different problems that have arisen on the road. In one union case alone, a legitimate request from the promoter for $1,750 was whittled down to $500 via a stream of letters. In this particular instance, Johnny was all set to pay the full amount requested.

It's somewhat of an anachronism coming at this time, considering that we have a hit record and that I've finally gained the necessary experience to do a proper job. The irony of the whole thing is that one of Johnny's main beefs is that he pays the overhead, such as office, telephone, and my travel expenses. If during the last two years he had an agency representing him as well as personal management, the amount he would have paid out would be more than double the type of expenses I have just enumerated, plus the fact that working at 15% and handling both booking and management is considerably lower than other similar arrangements.

Another of Johnny's concerns was that he has always felt that money he earned on the road never went to him, but went to the business. No matter how much I have attempted to point out that he is the business and that monies going into the business were used to pay obligations concerning Johnny, it was to no avail.

I am trying to give you a fragmentary picture of the situation, but it's impossible to apply logic or reason to the whole thing. I have never sought to have an "ace in the hole," since I honestly believed that no matter how emotional and irrational Johnny was, he was at least loyal, and I tried to reciprocate with a similar loyalty. To top everything off, I don't believe that he ever completely trusted me, as exemplified by the situation last year and several instances this year. I can't say that I blame him, however, since I'm sure he had reason in the past to build up such a suspicious nature. This is how things stand at the present, so I'm sure you can readily see that it doesn't make for the best frame of mind.

I really must get back to work now, so until I hear from you,
Saul

P.S. I might suggest that from here on, you write me c/o my apartment since I'm not sure whether I'll be back in the office again.[6]

Saul sat in his living room and stared at his new colour TV set. *Everyone says this country is the land of riches and luxuries, so I may as well find out for myself,* he had told himself when he splurged on both the television and a new black Cadillac. But there was no need to seek justification for these acquisitions. The half-dozen dates they had played in June before their second Hollywood Bowl show had gone well and afforded him a reasonable degree of solvency. The Bowl itself also went smoothly, and he already had performances booked well into 1964.

None of it made sense. Was Johnny stressed over the sudden death of yet another friend? Was he still jealous over George Jones? Or was it something deeper? And why target him, of all people? Maybe Johnny resented any suggestion that he needed Saul, or perhaps he was bristling at Saul's controlling nature. As Cash would later say to the audience from onstage —"put the screws on me, and I'm gonna screw right out from under you."

All things considered, Saul felt certain that there were no screw-ups he could point to for an explanation, at least none that he could see. It was difficult, and he had very little experience with which to compare it. Perhaps he simply wasn't good enough. Saul's mind scrolled over their last few months. Their second Hollywood Bowl show had gone off according to plan, though Johnny's voice was thin and barely carried to the end of a twenty-minute set. It had also ended awkwardly, but that was hardly his fault.

Following the show's all-star finale of "Gotta Travel On," when all the performers had come out onstage, Johnny Western had begun his usual banter to wrap up the show. Turning to Cash, he'd asked, "Johnny, do you have anything you'd like to say to the folks, or is this it?"

The question was then met with silence, as Cash simply turned and walked off the stage.

"There he goes …" Western had quickly riffed. "Well, that wraps it up, ladies and gentlemen, for the second annual KFOX country music spectacular here in the Hollywood Bowl. It's been a great pleasure to be here with you tonight."[7]

Whatever it was, Saul wasn't the only one confused by Cash's behaviour. Johnny had recently enlisted his baby brother Tommy's help with promotions on some of his summer tour dates. While on a drive from Casitas Springs to Los Angeles to finalize some details of the Bowl show, Johnny decided to stop in at a drug store. When he emerged clutching a paper bag, something clicked for Tommy, and at that moment he realized his brother obviously had a rampant drug problem. And in all honesty, "rampant" didn't even begin to touch it.

"I had become habituated to amphetamines and barbiturates and alcohol — all three at the same time. That combination is deadly poisonous," Cash later admitted. "I got up to a habit of as many as a hundred pills a day and a case of beer. And there's a lot of people OD'd on less than that."

It also soon became clear to Tommy just how inexplicably volatile the drug problem could make his brother.[8]

After the Bowl show, Cash offered Tommy a position in Nashville, in their newly relocated office, where he could continue handling public relations, record promotions, and overseeing his fan club. It's unclear whether he envisioned that Tommy might fully or partially replace Saul in some capacity, perhaps with the paranoid impression that a family member might be more trustworthy. Tommy agreed to the arrangement and rented a two-room suite at 812 Sixteenth Avenue in what is known as Music Row in Nashville. Decorating it in gold, orange, black, and green burlap strips, Tommy was proud of the organized, stylish space he created, but the contentment was short-lived. On three separate occasions over the next year, Johnny quietly visited the space at night after Tommy had gone home and viciously trashed it. Cigarettes were burned into the carpet, coffee slopped over the surfaces, wall fabric ripped, chairs turned over, filing cabinets pulled out, papers strewn all the way down the hall.

"I took off my coat and sat down on the secretary's chair, slid up against the door, put my head in my hands, and broke down and cried," Tommy told Christopher Wren in his Cash biography *Winners Got Scars Too*, about the second time he had found the office destroyed. By the third time it happened, he simply gave up. After packing up his belongings, he slipped the office key under the door of Cash's hotel room and left.[9]

In the months after Saul was let go, he kept busy, learning to perfect his French omelette, playing tennis, and becoming absorbed in chess. For a man who "thrived on pressure," however, he was climbing the walls with boredom. The extra time was also spent reconnecting with Barbara via a stream of letters, fuelled in part by the persistent insecurity his situation had exacerbated. It didn't sit well that she had refused his request to come to the Hollywood Bowl show, which fell on his birthday, with what seemed a thin excuse — that her roommate had moved out. Now that he had been away from her for two months, she should be happy, he said, now that she was free from the "theorizing, argumentative atmosphere" he created. Initially acerbic, he soon surrendered to the feelings of vulnerability that were overwhelming his life.

"Your recent letters, although correct and pleasant, are completely devoid of any warmth. I suppose this is a direct result of my letters to you. If so, I would like to change it. I still think of you constantly and warmly, and feel that given a chance, we still will find our way together," he wrote. "I must learn to love. I need help and understanding. In past relationships my whole thinking was predicated on what someone else could do for me and what they had to offer. It was always taking with me. Giving has never been part of my philosophy. The article you sent me, 'The Triumphant Spirit of Man,' was very interesting, especially where it says that a feeling of worth is the headiest concoction in the world, and is essential to the ability to love. I'm learning."[10]

At the core of it all was a grinding loneliness, often alleviated by incessant work, which now crept in at the edges of his psyche. One thing was certain, however; he must refrain from using loneliness as an excuse for apathy. He indulged in more than his fair share of self-pity, he knew that. It seemed that as he approached forty, the pattern of his thinking had changed and he found himself preoccupied with death. Unlike the eternally optimistic teenager, death was now a factor to consider: a tangible, imminent possibility. All around him people seemed to be dropping off from heart attacks. But whatever happened, he resolved to remain active and vital, to accept responsibility for his shortcomings and change what he could.[11]

As he and Barbara exchanged letters, the conversation turned to the more practical question of what direction he would now take in his employment.

"You will recall telling me during your last visit that you were getting stale — you had learned the ropes and there was no more challenge," Barbara wrote back to Saul, referencing his split from Cash. "You were no longer deriving satisfaction from your work. All these things are bad for you, so I'm glad the change has come along. Just don't let it hurt your hyper-sensitive pride; everyone knows how unpredictable Johnny is." Ever pragmatic, she suggested that perhaps this was an opportunity for him to start over, maybe use his connections to form a talent agency.[12]

"Your suggestion re: developing an agency makes sense, but I'm afraid that the talent you mention is not too readily available at the moment. I am toying with the idea of returning to London in the fall, providing Johnny's agreeable, and carry on booking his dates at home," Saul responded. "When Johnny pays me the balance of what he owes me, I would be solvent enough to dicker around in real estate as well.... I haven't abandoned the idea of going back to school. Los Angeles is a beautiful and exciting city, but I can't seem to get over the yearning to take occupancy of the house on the hill and fulfill some dreams I have and had."

The house he referred to was one they broke ground on the day he had left for the tour in Japan and Korea, and it was as much a symbolic accomplishment as it was a practical one. Fifteen years after he had vowed to return to Hollywood and make show business his life, come hell or high water, here he was. But cracks were appearing in that once-dazzling facade. "[In] Hollywood, under the phony tinsel is real tinsel, and you never really develop any kind of a relationship with anyone. No one really listens to you; they just are sort of feeding the idea through their brain as to how they can use you, and if they can't you're dispensable, and they slough you off, and I don't like that kind of a plastic atmosphere," Saul told journalist Candy Yates. "I'm not especially knocked out about being in the entertainment business. I think it's a self-indulgent, hedonistic, ego-ridden business filled with people that have no ethics and no principles." Though he recognized this was a generalization, and that there were notable exceptions, it truly was a unique cultural milieu all its own. And when Johnny had said they might move the office to Nashville — and possibly Saul along with it — the idea was even less appealing. If he felt discomfort in Hollywood, he was an alien in the South. The culture was warm and familial, sure, but the feeling of anti-Semitism was palpable twenty-four hours a day. "It was unmistakable. Some of these people were so naive that their feeling about Jews was just like, 'on their sleeve.' The only Jews they had ever met were merchants in some little town in Arkansas. But it was kind of a naive anti-Semitism. Just based on being a 'good old Southern boy,'" he told Yates.[13]

"We liked to give Saul a hard time," said Tennessee Three drummer W.S. "Fluke" Holland. "It was joking, but also not joking, and we'd make him mad. We'd make him laugh, and we'd find different ways to call him 'Jew.' Not in a racist way, but we used to like to try to work it into conversations, just to get a reaction out of him. All in all, everybody really respected [him] because he knew what he was doing. But he was like 'business,' and that's what some people didn't understand, how serious he was, and that's the reason we would kid him, and I don't know ... I don't think we ever really made him mad, but we probably hurt his feelings a lot."[14]

Within a month, Saul and Johnny had quietly reconciled. But it wasn't all champagne and cigars — there were conditions. As suspected, Cash wanted Saul to give up George Jones and focus all his energy on him. Saul was also now required to pay, with the exception of air travel, all his own road expenses. Cash also arranged to deduct their salaries from his gross, before calculating Saul's commission, which reduced his take.

There were reconciliatory gestures, too. As the men settled back into their routine, their feelings around the split were referenced in passing but never overtly explored. In writing to Cash about the upcoming dates he had scheduled on into 1964, Saul took pains to acknowledge that some of the bookings were bound to upset him and make him dissatisfied, but as long as he stayed with him, and remained "ambitious, determined and professional," he would endeavour to eliminate the "crummy" bookings entirely. After a long checklist of practical updates and items to attend to, Saul then signed off by informing Cash he would mail a duplicate copy of the letter in a couple of days, "in case you lose this one or don't bother reading it."

Cash was intuitive enough that he could now recognize this subtle jab as an expression of Saul's insecurity, and he quickly responded the same day.

"Sometimes I don't react to an idea or plan you speak of, but it's only because I'm wrapped up in being a performer that I have no interest in side tracks. I hope you didn't mail that duplicate copy. I read all your letters," Cash wrote back. "You're doing a great job. You're very thorough — very well respected among my acquaintances. You command respect without commanding it. You have no reason for any complex. Just inform me more about anything concerning my career or finances, please."[15]

In his time away, Saul found the strength to acknowledge and face his own personal demons. Though nowhere near the state that Johnny was in addictions-wise, he knew the daily rituals of smoking and drinking were wearing at him. Anxious by nature, and saddled with triggers, Saul had

June Carter, Johnny Cash, and Saul Holiff, backstage in London, Ontario, 1964.

W.S. "Fluke" Holland, Luther Perkins, Marshall Grant, Saul Holiff, June Carter, and Johnny Cash boarding a plane in Ireland, 1963.

Johnny Cash and June Carter board a plane for Zurich, Switzerland, 1963.

taken to imbibing a significant quantity of tranquilizers to calm his nerves. These things needed reining in, and he vowed to counteract their effects with a new positivity, a vibrant zest, and an urge to be immersed in life. Managing to ditch cigarettes and pills, the breaking point for his drinking problem had come during a stop in Holland after a tour of the United Kingdom and Ireland with Cash in October 1963.

"I feel 10 ft tall. It's now 24 days of no smoking under the worst possible conditions. Constant travel, being exposed to Johnny and the pressure of dates, planes, and new people," Saul wrote to Barbara at the time. "One night in Holland, after many drinks, I sat alone in my room. The silence was devastating. I swear that I could hear in my head the same sound, exactly, as high tension wires during a still night on some lonely highway. I realized that I've been drinking moderately to very heavy without a break for almost 20 years. The old joke 'I never knew he drank — until I saw him sober one day,' has a meaningfulness in many ways. I never realized how frequently I turned to booze — how constantly it was my crutch. Never — never did I realize the extent that drinking played in making social contacts more — or should I say less painful, putting me at ease etc. Never again."[16]

Resolute in his newfound sobriety, he felt proud when, at a later DJ convention in Nashville, he was confronted with endless record company "hospitality rooms," filled to overflowing with booze, and managed to abstain.

On November 22, 1963, Saul was en route from Texas to a show in Dallas for the *Big D Jamboree*. In the seat next to him on the tiny plane was Willie Nelson, a clean-cut singer-songwriter with a unique voice and a small but loyal following. Fresh off a show with Cash, Saul was rather uninterested in his travelling companion. Most of Nelson's most famous songs were hits for other people, and he was yet unaware Nelson was the one who had penned "Crazy" for Patsy Cline.

After the plane landed in Dallas, the two disembarked and were mystified by the scene they entered. "We got to the airport and found people acting strangely in the hallways, the people renting cars acting in a strange way," said Saul in a later interview with *Country Music News*. Stewardesses were openly crying in the airport lobby and holding on to one another. People stood in their tracks, covering their faces. No one was doing much of anything. It was as though time had stopped. Finally, after inquiring about what was going on, they were informed that President Kennedy had been assassinated.[17]

Largely heralded as a defining era for the civil rights movement, the 1960s were a time not only of intense conflict but also of major political change, embodied in historical moments like the signing of the Civil Rights Act. In the blistering late summer of 1963, Martin Luther King Jr. delivered his famous "I Have a Dream" speech; months earlier, Birmingham, Alabama, was at the centre of international attention when a campaign against segregation laws culminated in the blasting of protesters with fire hoses and attacking them with lunging police dogs. By the following June, three New York–based civil rights workers had been abducted and murdered by members of the Ku Klux Klan, who then buried them in an earthen dam. Throughout the spring and into the summer of 1964, sit-ins, protests, and race riots swept the country. In Rochester, New York, reports of police brutality set off several nights of riots in July that left four dead and more than eight hundred arrested. Less than two weeks earlier, the killing of James Powell, a fifteen-year-old African American boy, set off six straight days of rioting and chaos in Harlem. In the midst of this, tens of thousands of American troops were overseas in South Vietnam, with no end to the conflict in sight.[18]

The intensity of this time was not lost on Cash, who aligned himself ever more with the folk scene blossoming within this fertile political soil. Introduced to Bob Dylan's music with his album *The Freewheelin' Bob Dylan*, Cash was immediately a fan and wrote to tell him as much, saying he found it "refreshing" to hear someone like him sing the things he did. Dylan responded likewise, saying that growing up in Hibbing, Minnesota, all he had was Hank Williams and Cash's "I Walk the Line." The two singers swiftly began to correspond.[19]

The folk scene's significance was not lost on Saul Holiff either, though he disliked Dylan's music and felt that he picked up and adapted material from more authentic performers like Woody Guthrie and Pete Seeger, but his personal views were largely irrelevant. The direction the wind was blowing was clear, and he wanted to be certain their sails were accurately positioned to catch it. Cash asked Saul to book him for a stint at New York City folk hot spot the Bitter End, and began to draft plans for a protest song of his own.[20]

For his part, Saul felt more focused than ever. By 1964 they were back in the game — "Ring of Fire" had spent seven weeks at number one on the country charts, and album sales were approaching a quarter million, a number that Cash's Bob Dylan–esque release "Understand Your Man" had also now surpassed. In addition, he had secured an offer for Cash from Shelby Singleton, vice president of A&R for Mercury Records, for fifty thousand dollars a year and 8 percent royalties. It was an offer that bordered on insulting, but details aside, it was certainly a card they could use to pressure Columbia into a better offer. Cash agreed, and wrote to Saul that he wanted to use this offer and all other ammunition they had at their disposal to "milk" Columbia, adding that he preferred to aim for a five-year deal with the record company as long as the offer was right.[21]

Seeking inspiration, and sometimes merely an escape between tours, Cash would often disappear for days into Death Valley in a truck camper he named "Jesse" (after Jesse James). During this time Cash would at times write to Saul to try to explain this need for the desert, even though he knew his yearning to disappear would at times be inconvenient.[22]

"Saul, my only cure is solitude," he wrote in one letter. "Too many things work against my peace of mind. Only the desert, with its purity and silence can help me now." Johnny went on to say that he needed to be alone for as long as possible, as his mind was overworked and he was exhausted. He couldn't do anyone any good when he was in this state. Referencing a meeting he was supposed to attend, Johnny told his manager that though he genuinely regretted the cancellations, it was a matter of "cancel the interviews or cancel me, for always." Clearly, at times his schedule was overwhelming.[23]

Johnny was also deeply conflicted over a sense of loyalty to his wife and four children. A devout Catholic, Vivian had always made it clear that she would rather die than get a divorce. Beset by confrontations with June that were at times explosive, Johnny was often pulled back to his family and the desire to be a better husband and father. But he loved June. And despite her frustration around his drug use, which at times made her threaten to leave, she understood him and loved him back. They had grown from the same soil, and inhabited the same world. The pressure of this, combined with the expectations that came with the success of his latest releases, was at times untenable. And the drugs weren't helping. He knew that. Again, he planned to run as far as he could out into the quiet, unquestioning desert.[24]

Before he left, Cash sat down at the Sahara Hotel in Las Vegas to write a letter confessing his feelings to Vivian and telling her he was not coming home, but rather going out into the desert for three or four days. All he would take was a radio, his guitar, and a small Bible, he said, and he wouldn't go anywhere that wasn't safe or where rangers couldn't find him if they needed to. Vivian had told him so many times that he was sliding downhill, he said, and now he knew that was true, that he had to throw the tranquilizers away and focus on being a better husband and father. Mostly, he planned to just sleep and pray and not speak to anyone. Johnny signed off by telling Vivian he loved her, and asked her to believe in him and pray with him.

It seemed like a stab at reconciliation, but inexplicably, Johnny never mailed the letter.[25]

It was during this time of long sojourns out across alkali flats and under mesquite bushes, into dry creek beds and aboriginal burial grounds, that Cash said he became interested in the plight of indigenous Americans, telling interviewer Ed Salamon that he "felt like the American Indian had suffered great injustices through the treaties that were broken. And especially the dying, the starving women and children and men all with the removal of the Cherokee Nation west of the Mississippi, and I really had a great feeling for that — for them then. I still do."[26]

The previous year, when Cash had met folksinger Ed McCurdy backstage after the ill-fated Carnegie Hall show and the two had disappeared together, few knew where they had gone. But they had, in fact, ended up at a nightclub in Greenwich Village where Cash was introduced to Peter La Farge, a songwriter believed to be a descendant of the heavily persecuted Narragansett tribe. The three became close and started to hang out, swapping music, stories, and in the case of Cash and La Farge, drugs. As Cash tells it, while hanging out at the Bitter End one night, La Farge got up onstage and sang some of the Native American–themed songs he was known for. Of particular interest to Cash was his song "The Ballad of Ira Hayes."[27]

The song detailed the tragic true story of a Pima man, a marine who had fought in the Second World War and returned home a hero — forever immortalized by photographer Joe Rosenthal as one of six men who participated in the flag-raising at Iwo Jima. Tortured by the death and sorrow he had seen on the battlefield and subjected to immense pressure by his newfound, sensationalized role as a hero, Hayes returned to the Pima reservation. In his despair, he turned to alcohol. Broke and drunk, he slipped into relative obscurity, and just under ten years after he raised the flag, his frozen, lifeless body was found next to a rusted truck in Sacaton, Arizona.[28]

Cash had first heard the song while in Nashville visiting Gene Ferguson, Columbia Records's promotions director, who played it for him and suggested it was something he should record.

"So I did, and when I recorded it, I loved it so much; I had such a feeling for Ira Hayes. I had been to the Apache country out there, you know. I had seen the old women carrying the big bundle of sticks on their backs for their night's firewood and seen the poverty, and I had a feeling for it. So I really got into it there for a while. Then Peter La Farge himself came down and visited me and brought me more songs, so I decided to do a whole album of them," said Cash.[29] This album would later be called *Bitter Tears: Ballads of the American Indian*.

Cash not only empathized with Hayes's story, but both he and Saul had considerable respect for La Farge — his father Oliver La Farge was a bona fide intellectual who was educated at Harvard and received the 1930 Pulitzer Prize for his novel *Laughing Boy: A Navajo Love Story*. The book was hailed in particular for its use of Navajo characters and its accurate portrayal of Native American culture.[30]

As Saul prepared for the June 2 release of "Ira Hayes" he wondered how to best incorporate these interests of Johnny's, though some of his ideas missed the mark. "What do you think of an Indian Chief in full dress (complete war costume) on the *Steve Allen Show* to receive a presentation from you and possibly make you an Honorary Chief of the Pima Tribe?" Saul wrote to Johnny on May 23.

"No Saul, please. The Pima Indians never wore head-dress, or feathers," responded Cash. "They never wore war paint because the Piman [*sic*] have fought no battle in their 1,000-year history. They're farmers."

Cash added that they might even hate him for bringing up Ira Hayes's name, as they had "suffered a lot of embarrassment and bad-mouthing because of Ira's drunkenness."[31]

Saul's promotional ideas for Cash's television appearance on both *The New Steve Allen Show* and the *Tonight Show* on June 1 also fell flat with his client. Booked at the Hotel Delmonico in New York, Saul arranged for the hotel to provide a Rolls-Royce, stocked with a phone and cold beer, to pick up Cash from the airport. It would be an opportune time to get a photo of Cash enjoying himself in the car for a gimmick promo stunt or future album cover, Saul suggested.

"I WOULD NOT like a publicity picture in the Rolls-Royce," Cash responded. "Such 'class' is above any phase of my image to the people I sing to and the kind of songs I sing." The shift into folk music was not merely a cosmetic one, apparently. Cash seemed to want to not only change how his fans perceived him but also truly embody what that change meant.

There were always more ideas where those came from, however, and Saul was so energized by both his long stint of sobriety and the near-achievement of his New Year's goal of fifty push-ups a day that the rejections didn't appear to faze him. Taking Cash's concerns to heart, Saul went on to score some tentative dates at the Bitter End in August, as well as an invitation to the Newport Folk Festival in Rhode Island, where Johnny would share a bill with Bob Dylan and a mix of popular and traditional performers like Joan Baez, folk trio Peter, Paul and Mary, Pete Seeger, and Muddy Waters. The venue was widely viewed as one in which commercially successful folksingers paid tribute to the grassroots artists from whom they learned, according to singer Peter Yarrow from Peter, Paul and Mary.[32]

Curiously, despite the opportunity it offered to align himself with some of the most prominent folk voices of his generation, Cash didn't appear to be overly enthusiastic about the prospect of Newport. "Please find out when my spot is scheduled in the three days at Newport and if they want me to do one or two songs or what. I'll probably play it but I'm not worked up over the idea," he wrote to Saul in May.[33]

As it happened, Cash was scheduled for the festival's opening night lineup on Friday, July 24, but if his comments beforehand were any warning,

Saul may not have been terribly surprised when he was a no-show for this Newport debut. It was a situation that once again required precision repairs, and with some negotiation Saul managed to have organizer and Newport founder George Wein reschedule him for Saturday evening.[34]

"Ladies and gentlemen, the next performer was supposed to be on the program last night, but he couldn't get here," said Pete Seeger from the stage on Saturday night. "He was way out on the West Coast, and he found that somehow you can't get from Nevada to Newport, Rhode Island, in one day. But he did get here tonight. He's a songwriter and a singer, and I think many of you have heard him before. It's Johnny Cash."

Tendons in his jaw visible as he gripped his gum, Cash was haunting and ragged. But he had his voice. After a few familiar songs like "Big River" and "Folsom Prison Blues," he offered a rendition of the railroad-themed folk song "Rock Island Line," after which he repeatedly asked for water. "I don't drink anymore. I don't drink any *less*, but I don't drink any *more*," he quipped, chuckling to himself. Then he launched into a rambling tribute to Dylan. "Got a special request from a friend of ours to do a song tonight, and I'm very honoured. I ain't never been so honoured in my life, I can't ... Hey, Bob. Our good friend, Bob Dylan, we'd like to do one of his songs, and we've been doing it on our shows all over the country, trying to tell the folks about Bob, that we think he's one of the best songwriters of the age since Pete Seeger," said Cash in a preamble to Dylan's "Don't Think Twice, It's All Right."

Among other songs, Cash also played "The Ballad of Ira Hayes," introduced with a nervous-sounding joke about how they don't try to be "too commercial" in their recordings with Columbia, perhaps in an attempt to seem more folkie and less like a big label star.[35]

After the show, Dylan and Cash finally formalized their friendship in his hotel room with June and Joan Baez. Cash said they were "so happy to meet each other that [they] were jumping on the bed like kids." Cash presented Dylan with a gift of his guitar, an old Martin, and Dylan gave Cash a tape of his songs "It Ain't Me, Babe" and "Mama, You Been on My Mind." Within months, Cash would record both songs, and though he had almost lost his train of thought onstage in his praise of Dylan, the admiration was clearly mutual.[36]

"Johnny's voice was so big, it made the world grow small, unusually low pitched — dark and booming, he had the right band to match him, the rippling rhythm and cadence of click-clack," Dylan later wrote in his autobiography, *Chronicles, Volume One*. "When I first heard 'I Walk the Line' so many years earlier, it sounded like a voice calling out, 'What are you doing there, boy?' I was trying to keep my eyes wide opened, too."[37]

Having narrowly averted disaster once again at Newport, Saul was likely pleased with the final-day review from ever-influential folk music insider and critic Robert Shelton, who in summing up the final day of the festival for the *New York Times*, selected Cash's set as one of two "outstanding performances."

"Johnny Cash, the Nashville star, closed the gap between commercial country and folk music with a masterly set of storytelling songs," he wrote. Shelton also had high praise for his new album *Bitter Tears*, calling it "one of the best LPs to emerge from the 1960s folk movement."[38]

Problems for Cash soon ensued, however, when the reluctance of country DJs to play "Ira Hayes" prompted him to publish his outrage in a full-page ad in *Billboard* magazine on August 22, 1964. As far as Cash was concerned, it amounted to nothing less than censorship, and he had good reason to perceive it that way. Though protest songs were *de rigueur* for artists busy with the current folk revival, players in the conservative country scene were hardly keen to embrace a song about the plight of Native Americans.

"D.J.s — station managers — owners, where are your guts?" wrote an indignant Cash. "Classify me, categorize me — STIFLE me, it won't work.... 'Ballad of Ira Hayes' is strong medicine. So is Rochester — Harlem — Birmingham and Vietnam.... As an American who is almost a half-breed Cherokee-Mohawk (and who knows what else?) — I had to fight back when I realized that so many stations are afraid of 'Ira Hayes.' Just one question: WHY??"[39]

Though "Ira Hayes" did subsequently manage to get to number three on the country charts, the establishment in Nashville did not take kindly to Cash's words. In the September issue of *Close-Up Magazine*, the editor published his own full-page "Open Letter — to Johnny Cash," calling on him to "resign from the Country Music Association."

"Sir, like you I am also disgusted — but not for the same reason. I am disgusted with you," it began, and went on to say Cash had inferred that people who listen to country music were not intelligent. "I am sorry that it was good Country and Hillbilly Type Music Lovers who put you where you are today, in the music field. I am also sorry for you, Johnny Cash, that at your age you have never learned the old, old lesson, 'You don't bite the hand that feeds you.'... You have a lot to learn, and I hope you learn it on the way down."

Saul wasted no time in responding to the controversy in his usual paternal tone.

"A square by the name of Euripides once said, 'Waste not fresh tears over old griefs,' which I believe is consistent with your philosophy," he advised Cash in his next letter. He then went on to indulge in a post-mortem of their October tour, which hadn't gone well financially. This was due in part to their costs for extra talent, which were excessive compared to their grosses. "Hindsight is a good thing, but it doesn't help at the bank," Saul mused.[40]

Cash grumbled in return that yes, the extra talent on their tours had cost too much. "According to my conscience, or greed, we have carried far too many hillbillies, and I as a result of pride and ego, regret that certain "acts" were paid such large amounts," he said. "I cannot stand to pay high prices to those I don't believe in."

Despite this, Cash went on to add that he wanted to raise the wages of June Carter, Mother Maybelle, and openers the Statler Brothers. "And Saul, this will destroy you," he added. "Take a $1,000 bonus for yourself. You're the best agent, promoter, manager etc. in the world."[41]

"I congratulate you on your insight re your superlatives about me. It reminds me about the fellow who wanted to take his wife around the world ... but she wanted to go someplace else!!! I'LL TRY TO DO BETTER!!!" responded Saul. "The bonus you recommended for me is very, very much appreciated ... however, unless the December tour is a complete financial success, I would not feel right about the bonus and would prefer to pass it up at this time."[42]

The appreciation from Cash was understandable. Setbacks aside, there was much for the two to celebrate. In addition to the success of

"Understand Your Man" and "Ring of Fire," which had been nominated for a Grammy, holding out into 1964 without an official contract with Columbia had evidently worked in their favour; negotiations ended in a five-year deal with a five-hundred-thousand-dollar guarantee and 8 percent royalties. Saul also got them to throw in five full-page ads a year in music publications to support Cash's upcoming releases.[43]

Next on the list was to score Johnny more television appearances, with an eye toward his own network show. In late 1963 and early 1964, he had appeared on the show *Hootenanny* three times. By April of 1964, Saul was courting producer Stan Jacobson at Canada's national television network, CBC Television, with the entreaty that he was "interested in bringing about a syndicated TV show starring Johnny Cash, earmarked for the Canadian market, and judging from your background, we feel that you would be an ideal person to help bring this about." Saul didn't yet realize this overture would mark the beginning of something very big, indeed.[44]

Overall, Johnny and Saul's partnership was unmistakably back on track.

"I believe that as every day that passes by you are moving closer to America's foremost singing story teller in fact as well as name, and that you will come to be regarded as an artist of the very top rating with no special affinity to any particular facet of the music industry," Saul affectionately told Johnny.

"I am more full of piss and vinegar than ever. When I reach the top, I'll build another peak to climb," Cash responded.

The storm clouds were gathering, however, and these sentiments would serve to precede the most chaotic year of Johnny's life yet.[45]

8

ONE HUNDRED PERCENT TOP BILLING

Saul and Barbara were married in a small wedding at the city hall in Simcoe, Ontario, which was presided over by Judge G.A. Brickenden. Unable to attend the wedding because they were on a tour through Ontario, which Saul had left just days before the ceremony, June and Johnny sent along their letters of congratulations. In an attempt to maintain the illusion that they were not together, the notes were mailed separately, though they were written on the same hotel stationery. It was a detail Barbara found amusing. June also sent along a silver serving tray as a wedding gift.

The contrast between Saul and Barbara's above-board union and June and Johnny's secretive and increasingly heated affair was obvious, and yet neither had found the courage to leave their crumbling marriages behind. This may have been why both notes carried little more than vague platitudes about happiness and how marriage was the greatest gift God had to offer.[1]

Part of the agreement when Saul and Johnny reconciled was that he would now be managed from a headquarters in London, Ontario. The long separations from Barbara while in Hollywood had taken their toll, and Saul was ready for their relationship to become more serious. The two sensed from the beginning that they had an unusual connection — however complicated the reality of that might be — and it organically grew into a certainty that they would spend their lives together.

The Ontario tour wound up without notable disaster while Saul enjoyed some rare time off, snapping photos of Barbara during their week-long honeymoon in New York, where they caught the sensational Broadway opening of *Fiddler on the Roof*. Though it was late in the day, they then poked around at the World's Fair, which harboured the ambitious theme of "Man's Achievements on a Shrinking Globe in an Expanding Universe." Most of the attractions were closed, but Saul took a picture of Barbara in front of the Unisphere — a 140-foot-high stainless steel model of the Earth planted in Flushing Meadows Park in Queens — commissioned to celebrate the dawn of the space age and to symbolize the Fair's vague motto of "Peace Through Understanding." It then began to pour with rain. Laughing, the two ran through the puddles to a nearby pub, both separately remarking to themselves that it had been so long since they had truly found some time to relax.[2]

From there the two spent a week in Miami before flying in to Los Angeles to pack up Saul's Hollywood apartment. Back at their new "house on the hill" in London, there was a renewed focus on their partnership. Saul took some pleasure in further discussing aspects of his managerial career with Barbara, whose insight offered him perspectives he hadn't considered. The two transitioned fully into work on Cash's career as partners, with Barbara shouldering most of the booking and secretarial work. Within months the newlyweds realized they were at work on another project together. On a routine visit to the doctor, Barbara discovered she was pregnant with their first child.

"Barbara and I have listened and listened and listened to your new record. We truly believe that 'Time and Time Again' is equally as strong as 'It Ain't Me, Babe'; however, I believe that 'Babe' will be the side," Saul wrote to Cash a month after the wedding. A duet performed by Johnny and June, the original Dylan song was written as an ode to the rejection of audience demands, or even "a rejection of the mythology of true love," according to Robert Shelton. In any case, it was a strangely symbolic choice for the couple's first duet, but true to prediction, their cover went into the top five of the country singles charts and crossed over into the pop charts. At the same time, *I Walk the Line* — an album on which Cash re-recorded some of his Sun Records hits — and *Bitter Tears* were also featured in *Billboard*'s Hot Country album charts.[3]

Cash's full-scale launch into television was a goal Saul continued to aggressively pursue, but it wasn't easy. The CBC's Stan Jacobson wrote back to express his personal interest in a half-hour syndicated show, though he confessed his bosses would likely be reluctant to finance it. Turning to CBS Television, Saul sat down with producer Russell Stoneham early in 1965 to discuss a possible show or series of shows, and he departed with the feeling that it looked promising. Unfortunately, Johnny's reputation may have already been known to CBS, because a month after that meeting they rejected the idea, stating, "CBS at this moment has no inclination to develop such a show."[4]

The problem was likely that Cash's increasingly obvious signs of substance abuse presented a challenge in marketing him to television audiences. It just didn't make for great visuals. In January, he had shown up drunk for an appearance on the weekly rock 'n' roll television series *Shindig!*, which aired weekly on ABC. Set to perform the gospel hymn "Amen" and a variety of songs off his soon-to-be-released album *Orange Blossom Special*, Cash, who was reputed to know more country and folk songs than anyone alive, couldn't remember the words. He had to return the next day to record the song again. Producer Jack Good told writer Steve Turner that it took two hours to tape one song, and as a backup plan they brought in dancers "so there was somewhere to go if he was really out of it."[5]

Around this time, Cash had also flown to Los Angeles for a guest appearance on the first episode of a country music variety show on KTLA, a channel owned by Gene Autry. Hosted by Johnny Western, the show had Cash as one of its first acts, along with Glen Campbell and a few other big names in country music.

"Do you think I could borrow your car?" Cash asked, once the taping had wrapped. Western had just bought a brand-new gun-metal grey Cadillac Sedan DeVille a few months earlier that he was quite proud of.

"Sure, but where's your car?" asked Western.

"Well, uh, it's in the shop," said Cash, scratching at his neck.

Figuring they'd be busy with post-production at the studio anyway, Western agreed he could spare it for a few hours. Cash took his keys and disappeared. When he had not returned by the end of the day, Western hitched a ride home with one of the other performers. When there was no sign of him the next day, Western began to make calls. At 10:00 a.m. on the third day, Western's phone rang.

"Johnny, it's me. I've lost your car," Cash said in a gravelly voice.

"John? What do you mean you've lost my car?" Western said. He sat up and rubbed his eyes.

"I mean I don't remember the last couple days very much. The last I can remember — an' this is just a maybe — I was down buying some fruit in the middle of the night," sighed Cash. "It might, it *might* — be there. I'm sorry. Other than that, I don't know where your car is."

"Well, give me a number where at least I can leave a message for you if and when I find the car. If I don't find the car, we'll go from square one," said Western, who rose and got dressed. *Only Johnny Cash,* he thought, *would go down to the farmer's market in Hollywood to buy fresh fruit at four o'clock in the morning.* A friend picked him up, and they drove to the twenty-four-hour market.

"We drove around the parking lot, and lo and behold, there it was. The keys were still in the ignition, but the battery was dead. He had left the lights on," said Western.[6]

Cash managed to hold it together, at least onstage, for a tour in February through Ontario, but his ceasefire with Saul began to crumble. Often in the midst of amphetamine-induced paranoia, Cash was notorious for pointing the finger at even the most reliable members of his camp — including close childhood friend and bassist Marshall Grant — to allege the pilfering of funds. The funds to which he referred were not only always accounted for, but also often enormously trifling: in one case it was a matter of nine dollars; in another, forty dollars, which made it all the more exasperating for Saul.

"It has just come to my attention (from several sources) that I am supposed to have misrepresented the actual attendance in London on February 11. It seems that everyone in London is aware of a conversation that apparently took place, which supposedly involved yourself, where it was pointed out that there was a discrepancy in the total numbers of people attending the show," Saul wrote to Johnny about two weeks later. Reluctant to address the issue and disturb their peaceful relations, the issue was nevertheless driving him crazy. "I am supposedly guilty of some malfeasance. This rumour is vicious and has already done much to malign me. And of course I am somewhat concerned to know whether or not you were aware of it." He tersely signed the letter "S.H."[7]

At this point Cash had returned for a rare visit home to Casitas Springs. Enmeshed in conflict with Vivian, he was also in no mood to be accused of anything. It was hard enough to try and remember one day from the next, let alone what had or hadn't transpired during a show. "Now that you've raked me over the coals, I want to tell you that you're damn sure barking up the wrong tree," Cash wrote back. "I am the one that might have blown his top ... if I had believed things said of you. Please raise hell with someone else. I've had enough for everybody."

Cash was scheduled for a show the next day in the Gold Room at the Fairmont hotel in San Francisco, but when he returned home, he came down with a case of blood poisoning from an infected tooth and tongue, which combined with a flu to leave him bedridden for five days. In addition, he told Saul, he had piles of books and songs to go through for his western album and an upcoming tour. On top of that, a recording session in Nashville would take up four days that were supposed to be time off. "My camping equipment, fishing tackle, and guns are rusted and ruined from lying idle.... So am I," Johnny wrote.[8]

The western album Johnny referred to in his letter further explored his fascination with the desert, and was eventually released as *Johnny Cash Sings the Ballads of the True West*. Like its four predecessors — each a concept album — it didn't sell well. Though "Ring of Fire" had been certified gold by the Record Industry Association of America the month prior, and had given Cash his first gold record, Johnny hadn't cracked the top twenty on the pop charts since. As for Nashville, Cash was scheduled to record a series of new songs: "Streets of Laredo," "Mr. Garfield," and "Johnny Reb," after which he would embark on a big tour of the Northeast, kicking off with a show in Cincinnati on March 18 and ending with a gig at the Arie Crown Theatre in Chicago on March 28. If the illness and need for escape alluded to in the letter were any indication that Johnny was about to go off the rails, the subsequent recording sessions in Nashville confirmed it.

"Johnny got himself in trouble on pills and didn't show up to a recording session," Saul remembered. "The musicians were all paid. The session time was booked. The Statler Brothers were there to back Johnny Cash. The time was open. Don Law, the A&R man, said 'Okay Statlers, record something.'… So they recorded a song called 'Flowers on the Wall' and it became a giant pop hit."[9] The song was written by the quartet's original tenor, Lew DeWitt. He had only just put it to an original melody, and the band members tweaked the arrangement on the spot.

"We used the musicians that were there and available to us; the ones John had called for his session who were sitting there watching the clock tick. The Tennessee Three, a banjo and a rhythm guitar. If there had been a flugelhorn and an oboe, I guess we would have used that, too," Statlers singer Don Reid wrote in his autobiography, *Random Memories*. "Common people don't do great things. Great things happen to common people."

Once released, "Flowers on the Wall" quickly sold more than one hundred thousand copies, and by January of 1966 it had spent four weeks at number two on *Billboard*'s Hot Country singles chart.[10]

Though the Statler Brothers' career — which Saul also later managed — was on the rise, Johnny's was falling apart. At midnight on March 17, 1965, just as Cash was scheduled to embark on a ten-day tour of the northeastern United States, Saul's phone rang. It was guitarist Luther Perkins: Cash was in bad shape. The infected tooth and tongue had developed into some kind of bronchitis and laryngitis, and there was no way he'd make their first date in Cincinnati. The rest of the shows were also a question mark, as no one knew for certain exactly where Cash was currently located.

These no-shows were shaping up to be an unmitigated *disaster*. The tour's promoter was thirty-two-year-old Andy Serrahn, who got his start plugging Broadway stars at his one-man Variety Theatre in Wisconsin and had gone bankrupt three years earlier due to a number of cancelled productions. He was in no mood to repeat his earlier catastrophe.

A couple months earlier Saul had begun to feel out the possibility of a promotional partnership with the Variety, which would now likely unravel. And Johnny wasn't merely ill, he was *gone*. Stressed and powerless, Saul attempted to keep track of Cash's shenanigans. To cope as events unfolded, he paced his office and dictated a play-by-play log of events to Barbara.[11]

Wednesday, March 17: Midnight — Luther called.

Thursday, March 18: 1:30 AM — Wired Andy [Serrahn] to cancel Cincinnati show because of alleged case of acute bronchitis and laryngitis that has afflicted Johnny Cash. Rumours that Johnny recorded at Columbia Recording Studios on Thursday night, substantiated by Jan Howard.

Saturday, March 20: 6:00 PM — Marshall Grant called collect from Peoria to advise Johnny's appearance in Peoria was highly improbable. Andy Serrahn called 3 times in the evening so that I could speak to radio officials and building manager and make appropriate excuses.

7:00 PM — Called Andy and advised him of possibility of no show. Suggested he carry on with show since nothing was definite and I hadn't been advised by Johnny or anyone in Nashville.

7:30 PM — Called June Carter at hospital. She advised Johnny's condition was as described and that Johnny planned to join Maybelle and leave early Sunday morning for Davenport. June pointed out that Vivian was at the Andrew Jackson [hotel] and had been for the last several days.

Sunday, March 21: 10:00 AM — Called Maybelle. She advised no word from Johnny and would seek to locate him.

10:30 AM — Called Gene Ferguson. He advised that Johnny had visited his home Saturday night, March 20th, and that he later met him at Johnny's office to hear tapes on the session just completed. Ferguson advised Johnny Cash suffering extreme fatigue but otherwise okay.

1:00 PM — Andy called collect. I alerted him to the no-show situation at Davenport and advised about securing Roger Miller, who apparently was recording in Nashville.

1:30 PM — Called Maybelle. She advised Johnny asleep in his office; apparently out cold.

Monday, March 22: 11:00 AM — Called June at home. She advised Johnny in no shape to play shows and that she is powerless to intercede.

7:00 PM — Called Andy. Two hour discussion. Promised him that his financial involvement would be protected. He advised he would contact me *after* discussion with his lawyer. Statlers, Tex [Ritter] and band all advised by Johnny not to go to Green Bay prior to Saul Holiff being informed.

Tuesday, March 23: Noon — Called Maybelle. She advised Johnny didn't want to be disturbed. Sent two-page telegram recommending course of action to Johnny, to be delivered by cab. No answer.

2:00 PM — Johnny Cash called to say he would play dates and would "hang" Andy Serrahn if he thought Andy substituted other people on his show.[12]

The blow-by-blow account of Cash as he bobbed up and disappeared again throughout Nashville like a prairie dog read like that of a private investigator, but Saul likely wanted to keep a record for legal reasons. He had just missed an entire tour, and promoter Andy Serrahn was livid. If he was consulting a lawyer, as he said he was, there was the chance he would sue. Though he did not yet know it, Saul would in fact spend the next two years battling a lawsuit on Johnny's behalf in which more than fifteen thousand dollars in lost revenue was claimed. At this point, Saul just needed to stay one step ahead.

Makeup dates were quickly arranged for the shows missed in Green Bay, Madison, and Rockford in April and May, but Johnny missed those, too. Saul thought he had finally found a solution by booking Cash for a series of makeup dates in September, but Serrahn informed him he had hired singer-songwriter Buck Owens instead. Johnny's reaction in a later letter to Saul was summed up as: "To hell with Andy Serrahn."[13]

Adding to the tension was the fact that during Cash's tear through Nashville, Vivian was actually in town at the Andrew Jackson Hotel. It was a rare event for her to come out on the road and, as such, it was likely one of a number of last-ditch efforts to save their marriage. She seldom left their house in Casitas Springs, spending much of her time smoking, drinking coffee, crying, and staring out the window, waiting for Johnny's headlights to turn in to the driveway. Most often, Vivian went to bed disappointed and uncertain of Johnny's whereabouts, or whether he was even alive. She would later write in her memoir that on the occasions he did return, she would sit on the floor waiting as he lay in bed coming down from drugs and smoking — so that she could pull the lit cigarette from his lips once he fell asleep.[14]

Two days after Saul's anxious account of the missed tour and what had transpired, Cash was weaving through driving rain on the streets of Nashville in a 1964 Cadillac he had borrowed from June. Fresh from a meeting with Columbia Records rep Gene Ferguson, who was headed home with his wife, Dolores, Johnny trailed his tail lights as they slowly made their way down South Street. When Johnny leaned down to turn off the car's defroster (or so he claimed later), he suddenly swerved off the road and smashed head-on into a telephone pole.

"John was following my car when I noticed his headlights had disappeared, so I stopped and backed up to investigate," said Gene. "June's car was smashed to bits. John took off on foot down the alley, so I went after him. He broke his nose and [knocked out] four teeth. I put him in my car and drove him to the hospital. I remember it was a brand-new Buick Riviera with a white leather interior. [My car] was covered in blood. I asked the hospital not to record his name because I didn't want it in the newspapers. The hospital didn't even want to treat him. I took him home and called my family doctor, and he didn't want to treat him. Everyone knew Johnny was bad news."[15]

June was already in the hospital having an unknown operation of her own when Johnny was admitted. As she emerged from the operating room, a call came in from Saul, who by now had heard about the accident and was checking in on Johnny's condition.

"His face was blown up out to here," June told writer Christopher Wren.[16]

During those days it was customary for Cash to stay at Gene Ferguson's house whenever he was recording or working in Nashville, as it allowed him to be close to June, but lately his behaviour was becoming more and more unbearable. "When he was staying with me he'd sometimes take a ballpoint pen and write phone numbers on my couch," Gene told writer Steve Turner. "He'd go out into the rain with no socks or shoes on, and in the morning there would be mud right through the house."

The Fergusons rose the morning after the accident to find Johnny passed out in their den. Rather than sleep it off in the bed they had provided, he stayed up all night taking amphetamines, scattering records on the floor, and chugging Ferguson's beer. Terrified when he pressed an ear to Johnny's chest and couldn't hear a heartbeat, Ferguson phoned Luther Perkins, who dispensed a piece of advice that was classic in Cash circles. "He'll sleep twenty-four hours," said Luther. "If he awakes, he's alive. If he doesn't, he's dead."[17]

That day a small article about the accident was published in *The Nashville Tennessean*, saying that the car had been registered to a "Mrs. June Carter Nicks [sic] of Madison." Like Cash, June was still married — to her second husband, Edwin "Rip" Nix — an officer in the Nashville police department. Though the investigating officer was Charles Hay, word of the crash had likely travelled back to Nix, who, obviously, would have been familiar with her last name. Strangely, it was misspelled in the report, perhaps in a deliberate attempt to help Nix avoid scandal.

Privately, many people outside their inner circle by now suspected something was going on between June and Johnny, but publicly, it was a different story. The fallout from an affair could ruin their careers. Hay had also written "none" in the space for Johnny's licence, adding in the report that there was to be "no prosecution," despite police estimates there had been two thousand dollars in damages done to the car.[18]

"There was more than $2,000 [damage] to June's car, I can tell you that. And we did leave the scene," said Gene.[19]

Clearly exasperated, Saul wrote to Johnny on April 17: "Enclosed are copies of various telegrams and letters of interest to you. A copy of a telegram requesting information from you as to the best time to speak with you is also enclosed. No answer was received. Three previous telegrams have also been disregarded."

For once, Johnny's unreliability was of some benefit to Saul. After a scheduled USO tour in the Middle East was cancelled and a tour in the Far East fell apart, Saul ended up being home for the birth of his first child, Jonathan. Photos from that time show Saul revelling in the domesticity this time off afforded; shirtless and gazing down fondly at the tiny newborn tucked in his elbow. Uncertain of how to express his pride, he dashed off a telegram to Johnny:

June 9, 1965
To Johnny Cash. Confirming Jonathan Joel Holiff at 7 ¼ pounds. Terms — Life Guarantee. One Hundred Percent Top Billing. No Mikes, Spotlights or Extra Talent Required. Admission Free. Dontcha dare miss him. Paternally, Saul.

Jonathan was born June 8, 1965, and Saul had wanted the whole city to know about it. In his typical promotional style, he then had the telegram to Johnny turned into an advertisement that ran in the local

Saul with son Jonathan, reading the music trades, London, Ontario, 1965.

London newspaper, with the added text: "Jonathan hopes you'll all come to see his Daddy's shows … because his Daddy needs the money!"[20]

Johnny had missed so many shows that spring that Saul was likely trying to drum up some good publicity. And the ad definitely drew a reaction — Saul and Barbara received a slew of letters and telegrams, including one from singer Tex Ritter. One of the biggest names in country music, Ritter had appeared in numerous films and went on to host the *Town Hall Party* television broadcast in Los Angeles. He also sometimes joined the Johnny Cash touring show on the road as an added attraction. Addressed to "Master Jonathan Joel Holiff," his telegram read, "Welcome to our world. I know you'll be a great addition to it. You have selected grand parents who will shower you with love. I know you will return it and grow up to be a fine man. Regards, Tex Ritter."[21]

The outpouring of elation and goodwill following the birth, however, was short-lived. Three weeks later, Johnny phoned Saul to tell him he'd accidentally burned down a forest.

The last Saul had heard, Johnny was headed home, and he had called Vivian in Casitas Springs from the Los Angeles airport to inform her. She'd stayed up late that night with their four girls in the hope that he could see them before they went to school. However, her wait was once again in vain. When Johnny finally pulled into the driveway days later, her elation at seeing him was short-lived: he was soon preparing to take off again, this time into the mountains. It was a pattern that spoke to his constant state of unease. When he did show up, the good sentiment that accompanied his arrival quickly dissolved into fighting, punctuated by his swift departure into the night, after which he would be lost again for days or even weeks.

In her memoir, Vivian wrote about how she fell on her knees in the driveway crying, begging him not to leave, saying she felt certain something bad would happen. High and amped-up, he brushed her aside and tore off in a camper truck borrowed from his sister and brother-in-law, Reba and Don Hancock. With a short detour to pick up his nephew Damon Fielder, they then headed toward the Ventura County area of California's Los Padres National Forest. With much of its pristine 1.75 million acres available only by trail, it was the perfect place to unwind, away from the prying eyes of civilization.

It was about 4:30 in the afternoon when they pulled over near Sespe Creek so that the two could go fishing, Damon later recounted to author Robert Hilburn. Angry over his uncle's pill-popping and whisky-drinking during the drive, Damon had exchanged harsh words with Johnny and then left to fish in seclusion. The unmistakable scent of smoke soon reached him, and upon rushing back, he found Johnny flapping at a fire beside the camper, trying to extinguish it. The presence of a used-up book of matches nearby led Damon to believe that Johnny had actually set the fire himself, perhaps in a drug-induced attempt to stay warm.

The camper had become mired in the sand, Johnny later told the forest investigation service, and when he revved the engine, sparks and hot gases from a faulty exhaust pipe set the nearby grass on fire. The flames swiftly spread through the surrounding brush and fanned out over three mountaintops, eventually consuming 508 acres of forest and taking 450 firefighters a week to fully extinguish.

Realizing the danger the swiftly expanding blaze posed, Fielder said he attempted to flee the scene, but Johnny refused to come with him. In a panic, Fielder found a tree branch and hit him over the head, hoping to knock him out. However, it only caused him to stagger off into the creek, where he sat down. Fielder ran off down the trail and located a fire helicopter crew, who flew him back to get Johnny.

"It seems to me, when I went up there, he was wading around in a creek with his fishing gear and I couldn't figure out what in the hell this old boy was doing," said Carl Rivenburgh, who was the assistant fire control officer for the U.S. Forest Service's Ojai district at the time. One of the first on the scene, he interviewed Johnny and wrote him a citation. "He was kind of stomping around and chasing his gear; he had his fishing gear all scattered in it. Things that normal people didn't do.... He was either drunk or completely out of his head, but I didn't think about it. I had other things to think about."

The nearby wildlife sanctuary housed a variety of protected species, including a population of fifty-three endangered American condors — forty-nine of which perished in the fire, Johnny later wrote in his second autobiography. However, this was a claim Rivenburgh found unlikely. "They're not sitting around getting burned up in a forest fire," he said with a chuckle. "They're up flying thirty thousand feet in the air."

During the later court proceedings in Los Angeles, Johnny's defiance was on full display. When asked about how the fire had started, he responded, "I didn't do it, my truck did it and it's dead, so you can't question it." During depositions he was, by his own description, high on arrogance and amphetamines. When questioned about the condors, he responded, "I don't give a damn about your yellow buzzards."

A negligence suit was filed against Johnny and co-defendants Reba and Doug by the federal government two years later for $125,000. The following week, the Tribal Indian Land Rights Association of California jumped to Johnny's defence, declaring that unless the suit was dropped, they would "reclaim the entire Los Padres National Forest." In a statement, they argued that Johnny was being targeted for his *Bitter Tears* album, which focused on the unfair treatment of indigenous Americans. They even claimed him as a Cherokee, and insisted Reba and Doug — the owners of the camper — were Choctaw. However, despite their best intentions, Johnny eventually settled for eighty-two thousand dollars, one of the largest amounts ever recovered from a single individual at that time.[22]

There was little to indicate how Saul felt about the fire, but according to his accounts it required hundreds of unpaid hours with Johnny's lawyers and accountants to sort out, and the aftermath of scrutiny was intense. Vivian described "wanting to crawl into a hole" from embarrassment at questions directed her way in public.

But for now, Saul had even larger problems to contend with. Johnny's volatile and unpredictable behaviour was becoming known among talent buyers, who were whispering among themselves that he was "Johnny 'No-Show' Cash."

Ever on the offensive, Saul responded by launching an unusual ad campaign in *Billboard* magazine, emblazoned with the phrase "Eviction Notice To: Rumours In Our House" at the top. "The only rumour about Johnny Cash that IS true, is that he sells out wherever he appears," the ad emphatically stated, featuring a headshot of Saul at the bottom and the slogan "Wanted: For killing rumours." After raving about the quality of the show, Saul went on to tell promoters, "Ask the buyers, you'll find them on the way to the bank."

Despite the outward show of solidarity displayed in the ad, the tension involved in managing Johnny — the challenge of battling myriad external threats while Johnny decimated himself internally with drugs and wild car chases — was evident.

"I was brought up in a rational, nonreligious, open-minded house of logic," Saul later told author Steve Turner. "Suddenly I found myself in this chaotic, unpredictable, terrible atmosphere. Nothing could be finalized. Nothing could be definite. The cancellations were awful and I had to make good on them. I had to fend off lawsuits. There was never a tranquil period that lasted more than a week."[23]

Immediately after the forest fire, the edges of Saul's patience began to fray and his frustration emerged in a thinly veiled threat to quit. Though most of his correspondence with Johnny remained professional, if a little curt, at one point that summer he informed Cash that if he was concerned about the manner in which Saul represented him, he "would be agreeable to withdrawing from this area and concentrating on dates only, plus the usual prodding of Columbia and Hill & Range, press releases and distributing publicity and records," which he had been doing at his own expense for weeks anyway. With a new baby and a rejuvenated home life, perhaps it would be a relief to step back.[24]

"What do you mean 'withdraw from this area.' Let's work together and keep phrases like that out of our conversation. Black is black. Day is day," Cash wrote back, clearly alarmed. "Yes, again I say, I want you to represent me. Columbia … H&R … Sun. And to fill you in, I went to Memphis, dropped by to visit Sam Phillips. He screamed at me all night long, except for the three times I grabbed him by the collar and threatened to knock out teeth. His mind is completely soaked in alcohol, and I'll never speak to him again. Bad scene. Wish I could have afforded to hit him."[25]

But in dealing with Johnny, black was never black, and day was never day. Throughout July of 1965, Saul fielded calls from both Vivian, who said Cash wanted to work only four days that month, and June, who claimed that Cash wanted to work more at the end of July. Nothing made sense. By the end of August, Johnny and June managed to show up for a date together at the Canadian National Exhibition in Toronto but were acting so strangely it formed the basis of a scathing critique by reviewer Frank Kennedy. "Adults can receive off-colour material in its proper perspective. Teenagers and even younger children — and they come in all ages at the 'Ex' — shouldn't be exposed to it," wrote Kennedy in the *Toronto Daily Star*. Apparently no longer concerned with keeping their relationship a secret, Cash had rolled about on the ground in front of the stage licking his lips at June's heels while she performed. "Her coy pleadings to the 'sex maniac,' as she called him, crawling on his knees on the grass towards her, wasn't necessary," Kennedy sniffed.[26]

Following this lewd performance, Johnny then failed to appear as scheduled at the Franklin County Fair. Once again, Saul was fending off another lawsuit. "I pitched you to many of the No. 1 Fairs, and the response was practically nil. You apparently have missed some important engagements in the past and the word is out amongst major buyers: 'Hands Off,'" Saul furiously wrote to Johnny in late August. He then outlined the deep humiliation he had recently endured when their USO tour fell through — a tour that Cash himself had asked be scheduled.

"You agreed to a June tour in the Far East with [L.A.-based disc jockey and songwriter] Charlie Williams, and then advised me. It fell through due to an incredible lack of businesslike methods on the part of Stew Carnall and Charlie Williams, and this of course occurred after I had to cancel the USO tour that you first asked me to set. I have never discussed the embarrassment that this cancellation created in responsible circles. So that blew June as a worthwhile month, and it had to be salvaged in any way possible," he wrote. Adding to the insult, around this time Johnny had again accused Saul of financial discrepancies. Saul questioned the logic of this, writing, "You were further concerned about my allegedly signing chits at The Mint that came to the grand sum of $100-odd, only to be made aware, after accusing me of such a monumental theft, that *I wasn't even in Las Vegas* during the period the chits were signed. There are other instances such as this that are too numerous to mention."

As he wrote, Saul grew more enraged, thinking of the thirty-five thousand dollars he had just secured Cash as a result of negotiations he had just completed with music publishers Hill & Range, a deal that had not received so much as an acknowledgement. "Your comment on the whole negotiation was a classic Nothing. It's nice to be appreciated," Saul added. "You have never failed to let me know where I have goofed up in a business that is constantly changing, where I am called upon to package shows, buy talent, nurse-maid the promoter and guide him in every move, so that you can get the financial returns from a date that is not possible with the flat guarantees other artists work at. You tell me that you did well at Staunton, but who do you think conceived the date, and spent hours on the telephone guiding the local mooch?"[27]

In the midst of it all, Saul had attempted to reignite enthusiasm from Russell Stoneham at CBS to give Cash a chance at a television show. They had developed a top-quality pilot ready for screening that they wanted Stoneham to view, so they tentatively scheduled a meeting in New York for mid-July. However, in the chaotic aftermath of the forest fire, the meeting fell through. In late September, Saul and Johnny were in New York for an appearance on CBS Television's *Steve Lawrence Show* to play the show's finale number. It may have offered a perfect opportunity to salvage the lost meeting, perhaps even to manage to get Stoneham to agree to watch the pilot, or come to the show as an audience member. In any case, Cash bombed hard.

"He was in the midst of this real bad time. And I never told him this, to this day I never said a word to John about it, but the finale of the show was, we had Eddie Young and Minnie Pearl and Chet Akins and Floyd Crane — just everyone that was from Nashville that was big at that time," said Bill Walker, who was the show's orchestra conductor and arranger. "It was my first big-time show, and Johnny was to come out and start 'I Walk the Line.' At the end of him doing that, I was to grow the orchestra out of that and go on to do this big finale where all of the Broadway stars sang and the country stars sang and it was one of those big fifteen-minute monstrosities.

"And he, Johnny, came out, and he had Luther and he had the Tennessee Three then, it was Luther and Marshall and Fluke. And so they start up, boom chicka boom, and Johnny always used to go 'hmm, then boom chicka boom, hmm …' and this went on for about five minutes. He never did start the song. Never. This is my first meeting with Johnny Cash. So, the producer comes out to me and says, 'What is happening? Why isn't this thing starting?' So I copped out and I went straight to Saul Holiff at that time. And I said, 'Saul, you've got to fix this. What are we going to do?'" said Walker. Saul knew what to do — he simply walked over, pulled Johnny off the stage, and steered him out.[28]

Saul's head was reeling. He was juggling roles as manager, agent, press and public relations director, legal adviser, personal assistant, account-ant, and confidante. It seemed as though every time he gathered up and restacked the pieces of his client's career, Cash would stride over and kick them over. And the worst was yet to come. Though Saul's intuition was sharp — earlier that year it had saved his life when at the last minute he had "a crazy premonition" and decided to cancel his reservation aboard an ill-fated flight, which subsequently crashed, killing eighty-four pas-sengers — no one could have predicted the storm that was about to hit.[29]

All was calm for a few days after the television appearance. Cash gathered himself together and was "on" again, to an impressive degree. The band wrapped up a small but successful tour of the South with a show in Dallas on October 2. Johnny was booked on a flight to Los Angeles the next morning at 8:00 a.m., so Marshall Grant went to his room first thing and knocked on the door. When there was no answer, he opened it and was greeted with an empty bed. Thinking he must be somewhere nearby, Grant packed up Johnny's remaining belongings and called June, who also hadn't seen him. The night before, Johnny had requested all the tour receipts from Marshall — thousands of dollars — with the assurance he would deposit it in their bank account when he got back to California. He had been so clearheaded, and the tour had been such a roaring success, that Marshall hadn't thought twice about handing over the cash.

Eventually Marshall and June, who joined in on the search, found a bellhop who said he thought Johnny had checked out at about 2:00 a.m.[30]

By his own account, Johnny's taste for amphetamines was now so strong he couldn't find enough doctors to keep him supplied in Nashville and California, so he was sourcing pills on the black market via a network of drugstore connections. Rather than retire to the hotel room following their show that night, Johnny had decided to make his way to El Paso, having been told by a Nashville "pillhead" that he would find an endless supply in Mexico. He then hailed a cab across the border.

"I was nervous and a little afraid as I sat waiting a short time in Juarez while the driver got out of the car and went into a bar to get the amphetamines and barbiturates. I felt like the outlaw I had become, sitting in a hot dirty back street behind a bar in Mexico. When I got back to El Paso, I tied up the pills in two socks and put one of them inside my guitar and the other in the lining of my suitcase," Johnny later wrote in his autobiography *Man in Black*.[31]

Johnny didn't know that the Mexican dealer was under surveillance for selling heroin. The next morning, suspected of having made "a buy," Johnny was taken off a plane at El Paso International Airport by two narcotics agents and searched. They didn't find any heroin, but they did find the pills.

"American country singer Johnny Cash was arrested yesterday in Texas," said the voice of a TV news announcer as Saul watched in horror from his office in London. "The singer is charged with smuggling drugs across the Mexican border. He was arrested at El Paso International Airport Monday night while boarding a flight to Los Angeles. According to sources, Cash had 669 Dexedrine tablets and 475 tranquilizer pills on his person. Johnny Cash will be arraigned tomorrow morning."[32]

After a night in a roach-infested cell in the county jail, Johnny woke to calls from former record producer Sam Phillips, whom he hadn't talked to in months, since their near-fistfight in Memphis. Next to call was Don Law from Columbia, and by the time local DJ Neal Merritt from El Paso's country station phoned, Johnny realized the news was out. He recoiled in shame.

"I don't ever want out of this cell again. I just want to stay here and die. Because I'm too weak to face everyone I'll have to face. Knowing my family is heartbroken, knowing my friends and fans are hurt and disappointed — it's more than I can reconcile with them," he later wrote.

At the arraignment the next day, Cash posted a $1,500 bond and was released. However, he was anything but contrite. On his way out of the courthouse he "cursed a reporter and threatened to kick a reporter's camera," according to the Associated Press.[33]

It was front-page news across the country. "Pep Pills in His Guitar Lead to Singer's Arrest," blared the front page of the *Ventura County Star-Free Press*. An Associated Press photo of Johnny in sunglasses and handcuffs, flanked by a bondsman and a federal marshal, would go down in history as one of the most infamous images ever taken of the singer. However, all Johnny's daughter Cindy remembered was her feeling of terror at the thought that her friends at school would see it.[34]

Everyone managed the news of the arrest in their own way. June quit the Johnny Cash Show and retreated to her home in Madison, Tennessee. After he was released, Johnny had returned home to Casitas Springs and Vivian, not to her. It must have stung a little, even if it was for the sake of appearances. Near-constant fighting had marked June's relationship with Johnny up until that point, but the arrest now threatened her career. Johnny's drug problems had been an open secret in the music industry for years, but it was now international news, so she needed to keep her distance. And as she anticipated, the fallout was immediate.

Western Union Telegram, Nov. 12, 1965

Saul Holiff Care Hawaiian Hotel, Hollywood, California. Due to unfavorable publicity originating from El Paso, we wish to cancel the Johnny Cash performance scheduled for November 24, 1965, at Texas A&M University. This is our official notice of cancellation of contract. J. Wayne Stark, Advisor, Town Hall Committee.[35]

Cancellations began to pour in, and Saul gathered all his resources for the coming offensive. Though he also managed June and the Statler Brothers, Johnny was Saul's bread and butter. Barbara was now pregnant with their second child, and he couldn't let this run away on them. He swiftly devised a plan: if the fallout meant Johnny couldn't play any shows in the States, he would get him out of the country. Incredibly, within two weeks of the arrest, he had negotiated with lawyer Woodrow Bean (a former El Paso County judge) and the U.S. Commissioner to get a motion granted that would allow Johnny to both leave the country on bond and legally perform in Canada.[36]

"Relative to our conversation this past weekend, it is imperative that Johnny get together with his attorneys just as soon as possible so that we may be able to proceed on our investigation with all the facts that he

Telegram cancelling Johnny Cash shows, 1965.

has at his command. I can't impress on you too much the urgency of this meeting," wrote Bean, in the letter that accompanied the motion.

While Johnny was busy in Canada, Saul then launched a media onslaught to get out in front of the story. By the time Cash returned in mid-November, Saul had arranged for Dixie Deen, a beloved bluegrass composer and influential columnist for *Music City News*, to sit down for a lengthy interview with Johnny in Nashville just before his December arraignment. It was a brilliant piece of strategy; Deen was a close friend of both Cash and the Carter family, and Johnny felt comfortable opening up to her.[37]

"I don't pretend to be anything I'm not," Johnny told Deen. "I've seen the bad publicity, the horrible pictures of me in the papers within the last couple of months, and I don't even read what it says, because I know exactly what the papers want to do.... They want to make it sensational, and prove they are heroes by tearing down an image which they think has been built up. I am guilty of as many sins as the average person, but I don't say that I am guilty of any more than the average person. I may have a few different ones, but no more."[38]

The article revealed a vulnerable side of Cash, and combined with the bad-boy persona underlined by the arrest, it served to paint a compelling and — most important — sympathetic portrait of the troubled artist. It was exactly what the public needed to see. It also may well have worked to save Johnny's career in a time when scandal, as evidenced by Jerry Lee Lewis's downfall, often meant even the most promising careers could be abruptly snuffed out when a disapproving public turned their backs. The article steered their ship into calmer waters, and for the first time in weeks Saul felt as though he could catch his breath. The worst seemed to have been averted, and like many in Cash's entourage, he wondered if the arrest might have a sobering effect on the singer.

Once the particulars were arranged, Saul took Barbara and baby Jonathan to Jamaica while the rest of the world celebrated Christmas. In a pensive mood, he retreated to the sanctuary of his room at the Jamaica Reef Hotel to listen to jazz and smooth out the edges of his mind. It was a time for lists and letters; he often used resolutions to mark milestone moments. In an almost alchemical fashion, it served to bring order and control to a world he found distressingly and irritatingly messy. With the waves crashing on the beach below his balcony, he began to dictate a letter to Barbara.

Dec. 21, 1965
Mr. Johnny Cash
Casitas Springs, California
U.S.A.

Dear Johnny:
As 1965 draws to a close, and our fifth year of association approaches, I believe it's time to sum up some things from the past and present and, as usual, make some projections for the future.

I have given much consideration to what part I've played in your career during the past few years. Emperor Marcus Aurelius described it correctly when he said "Our life is what our thoughts make us." There was a period, a few years back, when it appeared that you had become completely indifferent to your career. I like to think that, through subtle and not-too-subtle prods from my end, I helped to channel and direct your energies back to constructive and creative effort. If this was my only service to you I feel satisfied. However, I did book a few dates, and there were situations like Buck Lake Ranch etc., from which I helped extricate you. Some of the dates were good, some not so good; some my fault, some couldn't be helped. Your asking price (depending on the circumstances) has now almost tripled — as compared to Marty Robbins, for instance, and others who are asking about the same, give or take 20% or so. Ballroom dates have been virtually eliminated, and club and military dates have been done away with.

There have been many times that surgical repairs had to be brought into play, public relations-wise.

I considered it my job to make such repairs and to always remember to respect you as an individualist and non-conformist who couldn't be expected to operate like a machine.

Now that it appears we will be going our separate ways, I thought it best to brief you thoroughly on what is upcoming, the balance of commissions owing etc.

Many other requests have been received, but all specific answers are being deferred, subject to your future plans....

Best wishes to you and your family for the New Year,

Yours truly,
Saul Holiff.[39]

It's not clear what exactly Saul meant by them each "going their separate ways." It's possible they were once again on the outs, but included in the letter was an extensive month-by-month list of all Cash's upcoming show dates and times from January to June.

A week later, at his arraignment, Cash pleaded no contest to charges of the illegal possession of drugs. In his weakness he turned to Vivian, who flew to El Paso to be at his side. Holding hands as they left the courthouse with lawyer Woodrow Bean, their photo was snapped by an Associated Press photographer. It ran in virtually every major daily newspaper in North America, and when a repentant Cash returned with his relieved wife to Casitas Springs, he likely thought — like Saul — that his troubles were over for the time being.

However, as Cash settled in for a quiet New Year with his family, the photo had dropped like a stone in a pond. Its effects rippled out into the most unlikely of places, and unbeknownst to any in their circle, it drew the ire of what would soon become a formidable foe: the Ku Klux Klan.

9

"SAUL, HELP ME!"

"Arrest Exposes Johnny Cash's Negro Wife," screamed the headline of the January 1966 edition of *The Thunderbolt*, a white supremacist magazine published by the National States Right Party based in Birmingham, Alabama. "The best kept secret since the Atomic Bomb has been the fact that Singer Johnny Cash has a Negress for a wife and they have four mongrelized children," the article went on. "Money from the sale of [Cash's] records goes to scum like Johnny Cash to keep them supplied with dope and negro women."

Included as "proof" of these claims was the Associated Press photo of Johnny and Vivian leaving the El Paso courthouse, reprinted along with the assertion that "controlled daily papers in the South" had suppressed the story.[1]

Except it, of course, wasn't true. Vivian was of Italian descent, and the hapless *Thunderbolt* writers had likely assumed she was African American because the blotchy quality of newsprint caused her complexion to look darker in the photo. In any case, the situation could not be taken lightly. It emerged at a time when racist sentiments in America regularly boiled over into violence and even murder. Throughout the 1960s, riots raged in every part of the country, from Florida to Cleveland, where a white minister was killed while protesting the workplace discrimination of blacks, to Selma, Alabama, where hundreds of peaceful black demonstrators had been attacked by state troopers wielding tear gas, nightsticks, and whips on what came to be known as "Bloody Sunday." As part of a long struggle for voting rights, marchers finally completed the journey from Selma to Montgomery later in the month, accompanied by Martin Luther King Jr. By August, Lyndon Johnson had signed the Voting Rights Act of 1965. At the same time, a black ghetto in Watts, Los Angeles, exploded into rioting, sparked by multiple unprovoked arrests and beatings of black citizens. Both the police and the National Guard were called in; thirty-four people were killed and hundreds injured.[2]

Amidst this chaos, the Klan, many of whom were avid *Thunderbolt* readers, were on the rise, flourishing anew in a racially oppressive South. "The Klan and allied organizations are now more active, and possibly stronger in numbers and influence than at any time since the Klan's heyday of the nineteen-twenties," John Herbers wrote in the *New York Times*, which estimated their active membership in 1965 to be at least ten thousand strong. Just days before he wrote the piece, the KKK had erected wooden crosses affixed with dummies of Lyndon Johnson and Martin Luther King Jr., set them alight, and then shot the effigies with pistols. Between 1963 and 1965, Klan members were implicated in at least eleven high-profile racially motivated murders in the South alone.[3]

When the *Thunderbolt* article first emerged, Cash hired Nashville lawyer John Jay Hooker and threatened a twenty-five-million-dollar lawsuit. Though the publication was directly connected to the KKK through longtime Klan member and party leader J.B. Stoner, who was also the imperial wizard of the Christian Knights of the KKK, the Klan proved to be a nebulous target. In the midst of incessant touring, the case soon faded into the background for Cash. Because the purpose of the article was likely to reduce his popularity in the South, when it appeared there was no immediate fallout the consensus in Cash's camp was that the *Thunderbolt* had likely realized their error and it would blow over. However, their failure to get out in front of the story would later come back to haunt them.[4]

It was easy to see why other issues were foremost in Saul's mind — Cash was scheduled for a string of shows on March 17, 18, and 19 at Toronto's prestigious O'Keefe Centre for the Performing Arts. It was considered a pivotal moment, the first time a country artist had ever played the venue, and as such, was expected to usher in a new era of appreciation for country music in Toronto. These concerts held personal significance for Saul: a gala affair on his home turf in an era when territory and appearances were paramount for promoters. To top it off, the general manager of the O'Keefe Centre was a six-foot-two, sharply clad, aristocratic Englishman who, in Saul's mind, was so well turned out he "made all other Englishmen look like total slobs."

Once again, every piece needed to be in place.

A press conference was scheduled for Cash at the Four Seasons Hotel in Toronto, at which Saul anticipated he could explain his El Paso drug charges. The week before the O'Keefe shows, Cash had appeared before a U.S. district judge to receive his sentencing and ended up with a one-thousand-dollar fine and a thirty-day suspended sentence. As a man in the public eye, he needed to be aware of his influence, cautioned Judge D.W. Suttle, who himself was a father of two teenage fans of Cash's music.

It was uncertain whether the press conference helped or hurt the cause. In a subsequent *Toronto Star* article, Cash was described as "gaunt-looking" and having a "fidgety way." A photo of a haggard-looking Cash

A clipping from the *Ottawa Journal*, found in Saul's scrapbook, illustrates how haggard Johnny was at the time.

ran with the piece, captioned with his quote, "I'm not nervous, I'm quick." As for the drug charges, he was characteristically frank. "It was my first conviction of any kind," he said. "Of course, I can't goof up like that again."[5]

The subsequent concerts were mostly a triumph — fans flooded the venue for sold-out shows every night, and the city's newspapers reeled off pages of giddy reviews. It was also a smash with audiences, with the inclusion of all-star performances by Tex Ritter, the Statler Brothers, the Carter Family, and Loretta Lynn.

But then there was Johnny. At times incoherent and erratic — one night he came out onto the stage and faced the wrong way — his performances nonetheless earned positive reviews. For the final show on Saturday evening, Cash dickered about for so long that emcee Tex Ritter finally had to shove him out onto the stage in his socks, where he stood blinking into the audience among the glittering shards of a bottle he had smashed. But despite a week-long binge of pill-popping and sleeplessness, of shattered jars and coffee grounds all over the dressing room, despite the addition and then sheepish cancellation of a sold-out Saturday afternoon matinee for which Cash was nowhere to be found, the evening show was pulled off and he brought down the house.[6]

On Saturday evening, Saul fell into his bed at the Four Seasons beside Barbara with a groan, grateful that the worst was over.

He was awakened by the sound of the phone ringing.

"Saul, you gotta get down to the motor home outside," June said quickly, without saying hello. "There's something wrong with Johnny."

The refrain was a familiar one. Receiver in hand, Saul briefly considered ignoring the call and going back to sleep. But they had to get to Rochester, New York, that day for an afternoon show and another that evening. He glanced at Barbara, and then at Jonathan in the crib beside her. Snoring at his feet was their poodle, Oedipus Rex.

An image of Abe Hamza, the promoter in Rochester, flashed in his mind. To Saul, he was *the* quintessential, mafia-type, upstate New York thug; a big man who smoked big cigars. These days, everyone in the business knew the deal with "No-Show" Cash, especially since El Paso. Hamza took pains to make it clear: if there were any problems, he'd break Saul's legs. This was not a man prone to idle threats. To cancel was not an option.

Saul rose and dressed. As he strode across the parking lot toward Cash's camper, the grim faces of the gathered crowd told him they were in trouble.

It was the apex of a week that had been all but unmanageable. Now, the scene was chaos.

For all intents and purposes, Johnny was dead. His body lay on the floor of his motor home, a half-peeled potato and a knife on the floor beside him.

"No one could pick up any pulse whatsoever," Saul later recalled. "Harold Reid of the Statler Brothers had his ear on Cash's chest and said, 'I can't hear anything,' another member of the group is saying, 'I wonder where he hid the pills,' another member is saying, 'I'm not going to cross the border at Buffalo because if they find any pills that he's hidden on the bus they'll confiscate the bus and we'll all go to jail,' another person is saying, 'Wellesley Hospital is just around the corner, why don't we dump him there?' another said, 'Toronto General Hospital is a much better place,' another said, 'Why don't we just take the chance and go as far as Buffalo and dump him before we get to Buffalo?'"

Saul's mind was reeling. Usually decisive, he felt unable to prioritize. It had been only five months since Johnny's drug smuggling arrest. Saul rubbed the stubble on his jaw. Snow began to slowly drift from the damp grey sky and settle on their shoulders. *This is a perilous situation*, he thought. They had no idea how ill he was. *Someone has to take charge.*

"I called a conference in the parking lot, behind the Four Seasons Motor Hotel, and we virtually had a board of directors meeting as to: Do we put him in a hospital in Toronto and cancel the Rochester show and risk utter mayhem and physical threats to ourselves? Do we risk going across the border and the possibility that customs will search the motor home and find the pills that he's hidden? He had a remarkable ability to hide pep pills in the most extraordinary places. It wouldn't matter where we would find them; he would find a place to hide them again. Do we simply stay in Toronto and have a moratorium and see what happens? Do we turn around and head for Detroit? What really do we do?"

No one in the entourage had slept much in the previous week, as Cash — partying the week away with nightclub owner and musician Ronnie Hawkins — felt that if he wasn't sleeping, why should anyone else be?

"There had been much pounding on doors at three, four, five o'clock with problems. 'Where can I get more pills?' was one of the more significant problems," remembered Saul. "There were scenes in the hotel of running up and down the hallway without clothes, which is somewhat awkward on Jarvis Street if you're across the street from the CBC. Matter of fact, it's awkward on Jarvis Street if you weren't across from the CBC. There was a film crew that had come in from Europe [and] were rather disconcerted about this. They hadn't had this to contend with before. I think they lost their lens in the commotion. There were a lot, *a lot*, of people wandering up and down the hallways who shouldn't have been wandering up and down the hallway, and there were emotional traumas galore. There were people checking out, part of our group who were leaving forever, and people joining our group that we hadn't even seen before. It was utter chaos. It was, truly, a scene of utter havoc."

And now this. As they stood in the parking lot, Saul shoved his hands in his pockets and hunched his shoulders against the chill.

"In some ways, because of the hostility, because of this extraordinary week, some of us were wishing to hell that we could put him in the hospital and that we could write it off and forget about the whole thing, and go home and apply for unemployment insurance," he remembered.

They went over their options again. No one knew for certain whether Cash would even survive the border crossing. If Cash didn't make the show, that meant Saul and Barbara had to also be concerned about their safety, and were worried about travelling with their baby. Saul glanced up at the sky. Conditions were worsening by the minute.[7]

"The decision, finally, was go. Go to Rochester and see what would happen. I phoned ahead and changed my reservations from the hotel we were supposed to stay at to another one so that the promoter would not know where we were staying," said Saul. June and Marshall covered Johnny with a blanket and prepared to cross the border.

"We made it to Rochester at about 2:30 in the afternoon. Barbara and I checked in and arranged for someone to look after the baby. We drove down to Rochester Memorial Auditorium. The motor home was parked in back. [We wondered] if there was any way I could get a doctor to give him some sort of injection to revive him, [but] this is what we saw: Johnny Cash sitting in the back, with a pot of coffee on the stove. And when I said, 'How are you doing?' he said, 'What the hell are you asking me how I'm doing for? What do you think I'm doing? I'm going to go out and do a show.' He was argumentative, full of piss and vinegar. He had made an extraordinary recovery, and he went out and he did two clear-headed, sensational, sold-out shows. I think we even got an honest count from the promoter that night."

With the Toronto shows behind them, Saul turned his focus to their next hurdle: a major European tour that had required months of preparation.

The plane touched down at London's Heathrow Airport for the Johnny Cash Show's first official tour of Great Britain on May 5, 1966. After an exhausting six-hour flight on which they were packed in with other tourists "like sardines," the entourage checked in at a cut-rate hotel with rooms that were, as Saul later told Barbara, "about the size of our lower stair closet." They checked out two hours later and found other more suitable accommodations at the Mount Royal Hotel.

Promoted by the dynamic duo of impresario Mervyn Conn and agent Joe Collins (father of Joan and Jackie), the tour kicked off with a press conference at the Pickwick Club on Great Newport Street, after which Cash performed "Streets of Laredo." Though he was tired, and completely sober, Saul went out on the town that night to what he considered "the finest evening of theatre" in his life — a performance of *You Never Can Tell* by George Bernard Shaw. The official opening of the Cash tour came the following day at the Empire in Liverpool, after which Johnny, Saul, and Merv Conn went gambling at a fancy club. Saul won three hundred dollars but had to reluctantly lend about sixty dollars to Mervyn, who seemed to be broke, which was mystifying to Saul, as it appeared he owned a fashionable apartment and drove a Jaguar.

"Hotel Pierre comfortable, very expensive — terribly stuffy. Johnny in good shape so far!! Liverpool very good box office-wise, but tonight looks poor," Saul quickly scrawled to Barbara in the minutes before the bus left for their next show in Birmingham. "Merv Conn comes by his surname naturally. He is a slim Alex Richmond type. Short, brash, slick, cunning and oh so ambitious. He makes Len Nymark [of Variety Theatre] seem sluggish by comparison. I'm very concerned that if an incident takes place (a no-show or Johnny being late), he will give us a very bad time. Just a few minutes ago he got into a hassle with the bus drivers because they took an expensive room here. Got me involved with it."[8]

For their part, Johnny and June quickly grew close with Merv, and gratefully accepted his offer to stay in his apartment so that the couple might avoid the scandal involved with staying in a hotel together. Merv graciously offered to sleep at his mother's nearby to give them privacy. Over the course of the tour the three became so comfortable together that June would visit Merv at his mother's house to wash her laundry.[9]

"Dear Barbara Jean — you now have a rival for my affections. I've fallen in love with London. Fickle of me!! I was in love with Paris last time, before that, L.A. This city, everything taken into consideration, is so much more civilized than anything in the USA that no comparisons are possible. It offers everything — Hyde Park and St. James Park make Central Park seem like a three ring circus," Saul wrote to Barbara, who was at home in the other London, round with the expectation of their second baby. For Saul, London's combination of history, tradition, pomp, and palaces mixed with the variety and colour of first-rate theatres and posh gambling clubs to provide an intoxicating environment.[10]

As the British tour wound to a close, Saul looked forward to what would be their crowning achievement: a final, one-night show at the prestigious Olympia Theatre in Paris, France. Arguably their most important date, bookended by a press conference and various television appearances, it was the first time a country and western performer had ever been scheduled in the venue, and as such, was another managerial coup for Saul.

As he met June, the Statlers, and the Tennessee Three at Heathrow Airport to board their flight into France, it gradually became clear that one member of their troupe was missing. Saul began to pace and check his watch obsessively as the minutes before their departure drained away. Jetlag and anxiety ground at his nerves; it felt as though he had been exhausted for the entire trip. *Where was Johnny?* He stopped pacing as the reality of the situation began to settle in and he realized what had happened. *He's with Bob Dylan. That drug-stunned bum. Of course.* Also on a tour of the United Kingdom and Europe at the same time, Dylan was cavorting about London with John Lennon and Joan Baez, playing shows and filming a documentary with D.A. Pennebaker for the ABC Television series *Stage '66*. Cash had wanted to meet up with him, and was now suspiciously missing.[11]

"He didn't show up for the flight," Saul wrote to Barbara when he returned to the hotel. "Spent four hours in Hyde Park today. My nerves were badly in need of recharging."[12]

Two days later, a letter was delivered to Saul's hotel room. It was Johnny, writing to tell Saul he wanted no dates booked for the last two months of 1966 and the month of December off completely. "January is another year," he wrote. "I am going to New and Old Jerusalem, or every business affiliation, including yourself, CBS, Columbia — the whole works — will be dissolved."

This trip to Israel would mark Johnny's first time in the country, due in part to June's strong encouragement that he return to his faith. The two were scheduled to fly into Tel Aviv within the week.

Without apology or even a mention of the missed show, Cash went on to criticize Saul's handling of the tour. "Your job as manager was to be there when needed on my behalf. No member of my cast will hereafter be directed or reprimanded by anyone other than myself, unless I'm shown without a doubt that I'm wrong."

Cash added that he felt Saul had "browbeat" tour promoter Mervyn Conn and others. "It is Mervyn that has saved the day and kept the ball rolling. You'll hate him more for my saying that, but I think he's a noble man to swallow pride and stay on his toes for me. He did this much; he was so efficient that I really had nothing to worry about. Even when I didn't deserve it, his dignity and aggression kept things on a high, respectable calibre. He's simply a friend, also, whether or not you believe it, so take it easy on my friends. No business talks today. I'm going to rest."[13]

There was no apology, no explanation, no acknowledgement even, of what had happened. Saul downed a bottle of Scotch and spent the next week walking around Hyde Park, contemplating his future. Middle age was creeping up on him, and he was afraid. Gripped by shame, he reflected on his thinning hair and sagging jowls, his ego-shattering, self-effacing deferment to Johnny. The humiliating letter had all but confirmed it. "The most crushing awareness: I'm not a genius, damn it. God is dead, or he would have noticed," he wrote to Barbara upon his return to the hotel. Their next child was due in a month, he had no other prospects, and payments were due on the new house; everything was riding on his relationship with Johnny. And it was a partnership he now sensed was finished. The sense of injustice over Cash's accusations hadn't diminished, but he didn't want to let on how much it hurt. Enough was enough. He sat down and drafted a terse response.[14]

Mr. Cash:

1. Don't want commission for this tour. 62 letters, countless calls, wires, notes and three months of preparation — manifests, work permits, etc. — so things would go smooth.

2. Browbeat? The incident you refer to according to Merv was after your call from Newcastle — when you complained bitterly about your treatment, the poor promotion etc. and requested cancellation of the last date. I called Merv to advise him accordingly. He was not browbeaten. However you would be more of an authority on the subject than I am.

3. Reprimand? Who? Where? When? Merv called from Glasgow to advise that your cast was late. He suggested that it was my place to reprimand your cast. I didn't.

4. Israel. Now that I've been advised by the travel agent that you are working on the 22nd it means that you will have 36 hrs. in Israel.

5. I arranged and selected Merv Conn — just like I did Lennie. They both became your close and fast friends.

6. As agreed 5 years ago, I resign and give one month's notice. (Gonna breathe air fit to be breathed.) I intend to be in Buffalo on the last date there — to collect my commission and come to what I hope is a peaceful arrangement for the balance of monies owing.[15]

Saul's suspicion was proven to be correct. While the rest of the troupe had waited fervently for Johnny to materialize at Heathrow Airport, he had indeed ended up in Dylan's company. Though never officially released, outtakes from Dylan's escapades were eventually edited into the documentary *Eat the Document* and revealed Cash backstage with Dylan in Wales, twenty minutes before he was scheduled to go onstage at Sofia Gardens. So high he could barely sing, Cash hung on to Dylan's piano in a stupor as they stumbled through a rendition of "I Still Miss Someone."

On his way to the airport, Saul mailed the letter and then boarded a first-class flight back to his home and family in London, Ontario. Upon his return, he was thrown into unexpected house repairs. Their well wasn't functioning, the septic tank had overflowed, and their furnace had stopped working. "Everything that could go wrong, did. I was a mechanical screw-up," Saul said.

It was a trying time, and though the resignation allowed him to be home for the birth of his second son, Joshua, on June 29, the circumstances also made it hard to enjoy his new role as a father. Most of the time he was so tired and concerned with what lay ahead that he was simply unequipped to handle any additional demands.[16]

In the weeks that followed his disappearance, Saul and Johnny's conflict triangulated to include June. Outraged that Saul had discussed his resignation with June and implied that he had been subject to unfair treatment, Cash typed out a feverish telegram from a stop on the road in Syracuse, New York. If Saul was unable to contact him, Johnny wrote, he would prefer that he wait to speak with him directly instead of discussing or condemning his behaviour with June, "due to the false conception you carry concerning my operations." Moreover, Johnny felt that Saul had managed to convince June that he was stabbing him in the back. "You are causing much mental anguish, to the thought that she turns from me when I deny your accusations," Cash added. If he had any criticism of Saul as a man or a promoter, he would be the first to know. He expected the same courtesy in return, and requested that if Saul felt the need to cry on someone's shoulder it be his instead of June's. They needed to focus on the last few months of business together without distraction, said Cash, who finished the letter by saying that if Saul gave him a chance, he would give him one back. [17]

This was about as much as their split was ever discussed. Cash soon invited Saul to visit him during a performance at the Red Rocks Amphitheatre near Denver. It was here that he somehow persuaded his ex-manager to come back on board. "It was an unspoken reconciliation that was almost bizarre," Holiff later said. It would not be their last. [18]

No sooner were Johnny and Saul reunited as a team than another split loomed on the horizon. Vivian had filed for divorce. For better or for worse, waiting for Johnny was something she simply did — during his three-year stint in the air force when he wrote her hundreds of passionate letters, and for the last several years as his visits dwindled to a trickle and she took up residence in the living room window, haloed in cigarette smoke, searching for his car. Until now it had been impossible for her to leave. Not only because of her Catholic faith and loyal nature, but also quite simply because she was still in love with him. "It is hard to walk away when there is a shred of hope," she wrote in her memoir. "And I always held out hope."

However, a recent trip to the doctor had changed everything. Thin, stressed out, and weak from constant crying, she listened as the doctor stared into her eyes and told her that if she didn't do *something*, someone else would be raising her four girls. The message got through. Terrified that it would end up being June Carter, she decided divorce was simply a matter of survival. But to survive, she would have to cut out her own heart. "A piece of me died on that day," she wrote of the Friday afternoon in June of 1966 when she signed the divorce papers. [19]

Adding to the deep humiliation and conflict was the fact that she couldn't even find Johnny to inform him of her decision. After the U.K.

tour and his trip to Israel, Cash briefly returned home to Casitas Springs and the two clashed, after which he left and did not return. Vivian was forced to take out an ad in the *Nashville Banner* asking him to appear in court in Ventura County on August 22, 1966. "Country and Western singer Johnny Cash doesn't know it yet, but his wife Vivian has sued him for divorce," read the August 18 edition of the *Oxnard Press Courier*. "The complaint charges extreme cruelty."

Johnny did not appear.[20]

That same day, Cash spoke to his accountant, Anzac Jacobs, on the phone, who then quickly drafted a letter to Saul. "[Johnny] stated that he had not been served any papers on the divorce proceedings and, as I told him, I am of the opinion that he won't be." It will instead be published as an ad in a Nashville newspaper, Anzac wrote. "In our discussion it was brought out that he had not secured the services of an attorney in the matter, as he was apparently leaving this up to you."[21]

Leaving this up to you. Saul had re-entered the hornet's nest of Johnny's life.

They retained the services of an attorney, who denied the charge of extreme cruelty and that Cash had caused grievous mental suffering. Two weeks later, a telegram arrived from Cash that requested that Saul fly into Nashville with Anzac Jacobs, so that together they could go over everything that needed to get done. It was the only way, Johnny insisted. "[I] will sit quietly and look at every angle," he wrote to his manager.[22]

There was a needy tone to the message that Saul couldn't ignore. But as he rolled up his sleeves and once again prepared to do battle on Johnny's behalf, he felt a sense of conflict. Vivian was lovely, a strong and tender woman who consistently eschewed the spotlight of the music business and whose personality was of such a rare calibre that he was felt a genuine fondness for her. The divorce would likely get nasty, and require tough negotiating. He did not look forward to it. In addition, Saul had helped draft a new will for Johnny in which he was named the executor of his estate. Other extraneous duties also jostled for his attention, including the tangled and complicated lawsuit from former manager Stew Carnall, still ongoing, that involved reams of letters and financial haggling in which he sought approximately $17,500 in back royalties and fees.[23]

The stress was taking its toll on Johnny. If guilt over Vivian and the children had fuelled his addiction, the current situation was gasoline on the fire. "I grieved for my little girls in California," Cash wrote in his autobiography *Man in Black*. "Things were beyond repair in my home. I had gone too far, stayed away too much. Too many bonds were broken. The girls grieved for me also, but it was harder and harder to face them each time I saw them."[24]

At this point he gave up sleeping on the couch at Gene Ferguson's and moved into a one-bedroom apartment with Waylon Jennings in Madison, Tennessee. During this time in particular, Cash couldn't stand to be alone. Once a week, June and Mother Maybelle, who both lived nearby, would come to sift through his dirty plates and clothes in an attempt to clean up. Unlike June, Maybelle never lectured Cash and was unfailingly supportive. Cash and Jennings — who was easily as messed up as Cash at this point — comically hid their mutual drug habits from each other. One night, in a pill-craving frenzy, Johnny broke into Waylon's brand-new limousine searching for drugs. Prying open the glovebox with a screwdriver, he shattered the plastic and scattered the contents everywhere, but found no pills. In the days that followed, the attempted theft only compounded the singer's sense of shame.[25]

"In time, I became afraid of everything. I would be a nervous wreck before a show; I was never sure of myself during a performance. I didn't believe people when they said things had gone all right," Cash later wrote in an editorial for *Guideposts* magazine. "Sometimes I was too sick to work. Sometimes I didn't even show up. It didn't take booking agents long to stop risking their money on me. Even though I knew this meant a loss of income to others in the show, people who were good friends, I didn't care. I didn't care about anything. I knew I was killing myself."[26]

Cash was a broken man. In a series of photos published in the *Ottawa Journal* at this time, he looked hollow-eyed, wrung-out, and skeletal. Snapped after his show at the Capitol Theatre on September 20, 1966, the accompanying text offered little more from Cash than the simple summary: "I just want to be myself, and for what I'm worth, I'm me."

The reporter who wrote the review seemed blissfully unaware of what had transpired just prior to the performance: The house was packed and the band was waiting onstage when Saul and local promoter Harvey Glatt went to Cash's motor home out on Queen Street, parked near the Capitol's stage door, and found the singer passed out inside. The two men quickly conferred and decided to each take an arm and carry Cash into the theatre. "We really had to help him all the way to the microphone," said Glatt.[27]

In this weakened state, Cash gathered what energy he had to head down south for a series of shows. It was at this moment that the KKK decided to attack him with renewed vigour. Though surely a cursory investigation would have revealed their error regarding Vivian's race, they went after him regardless. It's not certain why. Perhaps there was still some simmering resentment over his public support for Native Americans. Whatever it was, Cash had no idea he was under threat until his friend, glitzy country singer Porter Wagoner, mentioned he'd seen a flyer circulating at his show in Ponchatoula, Louisiana.[28]

Thousands of these flyers were circulated, accompanied by newspaper ads all over the South that said "FOR CASH CALL THIS NUMBER." Once called, the number connected to a tape-recorded message hosted by the Citizens Council in Mobile, Alabama, urging people to boycott Johnny Cash. After an introduction that quoted the *Thunderbolt* "article" about Cash having a black wife, it declared that "the race mixers in this country continue to sell his records to your teenage children."[29]

"There was a recorded message saying that they were going to blow up the Macon Coliseum and that they had bomb threats at the Ramada where we were staying," remembered Saul. "For the next two years we had Ku Klux Klan white hooded crazies barricading entrances into our dressing rooms and to our auditorium dates, into our concert halls with hate messages. This was a two-year campaign to destroy us. It was the most incredible experience."[30]

They pressed on with the tour in the South, with dates in Mobile, Birmingham, and Knoxville, while Saul went on the offensive. He engineered a face-to-face meeting with Robert Shelton, the imperial wizard of the United Klans of America, and threatened to sue the Mobile County Citizens Council for two hundred thousand dollars for slander and defamation. Another part of the pushback involved a public relations effort to steer the narrative. "That meant contacting newspapers to get the story out about what was correct, to offset articles that were printing these hate things," he said, adding that the campaign took "days and weeks and months."[31]

It was mostly successful — a piece in the *New York Post* presented Cash as a hero, trumpeting: "Singer Johnny Cash Fights the Voice of Hate."

"We'll repossess every asset they have, so that lies like this will not be built up to such monstrous proportions in the future," Saul said in the October 6 *Post* article. At stake was not only their prominence among Southern audiences, but their personal safety. The Klan threatened to kill Cash if he showed up for a show later that month in Greenville, North Carolina. The show went ahead as planned.

Motivated by protective feelings — Saul told the *Post* the hate campaign was "horrifying" and particularly painful for Cash and Vivian, as they were in the final stages of divorce proceedings — he also may have fought the harassment with such enthusiasm because it felt personal. *The Thunderbolt* regularly carried the viciously anti-Semitic views of party leader J.B. Stoner, who once addressed a KKK meeting in the late 1940s by saying, "I'll never be satisfied as long as there are any Jews here, or anywhere. I think we ought to kill all Jews."[32]

Buckling under its inaccuracies, the campaign eventually petered out and the concerts went off without incident, though at some shows members of the audience had tried to spit in Cash's face. The publicity that was engineered both created a paper trail for a planned lawsuit and presented Cash in a positive light. Though tactical, it came from a place of sincerity. Saul later said that he "regretted the optics," because their denials regarding Vivian could be mistaken by some to suggest "that there was something wrong with being black."[33]

Decades later, Cash would characterize that time by saying, "It's good to know who hates you, and it's good to be hated by the right people. The Klan is despicable, filthy, dirty and unkind. It's a shame sometimes that we have all these freedoms, 'cause freedom allows them to exist. I'd love to see them all thrown in prison."[34]

By all estimations, however, it looked like Johnny would be headed there first. Famously arrested in Starkville, Mississippi, for public drunkenness — which he later described as being picked up for "just pickin' flowers" — in his autobiography he acknowledged he was arrested seven times in seven years, everywhere from Texas to California. "I was on the verge of a nervous breakdown and I knew it," he wrote of this time. "I was usually on a hundred pills a day, but I got no pleasure from them, no peace. I couldn't stand my life, but I couldn't find my way out of it."[35]

After drinking himself into oblivion over the holidays, Cash returned to California on December 24 for a difficult last Christmas with Vivian and the girls, of which he later wrote that he felt "like a stranger."

The new year began with a major engagement in Miami on January 26 at the Dade County Auditorium. In good spirits — he had just signed

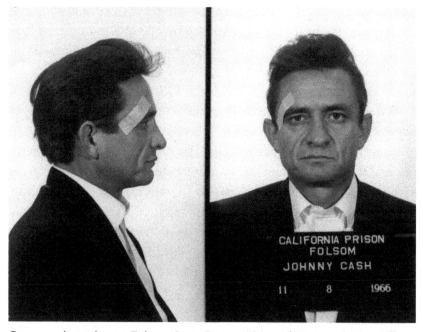

Gag mugshot taken at Folsom State Prison, 1966. When Jonathan Holiff later travelled to Folsom Prison to ask about this photo, the prison guards told him that it was not a real mugshot, as evidenced by the lack of a prisoner number. It is thought that the guards had convinced Cash to take the picture for fun, while he was there to play a show. In his research since, Jonathan has learned it is likely one of the only mugshots ever taken of a civilian at the prison.

singers Debbie Lori Kaye and Tommy Hunter on as clients — Saul decided to escape the cold of winter in London and make a holiday out of the show, so he flew Barbara and the babies out to Miami with him. They met up with his sister Ann, who now lived there. When it turned out that her daughter, Myra Richmann, was visiting from New York, Saul invited the whole family out to Cash's performance and gave them the best seats in the house.

"I remember that Saul didn't even have to advertise, because word got out and the place was filled to capacity. And I had never seen Johnny in person, and my mother and Saul and Barbara and I all had front-row seats, and the curtain went up, Johnny was announced, and the audience went crazy," Myra remembered. "And then Johnny came out, looked at the audience, strummed the guitar once, and waited a long time. I was feeling a little uncomfortable, I remember thinking, *Let's go!* You know, what's happening here? And the crowd was going crazy, so I figured he was waiting for the crowd to calm down. And then he looked down, and looked at Saul, and he said, 'Saaauuuuul, help me!' in the most pathetic voice. Saul went tearing out, stepped on my foot in the process, went running backstage, had the curtain drawn, closed, and refunded everybody's money. It was very dramatic, but obviously [Cash] was strung out. I remember feeling really sad for Saul, that he's gotta go pick up all the pieces and clean up after him."[36]

10

CARRYING CASH

The structure of concert promotions in the 1960s was not unlike that of organized crime, with its turfs and competitions, backstabbing and loyalties. More likely than not, it actually did involve local mafias in various capacities. As legendary concert promoter, agent, and producer Jerry Weintraub described it, it was a territorial game in which regions were divided up and ruled over by individual promoters.

"There was no such thing as a national tour. An artist moved from fiefdom to fiefdom, and the manager cut deals with local power brokers — the man who "owned" Philadelphia, the man who "owned" Buffalo — who made subsidiary deals with local police, local unions, local arena operators," wrote Weintraub in his book, *When I Stop Talking, You'll Know I'm Dead.* "If you tried to go around the local promoters and cut your own deals, you would find yourself frozen out of the territory. No one would rent you the hall if it was not through the local guy, who was, after all, kicking money back to the operator."

Most business was conducted in cash and sealed with handshakes. With a shifting cast of middlemen who each took their cut, the result was a business rife with kickbacks, fudged numbers, and, at times, payouts to artists that could cut a little thin. But it was a small, insular scene, and as such they all knew who was trustworthy and who was less so. For Saul, this environment only elevated the value he placed on honour and the strength of his word to almost sacred levels. In all dealings, he strove to

"Carrying Cash" — Saul Holiff's office desk covered in bundles of cash, circa 1960.

be ironclad in his promises. A handshake was as good as any contract, as far as he was concerned — even when it came to exorbitant amounts of money.

In Weintraub's case, when he secured his first tour with Elvis Presley in 1970 he simply met with Colonel Tom Parker in a casino at the Hilton International Hotel in Vegas and handed him a cheque for one million dollars. No receipt, no contract. Near the end of the tour, Weintraub wrote, he followed the Colonel into a back room where he was instructed to open two large suitcases and empty their contents onto the table. Confronted with a pile of cash earned through concessions, Weintraub recalled how the Colonel brought his cane down onto the bills with a *thwack* and pushed it into two piles. "That side yours, this side mine.... Is that fair?" he said. It was simply the way things were done.[1]

It was no different with Saul, who also regularly began and ended tours with wads of cash lining the worn leather briefcase he carried with him everywhere. "I've got $37,000 in here," Saul announced to author Christopher Wren one night, apropos of nothing, at a state fair in Topeka. At the end of the night or on the last stop of the tour, he would click open the briefcase, which was decorated with a Canadian flag, and the talent would line up to get paid out in cash.

"He used to scare the shit outta me. It was just like sittin' out here, he'd open up that little briefcase of his, he'd take out a fistful of hundred-dollar bills and just fan them out. He'd go 'What do you want?' And everybody'd be lookin' at him, no matter where we were — on the sidewalk, on the plane, in the hotel — he couldn't just do it subtle-like," said Bob Wootton, who later replaced Luther Perkins on lead guitar in the Tennessee Three. "I was scared someone was going to beat him on the head and take it. It worried me. At the end of the tour he'd come to your hotel room and count out the cash on your bed and make you sign for it."[2]

Saul Holiff, on the road with his famous Canada flag briefcase, which was often stuffed with bundles of cash. 1972.

Three weeks after the unfortunate show in Miami, the Johnny Cash Show was scheduled for an extensive two-week tour on the turf of Harry "Hap" Peebles, the biggest promoter in the Midwest. Well respected as one of the founders of the Country Music Association, he kept busy booking more than six hundred shows a year and set high standards for promotional work. This was not a man to cross. Though generally on good terms, Cash had once clashed with Peebles in 1961 over his incessant and unwanted romantic pursuit of Rose Maddox while on tour. Coming to her defence at a stop in North Dakota, Cash had slammed Peebles up against a wall and told him, "If you ever go near Rose again, I'll kill you." By 1967 the incident seemed to be mostly forgotten, but the entire Cash show soon realized they had other problems when they started the tour and, once again, Johnny was nowhere to be found.[3]

"Johnny blew off the first four dates," said Johnny Western. "The story was that Hap Peebles told Saul that Johnny had slipped on the ice in Nashville in front of Columbia Recording Studios, had fallen and cracked four ribs, and the doctor said he not only couldn't travel but he couldn't fly until his ribs were healed up. That was the official story."

However, the true story was a little more complicated. With the divorce from Vivian imminent, Cash desperately wanted to be with June, but she had made it clear she would never marry him unless he overcame his drug addiction for good. At this point it was a hopeless request, as Cash was deeper in it than ever. It was around this time, before the two-week tour, that they got into a bitter argument over the issue, and according to some accounts, June swallowed some of his tranquilizers out of spite. Incensed, she then left for the tour, and after some discussion, June, Saul, and likely Marshall decided the cast would do the shows as planned — without Johnny. The primary goal was to fend off a lawsuit, which combined with a fear of letting Hap Peebles down, but there was also an element of frustration involved over the lost revenue — this was work, after all.

"We did Fort Smith, Tulsa, and Oklahoma City without Johnny Cash, and then we heard this rumour that Johnny was furious that we were finishing the tour under his name and that he had had a confrontation with

Hap," said Western. Cash was indeed incensed, and unleashed his wrath in a letter addressed to June, which she then handed over to Saul.[4]

Johnny viewed the situation as a betrayal, and told June that when she joined the other members of their troupe to do the shows without him she had effectively turned her back on him. That act alone had more than repaid him for any wrongs he had done to her, he said. In his mind, he was hurt more by this than she had ever been hurt by him. It was unfathomable. Was she not able to see how in every way he was working to become a better and stronger man? He had taken the time to personally tell her father, Ezra Carter, as much — that he was going to "be the man they all were proud of," and he had sincerely meant it. These words were not uttered lightly; Ezra was a man Johnny deeply respected and with whom he had quickly bonded through their discussions of books and the nuances of religion. But now … what did this abandonment by June mean, exactly? Did she not see what they had as precious and valuable? Was this her way of dropping him? If so, "you need to think of doing it differently," he wrote. "For a long time you have been my future and I was yours," he continued, adding that it was hard to understand why she would potentially toss that future aside, and disregard all they had endured together, for a paltry two-week tour.

As for everyone else, and Saul, there were no words, he said. He needed an explanation from them personally. But if they insisted on continuing the tour without him, they must remove his name from any association with it, Johnny said. He also asked June to spare his feelings and be kind enough to not sing their duet with anyone else.

Much of Johnny's wrath was also directed at Hap Peebles, whom he thought needed to be reminded of his place as a local promoter, who was contracted first and foremost to present his show and little else, and who Johnny believed was under no authority to have acted the way he did. Feeling "disgraced, disregarded, disrespected and not believed," he wanted to ensure Peebles would be blacklisted. "You saw, and Hap will soon see, what you have done," Johnny finished.[5]

The duet Cash referred to in the letter was the popular section of their show in which he and June bantered, joked, and sang numbers like "It Ain't Me, Babe" and their newest song, "Jackson." Inspired by the play

Who's Afraid of Virginia Woolf?, "Jackson" was written as a back-and-forth between a married couple. It was intimate, funny, and carried a natural chemistry. Part of their show for some time, the recording was released just before the February tour and was a minor hit for the couple when it went to number two on the country charts. It also later formed part of an entire album of duets rather humorously dubbed *Carryin' On with Johnny Cash and June Carter*.[6]

Despite Johnny's perceptions of betrayal, the tour went on without him. "We all got backstage and said, 'Johnny's not going to make it for maybe two, three more days. We've got to continue on. Or as June would say, "Press on," so here we go,'" remembered Western. "[Saul] said, 'I want everybody stretched. Western, you're going to emcee the show and so forth, but instead of doing fifteen or eighteen minutes, you do at least twenty, twenty-two minutes.' The Statlers were totally capable of doing a bigger show than they had with Johnny, but they were his backup singers and were billed as part of the Johnny Cash Show. Gordon Terry, everybody, stretched and made the whole show go on."

In the audience at one of those shows was Bob Wootton, a huge Cash fan who taught himself to play guitar just like Luther Perkins. Short on money, he had saved up for some time to buy tickets and travelled to the Tulsa Civic Centre to see him with his wife and their neighbours. "I paid my good money to see Johnny Cash, and he didn't show up.... But I stayed, you know, they had a guy named Johnny Western, and he did his show, he didn't do Johnny Cash's stuff, and I enjoyed it, but I was just so disappointed. I mean, I had gone to see John one other time and I enjoyed the show, but he came this time to the Coliseum and I thought, 'Hey it's gonna be good.' But he didn't show up," said Wootton.

After the troupe managed to complete four shows, with various cancellations in between, Cash suddenly returned to the tour. "It was at the threatening stage, and I guess they had called and called and called and said, 'Either-or you get straight enough to do these shows or there's going to be lawsuits and it's going to be a very, very serious problem,'" said Western.[7]

The latest string of missed dates was definitely worrying, and not just for the obvious reasons. In the latter part of 1966, Saul had painstakingly orchestrated a lucrative deal with Moeller Talent, a major Nashville-based booking outfit, to act as the exclusive agent for booking the Johnny Cash Show into rodeos and fairs the next summer. At a dead end, with Cash's reputation quickly unravelling, Saul had needed Moeller's help for his summer bookings. The deal was of particular importance because it was essentially negotiated out of sheer desperation.

One of the engagements, organized by agency head and former banker W.E. "Lucky" Moeller himself, was dubbed by Saul to be "not only the largest sum of money to ever be received for an individual C & W performance, but twice as large as any figure previously recorded."

In the meantime, unable to find spring work for Cash in the U.S., Saul had resorted to putting up his own money as a promoter, and booked him on a seven-show tour of western Canada in April of 1967. However, Johnny would make it only partway through the tour.[8]

"We were in Edmonton and he was on a rampage of pep pills, and he had a Martin, an expensive guitar, very expensive guitar," Saul told

W.E. "Lucky" Moeller and Saul Holiff sign a lucrative but ultimately ill-fated agreement to promote Johnny Cash. Oklahoma City, 1966.

author Michael Streissguth. "He was in a darkened room, and he hadn't slept for a couple of days, and he's already missed one of the dates. And they're all my dates that I'd set up because nobody wanted to book him. You know, they couldn't trust that he would be there. He took the guitar and smashed it against the wall. I had said things to provoke him. And I guess he just didn't have the nerve to hit me with the guitar so he hit it against the wall and smashed it."[9]

It was the end of the line. This time, it would be Saul who would cancel the remaining dates and simply disappear — an action he would learn to perfect over the years. "I had one of the best disappearing acts," he said. "I just felt that there was a dignity involved and I could only go so far, and when I didn't want to go any further, I just left. I don't think I abandoned him. I think he didn't even know where I was. So yes, I did, but we always got back together."[10]

It wasn't only the buyers who were exasperated with Cash's unreliability. The fans were also beginning to see through the facade of his "laryngitis," "broken ribs," and other myriad excuses. Within two weeks of Saul walking off the job in Canada, the Johnny Cash Show arrived for a gig in Waterloo, Iowa. After Cash immediately passed out in the hotel bed, Marshall and June searched his room and flushed all the pills they could find down the toilet. Together they agreed to let him sleep, hoping a solid twelve hours would do him good, and somehow pulled off the show without him. But the fans, once again, were disappointed. "I was one of the many people who walked out and requested my money back," said audience member Mrs. Ray Kunhtzi, in a letter to the editor following the show. "I really felt very sorry for the rest of the cast. I know they are all capable entertainers, but I also felt justified in asking for a refund. Johnny Cash may be a big name in entertainment, but if he had so little respect for the fans of country music in this town or in any other place he may have failed to appear, then I think he's in the wrong business. I can tell you everyone who asked for their refunds were pretty skeptical about his 'nervous condition.'"[11]

News soon came in from Lucky Moeller about the extra shows, and it wasn't good. Despite his best efforts, he was able to secure only four summer dates for Johnny. Though they were "very sympathetic to the

Johnny Cash situation," he said tactfully, they had become aware of just how much that "situation" had affected his ability to sell dates to buyers. "I tried very hard this year to sell Johnny on some of these bigger and better fairs and there was always a doubt in the buyer's mind," Moeller wrote. "They wanted to buy Johnny, but they were afraid that he would not show up at the date."[12]

Even as he continued to miss shows, Cash found time to complain about the lack of bookings to Saul, who finally unleashed his mounting frustration. "Moeller has booked only fair dates, as agreed, and after submitting you to every buyer in the business was able to come up with only four dates," Saul said. "Your professional behaviour is totally reprehensible, showing a complete disregard for the rights and feelings of everyone around you."[13]

Of the four dates Moeller had painstakingly managed to secure that summer, Johnny then went on to miss three of them.

"We did our best to convince (the buyers) that he would be there and of course were let down with these three dates, which not only served as an embarrassing situation for us and no doubt we will be hurt next season by trying to place another package with them as an agent," Moeller said. Though they did not harbour ill feelings toward Cash, they did need to respectfully request their lost commission on the eleven thousand dollars in missed dates, he added. At the Missouri State Fair, a crowd of fourteen thousand had waited in the blazing heat on a Sunday evening for "No-Show" Cash. Finally, a local couple, R.C. and JoAnn Holmes, scrambled at the last minute and managed to fill in for him onstage. But the organizers of the Illinois State Fair were angry enough about Cash's absence that they decided to sue.

As Saul struggled to mount yet another legal defence on behalf of Cash, the federal government finally launched their own $125,000 lawsuit over the forest fire. The lawsuit with Stew Carnall also continued to rage unsettled. In terms of actual managerial work, as Saul finished up preparations with promoter Mervyn Conn for another major tour of the United Kingdom, he couldn't help but feel overwhelmed. "I am the only booker in show business who sets dates, looks after box office settlements, does all of the surgical repairs on missed dates — which include myriad letters, calls, wires, and meetings, and does it all with the privilege of paying my own costs on the road exclusive of travel. This is unique," he fumed to Johnny. Not only would he now have to arrange for the repayment of Moeller's commission, but he also had to do so knowing he would never receive his own commissions on the shows that Cash blew off. Nor would he be compensated for the days and months of work involved in arranging Cash's divorce, which was now imminent. The final straw came when Cash, beset by financial problems, not only requested that Saul further cut his commission down by 5 percent but also publicly accused him of double-dealing on record sales following a show in Saginaw, Michigan.[14]

"By confronting me on Sunday night about record sales and suggesting, by innuendo, that I had contrived to cut myself in for a third, you managed to embarrass me, humiliate me, demean me, and discredit me — unnecessarily — in front of everyone in the show, not to mention [promoter] Phil Simon and, of course, those associated with him who would be aware of this episode. It placed me in the position of appearing to conspire for a lousy four or five hundred dollars," Saul wrote. Not only was Cash missing as many dates as he was playing at this point, according to Marshall Grant, but what money he did make was disappearing just as quickly on lavish purchases. "You missed $40,000 worth of dates within one year, plus the additional reimbursement costs," Saul continued. "At a time when financial pressures existed, you added both the Carter Family and Carl Perkins at an approximate extra cost of $70,000 a year. You committed yourself to a $150,000 home, purchased land, a new Cadillac, a new fence, a new bus, antique furniture [and incurred] interior decorating charges."

Though Saul questioned the logic of Cash seeking to relieve his financial burden by cutting his manager's commission (down to 10 percent after talent was deducted from receipts), Saul agreed to it, on one condition — that Cash curtail his own expenditures and, most important, *miss no more dates*.[15]

That would be a tall order for Cash, who in an attempt to meet his expenses, had incurred two sizable loans from Columbia Records that totalled $125,000, and had secured the down payment for his new home

(left to right) Saul Holiff, Johnny Cash, June Carter, and Phil Simon, backstage at the London Gardens, 1967.

in Hendersonville only when a Columbia executive acted as guarantor on the loan.[16]

Even if he cut the unnecessary expenditures completely, the divorce with Vivian cost him dearly. After his objection to the divorce was withdrawn on August 30, Vivian was eventually granted half of the income from the music Cash had made while they were married, as well as half their assets, the house in Casitas Springs, $1,000 a month in alimony, and $1,600 per month in child support. Cash was also on the hook for her $6,500 attorney's fee. "You should recall that very little has been set aside for 1967 income taxes, and that a sizable amount must yet be raised to meet them," wrote Cash's lawyer Bruce Thompson. "I feel that it would be wise for you to give immediate attention to these financial matters."[17]

Twisting in the mire of his life, with chaos pressing in on all sides, Cash was sinking. The haggling over finances with Vivian became heated and at one point boiled over regarding his purchase of a new tour bus for

$9,600. He explained to her that they needed the bus to haul not only all the members of their entourage around but their baggage and instruments as well. The plan was to keep it at Marshall's and use it only as a business vehicle, he told her. It was also worth noting, he added, its use was for his touring, which in turn generated everyone's living expenses, including the alimony and child support. Johnny explained that the cost of the bus would be taken out of their joint funds over the next three months, which remained joint until the new year, and if she objected to that, the outcome would end up negatively affecting all of their finances, including hers.[18]

It was all too much for Cash, who by this point was barely eating. "I didn't want to die, but I'd given up. I'd accepted the fact that I was killing myself, and I was going to try to enjoy it," he acknowledged. Clearly it wasn't an ideal time to kick his habit; the stress of being sober only drove him deeper and deeper into drugs. The love of June Carter was likely the only bright spot in his life, but the drugs were driving her away now, too.[19]

The struggle to keep Cash alive had become routine for June and Marshall, who mounted an ongoing effort to dispense with Cash's pill supply, chase dealers away, clean up after him, and keep him fed and rested while encouraging him to get clean. But June had finally had enough. Just as it looked like his divorce was to be finalized, she told Johnny that when their current October tour through Michigan and Indiana ended, she was leaving him.

The announcement drove him to the brink of madness. One night after a show at the Morris Civic Auditorium in South Bend, Indiana, in desperation he turned to Saul, his "fixer," the man who always seemed capable of combing out even the most tangled of messes. As tears ran down his furrowed cheeks, Johnny pulled out a pen and began to write, as the years of pain he had endured came pouring out.[20]

It was October, 21, 1967, and other than a few details and loose ends, his divorce to Vivian was now a done deal, he began. The proceedings had taken exactly a year from when he entered the case, and he admitted that only a year ago, the prospect of finally having the freedom to be with June was a dream come true; a dream that June had made him hang onto for five years. But now that dream was falling apart, he said, as it was not something she wanted anymore.

"She wants this tour, then wants free in November. To stop our life together just as it starts," he wrote. "I'll have a hell of a time getting over her, as a matter of fact, I never will. But she wants new situations, then new companionship. No man has lasted long with her."

Feeling that his manhood had been "insulted and debased," Johnny admitted he was now retaliating, pushing back against June's rejection, which had cut him deeply. Previously, the couple had discussed a plan to see Johnny's children together after the tour, and he had also pledged that once the tour had wrapped he would go into a hospital for as long as he could. "I've promised till I'm blue in the face that I'll act right in California in November. She says she can't believe me, but that means she doesn't want to believe me, that would be a step toward her marrying me," he wrote. "She's 37 and I'm almost 36. I dropped a terrible marriage and four sweet kids and half my estate thinking that June was planning to marry me and enjoy a few short years with me." But now that all seemed lost. Though much of the time June and Marshall were in cahoots to try to save Johnny's life, Johnny wrote to Saul that he saw their conspiring as nefarious. They confided in each other and swapped stories about him, he said, and he believed that Marshall only confided in her to get into her "inner circle" and "come between me and the one who means most to me." And June wanted to believe the things he told her, he added. "She thinks exactly like Marshall now, talking about me to him, telling him lies, and hearing more lies, so they'll feel justified in betraying me by using my bad habits for a reason," he said. "I'd be the first to confess my faults, except that I'm always condemned and looked down upon before I can even admit them."

In addition to requesting that he pass the letter along to June, Johnny asked Saul to tell Marshall that he didn't need him anymore, and that he planned to replace him as bass player. "Sorry to put the load on you, but unless there is an immediate admission of betrayal and an apology to me as a good man, they can't be on my show," Johnny summed up, and then said that he needed to stop crying and get some rest. "This will definitely test June's intentions, her kindness, and goodness as well as make her open up her heart to me and show me whether or not she'll leave with these lies following."[21]

It's not known if Saul passed on the message to Marshall, but Cash's bassist did not end up leaving the show — at least not at that juncture. As dire as Cash felt, this was not his rock bottom, though June's rejection certainly sent him lower than he'd ever thought possible. That bottom came when, as Cash tells it, sometime in October he decided to drive to Nickajack Cave, a vast underground system of caverns along the Tennessee River at the base of Lookout Mountain, north of Chattanooga. "I'd had enough. I hadn't slept or eaten in days, and there was nothing left of me," Cash wrote in his autobiography. "I never wanted to see another dawn. I had wasted my life. I had drifted so far away from God and every stabilizing force in my life that I felt there was no hope for me."

Hoping he would die, Cash crawled deep into the recesses of the cave for hours until his light ran out. Then he lay down, waiting for God to take him. It was at this moment that he was overcome with a sense of peace, and realized that it wasn't for him to decide his destiny, but for God. Soon, he felt the need to leave. He scrambled back through the darkness and was met at the cave's entrance by June Carter, along with his mother, standing in the sunlight with a basket of food.

Except that's not really what happened. Fond of the Mark Twain quote "Never let the truth get in the way of a good story," Cash often later pinpointed this moment as the one when God saved him from killing himself and set him on the path to redemption, though it's not clear when, amidst the touring and divorce settlements, Cash found time to get lost in the depths of Nickajack Cave. What's more, it was flooded at the time Cash was supposed to have been lying on its floor — a fact that Cash historian Mark Stielper uncovered when he checked extensive weather records for the area. As a piece of the Cash mythology, however, it works — and the symbolism inherent within the tale is an honest account of Cash's tortured psyche at the time, not least of all when he was faced with the prospect of losing June, along with everything else. But there is another event that did occur at this time, that Cash credits as a pivotal moment in both his life and his relationship to drugs.[22]

As the tour wound to an end and June's departure became imminent, Cash loaded himself up with a supply of pills, slid behind the wheel of his new Cadillac, and headed south. It had been ten days since he wrote out his confessional to Saul, and shaking off whispers that he should perhaps be committed to a hospital or rehab centre, he held his foot to the gas pedal and sped over the border into Georgia. Maybe he'd try to find old Albert Fullam, a man who had once worked the rails with Jimmie Rodgers back in the day. Or maybe he'd just drive.[23]

"Do you feel better?"

Cash started at the voice, from where he lay on his back staring at the ceiling. As he sat up, he realized he was in a jail cell.

"How did I get here?" said Cash, as the man — Lafayette Sheriff Ralph Jones — unlocked the door.

"One of the night men found you stumbling around in the streets. He brought you in so you wouldn't hurt yourself."

With the door left open, Cash followed him down the hall and into an office. A resident had spied him knocking on random farmhouse doors in a stupor and called the police.

"How much time do you think I'll get for this?" Cash asked.

Jones shook his head and handed Cash his belongings, including the pills and money they had found on him when he was arrested.

"You're doing time right now, Johnny, the worst kind," he said, and watched as Cash stuffed the pills back into his pockets. "I'm a fan of yours, Johnny. I've always admired you. It's a shame to see you ruining yourself. I didn't know you were this bad off."

"Yeah, sure," Cash said, fiddling with the waistband of his pants.

"I don't know where you got your talent from, Johnny, but if you think it came from God, then you're sure wrecking the body He put it in," Jones said, and regarded him soberly.

Cash shrugged him off, but as he stepped out into the morning sun, he took a deep look at himself. "I knew I was a better man than that. Maybe it was the reference to God that suddenly cleared my mind," Cash later wrote. "Faith had always meant a lot to me; I have tried to express it in some of my songs. But until that morning it hadn't occurred to me to turn to God for help in kicking my habit."

On his return to Nashville, Cash's determination to turn things around allowed him to quietly reunite with June and Marshall, and with a declaration that he had decided to get off pills for good, he asked for their help. "See to it that I eat regular meals. See to it that I sleep regular hours. If I can't sleep, sit and talk to me. If we run out of talk, then let's pray," he told them.[24]

At Johnny's instruction, June sought the assistance of Tennessee-based psychiatrist Dr. Nat Winston. Prior to Winston's arrival, Cash had driven his tractor close to the nearby Old Hickory Lake and toppled in. Skeletal and shivering, Cash awoke to the form of Dr. Winston beside his bed. "I've seen a lot of people in the shape you're in," he said. "And frankly, I don't think there is much chance for you. I've never known of anyone as far gone as you are to really whip it. Only you can do it, and it would be a lot easier if you would let God help you."

During the next ten days, as Cash struggled with cravings, Winston — an Appalachian music aficionado who was friends with banjo legend Earl Scruggs — came to visit the singer on a nightly basis. As Cash began his drug withdrawal, the rest of his friends kept vigil.[25]

By the new year, Johnny's fourteen-year marriage to Vivian was officially over. As the members of his troupe watched nervously for signs of relapse, none of them could have imagined that in the midst of this darkness, Cash was merely ten days away from achieving what would be the greatest success of his career thus far.[26]

11

THE PROPOSAL

It was time for a renewed focus on the music, of that Saul was certain; a beacon that always brought Cash home in the midst of all the other drama, this basis was foundering. Three years had passed since his song "Understand Your Man" had gone to number one on the country charts, though "Jackson," his duet with June, was climbing the charts along with *Johnny Cash's Greatest Hits Volume One*. But he needed new material. Weak musical efforts with Don Law in 1967, which included "Put the Sugar to Bed," co-written with Mother Maybelle, and "You Beat All I Ever Saw," only served to confirm for Saul that Cash needed a new creative direction. It was an intuition he had felt for some time. Don Law, who was past the age of retirement, simply wasn't cutting it. Producer Bob Johnston had been on Saul's radar for years, and he had nudged Cash in his direction a few times. But he needed a push.

Raised in Texas, Johnston started out as a songwriter, following in the footsteps of his mother and grandmother, and began work as a producer for smaller labels in the late 1950s. After he found a home at Columbia Records, he became known for his work with Bob Dylan, most notably on his album *Highway 61 Revisited*. The next year, he followed it up with Simon and Garfunkel's *The Sound of Silence*. At thirty-four, he was decades younger than Law, and took pride in his tendency to side with artists. He trusted their creative vision and, as a result, he took chances that older, more established executives balked at. A year earlier, as the ink dried on the ill-fated deal Saul signed with Lucky Moeller back in December of 1966, Saul had drafted a letter to Cash, advising him that now was the time to drop Law and go with Bob Johnston.[1]

Dec. 29, 1966

Dear Johnny:

Under separate cover are many things — some of which are worth careful scrutiny.

Last week when we discussed Bob Johnston and Don Law, I didn't push the point too hard, one way or the other, but I have given the whole situation considerable thought since that time, and here are my feelings, for what they are worth ...

I urge you to declare yourself immediately and go with Bob Johnston. Contrary to the various malicious rumours about him, he is too smart to treat you in a high-handed manner or come on strong in any way with you. But he is man enough to <u>stand</u> up to you and take a <u>stand</u>.

Although you've never been exactly undernourished in the area of good material or the ability to come up with same, no one is infallible, and sometimes your good judgment has wavered. Bob Johnston is musically knowledgeable and creative enough to at least present palatable and exciting ideas for your consideration. That's more than anyone has done in recent years. I know how sick and tired you are of "yes" men, and I am personally pleased that every so often some ideas of mine have eventually proved worthwhile, recording-wise. However, the time is ripe for a change, and it should be <u>now</u>.

The word must come from you, however; if you feel reluctant to perform this dichotomy personally, I will <u>tactfully</u> pass the word on to Mr. Law.

Columbia quite naturally will abide by your decision. I believe that Johnston can be the catalyst to help bring you to the next plateau that we have so frequently talked about; especially now that you are in a highly motivated state of mind.

That's my harangue for today.

Regards,
Saul Holiff[2]

The letter was copied to Columbia marketing manager Bill Gallagher, with whom Johnston was already in discussions about his desire to take over their country operations in Nashville. Around the same time, vice-president and general manager Clive Davis was offered a position as head of CBS by Goddard Lieberson, which he accepted. When the dust settled, Don Law had been pushed into retirement by Davis and was then replaced by Johnston in March. But first, Cash needed to get on board with the changes. Out of loyalty to Law he had waffled on the decision for months as Law was slowly sidelined; by the summer of 1967 Cash finally invited Johnston out to his house to talk. Inspired by Johnston's belief in his artistic vision and that, as an artist, he — and only he — knew best when it came to the direction of his music, Johnny told Saul he was ready to switch producers.[3]

By the beginning of 1968, Cash and his new producer felt ready to try new things. Cash had quietly played prisons since the mid-1950s, including at the Folsom State Prison in California the previous year, and had long toyed with the idea of recording a live album in one. Something about it appealed more to his sense of identity than, for example, a set at Carnegie Hall. Bolstered by Johnston's confidence in his ideas, Cash brought the concept to him, thinking it was likely he'd reject it. On the contrary, Johnston immediately saw its potential. After quickly phoning around to find a venue, the warden at Folsom responded that they would be delighted to have Cash back. Though, according to Johnston, he and Cash immediately encountered resistance to the idea from Columbia, a date of January 13 was soon set for the live recording.[4]

Johnny Cash performs the song "The Legend of John Henry's Hammer" in what is the only known photo of Johnny Cash performing at Folsom State Prison in 1966.

Long before his arrest in El Paso and subsequent run-ins with the law, Cash became curious about prison life after watching the film *Inside the Walls of Folsom Prison* in 1953. Though not yet experienced with much beyond the farm and the air force, he felt a natural affinity for what dark loneliness and yearning might exist in the hearts of those men who were "on the inside." Turning his inspiration into music, this concept emerged in the lyrics and content of his early hit "Folsom Prison Blues," recorded with Sun Records two years later.

This affinity for prisoners never faded for Johnny, and as the convoy of vehicles wound up the road to the imposing medieval-style fortress of Folsom State Prison — opened in 1880 — it was likely evident to all those involved just how fitting a locale it was to record Cash's first live album. "I thought people would take notice of men that have been forgotten in everyone's mind. It would be good for them to hear the men's reaction," Cash later said.

In the years since he had first thought of what it might be like to be locked away, Cash's empathy for the men inside those granite walls had only grown; he now possessed an intimate knowledge of what it was to be on the wrong side of the law, and all that experience entailed.[5]

Clad in a black leather overcoat and suit, with June at his side in a fur-cuffed coat and demure white-collared dress, Cash was nervous. Though Dr. Winston's intervention had helped immensely, he was not yet free of his addiction. In the car on the way up, Cash quietly admitted to Bob Johnston that he had swallowed handfuls of pills before he left that morning, to bolster his confidence. The significance of the performance was clear to Cash, and weighed on him. This was not a show he could flub. But perhaps it was precisely his life's recent scrape across the very bottom that provided the best preparation. No other artist was as well positioned at that point to understand the plight of the incarcerated, and that lent an authenticity to his performance that resonated with the prisoners. "Convicts are the best audiences I ever played for," Cash liked to say. The political landscape was also ripe to receive a project of this nature. As civil unrest continued to rage across America, the "law and order" backlash from police and politicians was in full force. Nowhere was this sentiment more apparent than in presidential candidate Richard Nixon's promise to America that he would herald a return to traditional values. At this point in time, to record an album within the dark heart of one of America's most notorious prisons was nothing less than a decisive act of rebellion.[6]

Johnston surveyed the crowd of approximately one thousand inmates packed into the prison cafeteria, awaiting the show. The atmosphere was understandably tense. In conferring with Cash and emcee Hugh Cherry, Johnston advised that they not go with any flowery introduction, but that Johnny should simply stride out and immediately assert himself. The result was a simple declaration that would soon become iconic — "Hello, I'm Johnny Cash."

As Cash launched into "Folsom Prison Blues," the roar of approval told him all he needed to know. There was no need to worry. He was among friends.[7]

When it comes to Saul Holiff, the most enduring mystery of the Folsom Prison show is whether he was actually even there at all. Saul had long known that Cash's talent lay in being *seen*, and that his live performances went far beyond the rich timbre of his voice or the deep earthiness of his lyrics. If they could only capture the live-wire energy of those shows, he felt certain they would have something spectacular on their hands. It was a sentiment Cash often echoed himself. Carnegie Hall, his first live recording attempt, had been a bust. The concert at Folsom State Prison would not only potentially give birth to their next major album but also mark Cash's first project with Bob Johnston. So why wouldn't Saul have attended? After all, he had been the one to push for both developments, to varying degrees. But if he wasn't present, it's likely he was busy incubating Cash's next major career move: television. Also years in the making, the relationship Saul had carefully cultivated with CBC's Stan Jacobson since 1964 had finally borne fruit.[8]

Asked to produce yet another one-hour Hank Snow special for the Canadian network, Jacobson suggested to the top brass that they instead do one on Cash. A huge fan ever since he had stood, enraptured, and watched Cash perform a pared-down version of "Don't Take Your Guns to Town" on The Ed Sullivan Show in 1959, producer Jacobson had been searching for his chance to feature Cash on the CBC. "I loved him. As a writer on Country Hoedown, I connected with him. I loved his material. It was a kinship. I can't explain it," said Jacobson.

A spot was about to come free in Jacobson's schedule in mid-February, which was timely, as Cash would be in Brantford, Ontario, around that time for a performance, said Saul. Jacobson booked him, "sight unseen," and secured the rest of the Johnny Cash Show package, which now included Carl Perkins, for approximately twenty-five thousand dollars. The two quickly sketched out ideas — immediately after the Folsom show wrapped, the troupe would be in Baltimore, Maryland. Jacobson decided then and there that he would fly out with his assistant, Mary Blackwood, to check out the performance and discuss the television special with Cash in person.

Not long after their arrival, Jacobson ran into Saul in the hotel lobby.

"So what's a Jew boy from Toronto know about country music, anyway?" said Saul, by way of introduction. Somewhat ruffled, Jacobson sized him up before responding.

"For your information, I was born in Saint John, New Brunswick, I grew up in Fredericton, and I grew up with Hank Snow and Wilf Carter,"

Jacobson informed him. "I also wrote a show called *Country Hoedown*, and I have every one of Johnny Cash's albums, both from Sun and Columbia."

"Huh. Okay then," Saul nodded, and continued on his way.

If the purpose of Jacobson and Blackwood's visit was to seek inspiration in Cash's performance, there was little to be found. "It was just a ragged performance. He was all over the place," said Jacobson. "He was great, he was loose, he was nowhere." On the way back to the hotel, Jacobson and Blackwood rode in Cash's bus as he scratched at his face, twitched uncontrollably and swigged cup after cup of black coffee. Jacobson began to feel nervous. "Mary looked at me as if to say, 'You're gonna do a show with this guy?'" he said.

The taping of the show, dubbed *The Legend of Johnny Cash* as a nod to Jacobson's feelings about the singer, was scheduled over four days in CBC Studio 7, but was quickly completed in three. It was unexpectedly smooth and drama-free. To celebrate its speedy completion, Jacobson joined Johnny, June, and Saul as they dined at the Four Seasons Hotel across the road. At the table, the mood was warm and jubilant, and the conversation soon turned to marriage. Johnny and June shared a look and then turned to Saul and Stan. "We'd love to be married in Toronto. What can you tell us?" they asked. "This has been such a wonderful experience for us, and you've been so marvellous to us, we want to be married here."

"I think you need blood tests," Jacobson said, feeling pleased. "I haven't been married yet, so I don't know, but I can find out for you."[9]

Three days later, Johnny officially proposed to June — but not in Toronto. It was February 22, 1968, and the two were onstage at the London Gardens, a modest hockey arena in Saul's hometown of London, Ontario. Five thousand people watched breathlessly from their seats on folding metal chairs set atop sheets of plywood over the ice. Though not the plushest of settings, it was here that June came full circle and finally warmed to Cash's overtures.

"Johnny, you're embarrassing me in front of all these people," she said with a laugh. Johnny pressed her for an answer. For some reason he felt more comfortable asking her in front of an audience than he would have in private. Coming out of their shock, the spectators got in on the act and began to call out for her to say yes.

Unable to continue the show until she gave him an answer, June relented. "Yes, I'll marry you," she said, and Johnny leaned down and kissed her softly. Elated, the two broke into song.[10]

At his usual post backstage, Saul couldn't help but feel swept up in the emotion. Though Saul didn't necessarily see the hometown proposal as an explicit nod to himself, Johnny was possessed of an impulsive and loving nature that often led to thoughtful overtures. "In Victoria [British Columbia], for example, he would suddenly say some very flattering things in a gracious and generous way," Saul said. "So maybe he did make this kind of dramatic step in London, and just maybe it might have been connected to us all being close together at the time." It was embarrassing to admit, even to himself, just how much these gestures meant to him. At times Saul felt almost starved for appreciation. But that night, a warm blush of happiness spread over him.[11]

As Johnny emerged backstage at the end of the show, Saul was waiting.

"How long has it been now?" he said.

"Over three months since I had a pill, Saul," said Cash.

"Well, I heard that little proposal out there tonight and let me be the first to congratulate you. You've lost a lot in the last seven years. You need June, and she needs you now. You've proven everybody wrong, including me. I thought you would be dead by now," Saul said.

"I would have been, Saul, if God hadn't saved me."

"And that brings up a subject I need to talk to you about," Saul said. "Reconciliation with God doesn't mean you are reconciled with man."

"I'm working on that, too," Cash said. Saul looked him over and put his hands in his pockets. Johnny had gained at least thirty pounds and was in better shape than he'd seen him in years.

"You might consider playing some shows for a couple of promoters who went broke when you cancelled out on them," Saul said, finally.

"Arrange them," Cash said. "Any legitimate debt I owe, I'll pay. It's more important to me to clean the slate than it is for you or anyone else."

"I doubt that." Saul smiled at Johnny, and then at June. "Who are they going to gossip about in Nashville now?"[12]

Johnny and June were married in Franklin, Kentucky, on March 1 — just one day after they were presented with a Grammy for "Jackson." Merle Kilgore, who co-wrote "Ring of Fire" with June, was the best man. Characterizing this time to Christopher Wren as "the first spring in six years that I'd seen the trees bloom," Cash liked to boast about how their reception was alcohol-free and guests like Kilgore were "high on life." As the lone dissenting voice, Marshall Grant was privately certain that Cash had not fully kicked the drugs. Worried about June's future, Grant confronted her backstage after the proposal and told her flat out that she had made a mistake. What are you doing? he had asked. Don't you remember all those years when we worked together to keep him alive?

At the wedding reception he tried again, and pointed out the tough road that lay ahead of her. Determined to make it work, she shrugged and simply answered that they would "have to face it day by day."[13]

(Mostly) clean, and with June by his side, Cash's career ascended like a bird in flight. *The Legend of Johnny Cash* aired March 24, on a Sunday night that was unfortunately timed to coincide with the Stanley Cup playoffs. Incredibly, Stan Jacobson says that when he viewed the Nielsen ratings that week, his one-hour special beat out the NHL playoffs for the number one spot. Jacobson then quickly made a copy of the tape and mailed it to Saul with a message: "You want to do something with Johnny? Canada's no different than the States."

However, Saul needed little encouragement. He was booking requests for shows as fast as they came. Cash successfully completed a tour of the Midwest, and then in May he flew to the United Kingdom for another tour Saul had arranged with Mervyn Conn.[14]

By the summer, *Johnny Cash at Folsom Prison* began a ninety-week assault on the country charts, eventually peaking at number one for three weeks during July and August. On the pop charts, it spent 122 weeks in the top two hundred. Rave reviews took up pages in the *New York Times*, *Rolling Stone*, and even *Cosmopolitan*, who called the album "an extraordinary experience" and affirmed that "the rapport between this longtime loner and the thousand inmates is crackingly clear, and Cash extends himself for them." Even *Life* magazine writer Alfred Aronowitz, who recalled that Johnny once threatened to punch him in the nose, had to concede that on the "raw" and "uncomplicated" *Folsom* album Cash sang "with the conviction of someone who has grown up believing he is one of the people these songs are about."[15]

Not everyone was thrilled about the record. As the popularity of the album soared, a few music industry insiders noticed the song "Folsom Prison Blues" bore an uncanny similarity to "Crescent City Blues," a song penned years earlier by pop composer Gordon Jenkins. Gordon filed a lawsuit after hearing Cash play the song — later characterized by his son Bruce Jenkins as a "shameless rip-off" — on television. Upon hearing a recording of Jenkins's song compared to Cash's, the similarity was clear, so Saul quietly smoothed over the issue and arranged for a seventy-five-thousand-dollar settlement, as long as the matter was not disclosed publicly.[16]

Another major blow for Cash came when close friend and Tennessee Three guitarist Luther Perkins suddenly died. In the early morning hours of August 3 he had fallen asleep on his couch with a lit cigarette between his fingers, and died two days later in hospital from the injuries sustained in the ensuing blaze. Adding to the turmoil was the fact that Luther had called Cash late on the night of his death asking him to come over, but Johnny had put it off, thinking he could go by in the morning. The devastation was akin to the loss of his brother Jack, but somehow Cash weathered these setbacks without descending back into the depths of full-blown addiction, though he didn't remain fully clean either.

In the wake of their newly spoken vows and Cash's ongoing substance abuse struggles, June and Johnny both turned increasingly to each other and their faith as a guiding force in their lives. During the long nights at Cash's bedside in Hendersonville as he endured the ten-day torment of withdrawal, Dr. Winston asked June tough questions about what changes she, too, was prepared to make in her relationship with Johnny. Proud and independent, June examined the way she had lived much of her life and concluded that she would embark on a new path that focused on Johnny and their home life rather than her career. After seventeen years, she resigned from the Grand Ole Opry. Beset by guilt over her affair with Johnny and the failure of her two previous marriages, which had each given her a child, June also vowed to further immerse herself in God as a way to sanctify their union. With her encouragement, Cash followed suit, and this influence began to bleed into his creative choices, most notably in his proposal for the follow-up to *Folsom* — an original gospel album, recorded live in Israel.[17]

Ever since Cash — then an appliance salesman — had first stood sheepishly in the waiting room of Sun Records to request a meeting with Sam Phillips, he had done so with the desire to record a gospel album. At the time, Phillips quickly squashed the concept as not commercially viable, but the idea had never left Cash's mind. Just before he and June had visited Israel in 1966, after their first tour of England, their mission looked clear. "I'm going to spend a week in the Holy Land, tracing the paths of Christ, seeing all the places, getting the inside information, such as might exist for myself, and come up with the dialogue and songs for an album called *The Holy Land*," Cash told their friend, writer Dixie Deen. "I'm going to research and dig up the very earliest religious songs ever known to man, such as a song that was written during the time of Christ, if we can find one." As Cash's creative and financial power expanded with the success of *Folsom*, it felt like the time was right. It seemed that in the torment of the last six years he had lived his life for the devil, and he now wanted to show, in no uncertain terms, that he was living it for the Lord. Once again he found support in Johnston, who suggested he take June to Israel for a honeymoon, armed with a tape recorder and a camera to take down their ideas. After completing their second tour of the United Kingdom with a string of sold-out shows in England, the couple flew to Israel. They returned home flush with inspiration.[18]

If Columbia was uncertain about the religious turn Cash had taken, Saul was equally dubious. The prison show had been a stroke of genius; it not only positioned Cash as a "man of the people," no matter how down-trodden, but it also capitalized on his darker, outlaw side in a way that provoked a strong public reaction. "With a face that might have been ripped off a wanted poster, a voice that sounds as though it's coming through a bandanna mask, songs that may as well be fired from six-guns and a Bible under his writing arm, Johnny Cash has gone thundering through his career like a night-riding missionary, rousing the country music industry," Alfred Aronowitz had dramatically declared in his *Folsom* review.

But would his fans be as enthusiastic if the rest were stripped away and it was only … the missionary part? Saul was not convinced, and though Johnston's support was valuable, Cash didn't need another creative yes-man. Criticism was crucial. All things considered, Saul was too busy fielding and directing the renewed interest in Cash to pay it much attention quite yet. Offers for shows, television spots, documentaries, and even books flooded in as sales of *Johnny Cash at Folsom Prison* passed the five-hundred-thousand mark.

Now mostly unfettered by the limiting and draining influence of drugs, Cash went from success to success. A triumphant sold-out return to Carnegie Hall on October 23 permitted *New York Times* writer Robert Shelton — an early supporter of both Cash and Bob Dylan (who was also in the audience) — to finally review his performance as intended.

"Soul music of a rare kind — country soul from the concerned and sensitive white south — that Northerners tend to forget — was heard last night at Carnegie Hall as Cash made a stirring comeback to New York," Shelton wrote. "[Cash] doesn't hide from the fact that his career went under a cloud in the early nineteen-sixties. His performance was testimony that his own personal bouts with illness and control have been resolved, putting him at as strong a level as he has had since the middle nineteen-fifties."[19]

The remarkable part was, of course, that he was now even stronger, though the comparison was apt. Cash had not only regained the composure and clear-eyed focus of his early days, but he was now also possessed of a veteran stage presence and a solid, wide-ranging repertoire of music to draw from. It was a combination that was unstoppable. As Saul keenly continued to cultivate the possibility of a syndicated television show, a fascinating prospect emerged from Granada Television, an independent television company based in Manchester, England.

It was a nondescript day in November of 1968 when a group of creative visionaries sat around a conference table in the ground-floor office of Granada's London base in Golden Square to dream up ideas. Three months earlier, the producer and director of Granada's current affairs show *World in Action*, Jo Durden-Smith, had convinced the company's head of programming to allow him to produce a series of shows centred on the burgeoning 1960s music scene. Durden-Smith had argued that for thirty-nine weeks of the year, *World in Action* dominated the prime time slot on commercial television, so why not let his team create top-notch programming for the other thirteen weeks?

The idea was primarily pitched on the basis of ratings, but Durden-Smith was personally even more ambitious: he wanted to not only shift the culture within Granada but also create programming that would change the world. Already a proven documentarian who had delivered hard-hitting pieces on race politics in America and student revolutionaries in Berlin, he was given the green light.

This proposal came at a heady time for the entertainment industry in Britain, in which the old formulaic structures were crumbling. The unexpected arrival of bands like the Beatles and the Rolling Stones had the old guard so thoroughly shaken that they had turned to young, innovative content creators like Durden-Smith for advice on how to navigate this brave new world. As a result, in many cases these creative visionaries were suddenly given access to sizable budgets, facilities, and equipment that was unfettered by bureaucracy and oversight from more conservative influences.

It was Geoffrey Cannon — a twenty-eight-year-old creative consultant and vanguard rock critic who penned a weekly column for *The Guardian* — who first proposed the idea. One morning at about 10:30, he called Jon Cott and David Dalton, the other members of the creative team Durden-Smith had assembled, over to the table in their London-based office.

"I have a bad idea, and you will hate it, and it's against what we do, but I know it will be a hit," said Cannon. "How about getting Johnny Cash to do a second gig at Folsom Prison, and film it?" Shooting had just wrapped on their first project, *The Doors Are Open*, a documentary about the Doors and their performance with Jefferson Airplane at the Roundhouse in London's Chalk Farm. Filmed in black and white and interspersed with footage of street riots in Grosvenor Square, marching bands, and the Vietnam War, it was unlike anything that had ever yet been shown on national network television.

Could they do that with Cash? As Cannon put it, "The journalist in me, which I tried to suppress, could smell a story." Secretly though, Cannon hoped the idea would be swiftly rejected by his co-workers and that would be the end of it, and they could move on to other things. At that time in Britain, according to Cannon, those who were "in the know" viewed country and western music as unappealing and hopelessly redneck. The men instead responded with mild interest, and after a bit of shuffling someone dug up the phone number for Saul Holiff.

"John has no interest in going back to Folsom," Saul politely informed him. They were already in the midst of production for another Cash film with director Robert Elfstrom called *The Man, His World, His Music,* and Cash was currently on tour through Missouri, Wisconsin, and Iowa. When that finished, among other gigs, he was scheduled for a ten-day tour through the northwestern States and Canada that extended into December, and *then* he would visit the St. Francis reservation in South Dakota, with a special stop at the Wounded Knee Battlefield. On December 14 Cash was set to play the Tennessee State Prison, and then the entire troupe would depart for a two-week tour of the Far East in January. Even as far as February he was booked at the Florida State Fair, among other dates. Cannon thanked him and hung up.

"Having made the dud call, the idea started to worm its way into my consciousness, and I began to see that actually this was a good idea, for nothing like a concert made by a man who may have done time, singing songs about desperation to no-hopers and lifers in prison, had ever been transmitted on national networked television, and 'never-been-done-before' was one of our touchstones," said Cannon. A couple of days later, he picked up the phone again and called Saul's office in London, Ontario.

Still cordial, Saul reiterated that the situation had not changed; they were not interested. As Cannon prepared to hang up again, he heard Saul add, "but John is going to San Quentin. He'd be happy to make a film with you there." It was one of those life-defining moments, said Cannon, and as he held the phone to his ear, heart pounding, he knew that how he handled the next few seconds would be crucial in determining which direction this would head.

· "Um, hum, well, maybe that might be interesting, Saul. We'll think it over, no rush. When is a good time to get back to you?" Cannon replied. As he put the phone down, he called to the others and they gathered around the table. "We can make a film of Johnny Cash at San Quentin," he told them. For a moment, no one said anything, and then they all "stormed out to Bianchi's in Old Compton Street and over a five-hour lunch got pie-eyed on Elena Salvoni's wine and filled her ashtrays. On expenses — we took turns to entertain one another," he recalled. Back at the office, he phoned Saul again. "Okay, we've discussed it, and we're interested. Let's do it."[20]

12

THE CRASH

Striding in unison down the long hallway at Chicago's O'Hare Airport, Saul and Johnny were headed for a flight to Atlanta. They each toted brand new matching "Benny" kits, which were large travel bags about two feet long, that could hold as much as a week's worth of clothing. As they walked, the unexpected figure of Shel Silverstein approached. A formidable man, not unlike a dark-bearded sea captain with a great, bald head, he was a talented singer-songwriter and author of children's books, but was best known then for his work as *Playboy* magazine's travelling cartoonist.

"He had a song, he had it crumpled up on a piece of paper, and he shuffled around and said that he had this song and he handed it to Johnny, who shoved it down to the bottom of his Benny kit in amongst the debris and coffee stains and whatever," said Saul. The song, scribbled out on a sheet of lined paper, was an irreverent and humorous piece called "A Boy Named Sue," which traced the travails of a man given the unfortunate name of "Sue" by a father who had been absent most of his life, and the confrontation that eventually ensues between father and son.

As they pored over the song in the airport café, Cash pulled a jar of Chase & Sanborn instant coffee out of his Benny kit and ladled spoonfuls of it into his brewed coffee. It just might work as part of his set list for the upcoming San Quentin concert on February 24, Johnny thought. At first he had brushed off the idea of recording another prison concert, telling Saul he had no intention of producing a sequel to *Folsom*. "I don't want to repeat myself," he had said with a shrug. But the more Saul negotiated with Granada, the more both he and Cash could see its potential. *Why should we limit this to a one-time TV show airing?* Saul thought. *Why not do a live recording and turn it into an album?*

Once Johnny agreed, Saul turned to Columbia, who required more convincing. Their ambivalence was outrageous, Saul later told Barbara. "When he had settled down sufficiently to be able to deal with Columbia's unexpected response to the idea, Saul called them again and patiently laid out all the reasons why they should seriously reconsider their position in the matter," Barbara recalled. "Well, first they said that Granada should have to pay for the recording of the show, and then, one by one, tried every little cheap trick they could think of to have Columbia get away with avoiding every other cost that might be reasonably associated with such a project. Saul had to ride them on every tight-fisted point they raised, to finally bring everything to a satisfactory arrangement."

Saul and Barbara Holiff look over some papers in Saul's office, London, Ontario, 1968.

Saul felt that the Americans weren't enterprising enough to recognize that another live prison record could make it — even after Folsom Prison. But this was a British endeavour from beginning to end, and he was impressed by the company's audacity and sense of vision. It was an idea he was prepared to fight for. The documentary concept was ambitious, and distinguished itself from what Cash had done previously. Both Durden-Smith and director Michael Darlow envisioned that Cash's concert could be woven into a deeper examination of the American prison system and inmate psychology. It would be presented as a sociological study of sorts, and include interviews with prisoners on death row.[1]

An agreement was eventually reached to not only film but also record the show. In the subsequent negotiations with Columbia, director Darlow suggested they request a 4 percent cut in the recording. Anticipating it wouldn't amount to much, the head executive at Granada shrugged this off and instead instructed that they ask for just eight hundred British pounds in cash, a deal Columbia was only too happy to accept.[2]

As the date at the San Quentin State Prison grew nearer and Cash prepared for a January 15 departure for Japan, Taiwan, and Vietnam, Saul received news that there was major movement on the television front. After some negotiation, a deal had been struck with production company Screen Gems — taping on *The Johnny Cash Show* would begin in the spring and debut on ABC TV over the summer as a fill-in for the musical variety show *Hollywood Palace*. From Johnny and Saul's side, certain conditions were laid out and accepted, among them that the show be taped at Ryman Auditorium in Nashville, and that CBC's Stan Jacobson be brought onto the team as a writer.

Jan. 6, 1969

Dear Johnny:
For several reasons of varied importance, I feel that I should not go on the Far East tour. I arrived at this decision reluctantly, and it is emphatically not based on concern for my safety in Vietnam, or any other considerations except what I am going to spell out below:

The sudden decision to start taping your new series in April and May allows me only five working days (prior to leaving for the Far East) to cancel all the April and May bookings. This is not enough time. Some of those dates are rather involved, and will create the need for calls, return calls and more calls....

The sudden surge in your television activities comes just before our departure. Contractual agreements have to be made and agreed upon on *The Johnny Cash Story*, the television series, the prison spectacular and the upcoming Kraft and Glenn Campbell shows. I cannot be incommunicado in some place like Okinawa for 18 days....

Yours truly,
Saul Holiff[3]

To make matters more complicated, Saul was scheduled to move his home office, a job that couldn't be left entirely to Barbara, as her sister had become seriously ill and she was apprehensive about it. In his absence, Marshall Grant would handle all their tour details, like the contract and itinerary, as well as the collection of the nightly proceeds. As he signed the letter, Saul felt a sense of conflict. As someone who performed well under pressure, it was unusual for him to tap out on tours or important engagements. But aside from the very real priorities of Johnny, the television show, and Barbara and the kids, Saul was privately struggling with his own internal strife and it threatened to overwhelm him. Deeply invested to the tune of tens of thousands of dollars in a variety of airline stocks, it felt as though his blood pressure could be graphed in sync with the stock market's every fluctuation. The last several years had been particularly brutal. To cope, Saul often locked himself in his study and sat or lay on his sofa to tape-record long confessionals. It was cathartic, and served a similar function to psychiatric sessions. Drawn to gadgetry, over the years he had acquired all means of recording devices as they emerged, including a large reel-to-reel recorder he had set up in his office. Lately he had taken to utilizing a more modern and portable Sony three-headed recorder he'd picked up in Japan. It was useful to record events and their impacts on his psyche, not only for therapeutic reasons but also as documentation. During some drug-addled conversations in previous years, Saul had asked June to be a witness so that there was no confusion later about what had been agreed upon. Though these days he was more reliable, the need to record things in some capacity remained relevant as life with Johnny moved faster and became more lucrative.

Though he often confided in Barbara, it was never easy for Saul to discuss emotional issues with other people in a way that was satisfying. Letters worked better and allowed for the words to flow more smoothly from his mind, and the hush of a listening tape recorder worked much the same way; it allowed a sense of privacy and openness that was otherwise elusive. And now, with the movement of the stock market causing such distress, he was in dire need of some catharsis.

"I had gone through some real terrific emotional traumas, of reacting, severe reactions of fear, of fear to the point of nervous bowel movements, of buying stock and having them react violently and being desperately wrong. I remember losing ten thousand dollars in one week on shorting a whole bunch of stocks, I think airline stocks again, and they reacted totally the opposite of what I expected, they all went up. I think I lost somewhere between ten and eleven thousand dollars in forty-eight hours. My experiences in the stock market have been one series of, total series of, calamities," Saul confessed to his tape recorder one evening as he sipped his drink — a wonderful port from Cockburn's Port House in Portugal. In way over his head, Saul was borrowing heavily and racking up hour after hour of his time at home analyzing and making calculations, studying reports and entering various stock transactions.

When Cash returned from Japan in early February, Saul joined him on the road for a series of shows in the southern United States before heading northwest with him for a string of dates in California. Barbara accompanied Saul on the road, and they met up with Stan Jacobson in Monroe, Louisiana, where further discussions ensued around the television show. When the southern dates finished, Saul and Barbara headed to San Diego, for Johnny's next show and where Saul was scheduled for a complete physical at the Scripps Clinic. Prior to their arrival, he had eagerly anticipated their check-in at the El Cortez Hotel, as not only was it reputed to be the best in the city, it would also allow him to settle in and check his stocks. But Saul was bitterly disappointed. "It was a shitty, cruddy joint. We were suffering from extreme fatigue and everything was just a trauma. And by then, by the first day that we went into the hospital, the airline stock had started to go down. And by the time we got out of the hospital the airline stocks had gone down substantially and I was starting to get very, very nervous," Saul said.

Before Cash's concert, Saul and Barbara met with Granada's Michael Darlow and Jo Durden-Smith to go over the final details of the February 24 San Quentin show, which was in two days.

Darlow cut a clean, gentlemanly, well-turned-out figure, while Durden-Smith, who was startlingly tall, was the complete opposite, adorned in head-to-foot technicolour psychedelia that was topped off with a long ponytail. Barbara couldn't help but stare. She'd never actually personally encountered anyone dressed in the outlandish 1960s garb that was fashionable in some circles.

After San Diego they flew to Los Angeles to meet up with friend and promoter Marlin Payne and his wife, and by the time they disembarked, Saul's self-esteem had plunged as precipitously as his airline stocks. In a panic, he realized that he stood to lose a great deal of money. As they carried on with their scheduled activities the outside world seemed to pass by in a meaningless blur, oblivious to his internal turmoil. *I can't seem to remember a goddamned thing. What was that Hebrew phrase I just read about — "zachor" — to remember?* Saul thought. *As George Santayana wrote in* The Life of Reason: *"Those who cannot remember the past are condemned to repeat it." I experienced terrible emotional discomfort from my mistakes previously in the stock market, and here I am, on the threshold of another desperate mistake.* He felt humiliated by his own irresponsibility. The next day he and Barbara left for San Quentin.[4]

If the fortress of Folsom State Prison was intimidating, it was a playground compared to the notorious San Quentin. A maximum security facility located twelve miles north of San Francisco, it not only housed some of the state's most violent inmates, but was also home to its only death row, where prisoners were put to death in a grisly apple-green gas chamber.[5]

Two shows were originally scheduled, but by mid-January associate warden Jim Parks requested that Cash perform only once due to the security complications inherent in coordinating two audiences. After rigorous security checks, Saul and Barbara entered San Quentin well before showtime. The open-air northern dining hall was empty and laid out with benches and tables arranged in long, straight rows. Once Barbara was settled in her seat, stage left of the auditorium, Saul left her alone and went to his usual post backstage. From where she sat, Barbara's eyes travelled around the room. Posters had been made up in the prison print shop to advertise the show, which simply read "San Quentin welcomes Johnny Cash, Feb. 24 in the mess hall." At the bottom in tiny lettering it added, "BEST BEHAVIOUR ADVISED." At ceiling height she noticed a catwalk covered by wire mesh, behind which stood a number of guards with guns at the ready should there be any riotous behaviour among prisoners. Above one of the speakers, fifteen feet above the floor, a fork was impaled into the Celotex soundproofing — a relic of some mess hall scuffle, perhaps. She shivered slightly and rubbed the back of her neck. Another guest was soon admitted — a woman — and upon passing was introduced as a contributor for *Time* magazine. She took a seat about four rows ahead of Barbara. The prisoners were then given entry to the hall. One by one, they silently filed in and took their chairs. The crowd was slightly larger than at Folsom, with about 1,500 inmates in attendance. A prickling, uneasy sensation suddenly came over Barbara. Glancing over her shoulder, she noticed many of the men's eyes fixated on her. "Suddenly I had thoughts that most of these men had not been in the same room with a woman for many years, and I knew I had to dispel such notions or my nervousness would become apparent," Barbara said. She quickly looked away, but could still feel their steady gaze on the back of her head.[6]

The anxiety onstage was apparent too. The atmosphere seemed even more tightly wound than it had been at Folsom, perhaps due to the presence of the television cameras. After a couple of opening numbers from Carl Perkins and June Carter, Cash appeared in a blue open-collared shirt, long black coat, and grey pants. Armed with a set list that included several new songs, he delivered the now-signature introduction, "Hello, I'm Johnny Cash," and launched into "Big River." As the men roared in response, the energy in the room was so dense it was almost uncomfortable. As the show progressed, Johnny ribbed the guards and joked with prisoners, much to their delight. In looking for a red notebook in his briefcase, he quipped that it was "in my kit back there, where I got all my dope — I mean, where I got all my things," referencing his previous arrests, which only served to amp up the adrenaline in the room. By the time he got to the first of his new songs, "Starkville City Jail" — penned the day before the show and peppered with colourful lyrics based on his 1965 arrest in Starkville, Mississippi — there was an edge of rowdiness in the crowd. Ever the showman, Cash carefully maintained and amplified this tension as the show progressed. The next new song, "San Quentin," had been written at Michael Darlow's request, and though Cash was initially lukewarm on the idea, he followed through and it ended up being a daring indictment of life in the prison. As he made the declaration that San Quentin should rot and burn in hell, some men laughed at the audacity of it, and others erupted in cheers. Cash then launched into a second version of the song to guarantee a good recording, and the men continued to yell until they were hoarse. Granada's camera operators jostled to take in the scene, and captured more than one prisoner's eyes as they shone with a mixture of wistfulness and rage. At the song's finish some prisoners mounted the tables and chairs, shouting. Another inmate silently raised a closed fist in the black power salute. The guards shifted and glanced at each other, hands on their guns. The response of the prisoners hit Cash like a wave. In the sheer, teetering power of that moment, he felt certain they could have been led into a full-scale riot had he said the word, and confessed later to Bob Johnston that he had been "tempted."[7]

About a week before the show, Cash had hosted a party at his home in Hendersonville that was attended by Bob Dylan, Kris Kristofferson, Joni Mitchell, and Shel Silverstein, among others. It was then that he first heard "A Boy Named Sue" as Silverstein had intended it to be played. Onstage at San Quentin, on the spur of the moment, Cash rummaged around in his briefcase and pulled out the lyrics, likely shoved in there by June before he left. He laid the sheet on the floor, clearly intending to play the song, though they had never even rehearsed it. Carl Perkins and Marshall Grant quickly conferred and agreed to just go along with it.[8]

"That night, we had no monitors. The band couldn't hear *what* was goin' on. Finally, Carl Perkins started pickin' a few chords and the rest of us just joined in, like," said drummer Fluke Holland.

"The recording took place with Johnny sitting on a stool with the yellow page down on the floor and they had run through to try and get some idea of how they were going to do this, and the prisoners were in there going wild, I mean they really did," said Saul. "He recorded it, without another take, and with a lousy sound system, in primitive conditions, and that was the way it was released."[9]

This last-minute decision to play a novelty song that was not even included in the original set list would soon transform Cash from a successful career country singer into an international superstar. But as the phenomenal triumph of both *Johnny Cash at San Quentin* and the single "A Boy Named Sue" bore down on them all like a freight train, Saul hit his own rock bottom.

The day after San Quentin, Cash continued on his California tour for the rest of February, criss-crossing the state with dates in Salinas, Oakland, and Anaheim before he travelled on into Nevada and Arizona. It was during this tour that Saul struck an agreement with promotional company Artist Consultants to take on some of the dates and assist with the bureaucratic details he found tiresome. At the helm of the company were rock 'n' roll promotional veterans and partners Lou Robin and Alan Tinkley, who had also promoted the Kingston Trio, the Beatles, Simon and Garfunkel, and Bill Cosby, and who wanted to branch out into country music.

Thirty-nine-year-old Robin, who got his start promoting acts like Duke Ellington while he was still in college, had been aware of Cash for some time but until then had steered clear due to his unstable reputation. With the success of *Folsom*, however, his interest was sparked. "It showed he was probably getting more dependable and would show up for the concerts, where the previous ten years he wasn't," Robin said. "Booking him was very dodgy." As a result of their interest, a radio promoter named Barbara John arranged a meeting with Saul, Lou Robin, and Alan Tinkley in the summer of 1968, during which they bought the February dates for Cash and his entire entourage at five thousand dollars a night. Saul especially appreciated Robin's involvement in arranging many of the details for the San Quentin show, which relieved a considerable portion of the niggling work he disliked. It also allowed him to test out the mettle of these new promoters, whose reputation in the business was one of honesty and financial accountability. They proved to exceed his expectations. Robin, in turn, was also so pleased with the turnout at Cash's subsequent concerts after San Quentin that following a sold-out show in Oakland he felt compelled to offer Cash an additional five-thousand-dollar bonus at the end of the night. It was an overture Cash never forgot, and a strategic move that Saul found impressive. For Robin, however, it was just good business.

"We made so much money that night that we felt that the five-thousand-dollar fee wasn't enough, for what we made," he said. "We just wanted to be a little different than any other promoter."[10]

On the post–San Quentin tour, Cash was not only in capable hands with Robin, he was also in better shape than ever — and it looked as though everything Saul had envisioned, endured through, and fought so hard to manifest was imminent. But internally, Saul was disintegrating. After the San Quentin tour, he and Barbara flew to Los Angeles so that she could get a flight back to the children in London and he could rejoin the tour. As they checked in at the Hotel Continental, Saul felt himself sinking even deeper. The city was thick with smog, and the smell of food rising up the back of the hotel repulsed him. They moved to a different room, and within minutes Saul realized that he had left his housecoat on the back of the door; he quickly went back, but it had already been stolen. In an attempt to lift his mood they went shopping, but he couldn't even find the emotional strength to meet the eye of the man who worked there. Saul recounted what happened next in his recorder.

> I drove Barbara to the airport, and it was almost a traumatic experience for me to see her off. I desperately didn't want to be alone. I suppose I was at one of the lowest points in years. Now, get this for a sheer idiotic condition: Johnny is on the verge of a major breakthrough. He is not on the verge, he has broken through. He has just recorded at San Quentin, but *Folsom Prison*

Blues is number one. *San Quentin* hasn't even happened. "A Boy Named Sue" hasn't even happened, and Johnny is already on the verge of being a star. We've already had a meeting, and there's already going to be a television series in the summer. Uh, I'm on the threshold of making a great deal of money, and what's happening to me? I'm falling apart, physically and emotionally. I'm fat, I'm drinking too much, I have no exercise. The doctor has warned me in every conceivable way.

It is not a very pretty picture and, uh, and here I am, in, in … living at the Continental for three or four days. Jeopardizing my situation seriously with Johnny, being absent when I shouldn't be absent, threatening my very position with him. And in the meantime, [I'm] on the verge of virtually being wiped out by being in an enormous debit position in the market with an incredible amount of margin and paying a huge amount of interest and watching these stocks starting to plunge downwardly.

Oh, it was a desperate time. I remember I was unable to sleep. I'd go down to the coffee shop. I couldn't even look the waitress in the eye. My skin tingled and prickled, I lay in the room and I was agonizingly uncomfortable. The inaction, the loneliness, the self-disgust and the jeopardizing my kids' future and financially risking suicide, all of this coming together, all of it spelling virtual disaster at the time.[11]

At this point there was nothing that could stop Cash's stratospheric ascent, however, and despite Saul's instability he couldn't help but rise with it like a tide. *Johnny Cash at San Quentin* was released on June 7 to coincide with the debut of his new television show, and by August, "A Boy Named Sue" had hit number two on the pop charts and number one on the country charts, and went on to chart all over the world.

"It turned him from a pretty successful act to a superstar," Saul said. "I mean, we certainly went from a contract of $1,250 a night, with advertising off the top, to a hundred thousand dollars a run, for one night, at a time when that was an awful lot of money."[12]

With the attention came offers of all varieties. A.J. Perenchio, president of talent agency Chartwell Artists, took it upon himself to shop Cash around and presented Saul with an offer from the Bonanza Hotel in Las Vegas. They requested Cash for a three-year, $360,000 contract, in an overture that puzzled Saul.

"We don't seek agency affiliation at this time, and I'd like to go on record that we haven't authorized any agency to submit Johnny in Las Vegas or anywhere else," Saul wrote back to Perenchio in his refusal letter, somewhat amazed. The offers were welcome but also left a bitter taste in Saul's mouth. Just two years prior he was forced to book Cash in hockey arenas and high school gymnasiums because no one would touch him. At times it had felt that aside from the loyal members of Cash's troupe and his dedicated fans, he was the only one who had been willing to do battle on Cash's behalf. Now they were all swarming like birds of prey.[13]

May 7, 1969
Dear Johnny,

I am getting calls from many agencies. They are dangling all kinds of attractive offers in front of me, and are seeking out such offers without being authorized to do so. They are, in a way, like vultures, only what they are selling is alive, well and thriving. THEY WERE NOT AROUND WHEN WE NEEDED THEM — AND WE DON'T NEED THEM NOW.

These agencies (including William Morris) like to jump on a bandwagon and share in the good times without having done anything to contribute to the development of the artist or artists involved. They are predatory opportunists and, except for the very isolated instances, money paid out to them is money down the drain. Their gimmick is holding out the lure of movies and other similar inducements, plus their professional know-how.

This — as in an expression that you introduced to me many years ago — is a SNOW JOB.

I don't want you becoming a football in the business, with various agents scrambling around in an undignified manner, muddying up the waters and causing prospective buyers confusion and uncertainty.

I hope you appreciate the above, and the chaos that would result if steps are not taken to avoid it, and further that you support me in helping to take such steps. If you're a winner (and you are!) the doors are open and I could walk through them on your behalf as well as any agent in New York or Los Angeles.

Regards,
Saul Holiff

When word got out that a Cash biography might be in the cards, Saul was inundated with aggressive offers on that front, too. The first was from editor Bob Cornfield at the Dial Press, as established publishing house founded by Scofield Thayer, editor and owner of *The Dial* literary magazine, which had been around for at least forty years. Thoroughly charmed by Saul's hospitality during a recent visit to Los Angeles, in his offer Cornfield wrote that his visit there had not only been fantastic, but "for a boy from Brooklyn who never dared hope to get further than Ebbets Field, it was boggling as well."

The most urgent overture came from publishing giant Simon & Schuster, who in a flurry of letters and telegrams communicated in no uncertain terms that they were "VERY ANXIOUS TO DISCUSS CASH AUTOBIOGRAPHY." For his part, Cash wasn't so keen. Reconciled with his daughters, the summers they now spent waterskiing and making peach ice cream were the highlights of his life, and he wasn't particularly motivated to shoulder even more projects.[14]

The Dial Press tapped veteran journalist and *Look Magazine* senior editor Christopher Wren as their ideal candidate to author the book, as he had just written a lengthy profile of Cash, but he was also reluctant. Already close friends with Johnny, he was a natural fit to write it for Dial, and was just completing his first book, *The Super Summer of Jamie McBride.*

As Simon & Schuster's editor Michael Korda continued to barrage Saul with telegrams and letters that verged on the poetic ("THERE IS A SEASON AND A TIME FOR EVERY PURPOSE UNDER HEAVEN A TIME TO SOW A TIME TO REAP STOP THIS IS THE TIME TO START ON JOHNNY CASH'S BOOK"), Wren flew to Tennessee on his own dime to confirm his thoughts with Cash.

"I don't want to have a book done," Cash said. They were out in his garden in Hendersonville, picking beans. Wren had been sleeping in the cabin on the property.

"No, I don't really want to write it," agreed Wren, who would soon depart for Vietnam to cover the war once his current book was completed. That admission out of the way, the two men continued to pull at the slim green pods in peace. Free to speculate, they began to talk about what would go in a book if, theoretically, there ever was one. It would have to involve full access to friends and family, including Vivian, and no editorial control from Cash. On those points Wren felt certain. They had a lot of similar ideas, actually, and in fact the more they talked about it, the more Wren could see it as a tangible possibility. In spite of himself, he began to feel excited. Cash gave him a long look.

"Well, I think you should do it," Cash said.

"Okay, I will," Wren agreed with a laugh.[15]

"Columbia is having not only its greatest year in the company's history, but in the history of the recording business — and one of the main reasons for this bonanza is Johnny Cash," Columbia Records president Clive Davis proclaimed to the *Nashville Banner* in mid-October of 1969. "The man Cash is phenomenal in the true sense of the word." Cash was selling more records than any other recording artist in the world, including the Beatles, added Davis, who at that time was arguably the most influential man in music. *Folsom* had sold 1.75 million to date, and *San Quentin* was hot on its heels with 1.3 million in sales. Days earlier, Cash completed his fifth sold-out show in three days and went on to sweep the 1969 Country

Music Awards, picking up a record five awards that included Entertainer of the Year, Male Vocalist of the Year, and Album of the Year.[16]

At times, all this action was a drain for the performer, whose popularity was outpacing his ability to keep up. "Everybody wants me to double up — do two shows in one night — and I'm just one person," an exhausted Cash told reporter Blaik Kirby backstage in October. "This year I've done at least 250 concerts. That's the way I've been workin' for years; but with all the other things, the personal appearances, song writing, recording, television guest spots, writin' liner notes and makin' a movie, it's just too much."

The minimum Saul charged for a show rose steadily month by month; by the fall it had increased fivefold to twenty-five thousand dollars as records continued to fly off the shelves. The size of audiences followed suit and went from seventeen thousand at a County Fair in Allentown, Pennsylvania, on August 4 and 5 to twenty-six thousand at the Minnesota State Fair on August 26. That month, the Recording Industry Association of America certified *San Quentin* and "A Boy Named Sue" as gold records,

(left to right) Saul Holiff, unknown, Johnny Cash, June Carter Cash, in 1969 at a Screen Gems/Columbia Records press conference in Los Angeles. It was at this press conference that both Johnny and Saul were presented with gold records for "A Boy Named Sue" and the launch of Cash's television show was announced.

which were presented to Johnny at a joint press conference the following month by Irving Townsend of Columbia Records.

As Cash's manager, Saul received copies of each gold record, and further vindication of his efforts came in the form of Screen Gems International's announcement at the conference that ABC had added *The Johnny Cash Show* to its network schedule for the fall. The vision he had obsessed over for almost a decade was emerging as a reality: Cash would be broadcast into the nation's living rooms on a weekly basis for the next three years.

"I've always thought it ironic that it was a prison concert, with me and the convicts getting along just as fellow rebels, outsiders and miscreants should, that pumped up my marketability to the point where ABC thought I was respectable enough to have a weekly network TV show," Cash noted in his second autobiography.[17]

This respectability translated across the board, and Saul's phone rang off the hook as the media wrestled over one another to get a piece of Cash. Appearing in a slew of publications like the *Globe and Mail*, *Toronto Star*, and *TV Guide*, he was also granted a major profile in *Time* and featured on the cover of *Life* magazine. As for Saul, he hit his own personal best on November 10 when a show he produced for Cash at Toronto's Maple Leaf Gardens sold out before the box office even opened, beating out the previous attendance record set there by the Beatles.

"Johnny Cash is at the point of nearly hysterical, almost religious popularity," reviewer Jack Batten declared in his review of the Gardens show for the *Toronto Star*. "Flash bulbs popped like sniper fire, girls coiffed and styled like so many Jeannie C. Rileys clapped themselves silly, bucks of all ages whistled and stomped, and everyone in the house, all 18,000 of them, beamed for pure joy."[18]

It had been a beautiful evening — a Saul Holiff creation, complete with his signature pre-show cocktail party, this time high in the Sutton Place salon, replete with curvy cigarette girls and fawning fans. Backstage, Christopher Wren slouched in a corner with a tape recorder as June Carter, swathed in mink and burgundy satin, gave out lighting instructions. She had recently, triumphantly, announced her pregnancy after the baby was conceived during a summer trip with Johnny to the Virgin Islands. On the road with the Cash show, Wren's wife, Jaqueline, who was also pregnant, bonded with June over their mutual morning sickness, as they periodically pulled their cars over to throw up together.

While they waited in the dressing room, Rompin' Ronnie Hawkins ambled by and stuck a straw-hatted head through the door. "Y'all got a dollar I could borrow?" he said, as the rest of the entourage laughed and stood to hug him.

It was also a lucrative evening, with gross one-night revenue at well over ninety-two thousand dollars, a record not only for the venue but also for the city. But it wasn't the final highlight of an altogether standout year. No, the show that capped off 1969 for Saul personally came on one glittering, magical night in December.

It was actually Lou Robin who came up with the idea: to book Cash into Madison Square Garden, a first for Johnny and an enterprising endeavour the likes of which Saul likely might have dreamed up himself, had he been a little more flush with ambition and verve. It seemed these days that that drive was faltering a little; his mind was wandering. But yes, of course, why not? At nineteen thousand seats it was a daunting venue, but these days Cash was a musical Midas — everything he touched turned to gold. "It would be a great climax of his year," Robin emphasized, and Saul couldn't help but agree.[19]

For Robin, who had promoted a number of concerts in the venue throughout the 1960s, pulling off Madison Square Garden was tricky but far from impossible. "It was a bit of a crapshoot because it's a very expensive building to play, with the labour cost and the rent and ticket sales," said Robin. Located in Manhattan's Pennsylvania Plaza, the venue was famous for showcasing artists "in the round," with a rotating stage and an audience that encircled the performers on all sides — which would be perfect for a dynamic, prowling performer like Cash. Like Toronto, the show quickly sold out, and was packed with Hollywood luminaries like Robert Redford.[20]

Saul watched as Cash, in a swallow-tailed preacher's coat, fixed his black velvet bowtie and joked around with the other musicians backstage. Laughing with June, he appeared relaxed and in command of his game. As a performer onstage, he was defiant and exuded an otherworldly confidence that was like nothing Saul had ever encountered. But offstage, he really was an "aw, shucks" kind of a guy. This was his particular magnetism; he was not only respected but also adored. He was idolized by grown men; even successful artists like Bob Dylan couldn't take their eyes off him. There was a twinge deep within Saul, a sort of envy. *He's no yes-man, that's for sure. He's a forceful personality,* he thought. *But I have been able to influence him in certain areas, maybe even prompted him to do things that he may not otherwise have done.* He watched the others watching Johnny.

We work well together. I can read his mind. Cash caught his eye and gave a slow grin. *And I know he can read mine.*

Show time.

Saul craned to get a last glimpse of Cash as he ambled down the long, narrow hallway that led to the stage. As he emerged, the crowd erupted in a roar that made the hair on Saul's arms rise. The noise overwhelmed his senses and filled his mind, a lusty cry of nineteen thousand people all screaming and calling out at once. Saul's breath caught in his throat. Cash strode right into the centre of it, beaming. *Extraordinary*, he thought. *Absolutely extraordinary.*[21]

13

CAMELOT, NIXON, AND THE FAIRY TALE THAT WASN'T

Barbara stared at the ivory-coloured card in her hand, its looping, cursive script. Neither of them had been certain it would come, not knowing exactly how these things worked, but here was the confirmation, clear as day. She held it in the fingers of one hand, the other touching her lips absently. *I have nothing to wear,* she thought.

> The President and Mrs. Nixon
> request the pleasure of your company
> for an evening of entertainment at
> The White House
> on Friday, April 17, 1970
> at 8:30 o'clock

"Black Tie," it noted in small letters at the bottom.

I'll stop in at Holt Renfrew and pick something up. They were bound for a family visit in Toronto, and though it wasn't haute couture — she preferred the store in Winnipeg for special occasions — in this case it did not disappoint, and she found the perfect outfit within minutes. Pleased with her choice, on the 120-mile drive back to London she peppered Saul with questions about the event. As White House concerts had never been televised, she had no idea what to expect, but felt a sense of anticipation. Their nanny, Janet, would be available to watch the boys and could be counted on overnight, so that wasn't an issue. It might be an entirely new, pleasant experience, she mused. What might it entail? Barbara sat back in her seat and looked out the window. Then she froze.

"What happens after the concert?" she asked Saul, with a sinking feeling. He glanced in her direction, puzzled, and turned his eyes back to the road.

"I'm not sure what you mean."

"I can't do it," she said, her conviction growing as the words came out.

"What are you talking about?" Saul looked from Barbara back to the road, but she was staring at her hands, tucked in her lap. The whole evening unfolded in front of her, click-clack, like a Jacob's ladder toy. The music, the accolades, the hors d'oeuvres, and then the receiving line after the show, where they would line up to greet the president and Mrs. Nixon. That much she knew: she had seen it somewhere before, maybe in a news photo. It would be unheard of for anyone to find a way to purposely avoid this formality. She looked back at Saul's profile.

"I can't shake that man's hand, Saul. I can't do it."

Both of them knew Barbara had a face that could be read like a map; on this, there was little disagreement. It would be impossible for her to hide her disgust for President Nixon, especially if she had to face him. More than forty thousand American soldiers had been killed so far in Vietnam, and half a million were still stationed there. The United States had been embroiled in conflict for more than a decade, and the anti-war movement had only gained traction leading into 1970 as the pendulum of public opinion began to swing in the direction of de-escalation.[1]

Largely born from the struggle for civil rights, the anti-war movement simply picked up this momentum that had built throughout the 1960s, and then some. On all of these issues, Martin Luther King Jr.'s message had become increasingly incisive as, in the months leading up to his assassination, he advocated for widespread and militant non-violence. The war in Vietnam was "unjust, evil and futile," he cried, and urged people to connect the financial dots between war abroad and poverty at home. Boxer Muhammad Ali added his voice to the mix with his refusal to fight in the "white man's war" and was subsequently stripped of his world heavyweight title.

"My conscience won't let me go shoot my brother, or some darker people, or some poor hungry people in the mud for big powerful America," he said. "And shoot them for what? They never called me nigger, they never lynched me, they didn't put no dogs on me, they didn't rob me of my nationality, rape and kill my mother and father."

Thousands of others followed suit, burning and bagging up their draft cards at mass demonstrations. As stories like the massacre of hundreds of women, children, and elderly villagers at My Lai began to trickle out, they only further fanned the flames of public dissent. In the midst of this unrest, Nixon was elected on a platform of U.S. withdrawal from Vietnam. Once in office, he did begin to send troops home. But the war itself was by no means over, and under his guidance the bombing continued.

By the time Saul's invitation was packed into a mail carrier's bag and sent on its journey to his doorstep, the U.S. government had already begun to secretly and illegally bombard Cambodia. Nixon and Secretary of State Henry Kissinger were also in the midst of finalizing plans for an invasion — an act that resulted in the widespread destruction and death of the country's civilians and laid the groundwork for a Pol Pot dictatorship that slaughtered millions.[2]

In the days that followed, Saul put off answering the invitation in an attempt to convince Barbara to change her mind, but his arguments soon fell flat. Given that he was equally as opposed to the war and Nixon's policies, particularly the bombing of Cambodia, Saul had to concede. But his own attendance was non-negotiable — Cash was giving a command performance.

As for Cash, his convictions over the whole affair were far murkier. Pressed by the media to take a stance on the war at a press conference prior to his Maple Leaf Gardens show, Cash mentioned his January trip to Vietnam and said he "hated it" but felt compelled to support the boys. "You know, nobody hates war more n' I do. It scares the hell out of you when you lie in your bunk at night and hear shells five miles away. But after you've been over there you don't have the energy to throw rocks and yell," he said. "Somebody said that 'cause I've been to Vietnam that makes me a hawk. But I said, 'No. That makes me a dove with claws.'"[3]

Months later, however, as Cash said his closing remarks on his television show, he publicly backed Nixon. Asked about it later, he said he felt like he needed to take a stance because reporters kept asking him what his position was: "I said on TV that I felt safe in following President Nixon. And I said, let's remind our leaders that we must bring the boys back home. Let's do it faster than they said they can — if that's at all possible."

This support was all the encouragement Nixon needed to pull the highly influential Cash into his fold, via an invitation. News of the White House performance soon drew the outrage of fans who were partly drawn to Cash's work because of his support for prisoners and Indigenous Americans. Stan Jacobson, who was by now *The Johnny Cash Show*'s producer, was also wary of the effect his Nixon proclamation would have. "I went to him after and I said, 'John, you're being political now. There are a lot of young kids over in Vietnam being shot to death as we talk.' And he said, 'If you cut that [part of the show] out, I'll never talk to you again.' I said 'Really? Deep down? Well, fuck you.'"

Richard Nixon, Pat Nixon, June Carter Cash, and Johnny Cash at the White House, 1970.

Cash had been urged to take a stand on the war, but many were surprised when it came out as support for Nixon, given that a slew of entertainers were publicly joining the ranks of war resisters. Poet Robert Lowell and playwright Arthur Miller both refused White House invitations, and singer Eartha Kitt attended a luncheon there but used it as an opportunity to air her grievances about the war.[4]

According to Christopher Wren, who had travelled with the troupe to Pennsylvania Avenue in an olive-green army bus, Cash's attitude about accepting Nixon's invitation could be summed up in his simple belief that once a man was elected into public office, it was up to the people to back him. Onstage in the East Room of the White House, under an enormous chandelier, Cash reiterated this support, saying, "I said I've pledged to stand behind our president on his policies on Vietnam ... and to those who won't stand behind him, get out of the way so I can stand behind him."

As the turmoil and insecurity of the last year faded into background noise, Saul and Johnny emerged full speed into 1970. In addition to greeting the president (on a receiving line with 224 other white-gloved and bow-tied well-wishers that included Reverend Billy Graham and Stan Jacobson), Saul was named Canadian Music Industry Man of the Year at the annual RPM Gold Leaf Awards (which later became the Junos) in February. The spotlight of curiosity that had shone so intently on Johnny now widened to include his manager. Who was the man behind the scenes of the nation's biggest star? And was it true that he pulled the strings from an office in London, Ontario, of all places?

"They still can't believe where they're phoning. I mean, first they think it's Ontario, California — the 'London' part on the letterhead, they think is an error," Saul told reporter Peter Goddard, as they sat in his office perched above a high-rise apartment building at 185 Berkshire Drive. It was a strangely low-key space on the outskirts of London, overlooking quiet suburban streets and new housing developments. Inside, tables were topped with antique phones and flanked by leather chairs. On one wall there was a combination stereo, television, and bar. A floor-to-ceiling blown-up photo of Cash, taken at Folsom Prison, towered over his main desk; at its centre was a pale green push-button phone that rang incessantly. On any given day calls were fielded from Columbia Records, California governor Ronald Reagan, Warner Bros., New York governor Nelson Rockefeller, the Pentagon, and two Las Vegas hotels. "Things have suddenly gotten so busy that of the 100 long-distance calls I get per day, I can only return about 30," he told Goddard.

That summer another reporter, Paul King, followed Saul around as the Johnny Cash Show prepared for a concert at Toronto's CNE Stadium. Perched on a sofa in their trailer, Johnny and June sat together as Saul paced in front of them with his briefcase. Backstage was about as focused as Cash got, so Saul would habitually seize the opportunity to go over details of finances, upcoming shows, and promotional opportunities. The Cash empire was spreading. In addition to Saul's London office, an L.A.-based office at Columbia Pictures housed their production staff for the TV show, and Johnny had recently opened House of Cash Inc., a music

Saul Holiff shows off some of the memorabilia in his London, Ontario, office, 1968.

publishing firm. Earlier that year, Saul renegotiated Cash's contract with Screen Gems to "allow more favourable terms for Johnny." There were so many offers that Cash no longer needed to make decisions based on money — his newfound respectability had now also led to endorsements for Yuban coffee, Levi Strauss, Chrysler, and American Oil, among others.[5]

But first, the matter at hand — box office figures.

"They've put seats on the track for the first time in the exhibition's history," Saul told Johnny. "There's 2,500 people out there for a combined total of 23,000. With last night's crowd, it brings it up to 44,000. That breaks every live entertainment record at the grandstand."

"That's just great," June said, with a wide smile. She smiled a lot. Cash was regularly breaking attendance and financial records. At a show in Detroit just months earlier, Cash raked in $131,000 — a record in that city for one performer, according to Saul's figures, and the highest gross anywhere thus far for a country artist.[6]

Johnny Cash and Saul Holiff, backstage at the Canadian National Exhibition, Toronto, 1970.

At intermission, Saul attempted to engage Johnny again, starting this time with the details of his upcoming engagements. June continued smiling in her long white dress, hands folded in her lap. Johnny said nothing.

"Poor old Saul," he said, turning to King, who was there on assignment for *The Canadian Magazine*. "He's got a briefcase full of 14 things he's just bustin' to tell me about. I don't make it easy on him, do I?" Johnny began to laugh. Saul remained silent. "Aw, c'maaaawn, I'm only kiddin'," he added, and then said to King, "I consider these things important to my career, so I try never to make Saul wait too long."

"How often do you get together?" King asked, looking sideways at Saul.

"As little as possible," said Johnny. "No, really. Saul knows his job and does it perfectly. I never worry that things aren't done. He's a perfectionist. Like my dad useta say, 'Whatever you're goin' to be, be the best in the business.' Saul's the best agent in the world. He handles all aspects of my career. I feel sorry for guys like Presley who don't have an agent like him."

"Well *thank you*, John," Saul said, finally speaking.

He looks genuinely touched, thought King.

"I mean it," Cash said.

Intermission over, Cash returned to the stage and King watched as Saul pulled a wad of cash from his briefcase and began to hand it around to the Statler Brothers, Mother Maybelle, and Carl Perkins. Their travelling entourage had now swelled to twenty-one people, including an on-staff hairdresser, stylist, makeup artist, and nurse for June and Johnny's baby, John Carter-Cash. When Johnny and June descended from their airplane they were usually met by limousines, and even that luxury would possibly soon be upgraded, as Saul toyed around with the idea of bypassing airlines altogether and buying or renting their own DC-9.[7]

Money was by no means an object for either man anymore. At this point Cash's yearly earnings topped three million dollars, and Saul's cut worked out to more than 10 percent. The complimentary perks Saul negotiated for himself and his family were also top-notch. Not only did he pursue superb cocktails and the finest of dining experiences to a near-neurotic degree, but he also received whatever Johnny did. If he got a car and driver, so did Saul. If Johnny got the penthouse suite, Saul got the next best room. "I remember once when Saul realized he had been booked an economy class ticket by someone who should have known better, while Johnny was sitting up in first class. Saul just got up and walked off the plane," said Barbara.

Taking his cue from Elvis's manager, Colonel Tom Parker, Saul even got himself declared an official Kentucky colonel by Governor Wendell H. Ford.

"We have the best of just about everything in our lives. We have a marvelous lifestyle. Within reason, certainly within reason, we can have the best of everything. When we entertain, expense is of no consequence. We spend more in the process of entertaining in one evening than we used to dream of spending in a week for our entire living," Saul reflected in his diary. "We drive gorgeous cars and eat marvelous food and live extremely well. And so do our children."

The family's lavish Jarvis Street "house on the hill" — a custom-built dream home on a third of an acre in southwest London — was complete with bar, wine cellar, custom furnishings, and artwork, including Remington prints and Saul's prized possession, one of the few original Paul Peel paintings in private hands. It was also home to Saul's study, which he affectionately called "The Ego's Nest," a sanctuary into which he escaped to sip gourmet liquor and listen to Dave Brubeck and Tchaikovsky behind a locked door.

This time at home was increasingly rare; these days he averaged almost one hundred thousand air miles a year touring with Cash, from Melbourne to Denmark, Salzburg, Moscow, Helsinki, Madrid, Rome, Leningrad, Singapore, Hong Kong, Athens, Seoul, Vienna, Jerusalem, and more. "Upcoming is a trip to Germany and to England and to Scandinavia again. This will be my eighth or ninth trip to England, now, when once upon a time I never dreamed I'd ever see the Parliament buildings or cross Piccadilly Circus," Saul recorded in his diary.

When he was at home, he and Barbara also became known for their lavish house parties thrown on the patio in their manicured backyard, complete with valet parking and gourmet hors d'oeuvres. Jonathan, now five, watched spellbound one summer when the Statler Brothers inched down their street in a custom-painted bus that featured an enormous American flag. Every child in the neighbourhood came out of their houses to trail in its wake. Neighbours stood on their front porches, arms folded, and whispered about sightings of Johnny and June riding bicycles down the street, joking that Saul and Barbara's house was their very own Camelot, in a nod to the Kennedys.[8]

Despite outward appearances, it wasn't a fairy-tale existence in the Holiff household. It was difficult for Saul to conceive of his children as, well, children — with different needs and perceptions from his own. Barbara began to notice that Saul seemed to be unable to view the boys as anything but representations of himself. "The family, it was all about him and how it reflected on him. He didn't really think about any one of us as individuals, me included. It was him, and the rest of us," said Barbara. In the same vein as his own father, Joel, who had signed his letters with

Barbara Holiff with son Jonathan, at home in London, Ontario, 1965.

a postscript that they were penned "with the full consent of mother, as I am not a sneaky thing," Saul insisted that he and Barbara present a united front to the children. She often felt powerless to intervene. Despite her misgivings about some of his views, he was impossible to challenge. "I never saw anybody say no to him. Ever," said Barbara.

From about the age of five, the children were expected to behave as adults and act accordingly. Upon his return from various locales, Saul would bring home fine clothing for Jonathan and Joshua that were largely miniature versions of his own — cashmere sweaters from England, camel hair sweaters from Scotland, and tiny Italian suits — and be upset when they didn't show what he felt was an appropriate level of appreciation.

In an attempt to make up for a childhood in which his own education was cut short, he went to great lengths to expose the boys to culture, travel, and schooling. They were enrolled in French immersion and dragged out to the Stratford theatre festival and evening symphony shows, and castigated when they inevitably fell asleep.[9]

Defiant and spirited, Jonathan's nature stood in opposition to his more acquiescent and passive younger brother Joshua, and as such he grew to bear the brunt of Saul's expectations and narcissism. Perplexed as to why Jonathan didn't seem to display what he felt was a child's natural deference to adults, Saul often worried privately that he was becoming a discipline problem. But with Saul as his primary role model, who else was Jonathan to emulate? And Saul deferred to none; his word was final, his authority immutable. "There are givers and takers in this world, Barbara, and you're a giver," he once told his wife. "And you know what I am."

Like anyone, Saul was, of course, prone to be wrong about things, but this attitude was also bolstered by what had become a formidable intellect. The lifelong insecurity about his lack of formal education had pushed him to continually develop his mind, and he devoured books, endlessly scrutinized and tore out newspaper stories, and absorbed as much experience as he could on his travels with Johnny and Barbara.

"We went to Europe and we went to marvelous places that we had heard about all our lives, and kind of soaked in things that turned us on and made us aware of how bloody little we know," he recorded in his diary. "Since then, I've ordered and received [an] *Encyclopedia Britannica*, which I hope will help make up for lost time, although I haven't found the time to get into it yet. A little bit, but damn little, very superficial, like everything else I seem to do."[10]

Dinnertime was a particularly egregious time for father-son relations, as Saul would drink throughout the meal and become more and more bellicose until the dishes were removed, at which point he would ask Jonathan to stay at the table so that he could berate and lecture him.

One day Jonathan returned home from school at the age of eight or nine and, with all the hubris of youth, made a proclamation during dinner that he wanted to change his name. Sick of the teasing from his classmates and people stumbling over his three-syllable name, he concluded that he would now be known as Jon. To emphasize, he spelled it out, "J-O-N."

At this announcement, his father went quiet.

"Your name is Jonathan, not Jon," Saul seethed, brow low over his eyes. "Jon is a Christian name. You will not be known by Jon. And if you ever say that again, I'll hit you into next week."

At the time, Jonathan found his reaction completely bewildering. Of course he couldn't have known what was happening in Saul's life, the religious turn that Cash had taken in his career and the new pressures it had put his father under; that understanding would come later.

As Jonathan grew older the general message he received from his father gelled and centred on how he would "never amount to anything." At the resolution of his lectures, Saul would affirm that Barbara fully agreed with everything he had to say, and though she actually didn't, she was hard-pressed to get a word in edgewise. It was as if Saul's own self-loathing had extended to his eldest son, who now, for better or for worse, accurately mirrored his own characteristics. Frustrated, Saul reverted to what he knew about dealing with unruly people — namely, Johnny — and began to manage his children as though they were clients, even going so far as to make them sign contracts. Trust funds were started for each boy, in which Saul invested money that he and Barbara would have otherwise spent on cigarettes. Years later, when the trust funds matured, he informed the boys that he had itemized every expense they had incurred as children and then decided to repay himself from this fund for everything he had spent.[11]

The frequent absences from home didn't help the situation, and though Saul regularly confessed to his diary that he had a desire to do better, to be a more present and engaged father, the contrast between these entries and how they translated into reality was stark.

"When home, Saul tries to keep as much time as possible for his sons, Joshua and Jonathan," stated the caption on a photo that accompanied reporter Eric Bender's profile on Saul for the *London Free Press*. Saul had trotted the boys out on bikes and matching jerseys for photos, but it was all about appearances. The cycles and clothing were purchased specifically for the shoot, Jonathan remembered, and rather than toss a ball around in the backyard, Saul typically spent much of his time at home sequestered in his study. Without a specific invitation, it was an area that was strictly off-limits to both of the boys, but as soon as he had departed on yet another tour they would sneak in and explore its contents with a hushed awe.

Long and narrow, Saul's study housed an ornate antique breakfront cabinet at one end and an eighty-gallon saltwater fish tank at the other. Filled with languid, vividly coloured tropical fish, it was lit in such a way that it appeared they were suspended in space. When the undulating fish switched direction, seemingly by magic the lights would change hue. It was a mesmerizing, otherworldly feature of the room that held Jonathan in thrall. Adjustable teak shelving lined an entire length of one wall, with Saul's state-of-the-art sound system occupying the centre shelves. On both sides, every inch of the shelves was lined with hundreds of books, paperweights, souvenirs, and small sculptures. Photographs, plaques, and *Billboard* and *Cash Box* record charts were mounted throughout.

From one end of the room to the other stood row upon row of records, hundreds of them, stacked neatly against the wall beneath the lower shelves. Columbia Records sent a constant stream of their new releases to the house, and though Saul's study was immaculate, there were always a couple of half-opened boxes from the record company on the floor. Mounted amidst the gold records and framed wall photos were two identical plaques, each embossed in gold with a raised half-sphere that represented the Earth. Circled around the half-spheres were four rings, each terminating in a tiny airplane. Trans World Airlines had awarded these plaques to Saul in recognition of the great distances he had travelled on his global tours with Johnny — the equivalent of eight times around the world. But for his children, who ran their tiny fingers over its surface, they were monuments to his absence.

It was an absence that for them was forever superimposed with the face of Johnny Cash. His name was the one on everyone's lips whenever the boys asked for their father. A mountain of a man, a superhero in black, with a voice as deep as the ocean — the singer held a dreamy, fantastical place in Jonathan's mind. He was sure he could fly. And his appearance always seemed to coincide with some of most magical moments of their childhood, whether it was swimming in the pool with June at the Beverly Hills Hotel, the sound of Johnny's fatherly baritone as he introduced them

Johnny Cash and June Carter Cash at the Beverly Hills Hotel pool, Beverly Hills, 1970.

A young Jonathan Holiff with Johnny Cash on the set of an Amoco commercial. Nashville, 1973.

from a stage in Jacksonville, Florida, or his cowboy persona as he goofed around on a movie set in Santa Fe, New Mexico, where the boys were taught how to draw a pistol by a real professional stuntman.

On the back wall of the study, teak tables bookended a long black couch and were topped by lamps with enormous cylindrical white shades. Opposite the couch was a black swivel "egg" chair that Saul rarely used, in which Jonathan and Joshua took great pleasure, taking turns to spin themselves silly.

"You boys had better not do that when your father gets home," Barbara intoned from upstairs, a phrase that always filled them with fear. One time, Jonathan touched something in the study that was off-limits. Without warning, Saul lashed out and knocked him across the room. Running to his bedroom, Jonathan was careful to cover his mouth with his hands to stifle the shame of crying, not wanting to give his father the satisfaction of knowing he could hurt him. After conferring with Saul, Barbara was given permission to apply ointment to his back, but his crimson handprint remained tattooed there for a week. Later, Jonathan remembered what it was that he had touched — a giant machine that had been the centrepiece of his father's hi-fi system in his study — his brand-new tape deck.

The 1970s was a formative time in Cash's career, not only musically but because it marked his official entry into Hollywood films. Ten years earlier, Cash had starred in the critically panned *Five Minutes to Live*, his first feature film. But with the television show running full speed ahead, Hollywood experienced a renewed interest in all things Johnny Cash, and in the summer of 1970 filming began on *A Gunfight*, a dark western co-starring Kirk Douglas, Karen Black, and Jane Alexander. Shot on location in Santa Fe and Madrid, the film centred on the plight of a pair of retired gunfighters who decide to stage a gunfight in a local bullfighting arena to make money.[12]

"The people who funded this film were the Jicarilla [Apache] tribe from Santa Fe, New Mexico," said Saul. "In 1971, Hollywood was a disaster area. The only thing that was happening was that profits were dropping drastically in Beverly Hills, and the only active part the studios were playing was in producing television shows. The movie industry was in a state of disarray." Two million dollars in funds were sourced primarily through the tribe's extensive oil, natural gas, and timber industries, and this investment in Cash's film was part of a wider trend that saw new practices emerge from within an industry in crisis.

In the first three months of 1970 the number of independently financed films, like *A Gunfight*, jumped from just 12 percent three years prior to 43 percent. "The tribe's startling entry into the troubled movie business illustrates a major new trend in Hollywood today," Earl C. Gottschalk Jr. wrote in the *Wall Street Journal*.[13]

As associate producer, Saul accompanied Cash every step of the way, and wasted no time in promoting the idea that he was the next John Wayne. "He had a lot of those attributes," Saul insisted. "[But] I don't think he liked sitting around for hours between shots, and he got very restless. I don't think he cared for the Hollywood stuff that went with it."

This wasn't the case for Saul, who absolutely relished the time spent side by side on fold-out film chairs on set with Kirk Douglas, whom he admired and with whom he felt he had a lot in common. While Cash and Douglas were busy with their scenes, Saul strolled about the set, soaking

Saul Holiff and Johnny Cash on the set of the film *A Gunfight*, which also starred Kirk Douglas, 1970.

up the atmosphere and peppering the crew with questions about the filmmaking process. Again, it was a pivotal moment in which he felt as though he had fully arrived, in an integral part of the industry that had so dazzled him as a youth. *A Gunfight* was even distributed by Paramount Pictures, whose studios he first visited in 1945.

Over the years, Saul and Johnny often collaborated with Canadian actor and singer Lorne Greene of *Bonanza* fame, notably on a never-released duet of "Shifting Whispering Sands." On one occasion, he met with Greene at Paramount Studios to discuss further work when Greene leaned over and asked, under his breath, "Do you know who that is, over there?"

Saul shook his head no.

"That's one of the great moguls of Hollywood history."

"And who might that be?" asked Saul, not understanding what he was getting at.

"Adolph Zukor, and he's ninety years old, actually ninety-two," said Greene. In the end, Greene took him over and Saul chatted with the Hollywood icon, who, "along with maybe three or four others, really did in the loose sense of the word, invent Hollywood," said Saul.[14]

It wasn't just directors and producers who welcomed Cash into the world of Hollywood with open arms. Aside from acting, Cash also recorded music for films, including a drama called *I Walk the Line* and the comedy *Little Fauss and Big Halsy*, starring Robert Redford. "I can't tell you what a pleasure it was to be able to see your show Friday night," Redford wrote to Cash after his triumphant performance at Madison Square Garden in 1969. "I have long been a fan of yours, and never had the opportunity to see you perform in person. I thought the hour was great, and the highlight, of course, was being able to say hello and then the charge I got from the gesture you made in your reference to me personally in your show. I just about fell off my chair. I'm glad you will be working on *Fauss & Halsy*."[15]

Saul was now arguably managing one of the world's biggest superstars — Columbia's top artist with a dozen records on the charts, whose release of a major Hollywood film was imminent, and who had a hit television show just renewed for its third season.

"Cash has written more than 400 songs. He has made 23 record albums, sold more than 20 million records and grosses about $2 million a year," wrote Hubert Saal in *Newsweek* at this time. And though his craggy, timeworn face looked a fair bit older than his thirty-seven years, Cash evidently had many more years of success ahead of him. Drug use still lingered at the fringes, but it was clearly under control. Even his tumultuous relationship with Saul had lapsed into an easy rhythm, in what was the longest period of placidity they had endured to date. What could possibly go wrong?[16]

14

FROM JAILS TO JESUS

Raised in rural Arkansas, little J.R. Cash, as he was then known, heard his first hymn, "I Am Bound for the Promised Land," from his mother as the family truck bumped along a dirt road from Kingsland to their new family plot in Dyess. Growing up, some of Cash's earliest memories revolved around the Road Fifteen Church of God, which housed a fearsome young preacher who shouted and gasped while the congregation dissolved into a whole lot of crying and praying and "Hallelujahs." Then came the most prominent piece of the Sunday morning service for young J.R. — the singing and accompanying guitar, mandolin, and banjo, from which sprang his eternal love of gospel music.

By the time J.R. was twelve, a two-week revival came to their church, the First Baptist Church in Dyess, and he decided it was time to take a stand on his faith. His older brother Jack had already wore out his little Bible reading it every night by candlelight, and it looked like he might grow up to be a preacher, but J.R. hadn't yet felt any certainty when it came to his relationship to God. One night at the revival the invitation to song began, and the congregation, which numbered in the hundreds, began to sing "Just As I Am."

"As the song kept on flowing, I started thinking of all those songs I'd been hearing at home on the radio and how they were pointing out the direction for me to turn," Cash wrote in his autobiography *Man in Black*. "It was time to make a move. Either get up and turn around and walk out of the church, or answer the call and go down to the altar and give the preacher my hand, as he was asking us to do, and by so doing make a public show of repentance and acceptance of Jesus as Lord and Saviour." According to their beliefs, Baptists must publicly declare their faith in order to receive salvation, and young J.R. did just that, emerging quietly from the pew to grasp the preacher's hand.[1]

From these early spiritual roots two vines grew and curled around each other — a lifelong love of gospel music and of Jesus. As J.R. grew into John R. Cash, the ensuing years of addiction and promiscuity rendered him a wanderer, at times quite literally adrift in the desert as demons whispered in his ears. The conflict between Cash's sinning and the lyrics of the gospel songs he so loved to sing soon ate away at him.

"I used to sing 'Were You There When They Crucified My Lord?' while I was stoned on amphetamines. I used to sing all these gospel songs, but I never really felt them. And maybe I was a little bit ashamed of myself because of the hypocrisy of it all: there I was, singing the praises of the Lord and singing about the beauty and the peace you can find in him — and I was stoned. And miserable. I was climbing the walls," he said.

Later in his life, when *Penthouse* reporter Larry Linderman asked Cash, whose lanky form was stretched out on the carpet of the Las Vegas Hilton's imperial suite, "What finally caused you to give up drugs?" his answer was simple: "God. The times I was so down and out of it were the times when I felt the presence of God, or whatever you want to call it in whatever religion you might follow. I felt that presence, that positive power saying to me, 'I'm still here Cash, to draw on whenever you're ready to straighten up and come back to life.' Well that's what happened and I'm not playing church now."[2]

It was largely June Carter who brought Cash back to the flock after he had strayed, and let it be known that a relationship with her also meant a return to his relationship with God. On this point they bonded, and they immediately attempted to substantially incorporate faith into his life again. After the intervention with Nat Winston in 1967, it was June who took Johnny to his first post-withdrawal service at the First Baptist Church in Hendersonville. Cash later wrote about it in his autobiography.

"Look how good you're driving," June said, on their way to the church. "You're not weaving and jerking like you used to. I'm not even having to hold on to the dashboard."

"I think you're going to like me once you get to know me," Cash joked back. "I'm even beginning to like myself again."

Later that month he performed at the local Hendersonville high school, for the first time in years without pills. By January, as the success of the Folsom Prison concert began to build, spirituality became a more pressing issue when the wave of fame that subsequently washed over Cash's life brought along a questioning of his very identity.[3]

Post-Folsom, Cash's decision to record a collection of gospel music spoke to this desire to return to his roots, and also likely provided the impetus for Saul to fight for the San Quentin recording. Cash had not yet completely arrived, and Saul didn't want to see him relegated back into the country charts right when he was on the cusp of mainstream success. As Cash's power and influence expanded non-stop into 1970, he nevertheless felt obligated to use this new platform, especially the one he had on television, to again declare his faith publicly. It was onto this stage that one of America's most powerful religious figures then strode into Cash's life and, like the preacher of his youth, reached out to grasp his hand.

Born on a dairy farm in rural North Carolina, evangelical preacher Reverend Billy Graham had risen to international fame as an immensely charismatic public speaker. A Southern Baptist like Cash, Graham started out as a teenage door-to-door salesman and parlayed those skills into the construction of a massive evangelical empire. The secret to his enduring, widespread popularity was in part his unusual propensity for taking traditional religious beliefs and weaving them into a modern context that included wider issues of American and world politics.

There was no better time for this than the late 1950s and 1960s, when an anxious public, adrift within the moral questions of the era, felt drawn to Graham's potent, confident messages and flocked to his public "Crusades" by the millions. A close friend and informal adviser to Nixon, among other presidents, Graham heard about Cash when his son Franklin took note of the singer's popularity and religiosity and wondered if his media-savvy father could use him to draw even greater crowds to his sermons. Right after the Madison Square Garden show, Graham visited the Hendersonville house for dinner and invited Johnny and June to join his Crusades. The message was clear — Cash should waste no time in using his fame for spiritual purposes.

"[I] definitely saw the 'preacher' in Johnny," Graham told author Robert Hilburn. "You heard it in his testimony and listened to it in his music. June encouraged that 'preacher' in him as well." From that moment on, their friendship and collaboration swiftly blossomed, and Cash made his first Crusade appearance in Knoxville on May 24, 1970.[4]

"God has given you your own pulpit. You can reach more people in one TV show than in fifty Crusades," Graham advised Cash in the rush that followed his inaugural Crusade performance, according to Hilburn. And he would know — Graham's media skills were honed over decades with a radio show, half-hour television spot, films, and countless newspaper columns and magazine articles.

This advice from Graham coincided with Cash's growing disenchantment over his own television show. "It was all right the first year, but I soon came to realize that I was just another piece of merchandise to the network, a cog in their wheel, and when the wheel started squeaking and wobbling they'd replace me with another cog," Cash said. "I began to feel as if every part of my personal and family life was being merchandised and exploited; I felt as if they were stealing my soul."[5]

Encouraged by Graham's insistence that his power was divinely bestowed and should be used to further spread the word of God, Cash pushed for more gospel music and religious themes on his show. On November 18, 1970, Johnny closed an episode with a long monologue about God and the devil. "Well, here lately I think we've made the devil pretty mad because on our show we've been mentioning God's name. We've been talking about Jesus, Moses, Elijah the prophet, even Paul and Silas and John the Baptist," Cash said, as part of his closing thoughts. "Well, this probably made the devil mad alright, and he may be coming after me again, but I'll be ready for him. In the meantime, while he's coming, I'd like to get more licks in for number one."

More religious fodder followed. On one show, Cash declared himself a Christian; on another, he dedicated the entire show to gospel music and brought out Billy Graham to deliver a sermon. Ratings began to fall, likely due to a constellation of reasons. The American public may have experienced an aversion to this preaching or, as producer Stan Jacobson thought, were turned off by his support for Nixon and a tendency to take himself too seriously. Screen Gems had told Johnny the show would likely be renewed for a third season, so, regardless of the reason why, it came as a complete surprise when Johnny and June, along with Saul and Barbara, landed in Australia on March 24 for a tour and were approached by local media who wanted to get Johnny's reaction to ABC's decision to cancel his show. Apparently both Saul and Stan Jacobson had seen it coming, but no one had wanted to tell Cash.[6]

The cancellation did little to slow Cash's certainty that he was on the right path. The pressure to conform to the network's demands to boost ratings had already begun to rankle him deeply. If he had indeed felt his soul was in peril, then it wasn't the right fit for him anyway. But the platform had mattered; he was now receiving thousands of letters from all over the country — a flood of requests and accolades and prayers. Handfuls of tour buses regularly pulled up outside his gate in Hendersonville, and there was many a night he answered the door to a needy person who claimed to be sent there by God. The question that many of his fans wanted to know revolved around his faith: Was he truly a Christian in his heart, or did he just sing about the Lord? Cash felt anxious to give them an answer — publicly.

Fame brought with it a whole host of daunting questions and pressures. Cash was no longer simply a musician — people wanted, *needed* him to be a leader of some sort as well, and though he soaked up the adoration, he was uncertain how to navigate these expectations. Perhaps television was still an appropriate venue for him to offer his religious views. What about a television special? Or even a film about the life of Jesus? Both June and Billy Graham pushed for this idea. The time was ripe, they said.[7]

A few days later, the green phone at the centre of Saul's large teak desk began to ring. It was Johnny, and Saul quickly seized the opportunity to discuss upcoming business, most pressing being a tour of Sweden and England that had come together in a way he felt pleased with. "Now, I've got some good news. We've worked the English tour out, and it's not only worked out, but it's worked out incredibly," Saul said. "You talked about a prestige building, and you're just about to play, for the first time in history, the top building virtually in the English-speaking world. First of all, it has never, ever been rented other than to the Russian Bolshoi Ballet. It's where the Queen has her command performances, it's a fantastically beautiful place, comparable to what Lincoln Centre is like, you know, Philharmonic Hall? It overlooks the Thames, it's brand new, it's the Royal Festival Hall, and there's nothing superior to it in the world." He paused for a moment, twiddling with a pen on the desk. "Acoustically, it's the finest building in the world. And uh, we managed to get a Saturday night. We paid someone off to get out and it's the first ever. The only other American entertainer to ever play it was a benefit with Princess Grace Kelly and Frank Sinatra."

"*Mm-hmm*," said Johnny.

"And that was a command performance last year, which was televised."

"*Mm-hmm*."

"So we've got a beautiful combination that does the following things: the routing is such that we've got a Friday, Saturday, and Sunday, which includes Manchester, Royal Festival Hall, and Birmingham, and all three cities are outstanding. Manchester would incorporate Liverpool, which is only fifteen miles away, and there's six thousand seats. Uh, Glasgow, I can't recall the actual name of the building, but there's adequate seats and it's a fine building. If you recall, Birmingham was an excellent building," Saul trailed off. There was no response. Then he recalled something he knew Johnny would be pleased with. "We can bring the tour to an end so you can be home, relaxed, unpacked and be well-rested before you go on and do that appearance with Billy Graham," he offered. "We'll have to juggle it; it means many more phone calls ..."

At this, Johnny came to life. Just days earlier, on the evening of May 21 — six weeks after the news that his show had been cancelled — something remarkable had happened. When his friend Reverend Jimmy Snow made an appeal for believers in the pews at his Evangel Temple in Nashville, and asked them to get up and take a public stand on their love for Jesus, Cash had risen and been "born again." His mind had been reeling ever since.

"Well, listen, Saul. I've got something else on my mind now, at the same time. You know, I really have got it keeping me layin' awake at night thinkin' about goin' to Israel. Since we talked about doing a Holy Land special, I've updated my thinking. I believe, since the songs and the talk is about Jesus, and that's the thing I would do a much better job at, is talkin' and showin' about Jesus and his life, you know?... I don't know which, how you go about getting it on the networks, but it seems to me like at Christmastime if I had 'Johnny Cash Presents' um, 'Johnny Cash in Israel,' and then call it 'Following in the Footsteps of Jesus,' you know, for Christmastime,'" Johnny said.

"Well, I'm now, I'm gonna throw you a real curve then. At 3:30 on Friday afternoon I'm meeting with the Ted Bates Advertising Agency while you're rehearsing, and that's what I'm going to pitch to him is the idea of 'Johnny Cash in the Holy Land.'"

"For what network?"

"Uh, well, we can't discuss networks until we discuss their willingness to even participate," Saul said.

"How would they participate?"

"Well, they're the advertising company. They're the people who could go, who could go to a network and say, 'We want this.' I mean ..."

"Well, Saul, I feel like if I don't do it soon, somebody's gonna beat me to it," Johnny said.

"Yeah. I mean, now that you have told me, and, and I couldn't be more enthusiastic about the way you feel, I'll break my ass trying to bring it about."

"Well, Saul, make sure they understand now, we talked about me bein' an honest performer now. If I do a television special on Israel, I should do it about the life of Jesus, right? Uh, don't you think so?"

"Well, with slight modifications. I ... I would say that if, if you get too specifically tied into a-a-a ..." Saul trailed off. This was a tricky proposition.

"Well, it's following in the footsteps of Jesus, but it's showin' the land, you know," Johnny said. "And the people today."

"I would say that in your own way, in a subtle manner, you will follow the steps, footsteps of Jesus, and at the same time show the world what, you know, what the Holy Land looks like. But without hitting them over the head with it."

"Right."

"Now, the only comment I have is something that you said, in phraseology that maybe you don't mean; I still think that it should be labelled 'Johnny Cash in the Holy Land' rather than 'Johnny Cash in Israel.'"

"All right. Okay. Sure."

"So, let me go to work on it and that would be the first move, as Friday afternoon is the first meeting," Saul said, opening his appointment book.

"Well, Saul, I really do have a strong conviction about this. I think it's time for me to do it. Everybody is squirreling me to death about doin' a TV show, and I'm not interested in any of 'em. This is the only thing I want to do."

"Yeah, well there, there are several calls that I told you have come in and if you remember, I … I couldn't be more eager to work with you on this, because if you recall, I'm the guy that wanted desperately to try to help bring this about, if you remember."

"Right."

"So, I'll try it from both ends to start with, and I'll call CBS in New York and simply say, 'Johnny has never asked anything of you people, but he wants something now. He wants to do a special in the Holy Land, and he wants CBS International to help bring it about.'"

"Good. Okay."

"And, so I'm just going to tell you in advance I'm gonna bandy your name around to the point where you're, you're now asking them for something and you seldom … never do."

"Okay. Good."

Saul hung up the phone and stared at it for a moment. This was not a commercially viable venture. He sighed. It was going to take some negotiation. He thumbed through the pages of his book. What favours could he call in? Who would conceivably want to take this on? *We'll have to solicit virtually anybody in the industry that's interested in working with us*, he thought. The mayor of Jerusalem was due to be in London next week, and Saul was one of the conveners at his head table. Some co-operation from their end might make it viable.

In the back of his head he felt a dull sense of panic. At his office bar his fingers trembled slightly on the crystal decanter of Scotch. What kind of crazy idea was this? It was humiliating. And he would pursue it, goddamn it, he would bust his ass. But he knew the response he would get: "Who the hell cares about the Holy Land?"[8]

The first drink was downed as he stood there; he poured another. He was drinking too much again. In January, while en route from Mobile to Miami, Saul had stopped off in New Orleans to make a connection, stayed at an Eastern Airline lounge, and got smashed on Scotch and whatever else was around. By the time he arrived in Miami, he was still drunk and high. He had retired to his motel room near Miami International Airport, where the planes flew directly overhead, and smashed his fist against something, he couldn't remember what, but it brought blood. He rubbed a thumb over the knuckles, now healed. Despite being back on the booze, he was maintaining a regular jogging regimen. That was something. But he was definitely drinking too much.

Later in January he had boarded a Pan Am flight to Rio de Janeiro with Alan Tinkley and got as far as Caracas in Venezuela before they ran into trouble. During the two-hour delay they were served drinks, and again Saul had gotten plastered. Upon their arrival they discovered Rio was almost stiflingly warm, and his hotel — the Flora Verde, which overlooked the famed Copacabana Beach — was seedy and second-class. The room was small and he was unhappy, and for a moment he had considered just turning around and going home.

"Went to a private club where they were pandering," he recorded in his diary. "Tinkley was turned on, couldn't take his eyes off any of the females. I walked along the beach, was semi-propositioned by male prostitutes. The beach was jammed with every colour and shape and size, and I … I wasn't happy. I didn't feel comfortable." That sensation seemed to pervade much of what he did these days. Just prior to the Rio trip he had been invited to Tucson to check out a *Johnny Cash Show* taping and had met up with executive producers Harold Cohen and Joe Byrne. By this time, Johnny had conceded on taping some shows outside of Nashville. This one was set in Old Tucson and featured old-time country performers. It was an all-expenses-paid trip for Saul, but a similar feeling of exclusion prevailed. "I went to the set, I felt unnecessary and I was never made to feel otherwise. I took a pill that Harold Cohen gave me and fell asleep at the dining room table at a nice restaurant," he confessed in his diary. "It was another typical show where I was not called upon to do anything, and really, it was totally unnecessary for me to be there."[9]

Thoughts swirled as he drank. *I want to be liked, but I act in a manner that results in me being disliked,* he thought, turning the glass around and around in his hand. *I'm intolerant and smug and a smart-ass. I have a desperate need to impress and far too much vanity. I want to be noticed, with this ... this phony sense of bravado, like a peacock, but at the same time, I'm terrified of failure. I loathe myself and yet I have an overinflated ego. I'm a fraud.* He exhaled slowly through his nostrils.

It wasn't Barbara he had issues with — though at times it felt like she treated him with barely concealed hostility. And it wasn't Johnny, though he never could quite keep a grip on their relationship. At times it was like clutching a thrashing fish. A few months earlier Christopher Wren released his biography on Cash, *Winners Got Scars Too,* and in the copy Johnny gave to Saul it was inscribed: "To Saul. Thanks for your help in making things different now. We've come a long way. Let's go on." The gesture, however small, was appreciated. No, these issues weren't anyone else's but his.[10]

Saul tipped the remainder of the glass to his lips and replaced the crystal stopper. There was work to be done.

Unsurprisingly, the Ted Bates Agency passed on the religious special, as did the mayor of Jerusalem. Screen Gems, who were actually casting about for a Cash television project, were also unenthusiastic. Though Saul had reassured Johnny he felt eager and the timing was good, privately he was anxious and uncertain. During their earlier telephone conversation he had attempted to steer Cash toward the alternate idea that he play a concert in an ancient venue like Israel's Caesarea Amphitheatre. It could carry the same theme Cash wanted but with an added entertainment value as well.

"Then you've got the visual sight of performing in a place that somebody performed in two thousand years before you, at the time of Christ,"

Saul had suggested gently. But Johnny was unmoved. He was determined to talk about the life of Jesus, and to do it as a sort of travelogue. For his part, Johnny wasn't without his own sense of unease. It seemed as though everyone except June, Reverend Snow, and Billy Graham was trying to tear him from this new, righteous path. And that only served to strengthen his resolve.

At this time, Vegas also came calling. The Mint Casino had been a regular haunt during some of the more disorderly scenes of Cash's career, but he hadn't returned to the city since 1966. Now, Las Vegas casino magnate and developer Sam Boyd was cashing in some favours of his own and wanted to know if Johnny would make an appearance at the opening of his new hotel.

"I have not been able to prevail upon Johnny and June to go to Las Vegas no matter what the circumstances are. They have very strong feelings about returning to the State of Nevada and their beliefs are very deeply rooted," Saul wrote to Boyd's partner Joe Dale. "I personally feel bad that we can't cooperate with you and Sam. Both of you treated us well when we appeared at The Mint, and if we were ever inclined to do anyone a favour it would be Sam Boyd."[11]

A copy of the letter went out to Johnny, who was incensed. The sentiments around Vegas were true enough — the city of temptation and sin didn't feel like an appropriate destination for him right now. Not as he worked to find his new spiritual footing. "A place where Satan stalks about," June liked to say. And in the difficult years of the mid-1960s, the Mint had played host to Johnny when he was at his worst. On many nights when Johnny showed up high or drunk and was unable to perform, a fiddler named Abby Neal would round up whoever she could find to help get him through his sets. "We would hold Johnny by the back of his jacket through the big red curtain at The Mint while he did his show so he didn't fall off the stool," remembered luthier and musician Dave Bunker, who had worked the Vegas casino Golden Nugget with his band for almost ten years.

For whatever reason, Cash was irritated by Saul's attempt to explain the situation on his behalf and quickly jotted off his own response to Sam Boyd's associates, saying that he felt he should write to them personally because "Saul's letter to you left a lot to be desired for an explanation." After congratulating Boyd on the opening of his hotel, Cash explained that both he and June loved the state of Nevada, and that Saul had misunderstood their reasons for not wanting to perform there. The truth of it was that his life had recently undergone a renaissance of sorts, and all areas of his life from his family to his marriage were growing and developing, Cash wrote. In addition, his daughters would be visiting at that time, and as they visited only once a year, it was very important to him that he keep that time free for them. In the past, he had found Las Vegas to be a less than positive influence, he added, and he feared that to play there again so soon would pull down all he had built in the last few years. "What it boils down to is this — I'm not ready to come to Nevada. When I do, I intend to set the town afire instead of letting it burn me up," Cash concluded, but assured Boyd that as soon as he was ready, he would be the first one they contacted.[12]

When *A Gunfight*, the film Johnny made with Kirk Douglas, came out that August, reviews were mixed. Variously pointing out its plot flaws and the underuse of Jane Alexander and Karen Black's talent as actors, critics were mainly united on the perception that Cash had turned out a compelling performance.

"[Cash] does an impressive job as the shy, slow-speaking gunfighter, an explosive combination of ruggedness and gentleness," wrote Daniel Stoffman in the *Toronto Star*. "There's a natural, unpolished freshness to Cash's acting which is just right." A review in *Playboy* concurred, adding that "if audiences react coolly to the theme, they may warm up to Cash, who plays the role like the thorough professional he is — confident, laconic, virile and not the least intimidated by Douglas' steam-shovel presence."[13]

It wasn't long before the film dropped out of theatres and off the map, but given the reviews, Saul still had high hopes for Cash's major film star potential. These days, however, it was a low priority for his client. But the power of the screen and its potential to relay a message melded with Cash's not-yet-realized idea for a religious-themed special on Jesus, and if not on television, then why not on film? Both June and Billy Graham strongly encouraged the idea, and the wheels were set in motion.

They would have to source funding. Johnny recalled his frustration with the strong creative control that Screen Gems had exercised over his show, which was ongoing as they negotiated the possibility of rerunning some episodes. The case for simply funding the film himself was looking more attractive. But first, he needed to check in on the television special front, which was not entirely off the table yet, either. Once again, Johnny phoned Saul to discuss their options.

With greetings out of the way, Johnny broached the topic of Saul's ongoing correspondence with John Mitchell from Screen Gems regarding their desire to syndicate *The Johnny Cash Show*. Though a highly lucrative opportunity, Johnny had grave concerns about the possibility of rerunning episodes of his show, especially in light of his new, spiritual direction.

"I talked to June about those shows, and there's going to be really a lot of deletions and some work on a lot of those tapes before I'll ever agree to 'em bein' rerun," Cash said.

"Mm-hmm."

"Because that Johnny Cash is not the same Johnny Cash that is around now, see?"

"Uh-huh."

"And, I'm thinkin' about other things, too. I want to talk to you in a minute about another television special, and if we're gonna have a meaningful special or anything like that, won't those reruns hurt us?"

"Uh, yeah. Yeah. I, I personally feel that, you'd be better off if they were never rerun in the States."

"Well, I would, too. I don't want them rerun as they are. Just about every show needs to have some work done on it. I want to take out all the cussing, the hells, and the damns, and the smart-ass remarks," Johnny said.

"Well there's one way that he could do this and that is to edit the shows down to half-hour packages, which would probably do two things: make it more economical and tighten up the show and eliminate all this stuff that is undesirable. We could approach it that way," Saul offered.

"We'd have to talk about that, too; there's certain things I don't want eliminated, like 'Ride This Train.'"

"The thing is, you could keep all the best things and boil it down, and get it so that it really is *The Johnny Cash Show* and eliminate a lot of the extraneous guest material of a lot of guests that weren't desirable anyway," Saul said. "It would be a half-hour *Johnny Cash Show* package. Let me approach them on that one and get some feedback, and we'll take it from there."

"All right, and I wanna ask you about a special," Johnny said.

"Okay."

"Do they want a special with me?"

"Ah, the letter that he wrote simply said that ABC — if you want to hold on for a minute I'll find that letter and read that paragraph ... just a sec, I think I know where it is, one minute." Saul rustled around, looking for the letter he had received from Screen Gems not long after Johnny had first mentioned his desire to do a religious special.

"He says: 'I've been in discussion with the network, to be nameless at the moment, concerning a one-hour Johnny Cash special. I believe it's safe to say that I have an order for a special, subject to the following: One, the right to schedule it some time prior to December the 31st 1972, and two, an agreement with the network on the creative theme for the special.' Um, so whatever he means by that, I'm not quite sure ..."

However, this was not true. Saul was well aware of what Screen Gems president John H. Mitchell had meant. Eyes scanning down the page, he had decided to omit the letter's next paragraph, which went on to say, "Naturally, I brought up the subject of a possible special done in Israel because I know of John's continuing interest in such a project. At this time the network is not interested in Israel as the theme of a Johnny Cash Special. If a special is to be produced at any time in the near future, it is going to have to involve a U.S. theme."

Furthermore, Screen Gems would prefer to come up with their own creative idea for a theme show and pitch it to Johnny, not the other way around, Mitchell added. Saul declined to tell Johnny this part, too.

"There's only one that I would like to do, if we do a special," said Johnny. "And I would like to do, first of all, a live show. I'd like to do a live gospel music special, possibly from the War Memorial Auditorium here in Nashville. And I would like to have whoever the guests are, no matter who they are — we could get anybody we wanted to guest, I guess — to do a gospel song, see? Um, the Jesus movement is really goin' strong for us, all the *Jesus Christ Superstars*, *Godspells*, and all this, and I would like to show it the way it really is. I would like to close the special with about a ten-minute sermon from Jimmy Snow, with an altar call and people coming down to the altar, praying, raising their hands up, and then have the closing song over that, you know, at the end of his little sermonette."

"Mm-hmm."

"I really believe it would be a spectacular sight, as well as a good show," Johnny said.

"In other words, to put on film an actual, uh, um, um, segment of, of a real um ..."

"Of a real *revival*."

"Revival. That's, that's ..." Saul was at a loss for words.

"Of the people comin' down. I went to church yesterday, and last night, and the thing I saw in that church, if we could get that, on network television, boy it would *really* be something," Johnny said. "Those women and men comin' on their knees, raisin' their hands up, you know like they do to Jesus, and tears comin' down their face, and, uh, Jimmy could do a ten-minute sermon, uh, showing people's reactions, you know? It could be like a 'Johnny Cash Gospel Crusade, uh, Special,' you know?"

"Uh-huh."

"But have both sides of gospel. The music, and the traditions of my part of the country, of my people, you know?"

"Yeah. Lemme ... lemme try it out on him, and, and when I'm calling him about the other thing, I'll just pitch this idea to him and let him go to the network and see if he can create some interest in it. Because the timing right now for him to go to the network about such an idea, it couldn't be better. You know ..."

"It would be an easy show for me to do, you know, because it would be such a natural for me," Johnny said. "It's what I love doing."

"Yeah. Okay, then I'll, I'll go, I'll pitch that to him as well as asking for a further explanation about the rerunning of the tapes."[14]

Saul hung up the receiver and closed his eyes. Raised in a secular home that emphasized intellect and education, any kind of religious fundamentalism made him distinctly uncomfortable, especially evangelical Christianity. But this ... it was unprecedented. The new Johnny Cash was certainly different from the old Johnny Cash, of that there was no doubt. But with this new frontier came a whole new set of challenges. If Johnny truly wanted to go down this road with his career, and he clearly did, it would take some work, perhaps even an entirely different game plan. Saul sighed and reached for the phone.

15

THE RICHEST MAN IN
THE CEMETERY

The live gospel television special never happened. But as that idea faded, the concept of a film about the life of Jesus, shot on location in Israel, continued to take shape. With five hundred thousand dollars of his own money, largely raised through commercial ventures, like those for American Oil, Johnny decided to go ahead and fund it himself. Based on their earlier association on the documentary *Johnny Cash: The Man, His World, His Music*, Cash was leaning toward asking Robert Elfstrom to direct.[1]

The project was a minefield in terms of its commercial prospects, and privately Saul found the religiosity of it somewhat distasteful, but as a work of passion close to Johnny's heart, respect was due. It was what he wanted, and as such, Saul felt obligated to expend every effort in making it a success. But they were pressed for time. It was already the first week in August, and the sole break in their touring schedule was only a few months away. If this was going to happen, it needed to come together quickly. The pressure was mounting; it wasn't a typical project, so it was a challenge to pull all the usual players on board.

The push was on from Johnny, who wanted to gather everyone involved in the film together for a production meeting on August 13 and 14 while he played some fair dates in Allentown, Pennsylvania. Despite

Saul's best efforts, Elfstrom was nowhere to be found. Others were easier to pull together; there was no question Lou Robin was on board, and that was a relief. Now a crucial asset to the team, he worked closely with them on most major projects, along with Alan Tinkley and Marty Klein, president of the Agency for the Performing Arts. Former television producer Barbara John, who had orchestrated the lunch with Saul, Lou, and Alan back in the summer of 1968, was also an "in" for the film.

A script of some kind still had to be worked out, and Johnny had tapped ABC writer Larry Murray for the job. As that ball got rolling, Saul attempted to lure Jane Dowden, president of TV music production company Show Biz Inc., into signing on with the film. As he paced the carpet in his office trying to think of what else needed to come together, the phone on his desk began to ring. "Is this Mr. Holiff?" asked an operator. As Saul confirmed, he reached over and clicked the recorder he had attached to the phone. It wasn't clear why he felt drawn to record these conversations, but it satisfied something in his meticulous nature. Had the technology been available during Cash's most tumultuous years, it would have been useful to confirm details of agreements that were negotiated while Johnny was intoxicated. That was less of a problem now, but you just never knew.

"Hi, Saul? How you doin'," said Johnny.

"Okay." Saul glanced at the recorder to check it was rolling.

"I've got some letters and things, and I think it'd be good if we had a meeting in Allentown, huh."

"Well, uh, the only reason why I wanted to stall off is, first of all, I spent the last four days before Reba called trying to track Bob back down again, but he's out on an island and apparently they're called Deer Isle in Maine, and I spent two and a half days trying to phone a couple of numbers he gave me without getting any answer from those numbers. Now somebody said there's a telephone slowdown in certain sections of the country, and it may have been for that reason. So I wrote him a letter, special delivery, which I sent you a copy of. Can I just read it to you very quickly? I wrote this on Saturday. 'As you requested, please find enclosed copies of your budget sheets. I tried to reach you by phone on a couple of occasions but have not been too successful. Johnny has requested another

Saul Holiff on the phone in his London, Ontario, office, 1972. Visible in the photo is a cord attached to his phone, from a machine he used to record his calls.

meeting as soon as possible. He wants to review the budget (which is understandable) and also to nail down, more specifically, our future plans concerning the script, travel to Israel, a conference between you and the writer, et cetera. All of these matters must be resolved quickly. I suggest we rendezvous in Allentown on the 13th and 14th when Johnny plays the fair there. We'd be staying at the George Washington motel and could be contacted there by midday August the 13th. After word from you, I then could alert Barbara, Lou Robin and Larry Murray that a definite meeting had been set up. Please advise soonest.'

"And um, I could still try to get him by phone, but I don't know whether he's working or on holidays or what the hell he's doing," Saul finished.

"Well, I'll try to get him too, and tell him let's meet in Allentown. We'll bring Larry Murray up there too," Johnny said.

"Okay, I think that then I'll call Lou after this and get him to sit in on this because he's planning on going to Europe in the next two or three weeks, and he said that he would definitely come to Allentown. If that's okay with you."

"Let's do it."

"And then I've got to find out one way or another from Jane Dowden. Well, I spoke to Jane a week ago. She said she understood the urgency of it, and I may be repeating myself, I think I sent you a copy of the letter to her as well, but the fact is she may have understood the urgency but hasn't replied. So I just sent her a special delivery letter this morning, saying that it's absolutely essential that we know. I don't want to push them — that's the way I started the letter — but we really must know whether or not you and your associates are interested. So, so, that's just about where it stands, except the budget that Bob sent, is, you know, you'd need an interpreter to understand —"

"It doesn't mean anything whatsoever," Johnny interrupted.

"No, it doesn't, does it?"

"I don't think he can come up with a budget that will mean anything, Saul, until we have a meeting or until I have a rough draft from Larry Murray, which I'm gonna try and have him have ready for Allentown."

There was a pause. Saul decided it was time to express some of the caution he felt about Cash's choice of director, which until now they had discussed only peripherally. "Well, you know, it's only after talking to you and I put the phone down and I started thinking about it, and I realized what you were talking about. When you do a documentary you just shoot everything you see, hoping that some of it you can use."

"We don't have a script. He's gotta know his shots before he gets to Israel," Johnny agreed.

"Right. And I think that he can't quite get it clear in his mind that he is following a script rather than doing a documentary," Saul said.

"That's right."

"So I guess that after you set him straight, the whole thing will be approached in a different manner."

"I'm sure it will."

"But I think, the first time when he told me the price, Johnny, even without having talked to you, I had a feeling that his approach was being uh, improper. But not deliberately, and I had a feeling that you wouldn't accept what he had to say, so I —"

Johnny cut in. "Saul, I'm sure there are other directors, you know? Don't you think so?"

"Uh-huh. So I don't think you're locked into that situation, if you want to change it," Saul offered.

"Well, I think let's give it a few more days and maybe have the meeting in Allentown and then we'll know if we want to change it."

"Well, by then you'll know if he's levelling with you, if he's really sincere, or whether he just sort of sees a good thing and wants to capitalize on it," Saul said. Realizing this was perhaps a bit unfair, he added, "I'm not suggesting any of these things, because just like you, I'm not sure. He may be completely sincere, and on the other hand he may be seeing a good thing and want to take advantage of it. You'll know."

"Yeah. Well, I think we'll have a rough outline by the time we get to Allentown, and we can go from there."

"All right."[2]

For his part, Elfstrom had actually been completely taken by surprise when Johnny first called and asked him to direct the film. "He just got on the phone and said, 'Hey Bob, how are you?' And I said, 'Fine, what's up?' and he said, 'I want you to make me a film about Jesus,' and I remember responding, 'Jesus who?' I thought it might have been a music person, because many people have the first name Jesus. And he said, 'No, Jesus Christ.' And that kind of set me back," Elfstrom remembered.

Not only did he personally have, as he described it, "serious reservations" about all organized religions, at thirty-three years old, Elfstrom was young and somewhat inexperienced. "I couldn't imagine anyone less qualified to do a film about the life of Christ than me," said Elfstrom. "I had only done a feature film with Robert De Niro, earlier on, but I wasn't qualified as a feature film director at all. I was a very competent director of photography, especially with cinéma vérité, but there were probably two hundred directors more competent than me to do this film."

Ever protective of his client, Saul didn't need to worry about Elfstrom's sincerity. In fact, it was likely his integrity and respect for Cash that got him the job in the first place. In their earlier documentary work, he had made a personal decision to approach Johnny first as an artist and a poet, and balked at any pressure to focus on his substance abuse. "It was my decision as a director, and it was my relationship with John that started at that time — bearing in mind that I hardly knew who Johnny Cash was when I was offered to do [the documentary]," said Elfstrom. "But I stuck by my guns and didn't want anything to do with that; I thought it would have interrupted the Johnny Cash I knew, admired and eventually loved."

The production meeting in Allentown went ahead more or less as planned. A more detailed rendezvous took place on September 12 in Oslo, during which a budget and timetable were further formalized. That was about the extent of their planning, and little was truly in place by the time Elfstrom, Larry Murray, and Barbara John touched down in Israel the following month to scout out locations across the country. At this point the script was hardly more than eight pages, and Johnny and June's artistic vision didn't extend much further than the general concept of a musical travel diary, illustrated by images of Jesus walking all over Israel in his sandals.

"Anybody with any sense would know that you can't have 90 minutes of somebody's feet walking around Israel; it's not going to work," said Elfstrom. "But what they were saying was that they wanted to do a visualization on that, so the feet and the sandals were a metaphor and then everything else grew very spontaneously." They were all neophytes, really, Elfstrom added, adrift in a foreign and sometimes hostile territory and totally out of their zone of expertise.

"I accepted John and June on the sincerity of the commitment they wanted to make," he said. "I was trying, as much as possible, to execute a wish that they had."

It was the first week of November in 1971 when Johnny, June, Saul, Lou Robin, and a crew of about thirty friends and supporters boarded an El Al flight out of New York and headed to Tel Aviv to begin filming on what now had a working title of *In the Footsteps of Jesus*.

Upon their arrival at their base in Tiberias on the Sea of Galilee, they were met by an Israeli film crew hired by Lou Robin, who would work with members of Elfstrom's regular documentary team. Robin had taken care of all on-location arrangements, from booking a local studio to wrangling the Israeli government. Once again, Saul faced the consequences of his inclination to drift away from the tedium of day-to-day logistics. A welcome replacement was found in the steady capability of Lou Robin, and though it was a situation of his own making, at times this arrangement wore at Saul's ego. "I was in title only, the executive producer, but my responsibilities were really practically zero," Saul later admitted in his diary. "Lou Robin was the guy that kept it together and Barbara John was the girl that started it and once again I sort of coasted, sorta ... sorta kinda was present, but in body only."[3]

This left much time for sightseeing — and what a country through which to roam. Travelling everywhere by limousine, often together with Lou Robin, Saul coasted through groves of palm trees and crumbling ruins, stopping at sites straight out of the Bible: Nazareth, Cana, and Capernaum, an ancient fishing village with synagogues from the third and fourth centuries. They stopped for a photo on Allenby Bridge, which straddled the Jordan River; Saul rode a camel and crouched for pictures with local children. The film was also shot in many of these locations, including one scene in the river itself, where Johnny waded into the water to be baptized by Reverend Jimmy Snow, along for the ride as their religious consultant. Many of the film's scenes were shot in a Palestinian village outside of Jericho, a great walled city considered one of the oldest

Saul takes a photo of Johnny Cash as he is baptized in the River Jordan, Israel, 1971. They are on the set of his film *The Gospel Road*. (left to right) Jimmy Snow, Johnny Cash, unknown man.

in the world. The sites often bore remnants of the 1967 war, and Saul felt some trepidation at the palpable Arab-Israeli tension that at times was "outright hostile and angry."[4]

Despite his modesty, Elfstrom was actually an ideal candidate to direct the film precisely because of his lack of religious knowledge, which allowed him to completely trust Cash's vision. "He just wanted to do damn well what he pleased. He wanted to make *his* film about *his* Jesus and I think, if anything, probably the best characteristic I had was that I was not a threat," Elfstrom said. "I think I understood his emotional commitment to this. I didn't come with any baggage. If he said that, you know, 'Jesus walked on water,' I didn't have an argument with that. Or if his interpretation of the Last Supper was about Judas, I didn't have reservations about how he saw it. Frankly I didn't know a great deal about it. So my connection was more like an interpreter. John and June, they weren't filmmakers, but I was able at a certain level, to understand and interpret the silences between what they were saying."

Though Saul had worried Elfstrom might not be comfortable working from a script, his approach as a documentary filmmaker made the experience far more relaxed and improvised than a typical feature film — which was also ideal. "Basically what we did every day was determined when John came down to my room in Tiberias in Israel in his pajamas and we'd sit up half the night deciding what to do the next morning. We were winging it. And that was something that I was very comfortable with, and that was something that John was very happy about."

The casting was equally free-form and drew from whoever was available. With flowing blond hair parted in the middle and, as Barbara John put it, "perfect feet," Elfstrom was cast in the role of Jesus. June did a turn as Mary Magdalene, Johnny's sister Reba Hancock was the Virgin Mary, songwriter Larry Lee played John the Baptist, Jimmy Snow both served as a religious consultant and had a small role as Pontius Pilate, and even Saul was drawn in to play the Jewish high priest Caiaphas. Though he delighted in the power of the character and the period costuming, this choice in casting must have made Saul ponder its significance. It was Caiaphas who had organized the plot to kill Jesus and he who was involved in the trial that had led to his crucifixion. With his encyclopedic knowledge of the Bible, surely Johnny must have known that some Christians used the story of Caiaphas as a biblical justification for anti-Semitism. Was he trying to say something?

"They needed extras. I mean, I played a Roman soldier," said Lou Robin, who was recruited to push up the cross alongside their Jordanian limousine driver. They were on the back roads of Israel, on the other side of the hill from where they were shooting, preparing for the scene beside their wardrobe vehicle (which was basically a regular van) when an Israeli tank covered in soldiers pulled up alongside them. "I didn't know what to do. I couldn't wave, so I shook my sword at them. Dressed

(left to right) Johnny Cash, director Robert Elfstrom as Jesus, and Saul Holiff as Caiaphas, in costume while shooting *The Gospel Road*, Israel, 1970.

as a Roman soldier," laughed Robin. "I think they just shook their heads and went on."

As the crew prepared for their return to the States, Johnny felt as though their mission had been accomplished with the film, which would eventually be called *The Gospel Road*. On November 27, he sent a telegram to Barbara John, who had left early when the taxing film schedule of early mornings and long hours took a toll on her health. "Jesus film finished today," he wrote. "First rate full-length movie. More than pleased. Release next April."[5]

After a few show dates in North Carolina and Virginia, Johnny and June headed to Los Angeles in December to tape an episode of the *Glen Campbell* variety show where, on a whim, Saul decided to once again propose the idea of playing Las Vegas again to Johnny. "It was an impulse deal on my part. Right off the top we were supposed to go in Australia in March 1972, and he cancelled that for various reasons — the long travelling and so on, and the low net results financially — and I called him and I impulsively suggested that now was the time to play Vegas, and he said yes," Saul recorded in his diary. "I locked it up and put Marty Klein into it, who had sort of stuck with it all this time."

With the Australia dates cancelled, Saul booked Johnny into the same slot. Las Vegas Hilton president A.J. Shoofey had already attempted to woo Cash earlier with a special invite to Elvis's opening there in 1970, saying it "might be an excellent opportunity to chat with you concerning a similar performance."

Excited to have finally landed him, the engagement grew to become a series of prestigious Easter weekend shows. Feeling re-energized, Saul threw himself into the accompanying promotional work with renewed vigour, and not only negotiated an Elvis-sized pay rate of one hundred thousand dollars a week and the same first-rate hotel rooms, but also insisted that entertainment director Dave Victorson arrange for "an outdoor spectacular painted billboard on Sunset Strip in Los Angeles" at their expense, to advertise the show.[6]

The sign outside Saul's office was nondescript — Personal Management: Saul Holiff, President, Volatile Attractions. In some ways its lack of pomp was an accurate representation; when he returned from the hustle of travelling, Saul liked to retreat into relative obscurity to unwind. Nestled here in the office was one place he could do it, and best of all, it was quiet. At the back of the office was a broad teak desk that occupied nearly the entire width of the room, behind which he slowly rocked in a black swivel chair. At his back was a sliding glass door that opened out onto the sweeping expanse of London. Like its namesake, it featured the winding surface of the Thames River in the distance, which snaked its way around to Springbank Park. One of the best parks Saul had seen anywhere, really, it was the site of his regular jogging regimen, composed of three consecutive nine-minute miles.

As ever, he was preoccupied with health; the last scare was only about a year earlier when he'd found blood in the toilet basin after he had finished a jog around the rustic hills of Tucson. It was nothing serious, a burst rectum from jogging, but the sense of alarm it had induced left him rattled. Like everything else, he kept meticulous lists of all his health issues and wobbles over the years, and was ever on the lookout for something that warranted further attention. It seemed as though nothing could ever be left to chance: in health, in business, or in life. It could all dissolve at a moment's notice. The chair swivelled as he turned to face the sliding glass doors and the view beyond.

That summer he would turn forty-seven, in the week before Joshua's sixth birthday. Birthday parties were often a lavish affair for both boys, with cake and sweets and all the things he typically steered them away from. It was a far cry from his own childhood, in which he'd had a grand total of one party, for his fourth birthday, and it never ceased to delight him to remind his children of this misfortune on the occasion of their own birthdays.

It was also well into Saul's eleventh year with Johnny, officially, which carried its own interesting ramifications. Some aspects of his career vexed him; the constant travel was overwhelming to his senses, especially the noise, but the culture and stimulation some trips offered was second to none. In February he had flown to Europe again with Johnny, this time to Holland and Germany. Many locales were exotic, but just as many were not. *One can only go to a state fair in South Point, South Carolina, so many times,* he thought with a shudder.

There was never any secret made of his ambition to travel the world, make a million dollars, and retire. But now that he neared, or was perhaps at, that peak, there were only more questions. "I have been doing all the work that I possibly can do — which is practically nothing — in the office. I seem to have lost the desire, and I just can't seem to mobilize my energies to do a damn thing. Stopped taking tranquilizers temporarily, I hope permanently — started drinking again. I don't know which is worse," he confessed into his recorder.

At this juncture, the possibility of enacting the third phase of his plan — retirement — was plausible, tantalizing even. Financially, Saul's earnings had dropped to some extent but were still substantial. *If money is a security blanket, we're not what would be called significantly wealthy, but we're not exactly impoverished,* he thought. *Unless some disastrously foolish moves are made, frankly, we could phase down into semi-retirement or, for that matter, retirement, depending on the combinations of choices available to us.*

The lingering sense of dissatisfaction at work was tempered by an ongoing dream of returning to school. Saul's unrealized educational aspirations stood in contrast to Johnny's recent achievements, which included the award of an honorary doctorate, *if you please*, from the Gardner-Webb College in North Carolina for his work on prison reform and general "Christian service to others." Saul poured another drink.[7]

Then there was home life, which was, well … as much of a turmoil as ever. He knew his nervous, uptight demeanour did little to assuage the situation. Its source was never quite certain, but Barbara also suffered from some sort of ongoing anxiety. *These days, she seems to vacillate between modest to extreme hostility toward me,* Saul thought. Upon his return from a long absence he didn't exactly receive a king's welcome; the boys greeted him with casual acknowledgement, and the cats treated him with their usual masterful disdain. But there was some reason for hope in his relationship with his boys. Saul knew he could always do better, try harder, but when he compared himself with other men in the business, like Alan Tinkley and Lou Robin, they seemed easily just as caught up in work and travel as he was, perhaps more.

"It's been a week of extreme fatigue, but a week of encouragement as far as Jonathan and Joshua are concerned," he recorded in his diary. "There was a feeling of more reasonability on both sides. Both kids were, by and large, very pleasant to be with. I still find it difficult to tolerate the commotion and the debris, but there is a definite feeling of … They trust me, they feel good towards me. They are not intimidated by me, I know that now. At least at this point, anyway. There is an affectionate feeling there that is gradually building up, or is rebuilding or establishing itself. It's not where I would like it to be, but it's just about what I deserve at this point. No more, no less. I know how much more could be done. I know what should be done. I know that some people do a hell of a lot more, and then I know that some people do practically nothing who could be doing something.

"So I suppose that I can look for excuses if I want them, and I can justify my absences if I want to, but I know what I'd like to be doing with them, and I think they're reaching the stage where I want to be doing it with them. Maybe like the story of the guy who wants to help the little old lady across the street. I want them to do things, and probably they don't even want to do it. You know, I want to do it because I think that this is the way it should be. And they probably would be quite content to be doing their own thing."

Conditions with Johnny were about the same, though there was an ongoing tension between them that seemed irresolvable. Their communications had long been whittled down and streamlined to only what was necessary, or as Johnny once told a reporter, Saul got "all the chaff weeded out before we meet and we talk about all the essential things." Much of this took place by phone, typically about twice a month. Lately they were on the phone a little more, as it was busy and there were several large projects on the go. But plans were constantly changing. Johnny would give the impression they were going one way, and then suddenly turn and go another. Somehow Saul found it in himself to weather the storms, swallow his pride, and eat crow. But it was endlessly humiliating. *My relationship with Johnny seems to be just about where it has always been*, he mused with a sigh. *A mystery and a constant guessing game.*

The phone began to ring.[8]

"How's the Las Vegas dates comin' along?" asked Johnny, who was in Jamaica with June, taking some much-needed time off at the estate of CBS chief executive William S. Paley, in a locale where Billy Graham often vacationed.

"It looks extremely good, and I just got some glossy eight-by-tens of all the billboards that are up, and I'm putting them in the mail to you today in the hope that they'll be there when you get home. They're tremendous billboards; just absolutely beautiful — and everything seems —"

"Where? In Los Angeles?" Cash cut in.

"No, everywhere. In Los Angeles a beautiful billboard as you get off the plane, in Las Vegas a giant billboard as you approach the hotel — the whole side of their marquee is just one giant name: Johnny Cash. And I'm sending you the best ones that they sent me, and I think they should be there by Saturday. The bookings are very —"

"How are the advance sales going?"

"The advance sales, I was just going to say, are comparable to Presley's when he first opened at The International, as well, and they seem very pleased."

"Are we near sold out or anything?"

"I've tried to get an actual reading from them. They couldn't be specific. I don't know why it is they can't determine exactly how it stands," Saul said. "I suppose that the way it works is that they know in advance there's always the people that just simply line up at the rope before each show, so they take so many bookings, I think, and then they always know that there's going to be the pressure of those that just line up, so I can't say literally that it's sold out, but from their point of view they feel as if it is."

"Yeah." Cash didn't sound entirely convinced. Despite his earlier reservations, he was planning an unusual performance for Vegas that reflected who he now was, devil's playground or not. Free to play as much religious music as he wanted, he told Saul his idea was to pull off "a visual gospel, as well as music. I want to show them maybe quick stills from my film to help tell a story in song, you know." If this concerned Saul, there wasn't much he could say; he had other issues to deal with as they neared the date of the show. Every time he felt as though all the details were settled, Johnny would move the goalposts. The final issue arose when Johnny's sister Reba Hancock phoned Saul on March 10 to discuss the arrangement of complimentary tickets.[9]

"The Las Vegas situation shapes up as a potential disaster in that Johnny told me he didn't care about any big opening night deal, where we would invite half the country like Elvis did," Saul said. "I responded accordingly, and made the deal so we would have seventy complimentary tickets. And then Reba called me last night to say that Johnny has invited four hundred people. So, once again, the old, the old razzle-dazzle, I'm now caught in a bind, not of my own making. And I don't intend to make an issue out it, if he wants four hundred tickets, well, that's fine. I guess he can pay for them, if that's what he wants, or else I can tell the hotel that the engagement is cancelled unless they give them to us, and I'll say it's Johnny talking. I'm not going to be the fall guy. But the way this situation is going to be resolved will be very interesting. And Johnny will look at me with a mournful look, and say, 'You asked me to make up a guest list,' and he won't be able to be wrong; I'll be wrong. He will not remember saying that he didn't care about any fuss being made about opening night. I'll be wrong about that, too. And I'll be required somehow or another to resolve the opening night trauma. And whatever way I do it, it'll be wrong."

In addition, Cash had extended a special invitation to their old friend Johnny Western and his wife, but for some reason instructed Marshall Grant to make all the arrangements, a detail Saul found infuriating. "Marshall doesn't even know where the Las Vegas International Hotel is, [let] alone to make the arrangements," Saul said. "So there's an example of the still ever-present paranoia at work, and an exquisite example of the deviousness of this extraordinary character."

By the time he and Barbara were on the road to the Vegas show at the end of March, what enthusiasm Saul had worked up over the show had dissipated and was replaced with simmering resentment. In the weeks leading up to the show, Saul and Johnny had a bitter fight over a holiday postage graphic that Saul had approved, which featured a Star of David with the word *shalom* built into it. A major point of contention, Johnny felt it conflicted with his own religious beliefs.

To cope with all the ongoing issues, Saul installed a recorder in his car to take down his thoughts, and as he manoeuvred through the traffic in the Chrysler on the way to the airport, he turned it on and began to vent:

> My situation with Johnny is moving into a critical period. I feel a definite buildup of hostility on his part. He's challenging me endlessly, reversing himself, putting me in an embarrassing position, not advising me of different details that are going on, doing the old number on me, of keeping me guessing, keeping me off balance, making me feel as if I'm calling the shots and then suddenly pulling the rug out from underneath me again, and again, and again, and again. So, he doesn't know that I'm not as greedy as he is. Greedy I am, but not as greedy. I don't want to be the richest man in the cemetery. I want

desperately to start spending more time with my family, and I want desperately to start enjoying the things that I've worked so goddamned hard for in 10 years, and taken such incredible abuse, and such humiliation so often. I want to salvage my soul; he robbed it, he robbed me of my soul, and now I think he's trying to save it for me — through his fundamentalist Christianity jazz.

In any event, the conflict this week was on an issue that I never dreamed would ever occur. [Johnny] called me with righteous indignation, saying that I know his beliefs well enough, and there should be a cross on the envelope, and not a Star of David, and if not a cross, at least a combination of the two. And of course this is ludicrous, and this is the self-righteous bigotry at work again. Now it's religious bigotry, and at best I have a very low tolerance level to these religious cranky ideas that offend my sensibilities and any intellectual capacity that I have — I find it very offensive. And here I am, inundated with it; the very thing that I've always objected strenuously to.

So I know that my tolerance level is at an all-time low, and that it's inevitable that a rupture is on the horizon.[10]

16

THE GOSPEL ROAD

few months after he had settled in from the trip to Israel, Saul gave a talk at the local synagogue in London. It was very well received, broke attendance records even, and photos of the trip were circulated among the audience. Following the talk, they all watched Billy Graham's *His Land*, a film about Israel released the previous year. Both Saul and Barbara had looked forward to the film with anticipation, as it related so closely to Johnny's project, but they were ultimately disappointed. It was choppy and fell far short of its potential, considering the quality of the scenery and sites available in Israel, Barbara thought. Though they obviously had access to and utilized high-quality equipment, she felt it wasn't reflected in the final product, which was also overly steeped in evangelical ideology. Saul felt inclined to agree, and wondered about Johnny's increasing tendency to evangelize, especially during his Vegas show, after which rumours circulated that religious themes were finding their way into his shows more and more, and that audience members had even responded to "altar calls" after the performance.[1]

This final part was untrue, and had likely been a misinterpretation of the audience's enthusiastic response in the final act of Cash's show, which featured gospel numbers like "Peace in the Valley" while he projected stills from the film on a screen behind him. When Cash ended with a finale of "A Thing Called Love," many people left their seats and gravitated towards the stage to be closer to Johnny, reporter Robert

Hilburn described in his review. "I feel the Holy Spirit dwells in me at all times," Cash later explained. "The people feel that special something, and they come down to the front to shake my hand. That's what happened in Las Vegas."

The rumours nevertheless reflected a sentiment from some in the music business that Cash's religiosity was becoming tiresome. "There are several offensively pious men in country music. Johnny Cash and his God are a particularly tedious act," wrote leading influential music journalist and author Nick Tosches. "Each year, Johnny Cash's mind seems to grow more monomaniacal."[2]

Regardless of the scattered objections from audience, the show was lauded by the Hilton as a "phenomenal success," as the congratulatory ad they took out later stated. As Saul's meticulous charting of audience numbers showed, Johnny had drawn more people to his shows than any other act in Las Vegas that week. A substantial amount of money had also exchanged hands at the casino during his engagement, Marty Klein excitedly informed Saul after the show, and as a result the Hilton management could hardly wait to get Cash back to perform again. Dates were quickly firmed up for a return in the spring of 1973.

"Saul, as you know, aside from the fact that Johnny did sensational business, he did something emotionally to those people that has never happened before, and I doubt will ever happen again," Klein wrote to him at the end of May. Their next frontier could be the Sahara Tahoe, he added, where the desire to have Cash perform was so high that Klein felt certain there was "nothing that we would ask for that we would not receive, including the top money ever paid to anyone, $178,571 for the ten-day period," he wrote. Not only did he think it would be an even more stimulating venue for Johnny and June, the financial implications of combining both shows were staggering. "If you were to couple the Las Vegas date and a possible Tahoe date, you would be talking of over $357,000; plus all of the extras, which would be the all-time money received in these areas. In my opinion, if the decision is to play the Sahara Tahoe, the right decision will have been made. And Johnny Cash would unquestionably write another chapter in the history of the entertainment business in Lake Tahoe." It was a no-brainer.[3]

Editing on *The Gospel Road* continued in earnest, primarily at a studio in New York, while Cash took much of his spare time between shows and touring to record the film's soundtrack at the House of Cash Studios in Nashville. After his tour in Europe and prior to the Vegas show, Cash made a quick trip out to the editing room in New York to meet with Billy Graham and see a rough cut of the film. Nothing seemed to sway his sense of focus, and though Johnny was loyal to the prior performance obligations he had agreed to, other opportunities were largely just distractions for him.

Included within this category of "distractions" was a chance to play at the Royal Gala in England on May 22.[4]

"I know this is not feasible, but at least I have to tell you about it," Saul told Johnny in April. "The queen and the prince and the entire royal family would be there, and they have firmed up from the United States two acts, and they only want one other. They've got Rowan and Martin as the emcees, and they've got Liza Minnelli, and they would like to know if you would come, with all expenses and all, and this would be at the Palladium and it would be televised worldwide."

When he received the offer from ATV Network producer Sir Lew Grade, Saul had explained that Johnny was already committed to a show in Duluth on the 21st and that the only way he could go (if he agreed to go), would be to cancel it.

"So I'm just telling you, and the rest is up to you," Saul finished, somewhat nervously. It was clearly a tremendous opportunity. *I've never even addressed someone as "Sir" so-and-so before,* he thought. It had tickled him.

"I think we'd better not try to do that, Saul," Johnny said slowly.

Saul swallowed. "I didn't even dream that you would, but on the other hand I would be remiss by not telling you about it," he said.

"Yeah, well, I appreciate it, but I think we'd better not try to do that," Johnny repeated, quietly.[5]

Saul felt a sense of concern about the film, and was irritated by Johnny's hard swerve into religious fundamentalism, but ruminated over how to address it with him. Sure, he understood the level of importance this project held for Johnny and that it went far beyond the priorities of

(left to right) Unknown, Dan Rowan, Saul Holiff, Johnny Cash, Dick Martin, and Marty Klein on the set of the *Laugh-In* television show. Hollywood, 1971.

his secular career. It was a spiritual calling, a labour of love spurred on by a desire to do something worthwhile with his life. Those were admirable aspirations, but it was Saul's job to keep an eye on the business end of things, and he felt a gnawing sense of doubt about how the end product would be received by the public.

In June, during a show at the Saratoga Performing Arts Center in New York, Johnny once again displayed stills from the movie. After the performance, Saul found himself alone with Johnny in the dressing room. Sensing that perhaps now was the chance to express his misgivings, Saul broached the topic. He mentioned the film, and suggested that it might be controversial in ways Johnny hadn't anticipated and gently floated the idea that its religious message would likely not resonate with all audiences. The talk seemed to go over well, but a month later, during a phone conversation about an appearance on *The Dean Martin Show*, the subject of the film came up again and Johnny mentioned the conversation in Saratoga.

"There's a couple of things I want to say to you that I need to clear the air completely with you on," Johnny said.

"Mm-hmm."

"First of all, I knew way before we even did the film that there's a lot of people — maybe the majority of the people — are not gonna buy what I am saying in this film or what this film is sayin'. So, you see, I don't really have to be told that because I know that," Johnny said.

"I haven't, uh, now, you say you don't have to be told that, but who, who did any... who said that?"

"You did. You said, uh, you know, in the dressing room at Saratoga, you said, 'You realize of course, that a lot of people are not gonna agree with your film.'"

"Well ... when I say, when I make a statement like that, that's what is known as trying to be honest, because first of all, if you take a hundred people, twenty-five of them are of Christian faith and twenty of them are Muslims, and ten ... you know, that's what I meant."

"Yeah, but I knew that originally, see," Johnny said.

"Yeah."

"Before I even went into the film," he added.

"That misstatement in Saratoga wasn't meant to be derogatory."

"Well, I just felt like that you didn't have a lot of interest in this film, and I just wanted to know if you don't, then, uh, I'd go ahead and do what I can do without you."

"Well, I — all I wanted to do is help in any way I can to see to it that the film is seen by as many people as it's humanly possible to see, and as tastefully as it can be done and with as much dignity as it can be done," Saul said.

"Well, I appreciate that, Saul. You know there, there won't be any income, any money for anybody from the film until we get back our investment."

"Yeah. Well, frankly speaking, I said something then, and I say it again, I haven't the slightest interest in any financial return from the movie — not the slightest, even if it was a winner. I never have had, and

I just feel as if from your point of view, it's a work of love, and if you happen to make some money, more power to you. If you don't, uh, well, then at least to have the satisfaction of trying. From my point of view, I'm not interested financially."

"Well, good, I really appreciate that, I really do need you," Johnny said.

"That's a flat statement, incidentally. I mean, whether you win or lose, I don't want a nickel."

"Okay, Saul."

"I know that you're very sensitive about the whole subject and none of these remarks are meant to. — other than to be one of the few people that try to say to you exactly what they think without meaning to be harmful. I'm not trying to break things down, I'm just trying to maybe temper things a little bit by saying, not exactly what people think you want to hear."

"Yeah, right."

"I find that a lot of people tell you exactly what you want to hear," Saul continued.

"Yeah. I know that. I don't need that either," Johnny agreed.

"And that doesn't help."

"No, it doesn't."[6]

On a weekend in late September, Saul and Barbara attended a screening of the final version of *The Gospel Road* in Chicago, which was publicized as "The musical of Jesus Christ, sung by Johnny Cash." Saul privately noted that despite the early negotiations, letters, and phone calls he had undertaken to initially bring the film to fruition, there was no mention of his name in association with the project. Which was fine. The work he had completed was clearly done as a favour, but it was interesting nonetheless.[7]

Both Saul and Barbara had already seen an early cut of the film back in June when Johnny played at Saratoga in New York. Unbeknownst to Saul, who had then departed the next day for Jamaica, Barbara had drafted a detailed three-page critique afterward and mailed it to Johnny and June.

"I regret that I couldn't summon the courage to voice my amateur opinions with so many trained specialists present, but with the hope that it might be helpful to you to hear from one more 'typical' viewer, the following were my reactions," Barbara wrote, and then went through her opinions on such things as the title, which "comes across as irrelevant in that its meaning isn't developed in the film" and Mary Magdalene's repeated removal of her shawl, which seemed too sensual. Though June was excellent in the role, Barbara added, she also found it difficult to accept June's distinctly southern drawl as "belonging" in the film and wondered if an alteration could be made to replace her voice track.

There were also many positive aspects of the film, she quickly added. Handsome, flaxen-haired Bob Elfstrom presented "a beautiful classical image of at least one interpretation of how Jesus looked," the music and photography were generally good to excellent, and the Ascension scene "was handled with subtlety and didn't even come close to suggesting 'bodies rising into the air,' as someone commented at the screening."

Barbara closed the letter with a confession that she was ultimately a little confused as to June and Johnny's intent behind the film, especially regarding the modern crucifixion scenes, which were staged not only in Jericho but also in Las Vegas, Death Valley, and near the Hollywood sign in Los Angeles. "If it is to say, 'He is gone, but we wish He'd come back and help us out of the jam we're in now ...' — as June mentioned — then I think the modern crucifixion scenes are in conflict. (To some people, they say that if He did come back we'd just wind up crucifying Him again.) I hope this is of some value. It certainly comes with my best intentions, and I do wish you every possible success with the film," she finished.[8]

"I believe that's about the greatest letter I ever heard," Johnny told Saul after the letter had arrived. "I want you to send a copy of that to Bob Elfstrom."

"The interesting part about the crucifixion scenes is it's an original thought that hasn't been brought up before — that if Jesus was to come back, and if he was to be crucified again, um, there is a conflict of interest, isn't there," Saul said.

"Yeah. Oh well, y'know," Johnny said.

"But nevertheless, listen, this is just well intended by someone who takes things very seriously," Saul said.

"Of course. It's beautiful, Saul."

"So, read it over again in your own way with June if you would," Saul said. "And if you'd drop a little line to Barbara, it would only take a moment and it would probably thrill the hell out of her."

"All right, I will."[9]

Given the incisive and honest criticism Barbara delivered in the letter, Johnny's heartfelt response was interesting. Perhaps he and June felt encouraged that Barbara, and by association Saul, had taken the time to reflect so deeply on the film's message and, generally, on the topic of Jesus. Privately, they had both discussed at length Saul's conspicuous absence in their Billy Graham engagements. And as religion became ever more a driving force in Johnny's career, they both began to wonder whether Saul's priorities really lined up with theirs any longer.

The worldwide premiere of *The Gospel Road* took place on Valentine's Day in 1973 at a shopping mall theatre in Charlotte, North Carolina — birthplace and hometown of Billy Graham, who served as the evening's honorary chairman but, strangely, never actually materialized. Marching songs from a 110-member high school band played in the background as hundreds of fans, curious locals, and Billy Graham acolytes milled around the lobby, hoping for a glimpse of Cash. Saul and Barbara brought Jonathan and Joshua along in their little matching trench coats, though the film featured a crucifixion scene so bloody that at least one child in the audience dissolved into tears and called out, "No!"[10]

However, this was Graham territory, and as such, the response was duly enthusiastic. Dr. Eugene Poston, president of the nearby Gardner-Webb College for which the event was also a benefit, bizarrely told the assembled audience that "God planned this world premiere long before we were born," and was so inspired by the film that he briefly considered asking people to come forward and publicly state their faith before he realized it wasn't the appropriate time or venue. Johnny Cash was a man of the little people, one emphatic fan told *Washington Post* reporter Richard Maschal.[11]

When later asked by another reporter why he and June had decided to make a movie about the life of Jesus, Cash responded, "I felt … that would be the most meaningful thing that we could contribute with our lives.... The story of Christ is a story that needed very much to be told, I think, in a way so that people could relate to it. Christ was sent to earth as a human being, and if our film has one thing, it has Jesus as human and believable."[12]

The Gospel Road was received well in Charlotte, but how would it fare in mainstream America?

"We were really trying desperately to get it distributed beyond the conventional places," Saul told author Michael Streissguth. "I think I had a little something to do with that. Maybe it was more than just a little. But getting [it] out of the basements of Baptist churches in the South was quite an achievement." Whatever effort Saul managed to put in, it was Lou Robin who took on the heavy lifting, and managed to convince 20th Century Fox to purchase the distribution rights to the film from Cash for two hundred thousand dollars. Cautious about the film's strong fundamentalist approach, Fox prepared to first open it in the South, where "people take the Bible more literally than in New York, Chicago or Los Angeles," company executive Hal Sherman told the *New York Times*. They anticipated some resistance from theatre owners, he added, because "traditionally people go to church on Sunday and they want entertainment from the movies."[13]

Ultimately, Fox's own analysis proved correct. By December it finally opened in New York and even found its way to a first-rate cinema on the main street in Saul's hometown, but its deeply religious message made it a hard sell and Fox found they simply couldn't distribute the film through regular channels. Billy Graham's company World Wide Pictures finally stepped in and got a multi-year distribution licence from Fox so that they could play the film in churches throughout the country for free. "There were as many as five hundred prints out on loan at one time. The proceeds went to each particular church's needs," said Robin. *The Gospel Road*'s accompanying double album suffered a similar fate, and struggled to number twelve on the country charts, the worst performance yet for a Cash album that featured new material.

If Saul felt vindicated in predicting this type of outcome for the film, he never expressed it. As far as Cash was concerned, he maintained the film was his "life's proudest work," and if viewed through the lens of it being a daring and visionary expression of his most deeply held beliefs, it was an admirable accomplishment.

The entire affair made Saul come to a different conclusion, however. As the spring of 1973 turned into summer, he couldn't escape an intuitive sense that the writing was on the wall for Cash. In just three short years, Saul had accomplished his goal of managing an international superstar. But more and more he felt the need to climb down from that mountain. Privately, he began to mull over the pros and cons of quitting Johnny for good. One night in the solitude of his home study, he slowly rolled a sheet of paper into the typewriter.

"Factors that influenced my decision to leave Johnny Cash," he tapped out, and then paused.

"Pros: money, prestige — power, travel, glamour, free hotel, etc." He stopped again.

It was really the cons that had pushed him to make this list.

"Cons," he typed.

Then the words came tumbling out: "ego-shattering, tension, need of change and renewal, neck tension, humiliated, religion and politics, time with kids, hyper & manic, hyperventilate, tired, nervous (Travel!!), drink too much, eat too much, high pressure, justifying, deadlines, nice guy routine, no routine — no long range plans, salivate, packing and unpacking, crummy hotels, hives, lousy water, risk of hepatitis, gas shortage, mugging and theft, decline in economy, decline in Cash career, anti-climactic from now on, creepy people."

The typing stopped and he pulled the page from the machine. His eyes scanned down the list and he fumbled in his desk. With a green highlighter pen he carefully traced over the words "decline in Cash career."[14]

17

THE WISEST MAN I KNOW

The sun on the surface of Lake Tahoe flashed like camera bulbs in Saul's eyes as he broke into a jog. Clad all in white — T-shirt, shorts, and trainers that were broken in but clean, Saul quickly settled into his usual warm-up rhythm. It was now July 29, 1973, and he was in the best physical shape he'd been in for some time.

Throughout June, progress had been excruciating, and he had run vigorously and single-mindedly for the entire month but not lost any weight. In fact, he was now eight pounds heavier than a year and a half ago. But it was okay. The drinking was mostly under control, and he hadn't taken any hard liquor in weeks, though wine and sherry were still on the menu.

They were now at the Sahara Tahoe and in the midst of Johnny's debut, which was going quite well, aside from a small upset that occurred when Roy Orbison — Cash's close friend and neighbour — was booked there at the same time but *not* in the main showroom, which required some tactful negotiation.

When all was said and done, the outlook ahead was sunny: considerable planning had been completed for the remainder of the year, August tours in the States were ready to go, and September tours to the United Kingdom were set up. But for Saul there was a constant sense of irritation that it was never enough, that he couldn't seem to mobilize his energy to exercise as much as he wanted or complete the reading he felt was important. Before the departure to Nevada with Barbara, he took out his recorder and tried to sort out his feelings.

"Emotionally, I'm somewhat confused," he said. "More has been accomplished than I might normally have expected, yet it doesn't seem to satisfy me a great deal. Still seem to be disoriented in my own home, and tension still has not subsided."

Observation of the current affairs in the United States didn't help.

"Watched the [John] Dean television testimony at great length. It's fascinating to see the fall, and you might say the decline, of the American Caesar. Um, it vindicates our stand about Nixon, and indicates that the American government is about as corrupt and as rotten as about everything else we know in the American society, which doesn't give us much satisfaction; it just makes us awfully damn apprehensive," he said. "The Watergate investigations have become more and more complicated, and the United States has shown more and more its lack of any kind of communication, of any kind of integrity, any kind of honesty, a lack of shame, a lack of self-censorship, a lack of self — I forget what the Chinese call it, but an obvious inability to face facts. It's a sad state of affairs."

As he jogged, a motorboat slowly drifted in the distance across the lake's surface, trailing white froth. They had tooled around on a boat themselves up there last fall while on vacation with Marty Klein, with Saul in his Sahara Tahoe sweater and jaunty white captain's hat. It was a pleasure trip, but they had also managed to tie up some loose ends for Johnny's show, of which he was now in the third performance of a seven-day engagement. Everything was running smoothly, except this ongoing back-and-forth dynamic with Johnny that had been going on for months. It was an undercurrent that never seemed to quite reach a resolution before a new wrinkle appeared. As he ran, he reviewed their conflicts in his mind.

A tangle with Johnny had arisen earlier that year, in April, when Saul had received an irate call after a long and involved tour in New Zealand, Australia, and Japan. Johnny felt that Saul's absence from the filming of his Amoco/American Oil commercial in February had indicated he was not looking after his interests. From Saul's vantage point it was he who had dined and wooed American Oil for years now, initially as a potential sponsor for Cash's ill-conceived gospel specials and then as a lucrative source of revenue through a series of advertising contracts that were relatively easy for him to shoot and didn't compromise his integrity. Saul had been careful on that point.

Cash went on to say he had lined up the next series of commercials with American Oil in mid-May, without consulting Saul, which was a role that until now had been exclusively his terrain. Furthermore, the cheque for the tour had not yet arrived from the Australia tour, Johnny added. He then finished the conversation with the ominous phrase, "If you want to stay with me, you better look after these things." Saul had been unable to interpret what it all meant.

Running hard now, hardly aware he was running at all, Saul's mind loosened from the anxiety that so often bound his thoughts in repetitive permutations and patterns. Ten days after that call, on April 23, a telegram had then arrived from Johnny. The cheque from Australia had come through, he wrote, but the one for *The Flip Wilson Show* he had done the previous November had not. "Do you want this in advance as well, or will you wait until it arrives?" Johnny said, a comment Saul interpreted as nasty.[1]

The conflict had not been resolved by the time Johnny was scheduled for his return show in Las Vegas four days later. Saul had gone along to the show regardless, and upon his arrival at the hotel, had unpacked his recorder. "I came here with great trepidation, because I didn't know by the time Johnny arrived whether I was going to stay out the week, or be told that he wanted me to leave," he said. This was in addition to "the usual nervous strain of wondering how we were going to [handle] all the loose ends and reservations and people wanting complimentary tickets."

And then there was June. For the past few months, Saul had endured veiled insinuations from both her and Reba that he was less than forthcoming with gifts and gestures of appreciation for them on special occasions. The implication, of course, was that he was cheap, and it infuriated him. All the times he had gone to great lengths to be generous reeled through his mind, like when he had negotiated with Screen Gems to gift Johnny a brand-new Rolls-Royce. *If I had pushed hard enough for an additional cash bonus, they would have included it in*

Saul Holiff in front of a Johnny Cash billboard in Las Vegas, 1973.

the deal, and I would have received a commission. But no, the Rolls was a unique and special gift, and it gave me satisfaction to represent my client usefully and imaginatively.

The rise and fall of Saul's breath fell in line with the push of his legs as he increased his pace. Then there was that time he had spent countless hours purchasing customized gifts for every person who had been involved in the TV show, no matter how minor a role they had played — only to be later informed by Johnny that it was unnecessary and expensive, even though Saul had managed to convince Harold Cohen to get the network to foot the bill. On and on. The time he had sent a spectacular one-hundred-pound cake to the Cash household for John Carter's first birthday, with a request that a small piece be kept aside in the freezer so that he might have a taste — a request that had been ignored. Or how, in the aftermath of Johnny's triumphant open at Madison Square Garden, he had felt so inspired that he had the tickets dipped in gold and embedded in onyx and glass, and then sent the paperweights to June and Johnny, his parents, and Reba as gifts. Or the numerous presents and notes he had sent to housekeeping staff and executive personnel at the Ramada Inn in the hope it would make up for the sad fact that week after week they were forced to clean up rooms that looked like barn animals had resided within them. There were reams of examples, and receipts to boot. It wasn't so much that he needed the recognition, it just hurt that despite the effort, he was still castigated. That once again, he felt like an outsider.

As he rounded a bend, the magnificent snow-covered peak of Mount Tallac rose into view.

He was reminded of a time several years ago, just after the TV show had been picked up, when he had attended a celebratory dinner party at Johnny and June's house in Hendersonville with Barbara and Stan Jacobson. During the party they were to be presented with the keys to their new Rolls-Royce. Columbia representatives were invited. During the festivities, June had regaled the group with a story about the infamous witch of Belle Meade, which was an exclusive neighbourhood within Nashville.

"Do you know that there are witnesses who saw the witch of Belle Meade in two separate places at the same time?" June had said.

"She was probably booked by Saul Holiff," Jacobson had quipped, and Johnny chuckled. Saul joined in halfheartedly. Jacobson glanced at him. "Aw, I'm just kidding, Saul," he quickly added.

"I know," Saul had said, and raised a glass to his mouth. It was all in good fun. Except when it wasn't. The undercurrent of the sentiment had bothered him, as had June's recent insinuations. The joke's subtext was that Johnny's unreliability had somehow been the result of Saul's bungling. It was nothing, no big deal, but now it seemed that all these subtle humiliations and barbed comments throughout the years had accumulated to a point where he no longer had any patience for it.[2]

As he ran, Saul reflected on his family. Much of May had been spent travelling back and forth to Nashville, where Saul took both Jonathan and Joshua on separate one-on-one trips. On both occasions they had stayed at the Sheraton and visited Cash's home in Hendersonville, where Johnny and June put out "a banquet fit for a king," as Saul remembered it. They were generous and gracious: Johnny not only invited Jonathan to watch the filming of his Amoco commercial but also took Joshua along to participate in the taping of an NBC show that was to be the summer replacement for Dean Martin. Jonathan had gone to dinner at Mario's with some of the Amoco executives and behaved like a gentleman, which was a relief, as lately Saul had been having concerns about whether he presented a serious discipline problem.

"Just a short note from far away Alaska to tell you both that I love you and that I'm proud of you. School will be over by the time I see you next — so maybe we will finally get a chance to throw a ball around, hit a few and maybe go exploring and have a picnic," Saul had written to the kids in June, after a tour wrapped up that had gone through western Canada and up to Anchorage. "Up here in Alaska it hardly ever gets dark at this time of the year and the sun comes up around 3 a.m.!! It's much colder than London and you must fly to get here. There are roads in Canada that go up the long way through the Yukon. Be good and keep busy learning and playing. See you soon, Love Daddy."[3]

On the Fourth of July, Saul and the family were customarily with the Cashes at the Statler Brothers' yearly "Happy Birthday U.S.A." celebrations in their hometown of Staunton, Virginia, but instead that year Saul had shut himself in the office for half the day to complete work, and then spent the afternoon holed up in his study with his TC66 Sony recorder to get down a final summary of where his life was at. There had been a sense of urgency to it that he couldn't quite place.

"The kids seem to be enjoying life around the house, and enjoy being out of school. And we're tutoring — or at least I'm working with Josh on his mathematics — with moderate to practically negligible results, and they're doing exercises daily. I still would like to be able to get out and toss a ball around with them, kick a ball around with them, and get more involved physically with them, which I can't seem to get off my ass to do. Still terrible habits both in being lazy and my reading habits are lousy. My work habits seem to be atrocious. It's a question of … I've got so much to be grateful for, but I'm so goddamned lazy about so many things, apathetic, but by and large I've got a great deal to be grateful for. I just need to reorder my priorities and get off my fat ass, and get out with the kids and do things with them. Toss a ball around, get involved. Help a little bit around here. I feel guilty about it, I guess."[4]

Things would get better. He would do better. When they returned from this trip, he'd make more of an effort. At least he had maintained a regular jogging regimen; that was something.

As he completed his jog, Johnny and June's bungalow came into view. Saul slowed to a casual pace and then fell into a walk, breathing hard. Their own bungalow was just a couple of blocks away, with luxuries and staffing that was comparable to Johnny and June's, as he had requested. On a whim, Saul decided it might be a good time to stop in at Johnny and June's for a moment to quickly go over the rest of their schedule.

Tension was evident from the moment he entered the room. Johnny and June invited him in and offered him a seat. The sofa squeaked softly as Saul, still breathing hard, sat down next to June. They both turned and observed him. June spoke first and asked why he had been absent at their recent Billy Graham Crusades. "Do you have something against Jesus?" she asked. Maybe it was that Johnny played these concerts for free, she added. Maybe he was only interested in money. Saul stared at her, his heart still beating hard under his ribs from the jog.

"I consider those remarks to be anti-Semitic, June," Saul countered. "And I object to being portrayed that way." Not only was his presence unnecessary, he added, but there was also no logical reason it was even required at benefit concerts that he had had no hand in arranging. He paused for a moment. *Like I have the market cornered on money? Ah, but of course that's part of my history, isn't it? Somehow or another, it's always the Jews; they're the only ones who are really after money.* When telling Barbara the story later, June's comment would strike him as funny. The Cashes were, of course, as interested in money as anyone. But in that moment it stung.

A strange sense of calm came over him. He turned to face Johnny. "You know what? I think it's time that I gave you five months' notice." Both June and Johnny looked shocked and said nothing. Saul stood and left.[5]

In the months that followed, the incident at Lake Tahoe was never discussed. Like so many of their conflicts, it was as if it had never happened. Except this time, it was different.

The day Saul resigned, when he returned to their bungalow and told Barbara what had happened, his relief was palpable. Already wistfully perusing materials related to Victoria, a picturesque city nestled in Vancouver Island on the West Coast of Canada that featured a renowned university, his dream of completing a degree was now actually a tangible reality.

For some time, and at Saul's request, as Lou Robin had shouldered more and more of the day-to-day needs of Johnny's career he had also been witness to their clashes. "Saul would try to tell him what to do, and that was the worst thing you could do with John," Lou said. "They were tired of each other. Saul had covered for John for so many years, for all of John's antics, and he just got tired of it. And Johnny got tired of him trying to be the policeman."

Within a week of Saul's resignation, word filtered back to Lou, who realized it was time to formalize what had already pretty much developed into a managerial relationship with Cash. In mid-August, Lou and his partner Allen Tinkley picked Johnny and June up from the Detroit airport in a limousine to drive them to their next show at Michigan's Pine Knob Music Theatre. During the forty-five-minute drive to the hotel, they seized the opportunity to outline their case.

"We've learned a lot from Saul, and as long as you've let him go, we'd like to put our hat in the ring and try to pick up where he left off," Lou said.

"Well, that's okay, but I only have one problem," Johnny said.

"What's that?"

"All the people Saul kept away from me over the years are now gonna come back again," said Johnny. Until now, it had been Saul's domain to keep the vultures at bay — the people he had no interest in, who were useless or just tagalongs, people who tried to sell him something. "You'll have to be aware," he added.[6]

Over the months that followed, Saul and Johnny's partnership was in many ways better than ever — during a September show in Glasgow, they wagered five hundred dollars on the Muhammad Ali match that was on, which Saul won. "You couldn't find a better relationship going on. And I did leave in November. That's the truth," Saul told author Michael Streissguth. There was reason for Saul's insistence on this; as word of his departure hit the music industry, rumours began to circulate that he must have been either pushed to resign or flat-out fired. At the centre of this speculation was the question, who quits a superstar at the height of his career?

"It was more or less accidentally brought to my attention while I was in Nashville last weekend that you have advised certain people within the House of Cash that the reason for my split with Johnny is, to quote you, 'that he had a falling out with June and was asked to resign,'" Saul wrote to Johnny's sister Reba Hancock on October 19. "I take umbrage at your spreading false information, since, as I am sure you know, I resigned of my own volition, which of course was verified by Johnny's letter to me. It is unfair and unwarranted to give anyone an incorrect version."[7]

Included with the letter was a copy of the press release that had been sent out to all the individuals involved, as well as to all the trade papers and magazines in the industry, that announced Saul's resignation. Lou Robin's Artist Consultants were to take over the representation of Cash for concerts and other appearances, it stated, while Marty Klein of APA would look after Johnny's interests in regards to TV, movie, and commercial appearances.

"Holiff and Cash are parting on completely amicable terms after having shared, over the years, many ups and downs and ultimately much good fortune together," the release said, and went on to state the reason for Saul's resignation as "the fact that he has a very young family that, due to prolonged absences from home owing to business and travel obligations, he has seldom had the opportunity to see during their formative years."[8]

The letter to Reba was written on the heels of an incident at the Country Music Association Awards, which Johnny had hosted, that Saul found deeply humiliating. Upon his and Barbara's arrival, the two were ushered to an unmarked, broken bench covered in chalk dust, only to be then asked to vacate the area sometime later by a cameraman who described it as "unsafe." Once they left this "cubby-hole," as Saul described it, the couple was then squeezed into a spot behind the camera, in the area reserved for the cue-card man, who graciously allowed them to stay.

Immediately following the show, in which the Statler Brothers, whom Saul still managed, won an award, "the ushers took up positions on all of the aisles of the reserved section and refused us entry since we didn't have, in his words, 'passes,'" Saul wrote in horror to CMA executive director Jo Walker. "As a result we were unable to get to where the Statler Brothers and their families were standing to offer our congratulations."[9]

The edifice of status and deference Saul had worked so hard to build was already cracking. Though no doubt devastating to his ego (with typical self-deprecating humour, he actually launched a short-lived TV talk show on Cablecast at this time called *The Ego's Nest*), it did little to sully his sense of relief around his decision to leave, which at times blossomed into a sort of optimism. As the press release about their split made its rounds, there was a flood of surprised and curious responses from associates and music insiders. Within days, southern gospel singer Larry Gatlin wrote to request that Saul manage him. Though describing himself as "drained, tired and dispirited" in his good-natured refusal letter, Saul responded to the majority of queries with an uncharacteristic sort of Zen.

"I received today the press release about you and Johnny," wrote Harold D. Cohen, former executive producer of Johnny's TV show. "In some ways, I think you would agree, more than many others, I know the contribution you have made to his well-being and the price you have paid for it. If the termination of the relationship was your desire at this juncture, obviously, I revel in it for you. If not, I must believe that the benefits of your 'semi-retirement' are long overdue. You remember, I once said, 'You've earned every penny you made.'"

"It feels strange but somewhat exhilarating to be free again," Saul responded to Cohen. "I would apply for welfare, but I am sure they would turn down an ex-country & western manager!" Overall, Saul felt proud of the fact that he was the one who had walked away, on his own terms. It was virtually unprecedented in the business, as far as he knew — unless the client's career was already completely finished.

"It gave me some weird satisfaction to know that I was doing this of my own volition," he later told a journalist from the *London Free Press*. In a response to Variety Theatre International president Len Naymark's queries, he mused that "thirteen years is quite a long spell, and I feel that I need a crack at self-renewal and re-ordering of some of my priorities."[10]

As the curtain began its descent on their time together, Johnny chose a sold-out show at the London Gardens on November 3 as the venue to pay tribute to his manager, whom he described to the audience as a "great family man, and one of the wisest men I know." Then, perhaps to tempt him, Johnny told the crowd, "We've grown together for twelve years and now Saul plans to turn his back on some of the future wealth we may have in order to spend more time with his family in London." Johnny then presented Saul with two bottles of champagne.

Two weeks later, Saul's resignation became official.[11]

As they travelled the road to this juncture, "there was never one ill word, never a suggestion I would be leaving," Saul mused to author Michael Streissguth. "I think they looked upon me — I'm positive of it — as a good luck [charm]. Like, that I brought luck to their situation. Like I was some sort of medallion. It had something to do with being superstitious, I know that. And then, I probably might've felt a similar way."

Though Saul's press release was careful to enunciate the amicability surrounding the end of his tenure on December 9, there was one final showdown in store for the two men before they finally separated for good. And true to what Saul had intuited, Johnny's fortunes were about to shift dramatically.

18

CINNAMON HILL

Though the rest of their journey would now be walked on separate paths, the ties had not yet been completely severed between Johnny and Saul. Given the decade or so of legal wrangling over finances between Johnny and his former manager, Stew Carnall, Saul had the foresight to expect some delay or contention when it came to sorting out the last details of their relationship. After analyzing all the books and financial records, Saul sent off his final invoice with fingers crossed that all would be amicable.

However, when the response to this invoice arrived in February of 1974, it did so via Cash's lawyer. Something inside Saul snapped. The issues at hand were simple enough — commissions were due on contracts with the Country Music Awards show and American Oil. The amount in question was $22,500 — a substantial but not exorbitant amount — but the sense that he was about to get screwed was enough to cause decades of Saul's pent-up frustrations and humiliations to rise to the surface.[1]

A new sheet of office stationery was rolled into the typewriter, emblazoned with the simple Volatile Attractions logo. As Saul sat down to compose his response, he closed his eyes for a moment and then the words began to flow. What emerged was a draft letter that was never sent to Johnny, but it served as a complete, unedited airing of all the grievances Saul had accumulated over their time together.

Johnny ...

... Knowing you as well as I do, your most recent lawyer's letter did not come as a surprise to me. I anticipated this kind of approach. It's entirely consistent with the past, if one recalls how you dealt with Stew Carnall thirteen years ago.

Although I served as your road manager for many years at no additional compensation, and although you failed to honor the contract that existed between us which was written up October 3, 1961, and although I was forced to pay all of my own expenses with the exception of air travel, I did feel that it was not my proper function, as precedents in the trade will bear out, to be in constant attendance serving no useful purpose. It was absolutely necessary to return to the mounds of work that had accumulated in the interim. Your remarks to your lawyer about my not attending taping sessions were unwarranted, unfair and irrelevant. I believe that in the three-year period of commercial sessions I may have missed two or three — all for very good reasons. I am sure the courts will bear me out when seeking a typical example (precedent) to establish the guidelines and appropriate functions of a personal manager and/or agent.

A personal manager is not intended to be a hand-holder.

Only a handful of people know what you are really like, and I am one of them!! You did exactly as I would have expected. You did wrong. Your actions are unethical, decidedly not honorable and, depending on various interpretations, un-Christian. I shall resort to every legal means at my disposal to see that all commissions that are rightfully due me are paid in full. I assure you that I will approach this task with the same single-mindedness along with self-centeredness that you have displayed in your work. Your actions in this case do not live up to your public image. Again, this is entirely predictable. I assure you I will try to set the record straight.

For years, in the most devious, subtle and ingenious methods imaginable, you have managed to denigrate my position with you, humiliate me wherever and however possible, and rarely if ever acknowledge any contribution I may have made to help you further your career. I acted as your manager, agent, press and public relations director, conceived and expedited publicity materials, played a 24-hour-a-day role in preparing the groundwork for your divorce, met at great length with the I.R.S. in Ventura to help achieve a settlement that would not inflict a financial hardship on you at the time, spent literally hundreds of hours meeting with your lawyers and accountants on the West Coast to sort out the California fire lawsuit and the incredible Kafka-esque bookkeeping entanglements that I inherited from my predecessor.

I negotiated two of your Columbia Records contract renewals, exacted better terms, and helped retain the tax deferral arrangements when they were in jeopardy because of abuse of the conditions that they were predicated on.

Many days were expended in resolving the Ku Klux Klan attacks on you, and virtually hundreds upon hundreds of hours were spent to help thwart endless threatened lawsuits because of all the dates that you failed to "show" without any valid reason whatsoever. Over the years, only one legal action against you was successful, and that was resolved by simply re-scheduling the engagement at a reasonable guarantee. At no time was I compensated for any of these services, nor, in most instances, was there any comment made, period. It was all "expected." Thousands of dollars of commissions that would have been payable for all the work required to set up the many dates that you callously cancelled were lost as income to my Company.

The embarrassment that I was subjected to and the evasive tactics that I was forced to adopt are inconsistent with my nature and my background. I was driven to these actions to protect my client.

Over the many years and the many, many LPs that you produced, never did you ever pay me the smallest token of respect by suggesting that I might write some of the usual inane liner notes on the LP jacket. In many cases you simply left it up to strangers at Columbia Records. It's incredible that you are so insecure that you feared giving me or showing me any recognition whatsoever in case it might be interpreted as being a weakness on your part and that you weren't really Superman, after all....

My only concern is really not to make a character analysis or an assessment of your insulting actions towards me over the years. My main purpose is to point out to you, if that is at all possible, that I have been directly responsible for saving you many thousands of dollars by serving you in various capacities. I negotiated your contract with [music publishers] Hill and Range back in the mid-1960s and extracted substantially improved terms. You showed your appreciation by subsequently cutting me off from all commissions on publishing, BMI, record royalties etc. Our original contract that you drafted and handed me in October of 1961 clearly states that I was to receive 15% commission on all income that you earned, whether it be from one-nighters, record royalties or whatever. It also states that you were to pay all my road expenses. Over the years you failed to honor this contract, and endlessly eroded the terms of this agreement to the point where the agreement became a travesty and a charade.

I made the deal with Granada Television to do a musical/sociological television documentary at San

Quentin. A sequel to the Folsom Prison LP resulted. You never had any intention to produce a sequel. This television special was the catalyst that resulted in Columbia, at the very last minute and in the most improbable and unethical manner imaginable, attempting to become a part of a deal that they contributed nothing towards financially, artistically or in any other manner whatsoever, and which I managed to salvage, through a series of painful, lengthy dialogues with stubborn, unrealistic Columbia executives. The LP that resulted from the San Quentin engagement went on to earn enormous sums of money. I have not received any recompense.

I strongly recommended that you secure proper legal counsel and actuarial services consistent with the enormous upsurge in your income. You chose to select a bookkeeper who subsequently embezzled you out of hundreds of thousands of dollars, and an office manager who apparently didn't render the services that your business situation demanded and who was peremptorily let go, after a brief tenure. You now show your appreciation by advising your lawyer that I wouldn't be there to "service" your commercial sessions, and your lawyer further states that "... John indicated that he did not think it totally reasonable to pay you the commission on the American Oil contract renewal as you had resigned as his manager and were not serving the taping sessions. I must say I agree with John on this, after having reviewed yours and John's relationship over the years" (whatever he means by that). Incidentally, if you have any concern about my writing a book dealing with your years of shoddy behaviour and shameful actions, forget it. I personally do not think there is a market for it. I do hopefully intend to write a book following my sojourn at university, which would deal with personalities such as yourself, but it would be more of a sociological study.

I strongly recommend that you honor your commitments.

Yours truly,
Saul Holiff

P.S. Years ago — I believe at least fourteen — I made a comment backstage ... "You're just like the rest of them." I haven't changed my mind.[2]

Housebound with a severe case of flu, Saul found writing the letter cathartic but exhausting. Once completed, however, Saul held on to it and wrote again to Johnny's lawyer. A flurry of messages ensued, and by mid-February Saul had consulted his own lawyer. A couple of weeks later, Saul decided to address Johnny directly and mail what was likely an edited and different version of the letter. Cash then decided to take matters into his own hands and respond to Saul himself on March 5, without the mediation of a lawyer.

It was time to clear the air, and it was only right that he write back in his own words, said Johnny, as gossip and rumours had been circulating like crazy among lawyers and agents. Enclosed with the letter was a cheque covering Saul's commissions from American Oil; the CMA money would be sent once it was received from the awards show authorities. Furthermore, if there were any other financial misunderstandings, he was sorry, Johnny added, and grateful that Saul had cleared them up. With this payment of monies due to his manager, he felt confident it would ethically wind up the business end of things between them. But it was important for him to know that their personal relationship with each other would remain, emphasized Johnny, "because a man who was so much a part of my life for so many years is still in so many ways like a part of the family."

As for the other grievances, he said he didn't share the mixed emotions over their relationship that Saul seemed to feel. "I think it was a fine relationship. As you pointed out to me, you were responsible, in part at least, for the good reading habits I have developed for some of the better books that I've read. This, I feel, has given me a lot of growth mentally and spiritually," Johnny wrote, and added that Saul would never hear him or June say an unkind word about him to anyone. "We all know what Saul Holiff has meant to us, the hard times and the dirty work that you had to take on."

There was one thing that did hurt a little, however, and that was how in his letter Saul had raised the issue of the Ku Klux Klan episode, the divorce proceedings, and the California fire lawsuit. Those were incidents he would rather not be reminded of, Johnny wrote.

That said, in the weeks to come Johnny and June would be sending along a gift to Saul, a Patek Philippe wristwatch. This was not to be viewed as compensation for any unpaid work he had done but rather just as a gesture to show how "we love to give whenever we can," said Johnny, and "because it means so much to you." In addition, they wanted Saul, Barbara, and the kids to visit their new estate in Jamaica, which they had just purchased from an American businessman named John Rollins. A new swimming pool was under construction, and the main building — dubbed the Cinnamon Hill Great House — featured five air-conditioned bedrooms and a full staff that included a gourmet cook, Edith, two maids, a domestic assistant, a gardener, and a yard hand. "I know how you appreciate the finer things of life," Johnny said, deliberately tempting Saul. At Cinnamon Hill, all the luxuries afforded the Cashes would be theirs to enjoy, he added, before signing off, "God bless you and your family."[3]

Saul was floored. The sentiments were of a variety he had never really heard before from Johnny, and the gift of the watch, which was among the most expensive brands in the world, was heartfelt and personal. He felt his resentment begin to recede. This was what he had wanted. It was really all he had ever wanted: to be seen. And for the first time, albeit via letter, the two men stood and truly faced one another — the sober-minded Jewish businessman from London, Ontario, and the wild, cotton-pickin' Southern Baptist from Dyess, Arkansas. Immediately, Saul wrote back and ensured copies of his letter were sent to Johnny's homes both in Hendersonville and in Jamaica.

"Your very welcome letter certainly clears the air. I know only too well how denigrating and distorted remarks can cause one to take a jaundiced and skeptical view of business or personal associates," Saul replied. "We appreciate the invitation you have extended and hope very much to take you up on it. I am especially pleased at some of the thoughtful and kind sentiments you expressed in your letter. The gift of the Patek Philippe will obviously be very welcome. It was totally unexpected but then you always had a flair for doing the unexpected!"[4]

The tone was jovial, but Saul wasn't entirely at peace. Not yet. Saul mentioned to Johnny that there was still some unfinished business with June he felt driven to resolve, or at least express. It was time to cast off the weight of constant deference he had offered his client for so long, piece by piece. "It may seem ridiculous at this stage of the game to bring these matters to her attention, but I was never able to accept — then or now — criticism that I felt was unjust. As overdue as it may seem this helps complete the necessary catharsis for me," Saul wrote in a postscript in yet another letter to Johnny less than two weeks later.[5]

The full power of his pen then turned to June.

"During the last many months preceding my resignation in Lake Tahoe, there were many direct references and indirect inferences by yourself and Reba about my failing to show proper respect and sufficient interest as regards activities concerning Johnny. The impression that I clearly received from you and your sister-in-law was that I neglected to send appropriate gifts, flowers etc. on special occasions (e.g. openings at Vegas and Tahoe, the office party at the House of Cash, etc.)," he wrote on May 27. "To set the record straight, I am enclosing information that should refute most — if not all — insinuations made by you, Reba and others."

The gifts of the Rolls-Royce, the Madison Square Garden paperweights and the cake for John Carter were all recalled and painstakingly listed. As he went on, he remembered more and more. Christmas and birthdays, appreciative gifts that were sent to airline personnel, police officers, air freight workers, telephone operators, the First American National Bank, the florist shop, secretaries of key personnel and executives, and sales personnel at Columbia. Beautiful attaché cases that were mailed to Chief Viger and the members of the Jicarilla council in New Mexico, as well as Columbia executives, black and yellow wallet sets sent to Johnny's parents and to Reba. Hundreds of LPs to various people within the Cash sphere.

All of this was done to present a certain impression of Johnny to the world, and much of it was at Saul's own expense. A large floral arrangement had been sent to the House of Cash's open house and became a centrepiece on one of the tables, even though Saul himself had not been invited. "You did, however, advise me on the road that I had neglected to properly acknowledge this important occasion in your lives. I was put in a defensive and embarrassing position by your remarks," Saul recalled hotly.

"Several years ago, I commissioned a painting on velvet for Johnny. It was done by a highly regarded and very expensive artist in Los Angeles. Whether he cared for the painting or not was immaterial, but his response was, as usual, negative."

These were just some examples, some insignificant perhaps, but enough for Saul to feel he had effectively refuted the assertion that he was somehow not as forthcoming as was expected. Now was the difficult part. Perhaps one of the most challenging slights of his managerial career was in the suspension of his royalty commissions and compensation for road expenses, all issues that he felt were clearly embedded in his and Johnny's original managerial agreement, however informal that agreement originally was. It was time that he aired his secret suspicions: That this was primarily June's doing.

> In 1968, due largely to your influence on Johnny, commissions were suspended on record royalties, publishing royalties, BMI royalties, etc. It was claimed at the time that the separation and Johnny's impending divorce was creating a financial burden on both of you that was too difficult to handle at the time. The original agreement clearly stated that I was to receive the usual managerial commission from all sources of his income.
>
> Aided and abetted by your advice and counseling, the agreement was chipped away at and eroded by every conceivable means. In spite of the fact that I was acting as personal manager, booking agent, press agent, public relations director, budget planner etc., another part of the contract was arbitrarily and unfairly cancelled.

This involved payment to me for road expenses. I was required to cover many bases and go out on the road, look after settlements, resolve endless emotional conflicts and other squabbles and have to pay my own expenses for the privilege of doing so. This is unprecedented.

I have long debated with myself as to whether I should send this letter. I realize it is now ancient history. Obviously, you didn't coerce your husband. He went along quite willingly with all your suggestions and came up with quite a few of his own. Do you think it is possible for both of you now to realize why my attitude eventually hardened? It is also not very difficult for any reasonable and open-minded person to conclude that I might have reason to feel that I was unfairly and improperly dealt with.

It is not my intention to stir up any old or new animosities at this point, but after so many years of suppressing my feelings and having been exposed to endless subtle slights, denigrating remarks and painful humiliations, I had to get some of these things off my chest. I am sure that, like in the past, you both will rationalize all of the things that I have attempted to bring to your attention and give yourselves a clean bill of health with complete exoneration of guilt or wrongdoing."[6]

As he signed the letter, it felt as though a chapter of a book had closed.

But even this was by no means the end of Johnny and Saul's relationship, and things were about to take another unexpected turn.

There comes a time in every artist's career when the well of creativity runs dry or the work is simply not resonating with its audience as intended. For musicians, it can happen as early as the album that immediately follows a successful debut, often dubbed the "sophomore slump," or to veteran artists, no matter how untouchable their talents may seem. As Saul tried to express to Johnny in their telephone conversation regarding

The Gospel Road in 1972, there were few people in Cash's camp who would tell him the truth, and not just what he wanted to hear. Though this had inevitably led to strife between the two, the benefit of a strong counterweight — either from Saul or people like Stan Jacobson — often served to keep Cash keen and push his career in new directions.

Unfortunately for Johnny, this lack of outside criticism combined with both a sense of exhaustion from the pressures of his career and a desire to prioritize religion and family to create a perfect storm that eroded his artistic and commercial appeal.

What many didn't understand was that Cash felt no doubt that this new direction was a divine calling, and its effect on his career was in no way a deterrent. "As far as losing my following or something like that — well that doesn't worry me at all," Cash told author Charles Paul Conn. It was what God had chosen for him to do, and outside dissent only served to galvanize his resolve. "The criticism that came was something that he felt was his crown of thorns; it was his way of the cross, that was the burden that was given to him, the price he had to pay to deliver God's word," said Cash's close friend and family historian Mark Stielper.[7]

It was a tricky state of affairs for Lou Robin to inherit; on one hand, Cash was pretty much "out of the woods" in regards to the drug problem that had so severely curtailed his ability to complete tours and recording sessions. On the other, his spiritual pursuits now both consumed and validated him — a performance at the evangelical Explo '72 in Dallas had drawn an unbelievable audience of more than one hundred thousand people, for example — and though the lack of commercial prospects on this path concerned him, there was little that Robin could do to intervene. And frankly, Cash didn't want any intervention. The best Robin could do was to try to accommodate Cash's desires while also serving as a go-between for Columbia's interests.

"He sort of had a religious segment in his show [where] he'd do a couple gospel songs. That seemed to be adequate for the time, and the record company was happy, and he was putting out commercial records. And then every now and then he'd go back to 'Why can't they put out my mother's hymn book album?' which finally American Recordings did one Easter, with a gun to their heads from John," Robin said.[8]

If Saul had seen the writing on the wall that Cash's career was about to enter a slump in 1973, by the following year, it was a neon sign. As they headed their separate ways into 1974, whatever new material Cash managed to produce languished in the charts. The highest showing over a two-year period was a number fourteen placement on the country charts for "The Lady Came from Baltimore," though the album it came from, *John R. Cash*, didn't chart at all.[9]

That fall, Saul enrolled as a full-time student at the University of Western Ontario to major in history after a summer spent learning to speak French in Quebec. Now fifty years old, it was the first time he had tried to concentrate in a classroom since he was fourteen, save a brief stint in 1945 when he'd learned accounting. However, it was the fulfillment of "a lifelong dream of many years," and as such, he took to it with grave devotion. Despite a wide-ranging exposure to the world through travel, and to ideas through his voracious reading, Saul had always harboured an insecurity that while out in the world he regularly spoke with a sense of authority on subjects he in fact knew little about. That was something he wanted to change.

To round out his education, he also decided to take a course on comparative religion.

A little less than a month after his final missive to June, she responded with a letter in her signature curling, cursive script. "Another year for us both, Saul! It's almost birthday time, and I send you my best," she said on June 20, referring to her June 23 birthday that came the day after Saul's. "John and I are in Washington for the Religious Heritage Award — to be presented this evening. He's also trying to help with two bills in congress — the tape piracy and the copyright laws. Let's hope something can be done with both," she wrote, and then reminded him of their invitation to visit their home in Jamaica. The girls and John Carter were fine, Carlene Carter and Jack Routh had been married that past Saturday at home, and both she and Johnny barely got home from Jamaica for the wedding before they went straight on the road again. She added, "We miss seeing you both and send our best to your children. Love, June."

Though it did not address the issues Saul had mentioned, June had smoothed things over with her typical charm. Intentional or not, this move then served to keep the door of communication among all three of them propped open.[10]

As the Holiffs braved another bitter Ontario winter, Saul kept up meticulous attendance in his classes. At times it was stifling — jostling through the crowds of unkempt students, and negotiating with neurotic teachers was a challenge. The simplest of tasks sometimes stumped him, like navigating around campus, learning how to take notes, or finding things he needed in the library. It was an entirely foreign experience. As they debated biblical details in his comparative religion course, snow swirling past the classroom windows, Saul couldn't help but think of Johnny. In a fit of spontaneity, he decided to mail him the assignment he had completed on Moses. When it arrived, Johnny was incredulous, not only due to the topic but because he, too, had decided to formally study religion at the same time.[11]

"Dear Saul. Received and read with great interest your paper on Moses. It was really quite a surprise if you don't mind me being candidly honest, because I remember twelve years ago your telling June and I in the back seat of a car (where exactly I don't remember, but I do remember exactly what you said about Moses), you said, 'I think Moses was a fake and an Egyptian who became a Hebrew folk hero. As a matter of fact, I am planning to write a book called *The Case Against Moses* and maybe even one called *The Case Against God*,'" Johnny wrote. "But we do change, don't we, and I hope we grow."

Johnny was in the midst of taking his own a college extension course at the Southwest International Seminary in San Antonio, Texas. It was very fundamentalist, and their approach was to take the Bible literally in most cases, wrote Johnny. They believed in the virgin birth of Christ and his resurrection, and that Moses was a divine instrument of God who was sent to preserve and deliver His chosen people, the Jews, to give them a land and a seed through which the Messiah would be born. This was something even Moses had spoken of, Johnny said.

"There is much more I could tell you I believe about Moses; however, I would like to wait another couple of months before I give you a firm opinion on what I really think about your paper on Moses," he wrote, the reason being that he was only in the third month of his Bible studies, in which they had just finished Genesis and the Gospels, and next semester he would study Exodus and the Acts of the Apostles. "Therefore any gleanings or wisdom I might gain concerning Moses is an up-and-coming subject. Best of luck in your studies. This paper you sent me on Moses was the most welcome piece of mail I ever received from you."

The talk of religion pulled the two men closer, perhaps more so than they had ever been. In an attempt to explain why he had decided to pursue his religious studies more formally now, Johnny confessed that for years, June had prayed for him to have wisdom. "I told her one morning, 'Your prayers are not working; I'm feeling more evil and unwise all the time.' Then she said, 'Why don't you read Solomon?' I am sure my face must have turned red, because she was suggesting, 'If you want wisdom, read what the wisest man on earth had to say,' and that was the beginning."

In summary, Johnny described his pursuit of education as exhilarating, and a joy, and said he was breathlessly waiting for the next parts to come. His dedication and devotion to the scriptures and his deep belief in their truth didn't allow for much secular reading, Johnny wrote, but he had reflected on how Saul must have "gotten a lot of information and highlights from Wouk and Freud as well as the book *Jews, God and History*, which you and I discussed about ten years ago." This time he signed the letter, "Sincerely your friend, Johnny Cash."[12]

Had Saul given Johnny the impression he was interested in understanding the word of God as a spiritual quest rather than just an intellectual one? It was hard to know. The following month, the book *Adam to Daniel* arrived from Hendersonville with this inscription: "To Saul. This is one of my favourite books. Hope you will enjoy it as much as I did. John Cash."

On a break from his studies, Saul quickly wrote back.

"I was delighted to hear from you, and very impressed with what you had to say ... and, for that matter, the way you said it," Saul replied. "A few days ago I received *Adam to Daniel*. I am anxiously looking forward to reading it during the next school break."

The two men went on to exchange letters that discussed Moses at length, and shared detailed analyses of various texts from 1 Kings to Flavius Josephus's *Antiquities of the Jews*. Again, Saul mailed over his latest essay assignment. By April, Johnny had worked up the nerve to ask Saul a question that had been burning in his mind.[13]

Over the last nine months, Johnny had reflected a fair amount on his life as he worked day and night on his book *Man in Black*, which was now complete. In a letter to Saul, sent April 28, 1975, Johnny described it as a sort of spiritual autobiography that explored much of his life, including his music business, through a spiritual lens. In the story, many people come and go. Some are mentioned more than others, Johnny said, and others are left out — "simply because I couldn't fit them into the narrative flow," or their stories were too long and involved.

"You are mentioned from time to time in the book, and in one chapter I relate a conversation between you, June, and I which were said at different times and places," wrote Johnny, who enclosed a chapter of the book that referenced Saul. This was necessary, however, "to get said what I wanted said, and to show you as the friend and advisor that you always were," he continued.

In the letter, Johnny also apologized for not replying to the paper Saul had sent on Moses and Luke, but he was so busy excitedly relaying the news to everyone that Saul Holiff was studying the Bible and religion that he forgot to tell Saul himself how impressed he was with what he had written.

"You always were a wise man, but you are gaining and growing so much in and through the wisdom of the 'Word.' June and I are proud of you, and for you, because we know so well from our own Bible studies what joy there is in it," Johnny said.

"There is one question that burns in our minds, and I have to ask you: With what you have learned, do you believe that Jesus of Nazareth is the Messiah as prophesied by the Old Testament prophets? Do you believe in his Divinity?"[14]

It was a heavy question, and one that would certainly require a careful response.

Too busy to reply immediately, as he had just started a new psychology course that ran five days a week, Saul took his time mulling over just how to best approach the topic diplomatically. After about a month, he finally responded.

First, he addressed his inclusion in Johnny's book. "You were right when you said, 'I believe you can live with the things I said about you,'" Saul wrote. "I am pleased with what you said, and the way you said it. It certainly captures the emotions, tensions, and conflicts that we were all experiencing at the time."

As for the question of Jesus's divinity, well, that was a more complicated topic. "The enthusiasm you and June expressed about my essay is very encouraging, [but] I can't honestly answer your question about Jesus at this time. Years of preconceived notions and a propensity for sounding off about things that I haven't thoroughly investigated (or understood) has resulted in the need for a mental catharsis. It's a non-stop ongoing exacting process. I have to make up for a lot of lost time."[15]

Over the summer, Johnny's autobiography arrived. With a sense of anticipation, Saul opened the cover and read the inscription: "To Saul Holiff. We both know that you are much more a part of our lives than is told here. Thank you for living it with me."

By December, the family took Johnny and June up on their gracious invitation to visit the great Cinnamon Hill manor in Jamaica while they travelled to be with June's daughter Carlene, who was about to give birth. With instructions to the Holiffs that they were to use it as their own home, Johnny and June made certain the family were afforded all the luxuries they enjoyed. It was their "little dream world," June said in a note left behind for the family when they arrived. "This has been the greatest place to replenish mind, body and spirit. I hope it does the same for you. Please use our bedroom — just pick the easiest bedroom for the boys.... We love you and really will miss being here with you."

In case Barbara ran out of clothes, June offered up her own closet, which was stocked with designer outfits. The Southern hospitality extended by the Cashes was nothing short of extraordinary, and though Saul had now eased comfortably into retirement, he couldn't help but be reminded of all the extravagant perks he had once enjoyed that were now that much harder to access.

From the veranda that fronted the north side of the great house, one could look out onto Montego Bay, where it was speculated the poet Elizabeth Barrett Browning may have once sat to write. Built in the 1700s for Richard Barrett, her great-grandfather, Cinnamon Hill was a former sugar plantation surrounded by mahogany trees that were filled with the call of mockingbirds. The warm breeze that touched Saul's face carried the scents of jasmine, cinnamon, and orchid. On the first night Saul and Barbara retired to their room, he found a note from June — a poem, really, handwritten on her monogrammed stationery — which she had left on his pillow.[16]

"Dear Lord in your book of predestined, preordained, if it's not there — I wish you'd write down ole Saul's name," she wrote. "Back when excuses had to fall, it was Saul who took the call, and looked you straight right in the face, and followed Johnny every place. In bars, honky-tonks and ditches — Ole Saul caught the heavy pitches — and threw them back just as hard. He fought to keep John in the yard."[17]

Saul and Johnny never reconciled their business relationship, and over the years their communication slowed to a trickle and then stopped. For the remainder of Saul's life, when asked about Johnny, he maintained a pride in the fact that he had left on his own terms.

"I don't want to sound corny, but I gave Johnny up, Johnny didn't give me up," Saul told Candy Yates, host of the radio show *Cinematically Speaking*, in 1976. "I'm not especially knocked out about being in the entertainment business. I think it's a self-indulgent, hedonistic, ego-ridden business filled with people that have no ethics, no principles — this is a terrific generalization; there are notable exceptions — but I got out of it because I wanted out of it so I could rebuild my self-respect and be my own person again."

"What do you think of Johnny Cash, the person?" Candy asked.

"I would say he has all of the faults of a very successful entertainer."

"Which are?"

"A big ego, self-centred, self-serving, oh, I could just go on endlessly. Read *The Confessions of Jean-Jacques Rousseau* and you got it all in one nutshell. On the other hand, he's bright, he's got a fantastic memory. He respects a job well done. He's very demanding of himself, as well as anyone else. He's a perfectionist. He's inordinately clever. He's exceptionally well read, so he's got qualities that you can't help but respect and admire," Saul said.

In a way, Saul could have been describing himself. And, indeed, in Candy's breathless introduction, the way she characterized her guest wasn't much different.

"We taped our interview with Saul Holiff last night, and I am still reeling from the various reactions and impressions he left on me," she said. "Saul Holiff is incredible. He is fifty but looks about thirty-six, and has the drive, the vitality, and the awareness of a man barely into his twenties. He's sophisticated, but earthy. He's impeccable, he's articulate, he's witty, he's calculating, and he's super bright. And despite a lifetime of fast showbiz living, he's genuine."[18]

In the years that followed, Saul became more candid about why he left Johnny and management in general, which went beyond the simple desire to spend more time with his family. "I had to serve someone else's ego. I really deferred almost entirely to him," he told *London Free Press* reporter Mike Mulhern in 1980. "I kept my dignity intact, but just barely."

By this time Barbara had taken the boys with her and moved out West to settle in Victoria, a picturesque locale surrounded by verdant mountains and clean expanses of endless ocean, on the southernmost tip of Vancouver Island. Their marriage was "in a curious state," Saul confessed to the reporter. "An undefined state. It's an awkward time." Though he planned to join his family on the West Coast, he also felt compelled to stay in London where he still enjoyed an air of celebrity. For the last four years, his reputation had grown as a restaurant critic with his popular culinary review column Eat, Drink & Be Wary, which was carried in the *London Free Press*.

Despite Candy Yates's exclamations over Saul's energy and vitality during their interview, it was at this time that he began to obsess once again over his own mortality. Jonathan and Joshua were barely teenagers when Saul, in his characteristic way of relating to them as adults, sat the boys down and gave them a package of documents he had drawn up. "Put these in your files, boys," he said, which left them wondering what files they were supposed to be keeping, exactly. It was time to deal with the practicalities of life, he went on, and these papers pertained to his plan for the end of his life.

At this juncture Saul was about fifty-five, still jogging daily, and in good health. It was the first time either Jonathan or Joshua had heard words like *euthanasia* or the concept of "dying with dignity." There are a lot of people who want to choose how and when they will die, Saul said. They had formed a group called the Hemlock Society, and he was a member. The idea is simple enough, he explained. Rational, even. Rather than waste away in a hospital with an incurable disease and suffer all the attendant humiliation and suffering, you would take your own life. It was better for you, and it was better for your family.

Barely out of childhood, the boys found this to be a hugely abstract idea to get their heads around. At first it was a source of irritation, Joshua remembered, but over time he began to understand this rationale and developed a begrudging respect for his father's wishes. As the years went by, Saul dropped the topic, but the possibility that he would end his life at any point continued to hang in the air for decades. Every so often they would get a reminder of his plans, like the time Jonathan went snooping in Saul's floor safe at their house in Victoria and pulled out a bag filled with pill bottles — his suicide kit. Or when Joshua once found a gun hidden in their bookshelf — in all likelihood an insurance measure against robbery, but jarring nonetheless.[19]

In her time alone in Victoria before Saul arrived, Barbara had found her footing and delved further into the pacifism she had exercised so firmly when it came to Nixon's war policies. Nudged onward by the National Film Board's documentary *If You Love This Planet*, which featured a lecture by nuclear critic Dr. Helen Caldicott, Barbara joined the Greater Victoria Disarmament Group and the issue of nuclear disarmament became a central force in her life. Once reconciled with Saul, which he credited to his sister Ann's intervention, they continued to travel and entertain, but the anonymity of Victoria would never permit Saul the status he had retained in London. Despite the challenges, Saul pressed on in school and enrolled at the University of Victoria.[20]

The proudest achievement of his life, by his own estimation, came in 1983 when he graduated from the institution with an honours degree in history.

Other goals weren't quite as forthcoming. The reconciliation he so poignantly sought with his children, and detailed in his diary before the showdown at Lake Tahoe, never truly manifested in the way he had hoped. It seemed that after he resigned, he was indeed home as anticipated, but his estrangement from the boys only grew. Joshua he could manage, but conflicts with Jonathan became more and more volatile.

When communication broke down, as it often did, Saul resorted to pushing notes and letters under Jonathan's bedroom door.

"Until now, in addition to never voluntarily lifting a finger or contributing anything to your home since you were a child — you also have brought very little joy or pleasure to this household — as far as I'm concerned — just confrontation and disrespect!! Nothing else seems to exist for you outside of your own concerns," Saul fumed to Jonathan, who was now in his late teens. It was a sentiment that seemed to echo his words to another troublesome Johnny, decades prior. It wasn't long before his eldest son moved out.[21]

"I guess parenthood didn't work for me," Saul sighed in an audio recording made in 1998 for his sister Ann's grandson, the renowned journalist Steve Paikin. "Maybe if it had been a boy and a girl, maybe if they hadn't been so close together. But on the other hand, since both of us read a lot and had some idea of what we thought was the right thing to do, we took the boys everywhere, and they did everything and they tried everything, whether it be hockey, or judo, or swimming lessons at the Y, or camping, or French immersion, or dance lessons, or camera lessons, or trips. We took them to Bermuda and on driving trips across the country. You name it, they did it. We thought that all of this somehow or another would result in some kind of successful parenting. But I couldn't relax, and I couldn't show the patience or the understanding or the restraint that one needed. I could with Joshua; I could not with Jonathan. He was an extremely tough kid to cope with, as I'm sure he thought I was a tough father to cope with. He was very strong-willed and very outspoken, and troubled and troublesome. So we had hang-ups. I had hang-ups. It took an amazing amount of understanding that I lacked." He paused.

"You ask about … parenthood. Well, that's the toughest question of all. If I had been different, if the circumstances had been different, if I hadn't led such a chaotic life being constantly away, if I had been smarter, or stronger, or better adjusted, if I hadn't been such a screw-up. You know — 'if, if, if.' Excuse after excuse. But, I would have to say that if it had all happened over again, I probably would make all the same mistakes."

Though he took responsibility for many of the issues, Saul acknowledged that his upbringing had some effect on his parenting and sense of self-worth. "In some ways, publicly, I appeared to be mature and alert, rational and even reasonable. But in most ways, I was as screwed up then as I had been most of my childhood: bluffing, bullshitting, trying to impress, insecure, talking too much. I wasn't prepared for the kind of responsibility of parenthood at all," he said. "My past is brimming with unrealized ideas and projects. An overactive imagination, a driven personality, a predilection for talking far too much, energy to burn and a profound lack of confidence. It didn't help to have a father who went bankrupt when you were seven and go from affluence to nothing in the middle of a Depression; a father who felt that he was a bitter failure and unfulfilled and who seemed to make himself feel just a little bit better by continuously belittling and humiliating me however and whenever possible." He paused. "I deserved a lot of it."[22]

At the height of their conflicts, when Jonathan was about seventeen, Saul had come to him one night and said, "You're coming with me." The two had silently driven downtown to the Sports Centre in Victoria, where Johnny was performing. The downward spiral of his career and a receding presence in the charts had clearly taken its toll. Lost without the compass of music, he had slipped back into drinking and pills. A rambling appearance on German TV in the spring of 1983 had set off a new round of media speculation that Johnny had been sick or drunk, and that had further impacted his desirability.

Backstage at the show was the last time Jonathan ever saw his superhero, who was also worse for wear after health battles that had included stomach ulcers, severe back pain, pneumonia, and surgery after a bizarre ostrich attack. But he was still formidable.

"I remember Johnny and my father spent several minutes alone, speaking in the back corner. I always wondered what they said to each other," Jonathan said.[23]

This was also likely the last time Saul ever saw Johnny.

By December, Johnny had checked in to the Betty Ford Center for drug treatment, and in the summer of 1986, Columbia Records dropped him from their label.

In 1994, Saul mistakenly received a letter that was intended for Cash. Asked to forward it along, he took the opportunity to include a personal note.

Saul Holiff in a reflective mood in 1989, when he revisited his hometown of London, Ontario.

Dear Johnny:

It is now twenty years since we parted company, and with the benefit of hindsight and an awful lot of time to think, I realize now more than ever that if it hadn't been for your confidence, belief and trust in me so many years ago, I probably still would be back in London, Ontario, promoting hamburgers, hot dogs, clothes and mediocre rock 'n' roll and western acts.

For various reasons, justified or not, you apparently don't think very well of me. I know that in some instances in the past — and probably will in the future, too — I have done and said some foolhardy things. I profoundly regret using, so often and so impulsively, my mouth instead of my head.

But the bottom line ... is that I have always wanted to have, and hoped that I had, your best interests at heart, and have never ever intentionally wished to discredit you or embarrass you.

Hope all goes well with you and your family.

Sincerely,
Saul.[24]

It's unknown if Johnny ever responded to the letter or even received it. Health problems notwithstanding, in the late 1990s he began an upward slope that ended in an unprecedented career comeback, thanks to the vision and skill of hotshot producer Rick Rubin. In 1997, Saul and his family watched as Johnny's life and career were recognized during the Kennedy Center Honors broadcast on TV. "I see he's finally gone back to black," was all Saul said about it to Barbara, somewhat cryptically. Johnny's resurgence in popularity had in fact shocked him, and he jotted off a letter of congratulations.

"We were thrilled not only that you were one of the honorees, but with the absolutely marvellous production quality of highlights of your career," Saul said. "It was, without question, a most memorable tribute."

Johnny quickly responded, "It was so nice to hear from you after all these years. We often reminisce about the years we worked together, and always know that we think well of you and speak kindly of you. The night of the Kennedy Center Honors was a fabulous night. I've never felt so well esteemed in people's eyes before … and people that really matter to me."

On the occasion of Johnny's death in 2003, with the benefit of hindsight and decades of contemplation, Saul had a chance to revisit his feelings about his client as he fielded floods of calls from journalists seeking his thoughts.

"He's not what he appears to be. In many cases, he's more than he appears to be and, in some cases, possibly less," Saul said, a few years before his own death. "I would say overall it's a very happy story, you know, like a guy who prevailed against incredible odds and did extraordinarily well, as have the people around him. I mean, I didn't come out of this suffering either. Everyone who knew him might have different views on how situations could have been handled differently, but when you have as much power as he had, he was okay with people. He could have been like some of your horror stories you read about. He wasn't like that. On the other hand, he'd step out of character and drive a hard bargain when you least expected, and be tough, so you never knew what was coming down. If he thought you were trying to be a smart-ass, it was curtains."

When asked by reporter Adrian Chamberlain what his famous client was like, Saul characterized Johnny as a combination of both difficult and endearing. "He was the quintessential enigmatic everything. He was kind, he was cruel, he was thoughtful, he was selfish. And he was smart." He paused and smiled. "We had endless conflict."[25]

If, as he had said in his earlier letter, Saul had the perception that Johnny "apparently didn't think very well" of him, he would now never know for certain what his famous client truly thought of him. In Cash's first autobiography, Saul read that Johnny and June had long felt that they had found an understanding friend in him and that they knew "he suffered much embarrassment" due to Johnny's capers when he was on pills. But Johnny went on to write that Saul "was cool, level-headed, and always handled the most complicated of my business problems without burdening me down with the details of what he'd gone through in straightening out some of the messes I got myself into from missing show dates. He had never relayed the embarrassing questions he must have had to answer when I was in trouble. Saul made many of the most significant moves of my career and I owe him a lot."[26]

Unbeknownst to Saul, however, near the end of his life Cash did confess his feelings about his former manager to one close friend. Lifelong Cash fan Mark Stielper got to know his idol back in 1984 when Johnny's troupe came to stay at the hotel he had managed in Maryland. Impressed with his vast knowledge of their lives, Johnny and June soon developed a regular communication with Mark, which blossomed into a close friendship in which he became the informal family historian and was granted access to their files for various projects.

In the mid-1990s, Mark visited the sprawling Cinnamon Hill estate after completing an archaeological excursion in Rome. In the great drawing room of the house, as he told Johnny about his trip, their conversation turned to ancient Roman history. Johnny had often indicated that he'd be interested in a similar venture in Jerusalem, but at that time it looked less and less like something he would undertake. The talk turned from history to religion, and the two discussed which had more importance to the growth of Christianity: Saint Peter or Saul of Tarsus. "This led to a conversation about another Saul," Mark later wrote. At this point, as they sat looking out over the magnificent grounds of the former plantation, Johnny turned to Mark and confided, "I only really had one manager who could manage me. That was Saul."[27]

ACKNOWLEDGEMENTS

Foremost, I would like to thank the Holiff family for allowing me access to their lives and files, in particular Jonathan Holiff, who conducted years of extensive research prior to this project for his own award-winning documentary film, *My Father and the Man in Black*. He provided the bulk of the material for this book, and the amount of work he contributed to this project is immeasurable, from digitizing and dating the masses of information found in his father's archives — photos, documents, posters, letters, and news clippings — to searching out, sourcing, and transcribing old interviews, speeches, and audio diaries, as well as conducting scores of personal interviews himself. It amounts to what would have been years of effort had I conducted the work alone. The patience of Jonathan, Barbara Holiff, and Joshua Robinson in answering questions and clarifying details was also remarkable and much appreciated.

The Man Who Carried Cash would also not have been completed without the support of my family: To my brother, Will Chadwick, for finding a quiet place for me to live and write in his cabin on Protection Island. To my sister, Jane Chadwick, and her partner, Noel Villeneuve, for their support — and finding me a compatible laptop when mine died. To my mum and dad, Edna Chadwick and Maurice Chadwick, for the ongoing, endless child care help, massive encouragement, and unwavering belief in me. And to Ruby and Rowan, who are the lights of my life and who get me out of bed in the morning, in every sense of the phrase.

I appreciate the candid and open nature of those I interviewed or who supplied information for this book. Huge respect and thanks goes to Johnny Western — a delightful, old-school gentleman of the highest calibre, whose sharp memory and nuanced perspectives shed much light on those early days; Red Robinson, whose encyclopedic knowledge of the rock 'n' roll scene of the 1950s and 1960s is unparalleled; Lou Robin; Christopher Wren, who completed the first biography of Johnny Cash, which remains a classic for any fan; Tommy Cash; Robert Elfstrom, who completed the first (and many say the best) documentary about Cash; W.S. "Fluke" Holland; Dave Roberts; Geoffrey Cannon; Manuel; Robert Hilburn, who completed the most recent and most thorough Cash biography; Larry Paikin; journalist Steve Paikin; photographer Ralph Willsey; Marilynne Caswell; Western University archivist Barry Arnott; Belle Schwartz; Susan Bradnam; and more. The numbers of those who "were there when it happened" are dwindling, and I appreciate the participation and memories from all of you. Special appreciation goes to Cash family historian Mark Stielper, who Johnny Cash once said knew more about him than he did about himself.

Thanks to those who also helped, supported, informed, and assisted in various capacities along the way: Terence Fitzgerald, Sarah Webber Segal, Christopher Thompson, Ashta Cormier, Denisa Kraus, Eva Manly, Douglas White III Kwulasultun, Juliana Roe and James Booker Sr., Thora Howell, Lynne Bowen, Cale Cowan and Philip Wolf — the first editors to ever believe in me.

Special thanks to the whole team at Dundurn who nursed this project along: my editor Allison Hirst, Carrie Gleason, Margaret Bryant, Kirk Howard, Kathryn Lane, Cheryl Hawley, Jennifer Gallinger, my publicist Jaclyn Hodsdon, and Michael Melgaard, who believed in the book from the earliest stages. I especially want to thank my agents John Pearce at Westwood Creative and Chris Casuccio at Casuccio Creative, who were certain about this project from the very beginning, and author Ann Eriksson for introducing me to them and encouraging me.

NOTES

PROLOGUE

1. Barbara Holiff, interview by Jonathan Holiff, February 1, 2009; British Columbia Coroners Service report on Saul Holiff's death.

CHAPTER 1: THE WHITE COAT

1. Dmytrivka is where the family has traced their origins back to, but they do not know for certain that this was the village they came from.
2. Ann Paikin, interview by Steve Paikin, 1984.
3. Manus I Midlarsky, *The Killing Trap: Genocide in the Twentieth Century* (Cambridge: Cambridge University Press, 2005), 46–47.
4. Jonathan Holiff, in discussion with the author; Larry Paikin (Saul's nephew), in discussion with the author, November 24, 2016.
5. In 1939 Saul broke Morris's leg during a game of hockey, which attests to the ferocity of their competition.
6. Joel Holiff quote from an undated newspaper clipping found in Saul Holiff's scrapbook.
7. Saul Holiff, in an audio recording for his brother Morris's seventy-fifth birthday, 1997; Jonathan Holiff, in discussion with the author.
8. Morris Holbrook, *Music, Movies, Meanings and Markets: Cinemajazzamatazz* (New York: Routledge, 2012) 353; James Reaney, "Meeting a Beautiful Way to 'Beguine,'" *London Free Press*, November 16, 2003; Saul

Holiff, email to James Reaney, November 20, 2003; Artie Shaw obituary, *The Telegraph*, January 1, 2005, www.telegraph.co.uk/news/obituaries/1480154/Artie-Shaw.html.

9. Ann Paikin, interview by Steve Paikin, 1984; Saul Holiff, in an audio recording for his brother Morris's seventy-fifth birthday, 1997; Saul Holiff, interview by Steve Paikin, 1998; Saul Holiff, speech at the Jewish Community Centre, Victoria, B.C., 1997.

10. Saul Holiff, handwritten diary entries on envelopes, August 23–24, 1943, and September 24, 1943.

11. Morris Holiff, letter to Saul Holiff, April 24, 1943.

CHAPTER 2: "SHOWBIZ HAD TO BE MY LIFE"

1. Saul Holiff, postcard to Joel and Esther Holiff, September 4, 1945; Saul Holiff, diary entry, September 4, 1945; Saul Holiff, speech at the Jewish Community Centre, Victoria, B.C., 1997; American Film Institute, *The American Film Institute Catalog of Motion Pictures Produced in the United States: Feature Films, 1941–1950* (Berkeley: University of California Press, 1999).

2. Fred E. Basten, *Max Factor: The Man Who Changed the Faces of the World* (New York: Skyhorse, 2013); Joel Mokyr, ed., *The Oxford Encyclopedia of Economic History* (New York: Oxford University Press, 2003).

3. Lisa Mitchell and Bruce Torrence, *The Hollywood Canteen: Where the Greatest Generation Danced with the Most Beautiful Girls in the World* (Albany, GA: BearManor Media, 2012); Sherrie Tucker, *Dance Floor Democracy: The Social Geography of Memory at the Hollywood Canteen* (Durham, NC: Duke University Press, 2014).

4. Derek Sidenius, "Ex-Promoter Recalls a Life of Golden Peril," *Times Colonist*, November 25, 1984.

5. Saul Holiff, speech at the Jewish Community Centre, Victoria, B.C., 1997; "Arcades on Billboard Blvd. Hit by Petition," *Billboard*, March 25, 1944. The location of the dormitory is confirmed in the *Billboard* article.

6. Gerald Horne, *Class Struggle in Hollywood, 1930–1950: Moguls, Mobsters, Stars, Reds, and Trade Unionists* (Austin: University of Texas Press, 2001); Donald T. Critchlow, *When Hollywood Was Right: How Movie Stars, Studio Moguls and Big Business Remade American Politics* (Cambridge: Cambridge University Press, 2013); "Film Studio Siege Is Broken: Deputies and Police Open Picket Lines When State Guard Force Ready to Act," *Madera Tribune*, October 10, 1945. Two policemen and at least

forty-three strikers were injured in the riot on October 8, 1945, and mass arrests followed.

7. This was not such a farfetched idea, as Jack's story is not so different from Saul's. Born Jacob Warner in 1892 in London, Ontario, Jack was the son of Polish-Jewish immigrants, and before he followed his brothers into the film business, much of the family's life involved a similar struggle to Saul's.

8. Saul Holiff, speech at the Jewish Community Centre, Victoria, B.C., 1997.

9. Ibid.

10. Undated newspaper article in Saul Holiff's archives. It mentions he is a "Londoner" and "returned here by way of two of America's most storied cities," which indicates it is a local paper, probably the *London Free Press*.

11. Joel Holiff, letter to Saul Holiff, May 14, 1947.

12. Saul Holiff, diary entry, October 5, 1950.

13. Saul Holiff, will and suicide note, June 13, 1956. The will was dated, but I put the date on the suicide note for reference.

14. Saul Holiff, letter to Jonathan Holiff, April 20, 1998; Saul Holiff, handwritten notes, August 12, 1998. A note titled "An Outline of a Life" mentions "shock treatments."

15. Jonathan Holiff, in discussion with the author; Peter Goddard, "This Is What's New with Saul," *The Telegram*, November 8, 1969; Larry Paikin, in discussion with the author, November 24, 2016.

16. Charlie and Diane Schneider, Saul Holiff, "Anti-Semitism," *Generations: Growing up Jewish In the 20th Century*, 1997.

17. J. Burke Martin, "From Pratfalls to Cuckoo, LLT Play Broad Comedy," *London Free Press*, May 1, 1957.

18. Derek Sidenius, "Ex-Promoter Recalls a Life of Golden Peril," *Times Colonist*, November 25, 1984; Saul Holiff, contract with London Arena, April 24, 1957; Saul Holiff, radio spot on CFPL radio, May 9, 1957; Saul Holiff, show account statement of operations, June 30, 1957; Dick Newman, Show Beat, *London Free Press*, July 18, 1957.

19. Dick Newman, Show Beat, *London Free Press*, July 18, 1957; Bob Mersereau, *The History of Canadian Rock 'n' Roll* (Milwaukee, WI: Backbeat, 2015); Joe Scanlon, "$100,000 a Year: A Rock 'n' Roll Star, He Plans on Retiring at 21," *Star Weekly*, November 16, 1957.

20. Charles White, *Life and Times of Little Richard: The Quasar of Rock* (New York: Da Capo Press, 1994), 91–92; Anne Johnson, "Little Richard," in *Contemporary Musicians: Profiles of the People in Music*, ed. Michael L. LaBlanc (Detroit: Gale

Research, 1989); *Rolling Stone Encyclopedia of Rock & Roll* (London: Simon & Schuster, 2001), s.v. "Little Richard." www.rollingstone.com/music/artists/little-richard/biography#ixzz43NeGKbPI.

21. Saul Holiff, letter to Wesley H. Rose, October 21, 1957.

22. Dick Newman, "Rock 'n' Roll Show Thrills 4,000 Here," *London Free Press*, April 11, 1958; Jonathan Holiff, in discussion with the author.

23. Dave Roberts, a London-based DJ and former employee at record store Heintzmann's, in discussion with the author; Richard Carlin, *Country Music: A Biographical Dictionary* (New York: Black Dog & Leventhal, 2006).

24. W.S. "Fluke" Holland, interview by Jonathan Holiff, April 2006.

25. Saul Holiff, archives containing Sol's Square Boy information; Adrian Chamberlain, "Saul Tells Tales about George," *Times Colonist*, November 23, 1996.

26. Bill Lynch, letter to Saul Holiff, November 22, 1957. It's not known whether Saul actually attended the show, but if he did it would likely mark the very first time he ever saw Cash.

CHAPTER 3: WHEN SAUL MET JOHNNY

1. Walter Cordery, "Managing the Man in Black Opened Doors: Johnny Cash's Former Manager Reminisces about the Ups and Downs of the Country Music Business," *Nanaimo Daily News*, September 29, 2003; Dave Roberts, in discussion with the author, November 2015; Dave Roberts, "Looking Back," _____, August 15, 2008.

2. There is much uncertainty over when and what the first interaction was between Saul Holiff and Johnny Cash. A telegram from Bob Neal to Saul Holiff, July 17, 1958, states that Johnny was available on August 16 at the price of $1,250. This was confirmed in *Winners Got Scars Too* by Christopher Wren, where Saul says he first met Johnny in 1958 at a show in London where he was "a promoter." It is also here that he says the two "did not hit it off at all." He also mentions in an interview with Candy Yates on *Cinematically Speaking* in 1976 that it was in 1958 that he first "brought Johnny in" and Johnny spent the evening "glowering." However, his financial records from this time do not mention a Cash show in 1958 that he was financially involved in, so it is unclear whether he was the promoter or in what capacity he was involved, if at all.

3. Saul Holiff, contract with Johnny Cash, August 26, 1959. The contract was for Cash to play on September 10, 1959, at Lucan Memorial.

4. Michael Streissguth, *Johnny Cash: The Biography* (Cambridge, MA: Da Capo Press, 2006), 105; Christopher Wren, *Winners Got Scars Too* (New York: Dial Press, 1971), 126.

5. Robert Hilburn, *Johnny Cash: The Life* (Boston: Little, Brown, 2013), 120; Saul Holiff, interview by Howie Siegel, *Pajama Party* television show, Victoria, 1984; Paul King, "Want Johnny Cash? Call London, ON. and ask for Saul Holiff," *The Canadian Magazine*, November 7, 1970. Both Saul and Johnny recount this story of their first meeting in many different publications; the story is essentially the same in each one.

6. Saul Holiff, year-end calculations of income tax; Saul Holiff, interview by Candy Yates, *Cinematically Speaking*, 1976. The dates of the tour were confirmed in Saul's tax calculations.

7. Christopher Wren, *Winners Got Scars Too* (New York: Dial Press, 1971), 126.

8. Wren, *Winners Got Scars Too*, 102; Hilburn, *Johnny Cash: The Life*, 117.

9. Wren, *Winners Got Scars Too*, 130.

10. Saul Holiff, letter to Stew Carnall, January 15, 1961.

11. Johnny Western, in discussion with the author, November 2015; Jonny Whiteside, *Ramblin' Rose: The Life and Career of Rose Maddox* (Nashville: Country Music Foundation Press, 1996), 202.

12. Johnny Western, in discussion with the author, December 2014.

13. Michael Streissguth, ed., *Ring of Fire: The Johnny Cash Reader* (Cambridge, MA: Da Capo Press, 2002), 52. Previously published as "Write Is Wrong," *Time*, February 23, 1959. The article pegs the number at more than six million records sold for approximately fifty Cash-composed songs.

14. Johnny Cash, with Patrick Carr, *Cash: The Autobiography* (New York: HarperCollins, 1997).

15. Cordery, "Managing the Man in Black Opened Doors."

16. Saul Holiff, telegram to Johnny Cash, n.d., ca. 1961. Likely sent in early June.

17. Fluke Holland, interview by Jonathan Holiff, April 19, 2006; Saul Holiff, letter to Johnny Cash, June 4, 1961.

18. Johnny Western, in discussion with the author, November 2015; Marshall Grant, *I Was There When It Happened: My Life with Johnny Cash* (Nashville, TN: Cumberland House, 2006). Numerous other books reference their road behaviour in great detail.

19. Johnny Cash, letter to Saul Holiff, June 6, 1961.

20. Saul Holiff, letter to Johnny Cash, June 12, 1961.

21. Saul Holiff, telegram to Johnny Cash, June 16, 1961.

22. Johnny Western, in conversation with the author, December 2015; Wren, *Winners Got Scars Too*; Hilburn, *Johnny Cash: The Life*.

23. Dir. Al Greenfield, writer Martin Melhuish, interview with Johnny Cash, *Johnny Cash: Half a Mile a Day*, Documentary, 2000.

24. Wren, *Winners Got Scars Too*; Johnny Western, in conversation with the author, December 2015; Saul Holiff, his own account.

25. Johnny Cash, letter to Saul Holiff, June 15, 1961.

26. Johnny Western, in conversation with the author, December 2014.

27. Johnny Western, letter to Saul Holiff, July 1, 1961.

28. Saul Holiff, letter to Johnny Cash, June 17, 1961. In the letter, he says, "I would, however, strongly recommend the addition of two extra artists for this tour, such as Bob Luman and Rose Maddox."

29. Johnny Cash, handwritten letter to Saul Holiff, n.d., ca. July, 1961. The date is an estimate based on its contents.

30. "Saul Holiff to Promote Johnny Cash Abroad," *Billboard*, June 26, 1961; Saul Holiff, letter to Johnny Cash, July 2, 1961. Saul signed the letter "Your friend and fan."

31. "Funeral Service Today for Samuel G. Paikin," *Hamilton Spectator*, June 8, 1961; Ann Paikin, interview by Steve Paikin, 1984; Saul Holiff, letter to Johnny Cash, August 12, 1961; Johnny Cash, letter to Saul Holiff, September 1, 1961. The date that the Cashes moved into their new home varies in different sources, from days after Tara's birth to weeks, to October 1.

32. Saul Holiff, letter to Johnny Cash, September 4, 1961. It's not clear what Saul means by referencing Johnny's autobiography, as there was none published at that time, but it may have been an early private draft of one, or a lengthy profile written by someone else.

33. Dick Newman, Show Beat, *London Free Press*, October 1961.

34. Wendy Michener, "Big Letdown: Cash Customers See Little of Star," *Toronto Daily Star*, September 28, 1961.

35. Streissguth, *Johnny Cash: The Biography*, 106; "The Musical Businessman: Goddard Lieberson," *Time*, March 16, 1959.

36. Streissguth, *Johnny Cash: The Biography*, 106.

37. Dick Newman, Show Beat, *London Free Press*, October 1961; Saul Holiff, letter to David Baumgarten, September 23, 1961; Terence Fitzgerald, producer, in conversation with the author, August 21, 2016. Interestingly, the next afternoon after the renegotiation at Columbia, Saul met with David Baumgarten, executive vice-president in charge of personal appearances at MCA, to discuss

a side project that involved his potential participation in the management of singer Harry Belafonte. It's not clear where this conversation ended, but despite his focus on Cash, Saul kept up an active promotion of other artists, including Belafonte, whom he had scheduled for a show at the London Arena in early November. The show was cancelled due to a respiratory ailment, so he scheduled the Kingston Trio in its place, but his promotion of Belafonte soon fell off after this point and was not picked up again.

38. Whiteside, *Ramblin' Rose*, 203–4.
39. Johnny Western, in conversation with the author, December 2015.
40. Martin Melhuish, "Saul Holiff and 'the Johnny Cash Connection,'" *Country Music News*, Part 1, April 2007.
41. Johnny Western, in conversation with the author, November 2015. Johnny's phobia is talked about in many publications, but it is also mentioned in *Composed: A Memoir*, by Rosanne Cash.
42. Saul Holiff, interview by Candy Yates, *Cinematically Speaking*, 1976 (this story is recounted in varying versions in countless news stories and books); Saul Holiff, letter to Johnny Cash, February 12, 1974.

CHAPTER 4: THE SINGIN' STORYTELLER

1. "Johnny Cash Arrested Here on Drunk Charge," *Nashville Tennessean*, November 11, 1961; Saul Holiff, letter to Bill Morgan, January 4, 1962.
2. Melhuish, "The Johnny Cash Connection"; Steve Turner, *The Man Called Cash: The Life, Love, and Faith of an American Legend* (Nashville: Thomas Nelson, 2005), 88–89.
3. "Photos: Memories of The Cave Supper Club," *The Province*, November 29, 2012, www.theprovince.com/news/Photos+Historic+images+Cave+Supper+Club/4740822/story.html; Red Robinson, in conversation with the author, April 13, 2016. Cash's shows at the Cave ran from November 24 to December 3, 1961, and the interview happened sometime during this week, says Robinson.
4. Barbara Holiff, interview with Jonathan Holiff, July 2006.
5. Melhuish, "The Johnny Cash Connection"; Turner, *The Man Called Cash*.
6. Johnny Western, in conversation with the author, January 25, 2016; Columbia Records, memo to Johnny Cash, signed by Goddard Lieberson and Johnny Cash, May 12, 1961.
7. Bob Neal, letter to Johnny Cash, October 24, 1961.
8. Johnny Cash, letter to Bob Neal, October 26, 1961.
9. Melhuish, "The Johnny Cash Connection."

10. Turner, *The Man Called Cash*, 92.

11. Ralph Willsey, "Country Music's Royal Wedding: Johnny Cash Was Feeling Pretty Good When He Proposed to June Carter — 30 Years Ago Tonight," *Ottawa Citizen*, February 22, 1998.

12. Saul Holiff, collection, archived press kit from 1961. Saul insists in many different media reports that he is the one who came up with the "Singin' Storyteller" label, though it did get widely used by many others.

13. Johnny Western, in discussion with the author, January 25, 2016. "She just completely wigged out. She told Johnny, 'I've got to go, and that's it,'" said Western. "She never did come back to the tour; that was the last tour she ever worked with us as the girl singer."

14. Whiteside, *Ramblin' Rose*, 204–5.

15. Willie Nelson, with David Ritz, *It's a Long Story: My Life* (Boston: Little, Brown, 2015).

16. Mark Bego, *I Fall to Pieces: The Music and Life of Patsy Cline* (Holbrook, Mass.: Adams Publishing, 1996), 157.

17. Johnny Cash, interview by Ed Salamon, *The Johnny Cash Silver Anniversary Special*, WHN Radio, New York, July 4, 1980.

18. Andrew Leahey, "Flashback: Johnny Cash Makes Opry Debut, Meets June Carter," *Rolling Stone*, with video, July 7, 2014, accessed August 22, 2016, www.rollingstone.com/music/videos/flashback-johnny-cash-makes-opry-debut-meets-june-carter-20140707.

19. June Carter Cash, interview by Barbara Walters, *Barbara Walters: Interviews of a Lifetime*, 1995; originally aired December 6, 1983.

20. Johnny Cash, *Cash: The Autobiography*, 212.

21. "Big D Jamboree," Cathy Brigham, *Handbook of Texas Online*, last modified December 2, 2015, www.tshaonline.org/handbook/online/articles/xfb01.

22. Grant, *I Was There*, 108; Wren, *Winners Got Scars Too*, 134; Johnny Western, in discussion with the author, November 2015.

23. Johnny Cash Inc., declaration from headquarters, signed by Saul Holiff and Johnny Cash, December 13, 1961.

24. Johnny Cash, *Cash: The Autobiography*.

25. Saul Holiff, letter to June Carter Cash, December 25, 1961.

26. Mike Mulhern, "Holiff Cashing in Boyhood Dreams," *London Free Press*, June 20, 1980; Saul Holiff, letter to Jonathan Holiff, October 7, 1995.

27. Vivian Cash, *I Walked the Line* (New York: Scribner, 2007), 298; Turner, *The Man Called Cash*, 95; Wren, *Winners Got Scars Too*, 152 (the "Scrooge"

comment came in 1963); Rosanne Cash, *Composed: A Memoir* (New York: Penguin, 2010), 158.

28. Saul Holiff, letter to Johnny Cash, December 27, 1961; Saul Holiff collection, photographs of Saul Holiff circa 1961; December, 1961 snowfall records for London, Ontario, Historical Climate Data, Environment Canada, climate. weather.gc.ca.

29. Barbara Holiff, "Mister 17," December 5, 1961; Saul Holiff, letter to Barbara Holiff, January 5, 1962.

30. Barbara Holiff, interviews by Jonathan Holiff, August 16, 2005; January 10, 2006; January 22, 2006.

31. Barbara Holiff, interview by Jonathan Holiff (Barbara Part 1), August 16, 2005.

CHAPTER 5: CARNEGIE HALL AND JUNE CARTER

1. June Carter Cash, letter to Saul Holiff, January 3, 1962.

2. Bego, *I Fall to Pieces*, 157. The letter is from Patsy Cline to Louise Seger, January 22, 1962.

3. Authorization for Barbara Mandrell to go with the Johnny Cash Show under the personal direction of Saul Holiff, January 16, 1962.

4. Barbara Mandrell, interview by Larry King, *Larry King Live*, CNN, September 15, 2003; Barbara Mandrell, with George Vecsey, *Get to the Heart: My Story* (New York: Bantam, 1990), 69.

5. Margaret Jones, *Patsy: The Life and Times of Patsy Cline* (New York: Da Capo Press, 1999), 244; Johnny Western, in discussion with the author, December 2015.

6. Johnny Western, in discussion with the author, November 2014.

7. Ibid.

8. Margaret Jones, *Patsy: The Life*, 146–48.

9. Margaret Jones, *Patsy: The Life*, 182, 238; Johnny Western, in discussion with the author, December 2015. Western recalled it was very icy when they arrived, and that they all had to get ready backstage.

10. June Carter Cash, *Among My Klediments* (Grand Rapids, MI: Zondervan, 1979), 80; Johnny Cash, *Cash: The Autobiography*, 214; Johnny Western, in conversation with the author, December 2015. This story differs in its various versions as told by different people, but Western confirmed the shirt-ironing and said he had watched her do it.

11. Margaret Jones, *Patsy: The Life*, 245; Mandrell, *Get to the Heart*, 69.

12. Margaret Jones, *Patsy: The Life*, 241–42; Johnny Western, in conversation with the author, December 2015.

13. Barbara Holiff, interview with Jonathan Holiff, January 2006, (as recounted to her by Saul Holiff).

14. *Variety* magazine, November 25, 1964; Peter Lewry, *A Johnny Cash Chronicle: I've Been Everywhere* (London: Helter Skelter, 2001).

15. Johnny Cash, interview by Larry King, *Larry King Live*, CNN, November 26, 2002.

16. Frank Page, letter to Saul Holiff, March 1, 1962.

17. Johnny Cash, *Cash: The Autobiography*, 214.

18. Declaration, signed by George Jones and Saul Holiff, February 28, 1962.

19. George Jones, with Tom Carter, *I Lived To Tell It All* (Random House, 1996).

20. Jonathan Holiff, in discussion with the author, January 2016; Adrian Chamberlain, "Kind, Cruel, Selfish, Smart: Former Manager from Nanaimo Tells of His Days with The Man in Black," *Victoria Times Colonist*, September 13, 2003 ("He was as mercurial as they come").

21. George Jones, *I Lived To Tell It All*, 63–64, 74.

22. Tim Page and Carnegie Hall, *Carnegie Hall Treasures* (New York: HarperCollins, 2011), 19; Andrew Carnegie and Gordon Hutner (introduction), *The Autobiography of Andrew Carnegie and The Gospel of Wealth* (New York: Signet, 2006), 27–28; "The Richest Man in the World: Andrew Carnegie," *American Experience* series, PBS, 1997, www.pbs.org/wgbh/amex/carnegie.

23. Melhuish, "The Johnny Cash Connection"; Charles H. Taliaferro, letter to Johnny Cash from the American Consulate "regarding the immigrant visa case of Mr. Saul Holiff," May 9, 1962; Johnny Cash. letter to Stew Carnall, February 6, 1962; Nat C. Recht, attorney, letter to Johnny Cash Inc., April 25, 1962; rental agreement for Saul Holiff, Hollywood Hill Hotel Apartments, April, 1962.

24. Saul Holiff, letter to Barbara Holiff, April 13, 1962.

25. Turner, *The Man Called Cash*, 94.

26. Johnny Western, in conversation with the author, December 2015.

27. Melhuish, "The Johnny Cash Connection"; *Billboard*, May 5, 1962. The magazine reports that Saul also served buffalo to all those present during a Columbia Records recording session earlier in May.

28. Matthew A. Postal, *Time & Life Building* (New York: Landmarks Preservation Commission, July 16, 2002), www.nyc.gov/html/lpc/downloads/pdf/reports/timelife.pdf; Johnny Western, in discussion with the author, December 2015.

An interesting feature of the Time & Life Building is its location as the headquarters of the fictional ad agency Sterling-Cooper and Partners in season four of the HBO series *Mad Men*. In one episode the characters have dinner in the same restaurant on the forty-eighth floor.

29. Johnny Western, in discussion with the author, December 2015; David Kamp, "Live at the Whiskey," *Vanity Fair*, October 31, 2000; Terry Melcher obituary, *The Telegraph*, November 23, 2004; Nancy Adamson, "Mark Lindsay Talks about New Music, Cats, and Charlie Manson," *Midland Reporter-Telegram*, June 8, 2013. Interestingly, the Manson story goes as follows: Terry Melcher had resided on Cielo Drive in the Hollywood Hills with his girlfriend Candace Bergen, and when they decided to move out, he sublet the house to director Roman Polanski and his pregnant wife, Sharon Tate. It was this house that then became the crime scene for the series of brutal murders ordered by Manson to be carried out by his cult followers in the summer of 1969, in which Tate and four others were killed. One of the murderers, Susan Atkins, later claimed that Melcher himself had been the intended target after plans for a documentary about Manson and his followers had ultimately unravelled and he had declined to cut Manson a record deal. Though the veracity of this was never proven, it was an assertion that rattled Melcher for years.

30. Johnny Western, in discussion with the author, December 2015; Johnny Cash, *Cash: The Autobiography*, 218–20; Antonino D'Ambrosio, *A Heartbeat and a Guitar: Johnny Cash and the Making of Bitter Tears* (New York: Nation Books, 2009), 73–78; Grant, *I Was There* (claim that Cash was dirty); Hilburn, *Johnny Cash: The Life*, 228.

31. Johnny Cash, *Cash: The Autobiography*, 218–19; Johnny Western, in discussion with the author, December 2015; D'Ambrosio, *Heartbeat and a Guitar*.

32. Dir. Al Greenfield, writer Martin Melhuish, interview with Johnny Cash, *Johnny Cash: Half a Mile a Day*, Documentary, 2000.

33. Johnny Western, in discussion with the author, December 2015; Johnny Cash, *Cash: The Autobiography*, 221.

34. Johnny Western, in discussion with the author, December 2015.

35. Johnny Cash, interview by Larry King, *Larry King Live*, CNN, November 26, 2002.

CHAPTER 6: "MY CAREER IS ZOOMING"

1. Saul Holiff, letter to Barbara Holiff, August 8, 1963. Although this letter containing his sentiments about Hollywood was written the following year, I think it is a fair assessment of how he felt at the time in general.
2. Saul Holiff, interview, CKNW, 2003 ("I have horrible memories of it happening in Carnegie Hall in New York,"); Martin Melhuish, "Saul Holiff and 'the Johnny Cash Connection,'" *Country Music News*, Part 2, May 2007 ("He developed laryngitis … part of the joy of being a manager and a promoter").
3. Robert Shelton, "Troupe of Country Musicians Gives Program at Carnegie Hall," *New York Times*, May 11, 1962.
4. Johnny Western, in discussion with the author, January 2016; Bill Sachs, "Folk Talent and Tunes," *Billboard*, February 24, 1962.
5. Saul Holiff, Hollywood Bowl schedule for June 15, 1962, issued to all performers; Stephen Miller, *Johnny Cash: The Life of an American Icon* (London: Omnibus Press, 2003), 111.
6. Johnny Western, in discussion with the author, January 2016; Diane Diekman, *Live Fast, Love Hard: The Faron Young Story* (Champaign: University of Illinois Press, 2012), 77; Sachs, "Folk Talent & Tunes."
7. In 2003, while Johnny was bedridden and ill, *I Walk the Line* director James Mangold visited June and Johnny and got them to confess that the first time they had had sex was in Las Vegas at the Mint, which is detailed in "A Romantic Secret Turns Cash Film Around," by Sharon Waxman, *New York Times*, October 14, 2005. It has long been suspected that their affair started prior to 1965 (due in part to June's writing of "Ring of Fire" in 1962 about her torment at being in love with Johnny). Confirmation from either Johnny or June or both, that it was during this particular tour at the Mint, is also in *Johnny Cash: The Life* by Robert Hilburn on page 232. That June joined them for the last five days of the tour is also mentioned in the June 2, 1962, issue of *Billboard* magazine. The date of their affair is also confirmed in a letter from Johnny Cash to Saul Holiff on October 21, 1967, in which he says, "it was a dream coming true that June made me hang on to for five years," which suggests the affair had started five years earlier.
8. Turner, *The Man Called Cash*, 97.
9. Hilburn, *Johnny Cash: The Life*, 234. I make the assumption that Vivian and Saul weren't close due to the fact that he was not ever mentioned in her biography, though he did sometimes call her from the road to tell her that Johnny was coming home.

10. Accounts of this vary slightly, but this account is as described by Johnny Western in an interview with the author in December 2015. It is also described by Kathy Cash in Hilburn's *Johnny Cash: The Life*, 236.

11. Saul Holiff, letter to Barbara Holiff, June 28, 1962. Edited for length. It's not clear exactly what he was doing in San Francisco; it may have been for a show with Johnny, but that remains unconfirmed.

12. As mentioned by Johnny Western; also, when looking at videos and photos from 1962, it is clear he begins to take on the look with more frequency at this time.

13. Saul often favoured the sophistication of head-to-toe black himself, though there is no clear evidence his style influenced Johnny's; Saul Holiff, letter to Marty Robbins regarding the order of trousers and a blazer "for Carnegie" (which I assume means he was in the audience), January 17, 1962.

14. The Tennessee Three, interview by Jonathan Holiff, Duncan, B.C., April 2006; W.S. "Fluke" Holland, in discussion with the author, May 19, 2016; Tommy Cash, in conversation with the author, May 2016.

15. Manuel Cuevas, in discussion with the author, December 2015; Grant, *I Was There*, 101; Saul Holiff, as told to Jonathan Holiff.

16. Saul Holiff, letter to Johnny Cash, July 13, 1962.

17. Johnny Cash, letter to Barbara Holiff, n.d. Given the contents of the letter, it is estimated to have been sent around this time.

18. Johnny Cash, letter to Saul Holiff, August 10, 1962.

19. Saul Holiff, letter to Johnny Cash, August 13, 1962.

20. Saul Holiff, letter to Barbara Holiff, August 23, 1962.

21. Saul Holiff, letter to Colonel Tom Parker, January 17, 1962.

22. Tom Diskin (on behalf of Colonel Tom Parker), letter to Saul Holiff, January 29, 1962.

23. Alanna Nash, *The Colonel: The Extraordinary Story of Colonel Tom Parker and Elvis Presley* (London: Aurum Press, 2003), 36–58.

24. Despite lax border controls, the Colonel decided not to accompany him on these shows.

25. The USO flying them out together and "babies" comes from a letter Saul Holiff sent to Johnny Cash on August 13, 1962. June also refers to the Tennessee Three as "babies" in Christopher Wren's *Winners Got Scars Too*, page 138. I'm making an assumption that this is the route they took. Saul outlined two possible routes in his letter to Tom Parker, and later photos show him in front of a Japanese Airlines plane, so I'm assuming that was the one they chose.

26. According to Saul Holiff; Bob Rolontz, "Personal Appearance Chances for Country Artists Growing in Breadth and in Loot," *Billboard*, November 10, 1962; "Johnny Cash Sets Two 'Firsts' on Far East Jaunt," *Billboard*, December 22, 1962.

27. This was the precursor to the Country Music Awards. Evidence that this was arranged was in a letter from Saul Holiff to Johnny Cash, dated August 13, 1962, and in "Holiff Preps 2-Way Talk With Cash on Japan Visit," *The Music Reporter*, September 22, 1962. However, there is no evidence it actually happened, though audio of it allegedly exists.

28. Penny Von Eschen, *Satchmo Blows up the World: Jazz Ambassadors Play the Cold War* (Cambridge, MA: Harvard University Press, 2004); Dana Gioia, "Cool Jazz and Cold War," *The American Interest* 1, no. 3 (March 1, 2006): www.the-american-interest.com/2006/03/01/cool-jazz-and-cold-war; Dan Brubeck, in discussion with the author, November 9, 2015.

29. Al Ricketts, *On the Town*, as quoted in *Variety* advertisement, November 25, 1964; "Johnny Cash Sets Two 'Firsts' on Far East Jaunt," *Billboard*, December 22, 1962; "Johnny Cash Heads USO Bill for Tour of Japan & Korea," *Billboard*, August 11, 1962.

30. As recounted by June Carter Cash and Johnny Cash on episode 39 of Pete Seeger's *Rainbow Quest*, 1966. Their second USO tour wasn't until 1969.

31. "Johnny Cash Heads USO Bill"; Rolontz, "Personal Appearance Chances"; "Johnny Cash Sets Two 'Firsts'"; Saul Holiff, letter to Barbara Holiff, November 23, 1962 (dictated on November 22). The letter is only one page; any subsequent pages are missing. All other Japan tour information comes from *Billboard* magazine articles on August 11, November 10, and December 22, 1962.

32. Saul Holiff, letter to Sam Assaf, November 24, 1962; Jonathan Holiff, in discussion with the author.

33. Wren, *Winners Got Scars Too*, 143.

34. Johnny Cash, letter to Saul Holiff, March 5, 1974.

CHAPTER 7: THE FLAMES WENT HIGHER

1. Larry Brinton and Clay Hargis, "4 Opry Stars Die in Crash," *Nashville Banner*, March 6, 1963; Laura Cantrell, "A Chill Lingers at the Patsy Cline Crash Site," *Vanity Fair*, March 5, 2009, www.vanityfair.com/culture/2009/03/a-chill-lingers-at-the-patsy-cline-crash-site; Johnny Western, in discussion with the author, January 2016; June Carter Cash, *From the Heart* (New

York: Prentice Hall, 1987), 109; Bego, *I Fall To Pieces*, 186; Mark Stielper, in discussion with the author, July 22, 2016. Stielper befriended the Cashes late in their lives and became very close with them. He is generally regarded as the family's historian.

2. Mark Stielper, in discussion with the author, July 22, 2016. The story of June Carter driving through the streets of Nashville is as told by June to Stielper. Whether she was truly immersed in angst or not is debatable, but this is her version of the story. Other accounts state that the song was inspired by a book of Elizabethan poems, but Stielper said he has found no evidence of this in his research.

3. Mark Stielper, in discussion with the author, July 22, 2016; Singles Reviews, *Billboard*, January 12, 1963.

4. Jack Clement, interview by Jonathan Holiff, October 21, 2007; *Encyclopedia of Country Music*, 2nd ed. (New York: Oxford University Press, 2012), s.v. "'Cowboy' Jack Clement."

5. Jack Clement, interview by Jonathan Holiff, October 21, 2007.

6. Saul Holiff, letter to Barbara Holiff, July 11, 1963.

7. The "Put the screws on me" quote from Cash's performance at San Quentin prison, February 24, 1969. That Cash just walked off the stage is according to Jonathan Holiff in *My Father and the Man in Black*, and also from a recording of Cash's Bowl performance found on YouTube (www.youtube.com/watch?v=C5IS7OqsIDA).

8. Wren, *Winners Got Scars Too*, 148–49; Tommy Cash, in discussion with the author, June 2016. The case of beer and one hundred pills a day also confirmed in Ed Salamon's interview with Cash on *The Johnny Cash Silver Anniversary Special*, WHN Radio, in 1980.

9. Wren, *Winners Got Scars Too*; Tommy Cash, in conversation with the author, June 14, 2016; Bill Sachs, "Folk Talent and Tunes," *Billboard*, November 17, 1962.

10. Saul Holiff, letter to Barbara Holiff, July 24, 1963.

11. Saul Holiff, letter to Barbara Holiff, July 11, 1963.

12. Barbara Holiff, letter to Saul Holiff, July 15, 1963.

13. Saul Holiff, interview by Candy Yates, *Cinematically Speaking*, 1976.

14. The Tennessee Three, interview by Jonathan Holiff, April 19, 2006.

15. Saul Holiff, letter to Johnny Cash, May 23, 1964; Johnny Cash, letter to Saul Holiff, May 23, 1964.

16. Saul Holiff, letter to Barbara Holiff, October 26, 1963. It is uncertain

where he is, exactly. The letterhead is from Zurich, and he makes mention of "record companies" at a convention but doesn't say which ones. I am making a guess that he is using letterhead from Switzerland but is talking about a DJ convention occurring at that time in Nashville. It's also unclear whether Cash played a date in Holland or Zurich. No other Cash books or sources mention these locations.

17. Nelson, *It's a Long Story*; Melhuish, "The Johnny Cash Connection."

18. Gary Younge, "1963: The Defining Year of the Civil Rights Movement," *The Guardian*, May 7, 2013; Alan Taylor, "50 Years Ago: The World in 1963," *The Atlantic*, February 15, 2013; Alan Taylor, "1964: Civil Rights Battles," *The Atlantic*, May 28, 2014.

19. Johnny Cash, interview by Ed Salamon, *The Johnny Cash Silver Anniversary Special*, WHN Radio, New York, July 4, 1980.

20. Saul Holiff, interview by Candy Yates, *Cinematically Speaking*, 1976 (opinion on Dylan); Johnny Cash, letter to Saul Holiff, May 23, 1964.

21. Saul Holiff, letter to Johnny Cash, May 23, 1964 (sales figures); *Billboard*, August 22, 1970 (Singleton's position at Mercury at this time); Johnny Cash, letter to Saul Holiff, May 23, 1964.

22. Johnny Cash, *Cash: The Autobiography*. This is also mentioned in pretty much every book that talks about Cash.

23. Johnny Cash, handwritten letter to Saul Holiff, n.d.

24. Johnny Cash, *Cash: The Autobiography*, 200 ("Rather die than get a divorce"). June's attitude at this time is also referenced here on page 227, in which Johnny says she told him, "I'm going. I can't handle this anymore. I'm going to tell Saul that I can't work with you anymore. It's over."

25. Johnny Cash, letter to Vivian Cash, on letterhead from the Sahara Hotel in Las Vegas. Jonathan Holiff believes this letter was written in late 1963 or early 1964 based on a two-week stint in which Cash was scheduled to play at the Mint Casino. It has been cross-referenced with other Cash experts such as Peter Lewry, but it remains unclear exactly when it was written. It could have been as late as into 1965, as that was also a time when Cash regularly went out into the desert, though it seems unlikely that he would have written this to Vivian then, as his marriage was debatably in much worse shape.

26. Johnny Cash, *Johnny Cash Sings Ballads of the True West*, Columbia Records, 1965, liner notes; Johnny Cash, interview by Ed Salamon, *The Johnny Cash Silver Anniversary Special*, WHN Radio, 1980.

27. Johnny Cash, *Cash: The Autobiography*. Cash says he shared his Dexedrine and Thorazine with La Farge.
28. D'Ambrosio, *Heartbeat and a Guitar*.
29. Johnny Cash, interview by Ed Salamon, *The Johnny Cash Silver Anniversary Special*, WHN Radio, New York, July 4, 1980.
30. D'Ambrosio, *Heartbeat and a Guitar*; Johnny Cash, *Cash: The Autobiography*.
31. Letter from Saul Holiff, letter to Johnny Cash, and vice versa, both May 23, 1964.
32. Saul Holiff, letter to Barbara Holiff, November 18, 1963; Saul Holiff, letter to Johnny Cash, May 23, 1964; Ronald D. Cohen, *A History of Folk Music Festivals in the United States: Feasts of Musical Celebration* (Lanham, MD: Scarecrow Press, 2008).
33. Johnny Cash, letter to Saul Holiff, May 23, 1964.
34. Hilburn, *Johnny Cash: The Life*; Edward J. Rielly, *The 1960s* (Westport, CT: Greenwood Publishing Group, 2003); Cohen, *History of Folk Music Festivals*.
35. From a recording of Cash's performance at the 1964 Newport Folk Festival in Jonathan Holiff's archives.
36. Bouncing on the bed was described by Cash in *Cash: The Autobiography*, on page 204. The gifted guitar was mentioned in an interview with Dylan in *Winners Got Scars Too*, by Christopher Wren, on page 145. "He gave me his guitar, an old Martin. I still got it," said Dylan.
37. Bob Dylan, *Chronicles: Volume One* (New York: Simon & Schuster, 2005).
38. Robert Shelton, "'64 Folk Festival Ends in Newport," *New York Times*, July 27, 1964.
39. Advertisement in *Billboard* magazine, August 22, 1964. Full text of the ad edited for length.
40. Saul Holiff, letter to Johnny Cash, October 23, 1964.
41. Johnny Cash, letter to Saul Holiff, October 26, 1964.
42. Saul Holiff, letter to Johnny Cash, November 1, 1964.
43. Hilburn, *Johnny Cash: The Life*, 244. For some reason, there is no record of this deal in Saul's archives. "Ring of Fire" was nominated for a Grammy in the category of Best Country and Western Recording, but it lost.
44. Saul Holiff, letter to producer Stan Jacobson, April 24, 1964.
45. Saul Holiff, letter to Johnny Cash, May 23, 1964; Johnny Cash, handwritten letter to Saul Holiff, May 1964 (written on the back of Saul's May 23 letter).

CHAPTER 8: ONE HUNDRED PERCENT TOP BILLING

1. Johnny Cash and June Carter Cash, handwritten letters to Saul Holiff and Barbara Holiff on stationery from the Windsor Hotel in Sault Ste. Marie, September 19, 1964; Barbara Holiff, voiceover, *My Father and the Man in Black*, 2012.

2. John Steele Gordon, "The World's Fair: It Was a Disaster from the Beginning," *American Heritage* 57, no. 5 (October 2006); Donald Presa, *The Unisphere* (New York: Landmarks Preservation Commission, May 16, 1995), www. nyc.gov/html/lpc/downloads/pdf/reports/unisphere.pdf; Barbara Holiff, in discussion with the author, March 2, 2016.

3. Saul Holiff, letter to Johnny Cash, October 23, 1964; Robert Shelton, *No Direction Home: The Life and Music of Bob Dylan* (New York: Da Capo Press, 1986, 2003) 159; Robert Shelton, "Folk Music: Pompous and Ersatz?" *New York Times*, November 29, 1964. In the *Times* piece, Shelton calls the song Dylan's "propagandizing for non-dependent love."

4. Stan Jacobson, letter to Saul Holiff, May 25, 1964; Saul Holiff, letter to Russell Stoneham, February 15, 1965; Russell Stoneham, letter to Saul Holiff, April 23, 1965.

5. *Billboard*, November 14, 1964; Lewry, *A Johnny Cash Chronicle*, 49; Andrew Grant Jackson, *1965: The Most Revolutionary Year in Music* (New York: Thomas Dunne, 2015), 63; Turner, *The Man Called Cash*, 112.

6. Johnny Western, in discussion with the author, November 2015; Holly George-Warren, *Public Cowboy No. 1: The Life and Times of Gene Autry* (New York: Oxford University Press, 2009). Western said the appearance was for a new show called *Jambalaya*, but the only references I can find for a country and western show on KTLA is Autry's *Meadow Ranch*. Other sources, like Steve Turner, say Cash was in town for the *Shindig!* appearance when he lost Western's car.

7. Saul Holiff, letter to Johnny Cash, February 27, 1965. The forty dollars was mentioned in a letter from Saul Holiff to Johnny Cash dated July 9, 1965.

8. Johnny Cash, letter to Saul Holiff, March 2, 1965.

9. Saul Holiff, *Pajama Party* interview.

10. Saul Holiff, *Pajama Party* interview; Harold Reid and Don Reid, *The Statler Brothers: Random Memories* (Yell Records, 2008) 28–29.

11. "Variety Theatre Promoter Broke," *Milwaukee Sentinel*, January 17, 1962; "Green Bay Promoter Andy Serrahn, Whose One Man Variety Theatre Failed Here Three Years Ago, Is Back in the Business of Staging Shows in

Wisconsin, States the Column 'Bits of Show Business,' *Milwaukee Sentinel*, December 14, 1964.

12. Saul Holiff, memo, March 23, 1965. Emphasis added.

13. Johnny Cash, letter to Saul Holiff, July 14, 1965.

14. Vivian Cash, *I Walked the Line*.

15. Gene Ferguson, interview by Jonathan Holiff, February 2010.

16. Wren, *Winners Got Scars Too*, 170.

17. Ibid.

18. "Johnny Cash Slightly Hurt in Auto Crash," *Nashville Tennessean*, March 26, 1965.

19. Gene Ferguson, interview by Jonathan Holiff, February 2010.

20. Saul Holiff, telegram to Johnny Cash, June 8, 1965; Advertisement in the *London Free Press*, June 15, 1965.

21. Tex Ritter, telegram to Jonathan Holiff, June 12, 1965.

22. Hilburn, *Johnny Cash: The Life*, 278–79; Carl Rivenburgh, in discussion with the author, December 2014; "Johnny Cash Sued by U.S. for Forest Fire," *Associated Press*, June 28, 1967; "Tribe Eyes Warpath on Cash Ruling," *Pasadena Star News*, July 6, 1967; "U.S. Sues Singer for Forest Fire," *Capital Times*, July 5, 1967.

23. Turner, *The Man Called Cash*, 112.

24. Saul Holiff, letter to Johnny Cash, July 9, 1965.

25. Johnny Cash, letter to Saul Holiff, July 17, 1965.

26. Frank Kennedy, "Hoot's Off-Colour Material in Bad Taste," *Toronto Daily Star*, August 23, 1965.

27. Saul Holiff, letter to Johnny Cash, August 24, 1965. Saul refers to former manager Stew Carnall and Charlie Williams, a disc jockey and songwriter based in Los Angeles. Emphasis added.

28. Bill Walker, interview by Jonathan Holiff, March 15, 2007.

29. "Ex-Londoner Says Premonition Saved Him from 84-Death Crash," *London Free Press*, February 11, 1965. Saul was scheduled to fly from Kennedy Airport in New York to Charlotte, South Carolina, to meet Johnny, who was due to film a bread commercial. While waiting for the flight in his hotel room, he picked up a *Maclean's* magazine and at random read an article that detailed an Air Canada crash that had taken place in Montreal the previous year. Saying he got "a crazy premonition," Saul called and cancelled his flight, which subsequently crashed.

30. Grant, *I Was There*, 136; Wren, *Winners Got Scars Too*, 160.

31. Johnny Cash, *Man in Black* (Grand Rapids, MI: Zondervan, 1975).

32. As recalled by Barbara Holiff. The text of the TV news announcer from the actual London TV broadcast, courtesy of Jonathan Holiff, *My Father and the Man in Black*.

33. Associated Press, "Johnny Cash Out on Bond on Drug Smuggling Counts," *London Free Press*, October 6, 1965.

34. Turner, *The Man Called Cash*.

35. Texas A&M University, telegram to Saul Holiff, November 12, 1965.

36. According to Jonathan Holiff; Woodrow Wilson Bean, letter and motion to Saul Holiff, October 18, 1965.

37. Mark Stielper, conversation with Dixie Deen, relayed via email to Jonathan Holiff, November 29, 2005.

38. Dixie Deen, "Everything Ain't Been Said," *Music City News*, January 1966.

39. Saul Holiff, letter to Johnny Cash, December 21, 1965.

CHAPTER 9: "SAUL, HELP ME!"

1. "Arrest Exposes Johnny Cash's Negro Wife," *The Thunderbolt*, January 1966.

2. Roy Reed, "Alabama Police Use Gas and Clubs to Rout Negroes," *New York Times*, March 8, 1965; Howard Zinn, *A People's History of the United States* (New York: HarperPerennial, 1990), 450–51; *March from Selma to Montgomery*, History channel video, www.history.com/topics/black-history/civil-rights-movement/videos/march-from-selma-to-montgomery.

3. John Herbers, "The Klan: Its Growing Influence," *New York Times*, April 20, 1965.

4. Stephen E. Atkins, *Encyclopedia of Right-Wing Extremism in Modern American History* (Santa Barbara, ABC-CLIO, 2011); according to Jonathan Holiff; Wren, *Winners Got Scars Too*, 166. It is interesting to note that Stoner was eventually arrested in 1977 for his involvement in various church bombings during the 1950s and 1960s and eventually convicted for the 1958 bombing of a church in Birmingham, Alabama, for which he received a ten-year prison sentence.

5. Saul Holiff, speech at the London Rotary Club, 1978; Charles Gerein, "Singer Cash Explains Drug Charges," *Toronto Daily Star*, March 16, 1966; "Toronto Country Show at O'Keefe," *Billboard*, April 2, 1966.

6. Cordery, "Managing the Man in Black Opened Doors" (regarding the bottle incident).

7. Hotel scene as recalled by Barbara Holiff. All quotes are from a London

Rotary Club speech Saul delivered in 1978. He dubbed the tale "Nightmare in Toronto." Some passages have been edited slightly for length and clarity. I have concluded that it may have been Lew DeWitt of the Statlers who had his head on Cash's chest and not Harold Reid — Saul mentions that Harold had a medical background, but it was in fact DeWitt who worked briefly as a psychiatric aide at Western State Hospital, according to *Classic Country: Legends of Country Music*, by Charles K. Wolfe. As an interesting aside, fans have theorized this work influenced the lyrics for their hit "Flowers on the Wall," but this is unconfirmed.

8.   Saul Holiff, letter to Barbara Holiff, May 8, 1966. Alex Richmond was a family friend.

9.   Lewry, *A Johnny Cash Chronicle*; Saul Holiff, letter to Barbara Holiff, May 8, 1966; Charlotte Heathcote, "Mervyn Conn's Rootin' Tootin' Life with the Stars," *Daily Express*, January 29, 2012.

10. Saul Holiff, letter to Barbara Holiff, May 10, 1966.

11. Saul Holiff, interview by Candy Yates, *Cinematically Speaking*, 1976; Saul Holiff, interview with Steve Paikin, 1998; Lewry, *A Johnny Cash Chronicle*; Bob Dylan and D.A. Pennebaker, *Eat the Document*, ABC Television, 1972. Outtakes of this documentary feature a cameo by Baez and a clearly intoxicated Dylan with Lennon in a taxi. www.youtube.com/watch?v=1GOKN268kAk. The film's release was delayed by Dylan's motorcycle accident in the summer of 1966, and ABC eventually refused to air the feature, as they thought Dylan's edit had made it incomprehensible to mainstream audiences. Jordan Runtagh, "Remembering Bob Dylan and John Lennon's Drugged Out Limo Ride," *Rolling Stone*, May 27, 2016, www.rollingstone.com/music/news/remembering-bob-dylan-and-john-lennons-drugged-out-limo-ride-20160527.

12. Saul Holiff, letter to Barbara Holiff, May 10, 1966.

13. Johnny Cash, letter to Saul Holiff, n.d. Researched by Jonathan Holiff to be referring to this period, specifically.

14. Saul Holiff, letter to Barbara Holiff, May 10, 1966; Saul Holiff, interview by Steve Paikin, 1998. There is a chance that they may have discussed the issue in some other format, or that Cash apologized for the no-show, but I am making the assumption here that he did not, given what else is said in their letters that this was the only communication the two had about the issue.

15. Saul Holiff, letter to Johnny Cash, n.d. Researched by Jonathan Holiff to be from this time. Small edits have been made for clarity.

16. Saul Holiff, interview by Steve Paikin, 1998.

17. Johnny Cash, telegram to Saul Holiff, June 3, 1966.

18. Adrian Chamberlain, "'Kind, Cruel, Selfish, Smart': Former Manager from Nanaimo Tells of His Days with The Man in Black," *Times Colonist*, September 13, 2003.

19. Vivian Cash, *I Walked the Line*, 303–5.

20. "Johnny Cash's Wife Suing for Divorce," *Oxnard Press-Courier*, August 18, 1966.

21. Anzac Jacobs, letter to Saul Holiff, August 18, 1966. It must have been confusing for Jacobs, who had processed the financial details of Saul's resignation only months prior.

22. Johnny Cash, telegram to Saul Holiff and Anzac Jacobs, August 18, 1966.

23. According to Barbara Holiff; James E. Dixon, Stew Carnall's attorney, letters dated September 29, 1966 and October 25, 1966; "Will of John R. Cash," from Saul Holiff's collection.

24. Johnny Cash, *Man in Black*, 114.

25. Johnny Cash, *Man in Black*, 122; Michael Streissguth, *Outlaw: Waylon, Willie, Kris and the Renegades of Nashville* (New York: It Books, 2013), 59; Turner, *The Man Called Cash*, 117.

26. Johnny Cash, "I'm a Free Man Now," *Guideposts* (November 1970), 3–6.

27. "Johnny Cash(es) In at the Capitol," *Ottawa Journal*, September 21, 1966; Harvey Glatt, interview by Jonathan Holiff, *My Father and the Man in Black* (London, ON: New Chapter Productions, 2012), DVD.

28. Turner, *The Man Called Cash*, 114.

29. "Hate Groups Gun for Johnny Cash in a Racial Error," *Variety*, October 5, 1966; "Cash to Sue White Citizens Council for $200,000," *Jet Magazine*, October 27, 1966.

30. Saul Holiff, speech to the London Rotary Club, 1978.

31. Streissguth, *Johnny Cash: The Biography*, 129.

32. John Garabedian, "Singer Johnny Cash Fights the Voice of Hate," *New York Post*, October 6, 1966; Wren, *Winners Got Scars Too*, 166; Atkins, *Encyclopedia of Right-Wing Extremism*.

33. As told to Barbara Holiff by Saul Holiff.

34. Bill Flanagan, "Johnny Cash, American," *Musician Magazine*, May 1988.

35. Johnny Cash, *Man in Black*; Johnny Cash, "I'm a Free Man Now," 3–6.

36. Myra Richman, interviewed by Jonathan Holiff, April, 2009.

CHAPTER 10: CARRYING CASH

1. Jonathan Holiff, in discussion with the author, November 2012; Jerry Weintraub, with Rich Cohen, "All the King's Men," in *When I Stop Talking You'll Know I'm Dead: Useful Stories from a Persuasive Man* (New York, Twelve, 2011) 73–98.
2. Wren, *Winners Got Scars Too*, 123; The Tennessee Three, interview with Jonathan Holiff, Duncan, April 19, 2006.
3. Whiteside, *Ramblin' Rose*, 188–205; *Encyclopedia of Country Music*, 395; Johnny Western, interview by Jonathan Holiff, July 2015.
4. Wren, *Winners Got Scars Too*, 181–82; Johnny Western, interview by Jonathan Holiff, July 2015.
5. Johnny Cash, letter to June Carter Cash, n.d. Based on the contents, circumstances, and both Bob Wooton's and Johnny Western's memories of that tour, Jonathan Holiff estimated its date to be February 16, 1967.
6. Hilburn, *Johnny Cash: The Life*, 309–10.
7. Bob Wooton, interview by Jonathan Holiff, Duncan, B.C., April 19, 2006; Johnny Western, interview by Jonathan Holiff, July 2015.
8. *Encyclopedia of Country Music*, 333; "Moeller Reps Cash Show; Guarantee Called Largest," *Record World*, November 12, 1966; according to Jonathan Holiff, *My Father and the Man in Black*, 2012, DVD.
9. Streissguth, *Johnny Cash: The Biography*, 133–34.
10. Melhuish, "The Johnny Cash Connection."
11. Grant, *I Was There*; "Reader Disappointed in Singer's Cancellation," *Waterloo Daily Courier*, April 27, 1967.
12. "Lucky" Moeller, letter to Saul Holiff, October 2, 1967.
13. Saul Holiff, telegram to Johnny Cash, May 6, 1967.
14. "Lucky" Moeller, letter to Saul Holiff, October 2, 1967; Saul Holiff, letter to Johnny Cash, October 31, 1967; "Star Doesn't Show So City Couple Performs at Fair," *Jefferson City Daily Capital News*, August 22, 1967.
15. Saul Holiff, letter to Johnny Cash, October 31, 1967.
16. Streissguth, *Johnny Cash: The Biography*, 135. Incurring these loans also further eroded Cash's bargaining position with Columbia, with whom his recording contract was up for renewal on October 31, 1967.
17. Divorce Agreement between John R. Cash and Vivian D. Cash, third draft, page 9; Bruce Thompson, lawyer, letter to Johnny Cash, December 19, 1967.
18. Johnny Cash, handwritten letter to Vivian Cash, October 20, 1967.
19. "Johnny Cash Walks a New Line," *Nashville Tennessean*, April 20, 1969.

20. That this letter was written after he played the Morris Civic Auditorium is according to Cash family historian Mark Stielper.

21. Johnny Cash, handwritten ten-page letter to Saul Holiff, October 21, 1967.

22. Jerry Fink, "Tributes include Cash's drummer of 37 years," *Las Vegas Sun*, January 16, 2008; Johnny Cash, *Cash: The Autobiography*, 231–32; Mark Stielper, in discussion with the author, July 22, 2016.

23. Johnny Cash, "I'm a Free Man Now"; Turner, *The Man Called Cash*, 120.

24. Johnny Cash, "I'm a Free Man Now."

25. Johnny Cash, *Man in Black*, 126–27; "Mountain Folk to Gather for Appalachian Homecoming October 6–9," *Nashville Daily News*, September 21, 1988.

26. Bruce Thompson, letter to Johnny Cash, December 19, 1967.

CHAPTER 11: THE PROPOSAL

1. Hilburn, *Johnny Cash: The Life*, 306; *Encyclopedia of Country Music*, 251; William Grimes, "Bob Johnston, 83, Dies; Produced Bob Dylan and Johnny Cash albums," *Rolling Stone*, August 17, 2015.

2. Saul Holiff, letter to Johnny Cash, December 29, 1966.

3. Frederick Dannen, *Hit Men: Power Brokers and Fast Money Inside the Music Business* (New York: Random House, 1991), 69; *Encyclopedia of Country Music*, 274; Hilburn, *Johnny Cash: The Life*, 316.

4. Hilburn, *Johnny Cash: The Life*, 317–18; Turner, *The Man Called Cash*, 123–25. Michael Streissguth mentions in his book *Johnny Cash at Folsom Prison* that Cash had thought of recording in prison since 1962, the date of the first Carnegie show, which was what gave me this idea.

5. Michael Streissguth, *Johnny Cash at Folsom Prison: The Making of a Masterpiece* (Cambridge, MA: Da Capo Press, 2004); Wren, *Winners Got Scars Too*, 198; Alfred G. Aronowitz, "Music Behind the Bars," *Life*, August 16, 1968.

6. Wren, *Winners Got Scars Too*, 197; Richard Nixon, "Address Accepting the Presidential Nomination at the Republican National Convention in Miami Beach, Florida, August 8, 1968," *The American Presidency Project*, www.presidency.ucsb.edu/ws/?pid=25968.

7. Turner, *The Man Called Cash*, 124; Hilburn, *Johnny Cash: The Life*, 327.

8. Robert Hilburn, interview by the author via email, August 31, 2016. Hilburn was the rock critic for the *Los Angeles Times* then, and personally travelled with Cash to Folsom Prison for the concert. He told me he does not recall seeing Saul Holiff there.

9. Stan Jacobson, interview by Jonathan Holiff, May 6, 2006.

10. Johnny Cash, *Man in Black*. Also as recalled by nineteen different audience members who were at the concert, interviewed by Jonathan Holiff in 2006 at an anniversary event in London. There is some discrepancy about which song preceded the proposal and which one followed, but it's safe to say "Jackson" and "If I Were a Carpenter" were two that audience members recalled.

11. Willsey, "Country Music's Royal Wedding"; Johnny Cash, *Man in Black* (in which Cash writes, "I'd never seen [Saul] as happy as he was that night in London after the show").

12. Johnny Cash, *Man in Black*. "The concert was at Treasure Island Gardens, now the London Velodrome. I believe it was later known as London Gardens, but not in 1968," said photographer Ralph Willsey (who was there), in discussion with the author February 20, 2017. From what I understand, the Treasure Island Gardens was also known as both the London Ice House and the London Gardens.

13. Wren, *Winners Got Scars Too*, 196; Johnny Cash, *Man in Black*; Streissguth, *Johnny Cash: The Biography*, 154.

14. Stan Jacobson, interview by Jonathan Holiff, May 6, 2006.

15. Nat Hentoff, "Cosmo Listens to Records," *Cosmopolitan*, August 1968.

16. Bruce Jenkins, *Goodbye: In Search of Gordon Jenkins* (Berkeley, CA: Frog Books, 2005), 280–81. In this book, Gordon Jenkins's agent Harold Plant says the issue was brought up with Cash's "personal manager," who had asked if they could meet and whether he had any material to substantiate the claim. The book says that one of the terms of the settlement was that they not disclose it publicly, but the dollar amount was discovered by Bruce Jenkins later.

17. Wren, *Winners Got Scars Too*, 190–91; June Carter Cash, *Among My Klediments*, 93–94.

18. Dixie Deen, "Everything Ain't Been Said"; Turner, *The Man Called Cash*, 146.

19. Robert Shelton, "Johnny Cash Sings to a Full House," *New York Times*, October 24, 1968.

20. Geoffrey Cannon, interview by the author via email, April 26, 2016; John Finch, *Granada Television: The First Generation* (Manchester: Manchester University Press, 2003); Leslie Woodhead, "Jo Durden-Smith: Documentary film-maker with his finger on the pulse of the 60s generation." *The Guardian*, May 21, 2007, www.theguardian.com/news/2007/may/21/guardianobituaries.media.

CHAPTER 12: THE CRASH

1. There are many sources for this section, and a variety of different stories about how "A Boy Named Sue" came to be. I defer to Saul's story for obvious reasons, as much of the book focuses on his perspective, but also because he recounted it at least four times — once in an interview with Candy Yates in 1976, in a speech to the London Rotary Club in 1978, again in an interview with Father Bernard Heffernan for *Country Music News* on August 1, 2001, and once more for *CMN* in a piece that was published in 2007. The story virtually never changes in each version: he insists they bumped into Silverstein at O'Hare airport and he handed Cash the song. Cash biographer Michael Streissguth's version is that it was delivered through music publisher Don Davis, and biographer Steve Turner says the song came from Silverstein after a party at Cash's Hendersonville house attended by Bob Dylan, Kris Kristofferson, and Joni Mitchell. I believe that many pieces of this could be true, and that the party did happen prior to San Quentin as described. Perhaps Cash had already received the lyrics in the airport prior to this point. "I don't want to repeat myself" and other aspects of the negotiations with Columbia were as recalled by Barbara Holiff, in discussion with the author on May 1, 2016, who was there when the calls were being made from their home.

2. Turner, *The Man Called Cash*, 132.

3. Saul Holiff, letter to Johnny Cash, January 6, 1969. This was a three-page letter that has been edited down, as much of it was about detailed tour, business, and financial discussions.

4. Saul Holiff, audio diary, recorded in the fall of 1971; Barbara Holiff, in discussion with the author, May 1, 2016; Michael Darlow, letter to Saul Holiff, January 21, 1969.

5. Christianson, Scott. *The Last Gasp: The Rise and Fall of the American Gas Chamber* (Berkeley, CA: University of California Press, 2010).

6. Bill Miller, with Mark Vancil and Jacob Hoye, *Cash: An American Man* (New York: Simon & Schuster, 2004), 51; Barbara Holiff, in discussion with the author, May 1, 2016; Ralph J. Gleason, "Johnny Cash at San Quentin," *San Francisco Chronicle*, February 26, 1969; Lou Robin, in discussion with the author, May 12, 2016.

7. *Johnny Cash at San Quentin*, 1969, audio recording, Jonathan Holiff's archives; Johnny Cash, "San Quentin," live at San Quentin prison, www.youtube.com/watch?v=1zgja26eNeY; Gleason, "Johnny Cash at San Quentin"; Turner, *The Man Called Cash*, 133.

8. Grant, *I Was There*, 167; Miller, *Life of an American Icon*, 180–81.

9. W.S. "Fluke" Holland, interview by Jonathan Holiff; Saul Holiff, interview, *Johnny Cash: Half a Mile a Day*, Documentary, 2000.

10. Lou Robin, in discussion with the author, May 12, 2016.

11. Saul Holiff, audio diary, recorded in the fall of 1971.

12. Saul Holiff, interview, *Johnny Cash: Half a Mile a Day*, Documentary, 2000.

13. A.J. Perenchio, letter to Saul Holiff, April 25, 1969.

14. Rosanne Cash, *Composed*, 19; Bob Cornfield, letter to Saul Holiff, April 21, 1969. In a later letter, they made an offer of a fifteen-thousand-dollar advance to Cash.

15. Christopher Wren, in discussion with the author, May 17, 2016; "New Cash Biography Is the Whole Truth," *Nashville Tennessean*, September 9, 1971.

16. "'Round the Festival," *Nashville Banner*, October 18, 1969.

17. Johnny Cash, *Cash: The Autobiography*. The press conference was on September 23, 1969.

18. Blaik Kirby, "Johnny ($93,000) Cash sets Gardens record," *Globe and Mail*, November 11, 1969; Blaik Kirby, "The Country King Has a Cause," *Globe and Mail*, October 18, 1969; Jack Batten, "Johnny Cash Deserved Record Gardens Tribute," *Toronto Star*, November 11, 1969. According to Kirby, the crowd numbered 18,106 and the earnings were a total of ninety-three thousand dollars. Saul's records show a gross of $92,813.

19. Marci McDonald, "To you it's country — to him it's 'Johnny Cash music,'" *Toronto Daily Star*, June 7, 1969; Lou Robin, in discussion with the author, May 12, 2016; Marci McDonald, "Cash Sure Is Makin' It Okay," *Toronto Star*, November 11, 1969.

20. Lou Robin, in discussion with the author, May 12, 2016; Robert Redford, letter to Johnny Cash, December 9, 1969.

21. Saul Holiff, interview, *Johnny Cash: Half a Mile a Day*, Documentary, 2000; "Sam [*sic*] Holiff Guiding Hand for Johnny Cash and Others," *Ottawa Citizen*, December 20, 1969 ("I can read his mind, and I know he can read mine"); Eric Bender, "Excellence His Hang-Up," *London Free Press*, October 7, 1972 ("We know each other so well he can sense what I want"); McDonald, "To you it's country."

CHAPTER 13: CAMELOT, NIXON, AND THE FAIRY TALE THAT WASN'T

1. Barbara Holiff, in discussion with the author, May 2016.

2. Howard Zinn, "The Impossible Victory: Vietnam," in *A People's History of*

the United States (New York: Harper Perennial, 1998); "From the Archive, 29 April 1967: Muhammad Ali Refuses to Fight in Vietnam War," *The Guardian*, April 29, 2013, www.theguardian.com/theguardian/2013/apr/29/muhammad-ali-refuses-to-fight-in-vietnam-war-1967; Martin Luther King Jr., "Why I Am Opposed to the War in Vietnam," delivered April 30, 1967, at the Riverside Church, New York, www.lib.berkeley.edu/MRC/pacificaviet/riversidetranscript.html.

3. McDonald, "Cash Sure Is Makin' It Okay."

4. Stan Jacobson, interview with Jonathan Holiff, May 6, 2006; Wren, *Winners Got Scars Too*; Zinn, *People's History of the United States*; Hubert Saal, "Johnny on the Spot," *Newsweek*, February 2, 1970; Larry Linderman, "*Penthouse* Interview: Johnny Cash," *Penthouse*, August 1975.

5. Bill Webster, "'Guardian' for a Super-Star: Saul Holiff Story Arm-in-Arm with Cash's Phenomenal Success," *London Free Press*, November 8, 1969; Goddard, "What's New with Saul"; King, "Want Johnny Cash?"; Saul Holiff, letter to John Mitchell, Screen Gems president, March 17, 1970.

6. "Cash and Manager Holiff — A 'Handshake Agreement,'" *Billboard*, May 23, 1970.

7. King, "Want Johnny Cash?"; "Cash and Manager Holiff," *Billboard*.

8. Jonathan Holiff and Barbara Holiff, interviews with the author, 2014–16; Bender, "Excellence His Hang-Up"; Saul Holiff, audio diary, October, 1971.

9. Jonathan Holiff and Barbara Holiff, audiotaped conversations, January 10, January 22, and January 31, 2006; Joel Holiff, letter to Saul Holiff, May 14, 1947.

10. Saul Holiff, audio diary, recorded September 17, 1972. Slightly edited for clarity.

11. Jonathan Holiff, in discussion with the author, 2013–16; Joshua Robinson, in discussion with the author, March 2013, June 2016.

12. James Bawden, "A Gunfight: The European Western [headline ends]," *Toronto Star*, August 1, 1971.

13. Saul Holiff, speech to the London Rotary Club, 1978; Rick Setlowe, "Apache Tribe Financing $2 Mil Kirk Douglas-Johnny Cash Pic," *Variety*, March 27, 1970; Thomas Schatz, "Film Theory Goes to the Movies," in *The New Hollywood*, ed. Jim Collins, Ava Preacher Collins, and Hilary Radner (New York: Routledge, 1993), 8–37; Earl C. Gottschalk Jr., "Gambling Bucks: As Big Studios Fade, Chief Charlie, Apache, Bankrolls a Western," *Wall Street Journal*, June 18, 1971.

14. Saul Holiff, speech to the Jewish Community Centre, Victoria, B.C., 1997; "Cash and Manager Holiff," *Billboard*.

15. Robert Redford, letter to Johnny Cash, c/o Saul Holiff, December 9, 1969.
16. Hubert Saal, "Johnny on the Spot." *Newsweek*, February 2, 1970.

CHAPTER 14: FROM JAILS TO JESUS

1. Johnny Cash, *Man in Black*.
2. Linderman, "*Penthouse* Interview: Johnny Cash."
3. Johnny Cash, *Man in Black*.
4. Grant Wacker, *America's Pastor: Billy Graham and the Shaping of a Nation* (Cambridge, MA: Harvard University Press, 2014), 5–31; Hilburn, *Johnny Cash: The Life*; "Cash and Manager Holiff," *Billboard*.
5. Wacker, *America's Pastor*, 5–31; Linderman, "*Penthouse* Interview: Johnny Cash."
6. Barbara and Jonathan Holiff, in discussion with the author, July 2016; Stan Jacobson, interview by Jonathan Holiff, May 6, 2006.
7. Richard Carlin, *Country Music: A Biographical Dictionary* (New York: Routledge, 2003); Johnny Cash, *Man In Black*, 176.
8. Saul Holiff and Johnny Cash, recorded telephone conversation, May 1971. Edited for length and clarity.
9. Saul Holiff, audio diary, recorded September 17, 1972.
10. Saul Holiff, "A Legend in My Own Mind," a notepaper in his records listing all of his failures and personality shortcomings, June 1995; Johnny Cash, inscription within a first edition copy of *Winners Got Scars Too*.
11. Saul Holiff, letter to Joe Dale, May 18, 1971.
12. Dave Bunker, in discussion with the author, June 22, 2016, and as recalled by Bunker on his website at http://davebunkerguitars.com/memory_lane. html; June Carter Cash, "Ole Saul," a poem written for Saul Holiff; Johnny Cash, letter to Joe Dale, May 18, 1971.
13. Daniel Stoffman, "Johnny Cash Shines in His Role," *Toronto Star*, August 7, 1971; [review clipping unnamed] *Playboy*, August 1, 1971.
14. Saul Holiff and Johnny Cash, recorded telephone conversation, August 1971.

CHAPTER 15: THE RICHEST MAN IN THE CEMETERY

1. Michael Streissguth, ed., *Ring of Fire*. Previously published as George Vecsey, "Cash's 'Gospel Road' Film is Renaissance for Him," *New York Times*, December 13, 1973.
2. Saul Holiff and Johnny Cash, recorded telephone conversation, August 2, 1971.

3. Robert Elfstrom, in discussion with the author, June 28, 2016; Streissguth, *Johnny Cash: The Biography*; David Yonke, "'The Gospel Road' Leads into Holy Week," *Toledo Blade*, March 31, 2007, www.toledoblade.com/Religion/2007/03/31/The-Gospel-Road-leads-into-Holy-Week.html; Saul Holiff, audio diary, recorded November, 1971. It's unclear when the original conversation between Elfstrom and Cash took place. Elfstrom remembers Cash calling while he was on Deer Isle, but it's clear from the earlier phone conversation with Saul that they had already been in talks to some degree with the director.

4. David Noel Freedman, ed., *Eerdmans Dictionary of the Bible* (Amsterdam: Amsterdam University Press, 2000); Saul Holiff, photos from archives; Streissguth, *Johnny Cash: The Biography*.

5. Robert Elfstrom, in discussion with the author, June 28, 2016; Lou Robin, in discussion with the author, May 22, 2016; Johnny Cash, *Man In Black*, 196; Yonke, "'Gospel Road' Leads into Holy Week."

6. Saul Holiff, audio diary, ca. September 17, 1972 (date uncertain); A.J. Shoofey, Las Vegas International president, letter to Johnny Cash, August 5, 1970; Cordery, "Managing the Man in Black Opened Doors"; Nick Naff, Las Vegas Hilton interdepartmental correspondence to A.J. Shoofey, cc Dave Victorson, January 6, 1972.

7. Saul Holiff, audio diary, March 11, 1972; "Singer Johnny Cash Has Act Doctored Up," *Los Angeles Times*, September 30, 1971.

8. Goddard, "What's New with Saul"; Bender, "Excellence His Hang-Up"; Saul Holiff, audio diaries, recorded February 22 and through March 1972.

9. Saul Holiff and Johnny Cash, recorded telephone conversation, March 1972.

10. Saul Holiff, audio diary, February 22, 1972.

CHAPTER 16: *THE GOSPEL ROAD*

1. Saul Holiff, audio diary, February 22, 1972. Barbara narrates this part regarding the Billy Graham film.

2. Nick Tosches, *Country: The Twisted Roots of Rock 'n' Roll* (Boston: Da Capo Press, 1977).

3. Robert Hilburn, "Cash a Superstar in Vegas Opening," *Los Angeles Times*, April 1, 1972; "Holy Spirit's Alive in Me, Cash Says," *Nashville Tennessean*, August 20, 1972; Marty Klein, letter to Saul Holiff, May 23, 1972. Audience counts for shows in Las Vegas are from Saul Holiff's archives, April 1, 1972.

4. "Johnny is returning to New York, supposedly to meet Billy Graham to see a rough cut of the movie or the television show or whatever in Israel or that

was made in the holy land, or Palestine, or His land," Saul recorded in his diary in March. It is not one hundred percent certain that the trip happened, but if it did, it was just prior to Johnny and June's vacation in Jamaica.

5. Saul Holiff and Johnny Cash, audiotaped telephone conversation, March 1972.

6. Religious irritation is according to Jonathan Holiff's own research and analysis; Saul Holiff and Johnny Cash, audiotaped telephone conversation, July 1972 (edited and condensed).

7. Saul Holiff, audio diary, August 1972.

8. Barbara Holiff, letter to Johnny Cash and June Carter, June 26, 1972; Hilburn, *Johnny Cash: The Life.*

9. Saul Holiff and Johnny Cash, audiotaped telephone conversation, July 1972.

10. From a photo in Saul Holiff's archives that shows Joshua and Jonathan at a *Gospel Road* premiere. I am not 100 percent certain it was the one in Chicago, so this may be taking artistic licence.

11. Sam Covington, "Johnny Cash's Rich Baritone Movingly Carries Premiere," *Charlotte Observer*, February 15, 1973; Richard Maschal, "A Man for the People," *Washington Post*, February 16, 1973.

12. *Gospel Road* film premiere clip from *My Father and The Man in Black*, courtesy WPA Film Library, Orland Park, IL. I'm not certain which film premiere this clip was shot at.

13. Vecsey, "Cash's 'Gospel Road' Film"; Lou Robin, in discussion with the author, July 18, 2016.

14. Undated typed note from Saul Holiff's archive. Jonathan Holiff estimates it was written somewhere between late 1972 and early 1973. Saul also highlighted the word *salivate* for unknown reasons, but for the sake of effect I left it out.

CHAPTER 17: THE WISEST MAN I KNOW

1. Johnny Cash, telegram to Saul Holiff, April 23, 1973.

2. Saul Holiff, audio diary, July 4, 1973; Saul Holiff, letter to June Carter Cash, May 27, 1975; Stan Jacobson, interview by Jonathan Holiff, May 6, 2006.

3. Saul Holiff, letter to Barbara, Jonathan and Joshua Holiff, June 19, 1973.

4. Brad Zinn, "Statler Brothers 50 Years Later," *Staunton News Leader*, February 21, 2015, www.newsleader.com/story/news/local/2015/02/21/statler-brothers-years-later/23818907; Saul Holiff, audio diary, July 4, 1973.

5. The scene is both as recalled by Barbara Holiff, based on what Saul had told her when he returned to their bungalow, and as told to Michael Streissguth in *Johnny Cash: The Biography*, 175.

6. Lou Robin, in discussion with the author, May 12, 2016.

7. Saul Holiff, letter to Reba Hancock, October 19, 1973.

8. Volatile Attractions, "Cash, Holiff Split," news release, October 17, 1973.

9. Saul Holiff, letter to Jo Walker, October 19, 1973.

10. Saul Holiff, letter to Larry Gatlin, October 29, 1973; Harold D. Cohen, letter to Saul Holiff, October 28, 1973; Saul Holiff, letter to Harold and Phyllis Cohen, December 18, 1973; Mike Mulhern, "Holiff Cashing in Boyhood Dreams," *London Free Press*, June 20, 1980; Saul Holiff, letter to Len Naymark, December 17, 1973.

11. Joe Matyas, "True Star: Cash Big Tree of Country Music," *London Free Press*, November 5, 1973.

CHAPTER 18: CINNAMON HILL

1. James F. Neal, letter to Saul Holiff, February 7, 1974.

2. Saul Holiff, letter to Johnny Cash, n.d. Jonathan Holiff believes this letter was never sent to Cash, because it is one of the rare letters in Saul's collection still on its original stationery, and it is undated and unsigned. On March 5, 1974 (see previous note), Cash responds to what he refers to as Saul's "letter of February 26." It is not known what letter he refers to — if it is this one, or perhaps an altered version that also mentions the same topics.

3. Johnny Cash, letter to Saul Holiff, March 5, 1974.

4. Saul Holiff, letter to Johnny Cash, May 15, 1974. The second page is missing.

5. Saul Holiff, letter to Johnny Cash, May 23, 1974.

6. Saul Holiff, letter to June Carter Cash, May 27, 1974.

7. Charles Paul Conn, *The New Johnny Cash* (Grand Rapids, MI: Fleming H. Revell Company, 1973), 72; Mark Stielper, in discussion with the author, July 22, 2016.

8. Lou Robin, in discussion with the author, May 12, 2016.

9. Hilburn, *Johnny Cash: The Life*, 432.

10. June Carter Cash, handwritten letter to Saul Holiff, June 20, 1974.

11. "Barney's People" *The Victoria Star*, September 26, 1984.

12. Johnny Cash, letter to Saul Holiff, January 16, 1975. It has been edited for length, as it also contains a detailed religious discussion.

13. Saul Holiff, letter to Johnny Cash, February 23, 1975.

14. Johnny Cash, handwritten letter to Saul Holiff, April 28, 1975.

15. Saul Holiff, letter to Johnny Cash, May 20, 1975.

16. Saul Holiff collection, inscription inside the front cover of *Man in Black*;

June Carter Cash, letter to Saul and Barbara Holiff, December 25, 1975; Johnny Cash, *Cash: The Autobiography*, 40, 47.

17. June Carter Cash, portion of a handwritten poem, December 25, 1975, *My Father and the Man in Black*, 2012.

18. Saul Holiff, interview by Candy Yates, *Cinematically Speaking*, 1976.

19. Jonathan Holiff and Joshua Robinson, in discussions with the author, June 2016.

20. "Barney's People" column, *Victoria Star*, September 26, 1984.

21. Saul Holiff to Jonathan Holiff, handwritten letter, August 15, 1984.

22. Saul Holiff, interview by Steve Paikin, 1998. These quotes are intact but have been heavily condensed from a long recording.

23. Peter Lewry, ed., *Johnny Cash: The Man in Black*, fanzine, March 2012; Lou Robin, letter to Saul Holiff, December 12, 1983; Hilburn, *Johnny Cash: The Life*; Associated Press, "Cash Follows Elizabeth Taylor into Centre for Drugs Treatment," *Times Colonist*, December 22, 1983.

24. Saul Holiff, letter to Johnny Cash, October 16, 1994.

25. Adrian Chamberlain, "'Kind, Cruel, Selfish, Smart': Former Manager from Nanaimo Tells of His Days with The Man in Black," *Times Colonist*, September 13, 2003.

26. Saul Holiff, letter to Johnny Cash, January 2, 1997; Johnny Cash, letter to Saul Holiff, February 6, 1997; Johnny Cash, *Cash: The Autobiography*, 156.

27. Mark Stielper, emails to Jonathan Holiff, November 27 and 28, 2005. For the record, during an interview with the author on July 22, 2016, Stielper declined to tell this story, though it was communicated to Jonathan Holiff in 2005 with no stipulated reservations or limitations.

Willie Nelson
wrote the song
"Crazy" -
- Patsy Cline - 1961

movie - A Gunfight

2003 - Johnny Cash
died.

IMAGE CREDITS

206   Saul Holiff Collection. Photographer unknown.

209   Saul Holiff Collection.

210   Saul Holiff Collection. Photographer unknown.

214   Saul Holiff Collection. Photographer unknown.

218   Photograph by Victor Aziz Photography Ltd. Saul Holiff Collection.

227   Saul Holiff Collection. Photographer unknown.

240   Photograph by Victor Aziz Photography Ltd. Saul Holiff Collection.

253   Saul Holiff Collection. Photographer unknown.

260   Saul Holiff Collection. Photographer unknown.

262   Photo by Victor Aziz Photography Ltd. Saul Holiff Collection.

263   Photograph by Jorgan Halling/Saul Holiff Collection.

266   Photo by Saul Holiff. Saul Holiff Collection.

270   Photograph by Barbara Holiff. Saul Holiff Collection.

271   Saul Holiff Collection. Photographer unknown.

273   Saul Holiff Collection. Photographer unknown.

294   Photo by Victor Aziz Photography Ltd. Saul Holiff Collection.

299   Photo by Saul Holiff. Saul Holiff Collection.

301   Saul Holiff Collection. Photographer unknown.

312   Saul Holiff Collection. Photographer unknown.

322   Photo by Barbara Holiff. Saul Holiff Collection.

351   Photo by Susan Bradnam. Saul Holiff Collection.